SEALING
THEIR FATE

SEALING
THEIR FATE

The Twenty-Two Days
That Decided World War II

DAVID DOWNING

Da Capo Press
A Member of the Perseus Books Group

CONTENTS

For my American parents-in-law, Bill and Betty Gilmore, who were married during these three weeks, and then separated for almost four years by their country's sudden involvement in the war

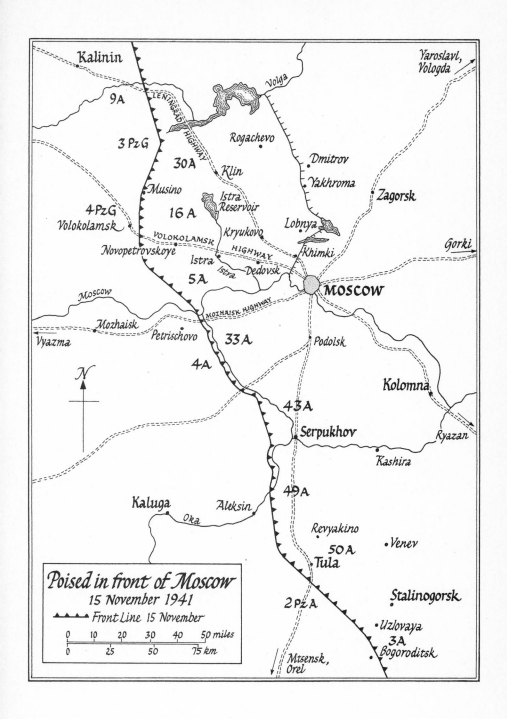

Poised in front of Moscow
15 November 1941
▲▲▲ Front Line 15 November

0 10 20 30 40 50 miles
0   25   50   75 km

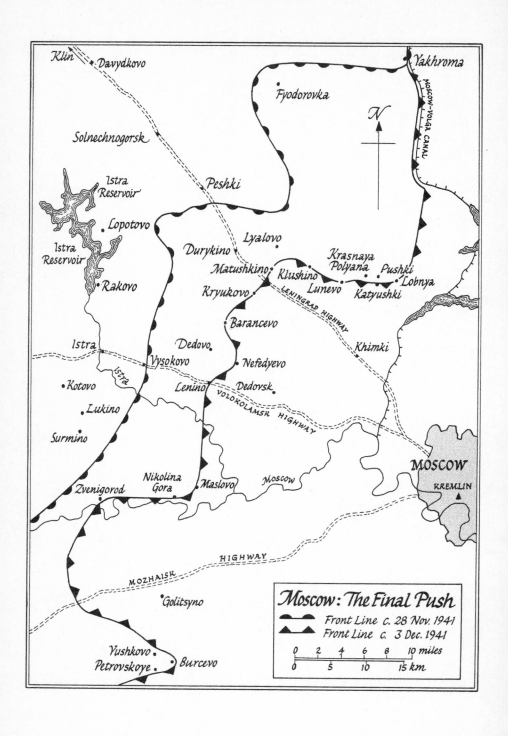

Klin • Davydkovo • Yakhroma

Fyodorovka

MOSCOW–VOLGA CANAL

N

Solnechnogorsk

Istra
Reservoir
Peshki

Lopotovo

Lyalovo

Istra
Reservoir
Durykino
Krasnaya
Polyana
Pushki
Lobnya

Matushkino
Klushino
Lunevo
Katyushki

Rakovo
Kryukovo
LENINGRAD HIGHWAY

Barancevo

Dedovo
Khimki

Istra
Vysokovo
Nefedyevo

Kotovo
Lenino
Dedovsk

Lukino
VOLOKOLAMSK HIGHWAY

Surmino
MOSCOW

Nikolina
Gora
Maslovo
Moscow
KREMLIN

Zvenigorod

HIGHWAY

MOZHAISK

Golitsyno

Yushkovo
Petrovskoye
Burcevo

Moscow: The Final Push

Front Line c. 28 Nov. 1941
Front Line c. 3 Dec. 1941

| 0 | 2 | 4 | 6 | 8 | 10 miles |
| 0 | | 5 | 10 | | 15 km |

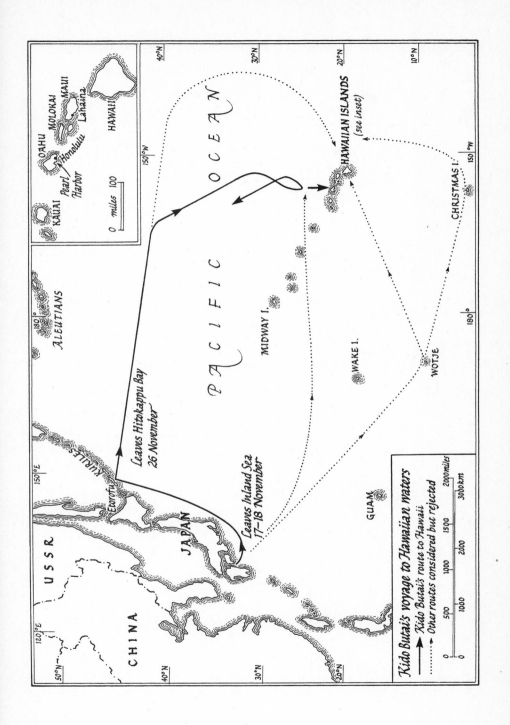

Kido Butai's voyage to Hawaiian waters
.... Kido Butai's route to Hawaii
------► Other routes considered but rejected

Leaves Hitokappu Bay 26 November

Leaves Inland Sea 17–18 November

USSR

CHINA

JAPAN

ALEUTIANS

KURILES

Etorofu

PACIFIC OCEAN

MIDWAY I.

WAKE I.

WOTJE

GUAM

HAWAIIAN ISLANDS
(see inset)

CHRISTMAS I.

KAUAI
OAHU
Pearl
Harbor
Honolulu
MOLOKAI
MAUI
Lahaina
HAWAII

0   miles   100

0   500   1000   1500   2000 miles
0   1000   2000   3000 km

50°N
40°N
30°N
20°N

40°N
30°N
20°N
10°N

120°E   150°E   180°   150°W

180°   150°W

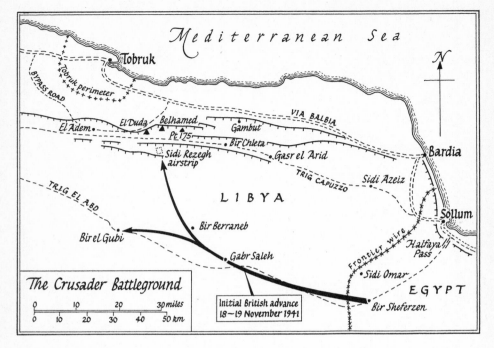

Mediterranean Sea

Tobruk

Tobruk perimeter

BYPASS ROAD

El Adem • El Duda • Belhamed • Gambut
Pt 175 • Bir Chleta
Sidi Rezegh airstrip • Gasr el Arid
VIA BALBIA

TRIG EL ABD

LIBYA

TRIG CAPUZZO • Sidi Azeiz

Bardia

Sollum

Bir el Gubi • Bir Berraneb

Gabr Saleh

Frontier wire • Halfaya Pass

The Crusader Battleground

0   10   20   30 miles
0   10   20   30   40   50 km

Initial British advance
18–19 November 1941

• Sidi Omar
EGYPT
Bir Sheferzen

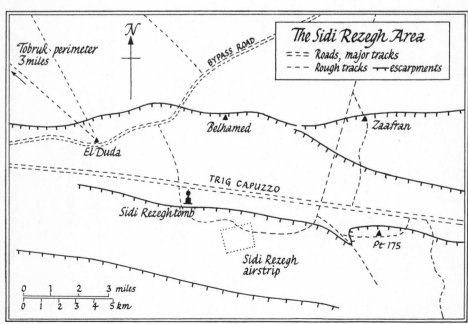

N

Tobruk perimeter
3 miles

BYPASS ROAD

The Sidi Rezegh Area
═══ Roads, major tracks
– – – Rough tracks ⊢ escarpments

Belhamed   ▲ Zaafran

El Duda

TRIG CAPUZZO

Sidi Rezegh tomb

Sidi Rezegh
airstrip

Pt 175

0   1   2   3 miles
0   1   2   3   4   5 km

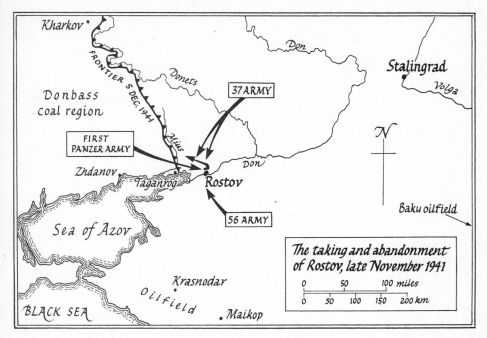

Kharkov

FRONTIER 5 DEC. 1941

Don

Donets

Stalingrad

37 ARMY

Volga

Donbass
coal region

FIRST
PANZER ARMY

Mius

N

Don

Zhdanov

Taganrog

Rostov

Baku oilfield

56 ARMY

Sea of Azov

Krasnodar

Oilfield

BLACK SEA

Maikop

**The taking and abandonment
of Rostov, late November 1941**

0		50		100 miles
0	50	100	150	200 km

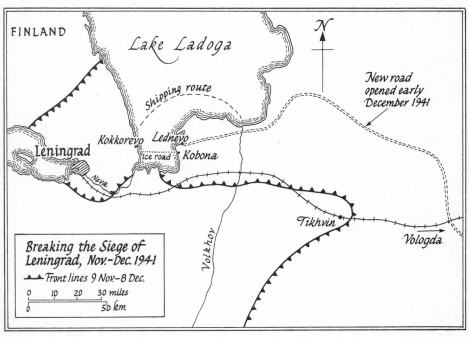

FINLAND

Lake Ladoga

N

Shipping route

New road
opened early
December 1941

Kokkorevo   Lednevo

Leningrad

ice road   Kobona

Neva

Volkhov

Tikhvin

Vologda

**Breaking the Siege of
Leningrad, Nov.–Dec. 1941**

▲▬▲ Front lines 9 Nov.–8 Dec.

0	10	20	30 miles
0		50 km	

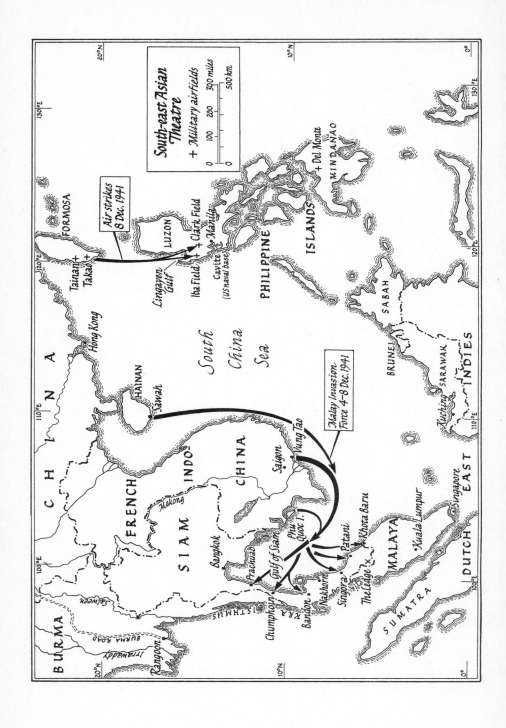

PROLOGUE

November 1941. The war in Europe had been under way for two years and two months. In that time Germany's armed forces had dismembered Poland, before turning west against Denmark, Norway, Holland, Belgium, Luxembourg and France. All had been occupied, leaving France's British ally to flee back across the English Channel. A German invasion of the British Isles was contemplated for the early autumn of 1940, but was indefinitely postponed when Göring's Luftwaffe failed to secure the essential control of the skies. Stalemated in the west, Adolf Hitler decided that the only road to British defeat led east. With Stalin's Soviet Union subjugated, and its vast resources – most notably of oil and grain – at Germany's command, he would have the power to face down both Britain and its fast-arming friend across the Atlantic. On 22 June 1941, following a Balkan side-trip to punish Yugoslavian defiance and prevent British intervention in Greece, Hitler took the plunge and invaded the Soviet Union. Success was swift in coming: millions of Soviets soldiers were killed or captured, thousands of tanks and planes destroyed. By mid-July the German panzers had advanced two-thirds of the way to Moscow.

There was, however, no end in sight – Nazi brutality ensured that neither individual soldiers nor the regime in Moscow were offered any incentive to surrender. Soviet industry was moved east beyond German reach, further millions drafted into the Red Army. In late July the Wehrmacht, constrained by the increasing logistical difficulties inherent in operating so far from its bases, was forced to choose between taking the Ukraine and taking Moscow. Hitler opted for the former's grain, and the prospect of seizing the Caucasus oilfields which lay beyond. Another huge victory ensued, but the time taken, and the wear caused to the motorized forces, meant that the march on Moscow could only resume in late September. Early successes were choked off by the autumn rains, and the adverse conditions which these created for motorized warfare. Further advances would be possible once the ground froze in November, but only for a few short weeks, until the first heavy snowfalls once again rendered movement next to impossible.

Many German military leaders doubted the wisdom of resuming the advance, but none offered a coherent alternative. Time was not on Nazi Germany's side. As the German population and war economy struggled to keep pace with the Wehrmacht's needs, German military strength was eroding, both absolutely and relatively. If Moscow was not taken in these few weeks, the chances were high that it never would be. And if Moscow was not taken the war was effectively lost.

As far as the German political and military leadership were concerned, the war in Russia dwarfed all other aspects of their global struggle. In North Africa and the Mediterranean the chances of inflicting a major and perhaps decisive defeat on Britain had been allowed to slip by. Three German divisions under Rommel had been sent to save the Italian forces in North Africa, but he lacked the planes (needed in Russia) or the U-boats (needed in the Atlantic) to safeguard his Mediterranean lifeline, and without adequate supplies a limited success – like the capture of Tobruk – was the best he could hope for. The British, on the other hand, had few problems supplying their army in North Africa, and were about to launch a major offensive. Over the next three weeks, Crusader would demonstrate that logistics were much more influential in deciding battles than brilliant generalship, well-designed weapons or technically proficient soldiers.

Between Russia and the English Channel, the war was only beginning. British bombing of Germany was sporadic and largely ineffective, and resistance movements in the occupied countries were, with the notable exception of those in Yugoslavia, still gathering in the shadows. While Russia's Jews were being slaughtered in their hundreds of thousands by execution squads, the future of Western and Central Europe's Jews – persecuted, ghettoized, but not yet killed in huge numbers – was about to be set in bureaucratic stone.

Six thousand miles to the east, another war had been under way for four years and four months. An armed clash at the Marco Polo Bridge south of Beijing in July 1937 had been used by the Japanese Army to justify an all-out invasion of central and southern China. Most of the major cities had fallen quickly, but further victories proved harder and harder to come by. By the summer of 1941 over 200,000 Japanese soldiers had given their lives for what looked increasingly like a forlorn hope. Reasoning that British and American aid to the Chinese was the main stumbling-block to their success, the Japanese sought to block the supply by occupying Indochina. The American reaction – embargoes on scrap iron and fuel which would eventually immobilize Japan's armed forces – left the Japanese in an even bigger hole. The leaders in Tokyo had a choice to make: climb out with hands held high or keep on digging. The former was out of the question.

MONDAY 17 NOVEMBER

Soon after sunrise the battleship *Nagato*, flagship of Admiral Isoroku Yamamoto, weighed anchor off Iwakuni and set sail for Saeki Bay on the eastern coast of Kyushu. The voyage across Japan's Inland Sea took around five hours, and it was past one o'clock when *Nagato* rounded the northern lip of the bay and the scattered ships of *Kido Butai*, the Japanese First Air Fleet, came into view.

At around 15.00 a small boat ferried Yamamoto and his staff officers across to the carrier *Akagi*, flagship of the First Air Fleet's commander-in-chief, Admiral Chuichi Nagumo. A hundred or so key officers from the other ships were already waiting on the *Akagi* flight deck to hear Yamamoto's farewell address. Unlike most of the twenty thousand men they commanded, these officers knew where *Kido Butai* was headed, and why. Many, like Nagumo and his chief of staff, Rear Admiral Ryunosuke Kusaka, had struggled long and hard to dissuade Yamamoto from proceeding with this operation, and, though the time for voicing them had passed, enormous doubts remained.

If anyone expected a gung-ho address from Yamamoto, eager for the fight and contemptuous of the enemy, they were disappointed. Addressing the ranks of white-uniformed men on the wind-blown flight deck, the commander-in-chief eschewed heady rhetoric and seemed less interested in inspiring his subordinates than in deflating any residual overconfidence. Japan had defeated many worthy opponents in the past, he said, but the Americans would be the toughest of them all. The fleet was relying on surprise, but it was always possible that the enemy would be waiting for them, and they might well have to fight their way to the target. This should not deter them – it was, after all, the custom of bushido to select an equal or stronger opponent.

Scanning the faces of Yamamoto's listeners, his chief of staff registered 'unshakable loyalty, determined resolution, even a degree of ferocity. But they were all self-composed. We cannot but expect some damage to us, yet I pray by the grace of heaven they will succeed in their objective.'[1]

All adjourned to the wardroom for a sombre farewell feast. The traditional dried cuttlefish were consumed for happiness, handfuls of walnuts for victory. Glasses were raised to the glory of the Emperor. Before returning to the *Nagato*, Yamamoto surprised and pleased the assembled officers with an impromptu expression of confidence in the outcome.

An hour or so later Nagumo and Kusaka paid the return visit courtesy required, and drank a last toast to Operation Z's success. On their way back to *Akagi* they could see the carriers *Soryu* and *Hiryu* already under way, heading for the mouth of the darkening bay with their four destroyer escorts. Other ships followed at regular intervals through the evening, and aboard *Nagato* many of the crew lined the main deck to watch and wave them goodbye. Yamamoto was one of them, watching each ship through his binoculars until her silhouette faded into the horizon.

Akagi and her two-destroyer escort were the last to leave, weighing anchor just before midnight. With lights out and radios disabled to prevent the accidental transmission of signals, they slipped out into the broad Pacific, hopefully lost to the eyes and ears of the enemy.

Earlier that Monday, the Japanese liner *Taiyo Maru* had arrived back in Yokohama from Honolulu, bearing three intelligence officers and a wealth of information about ocean conditions and American military preparedness. They were collected by launch before the liner docked and rushed by car to the Navy Ministry in Tokyo, where high-ranking members of the Naval General Staff, Operations Section and Intelligence were anxiously waiting to hear their report.

Lieutenant-Commander Suguru Suzuki did most of the talking. After leaving Yokohama on 22 October, ostensibly on a purely commercial voyage, the liner had taken an unusual north-easterly route for the first couple of days, and then followed *Kido Butai*'s intended route across the normally empty reaches of the northern Pacific. One of the three agents had been on deck every hour of the voyage, noting down the weather and sea conditions, constantly scanning the horizon for other vessels. The only storm had been short, and the *Taiyo Maru* had been less than two hundred miles from Oahu when the first American plane appeared in the sky.

During their five days at anchor in Honolulu, the agents had stayed aboard the liner. Nagao Kita, the Japanese consul general, had visited them on the first morning and taken ashore the Navy Ministry's list of over a hundred questions, covering everything from the American fleet's weekend routine to the precise location of each and every military installation on the islands. Over the next few days, Kita had smuggled written answers past the American security guards with what seemed indecent ease: the various police and military agencies had all been too busy checking arriving and departing passengers to concern themselves with Japanese officialdom. When the liner left on 5 November, most of the questions had been answered. The *Taiyo Maru* had followed *Kido Butai*'s intended route of return, a more southerly course this time, close to the American outpost of Midway. The sea had been just as empty, the weather and conditions even better than on the outward voyage.

The mission had clearly been a success, but the more sanguine members of Suzuki's audience were not overly impressed. Many of the key questions remained unanswered. A single liner could apparently cross the northern Pacific unobserved, but a fleet of more than thirty warships? There was no definite information about American reconnaissance sweeps, no guarantee that the fleet would not be betrayed by a chance encounter with a submarine or merchantman. There was no surety that the American carriers – or any of the enemy's other capital ships, the battleships and heavy cruisers – would be in harbour when the attack was launched. It was still, as many of them had always insisted, a terrible gamble.

Still, much information of use to the task force had been gathered, and Suzuki was sent home to pack for another trip. He would head north next day on the battleship *Hiei*, bound for *Kido Butai's* final assembly point in Etorofu's Hitokappu Bay, to brief Nagumo and the flight leaders.

Kido Butai's attack on Pearl Harbor was one of three major Japanese offensives provisionally scheduled for the same twenty-four hours. It would be 7 December in Hawaii, but further west, across the International Date Line, it would be 8 December when Japanese forces attacked on the one hand Thailand and northern Malaya, and on the other the Philippines.

To say that the British and American authorities in Malaya and the Philippines were expecting these attacks would be something of an overstatement. They were expecting the Japanese to try something or other at some indeterminate time in the future, but in all other respects wishful thinking was the order of the day. Neither the British nor the Americans were ready, and both managed to convince themselves that the Japanese would wait until they were. In the Philippines, the American C-in-C, Douglas MacArthur, had recently told the newly appointed head of his air force, General Lewis H. Brereton, that a Japanese attack was unlikely before April. Brereton's early impressions of his new command's readiness had been far from encouraging, but he had hardly begun setting things right when MacArthur sent him off to check the facilities for forwarding future reinforcements across the south-western Pacific.

Brereton was in Australia on 17 November, a long way from the morning exercise being played out over Luzon. The 93rd Bomb Squadron's B-17s launched a mock attack on their Clark

Field airbase, some sixty miles north of Manila, and the 20th Pursuit Squadron's P-40Bs rose to intercept them. The latter found the former, but their engines proved so underpowered that the B-17s just left them behind. 'Our planes,' as one interceptor pilot wrote home to his sister, 'are not good enough to fight with.'[2]

A further five time zones to the west, Lieutenant Kurt Gruman of the German 87th Infantry Division was enjoying another clear sunny day in the countryside north-west of Moscow. The myriad bushes and trees draped with glittering snow and ice were 'almost like a fairy tale', only subverted by 'the bitter thunder of guns' in the distance.[3] During the day he and his comrades were able to stand the cold, but at night it was beginning to torture them.

The temperature in the Moscow region had suddenly dropped around 7 November and seemed prone to further plummeting falls every few days. Wheeled movement was now possible both off-road and on, but only for a limited period – December's heavy snow would prove as much of a handicap to mobility as the late-autumn mud. And in every other respect the arrival of winter was bad news for the Germans. Their army had not been equipped to function in such temperatures. Weapons, tanks and lorries, even trains, all struggled to cope, while the soldiers were still wearing denim tunics and trousers and steel-soled boots that conducted the cold. The winter clothing was supposedly on its way, but no one seemed to know when it would arrive. Frostbite was rapidly becoming commonplace, and stories began circulating of German night sentries found frozen solid when morning came.

It was almost as cold in the gloomy East Prussian forest six hundred miles to the west, but the two purpose-built compounds occupied by the Führer, his immediate entourage and those who were supposedly running his Russian campaign were well heated, and a true appreciation of conditions in the field required either imagination or a willingness to listen. Neither quality was much in evidence in mid-November 1941, either in the Wolfsschanze or at the nearby OKH (*Oberkommando des Heeres*, the Army High

Command) headquarters. On their wall and table maps Moscow looked tantalizingly close, only fifty miles from the German front line, the sort of distance the panzers had been devouring in a couple of days a few months earlier. It was realized that conditions in November were more difficult than they had been in July, but Operation *Typhoon*'s October surge towards Moscow had been slowed by supply problems and mud, not the Russians. Now that the ground was hard again, a fifty-mile advance was surely achievable.

Hitler had made his decision, and OKH had turned it into an operational plan. On 12 November Chief of the General Staff General Franz Halder had boarded his personal train at Angerburg and journeyed overnight to Orsha, where Army Group Centre's commander, Field Marshal Fedor von Bock, had his headquarters. The chiefs of staff of all the German armies and army groups on the Eastern Front had been summoned to the conference which took place that day in a siding beside the town station. Many came expecting to debate the wisdom of a further offensive in 1941, but they were disappointed. Comments and questions were welcome, but the decision had already been taken.

Halder's presentation was unconvincing. He emphasized the enemy's weakness and supposed lack of reserves, but he and his audience were depressingly aware that their actual intelligence of Soviet troop movements reached little further east than Moscow. Halder also ignored or glossed over his own army's supply difficulties and reserve shortfalls. When the Quartermaster Field Office Chief protested that von Bock's armies could not be supplied as far forward as Moscow, Halder accepted his calculations yet insisted that OKH did 'not like to stand in Bock's way, if he thinks he can succeed'.[4]

Von Bock, it turned out, was Halder's only powerful ally at this meeting. The chiefs of staff listened with incredulity to the maximum and minimum advances which Hitler and OKH were now demanding in the expected six-week window of opportunity which lay between mud and deep snow. The maximum line ran from Vologda to Stalingrad via Gorky, two hundred and fifty miles beyond Moscow, the minimum a less ambitious but still breathtaking hundred miles beyond the Soviet capital.

The chiefs had their say. Army Groups North and South were opposed to any further offensive. Von Bock's chief of staff, General Hans von Greiffenberg, loyally refused to rule out an advance, but was keen to point out the difficulties. The chiefs of staff of the three infantry armies and three panzer groups, which made up Army Group Centre, all poured scorn on the proposed objectives. This was not May and they were not fighting in France, one exasperated chief told Halder.

It made no difference. Halder handed over the written orders, and the conference broke up. On 15 November the left wing of Army Group Centre would begin its push, the infantry of General Adolf Strauss's 9th Army moving east to cover the left flank of General Georg-Hans Reinhardt's 3rd Panzer Group as it advanced towards Klin and the Volga Reservoir. Further south, General Erich Hoepner's 4th Panzer Group would attack General Konstantin Rokossovsky's 30th Army on either side of the Volokolamsk highway leading into Moscow. On the right wing the German forces needed more preparation time, but the 2nd Army and 2nd Panzer Army would be in motion by 17 November, the former guarding the right flank of the latter as it swung in behind Moscow for the intended rendezvous with Reinhardt. Almost due west of the Soviet capital, the 4th Army would hold, pinning the Soviet forces that faced it while the panzer groups wreaked havoc in their rear. It had worked before, and Halder and von Bock clung to the precedents – not, perhaps, because they really believed it would work again, but because the alternatives were too awful to contemplate.

By that morning of 17 November the armoured spearheads of the 3rd and 4th Panzer Groups had punched several gaps in the defensive lines entrusted to the Soviet 30th and 16th Armies. General Georgi Zhukov, in overall command of the armies defending Moscow, had ordered his subordinates to launch probing attacks on the German infantry divisions which the German panzers had outpaced, hoping to find a vulnerable spot, anything to slow the gathering German tide. One such mission was allotted to the 44th Mongolian Cavalry Division, which had only just arrived from Tashkent in Central Asia.

The spot selected for its probing attack was a section of the front around fifteen miles north of Volokolamsk. It was held by the German 116th Infantry Division, with forward units stretched out along the slight ridge that ran east of the villages of Musino and Partenkovo. Three artillery batteries were deployed among them.

Dawn was a hazy affair, but the sun soon burned off the mist, and by 09.00 the German soldiers had a clear view across the mile of snow-dusted field that lay in front of them. At around 10.00 a forward observer spotted Red Army horsemen in the wood beyond, and the German infantry and artillery units were put on alert. An hour and a half later, four light tanks, T-26s, emerged from the trees and slowly advanced into the field. The Germans, guessing that this was just a probe, held their fire. Twenty minutes more, and a large cavalry force began emerging from the wood, forming up in long ranks on the far edge of the field.

'It was an indescribably beautiful sight,' one German soldier later recalled, 'as on this clear and sunny winterscape, stirrup to stirrup, bent over their horses' bodies and with brandished flashing sabres, the cavalry regiment raced in full attack across the field. It was as if the age of Mongol assaults had returned.'[5] Other Germans were more astonished than entranced: 'we could not believe that the enemy intended to attack us across this broad field, which lay open like a parade ground before us.'[6]

But they did. The artillerymen opened up with their 105-millimetre howitzers and quickly found their range. Men and horses were blown to pieces, spraying broken flesh and blood across the white snow. Panicked horses ran wild across the smoke-covered field, their discarded riders easy prey for the German machine guns. Those who could turned tail and ran.

'It was,' the second German soldier remembered, 'impossible to imagine that after the annihilation of the first squadrons the nightmare sight would be repeated.'[7] But it was. The Soviet cavalry re-formed for a second charge, this time supported by two horse-drawn 76.2-millimetre howitzers of their own. It made no difference. Three hundred and fifty 105-millimetre shells tore into horsemen and guns, forcing the survivors back to the shelter of the trees. Hundreds of Red Army soldiers had died, and not a single German had received as much as a scratch. Few victories, in this or any other war, had been so comprehensive.

And yet. That evening, huddling for warmth in what shelter they could find, the German soldiers outside Musino might have asked each other some deeply disturbing questions. What sort of enemy charged across an open field brandishing sabres at machine guns and howitzers? A stupid one? Or one that was willing to sacrifice life upon life from a seemingly inexhaustible supply? And if the latter, how could such a foe be beaten? And what would happen if the day ever came when *he* was the one with the superior weapons?

That night another German division found out. Earlier that morning, 185 miles to the south-east, General Heinz Guderian's 2nd Panzer Army had launched its offensive. The main attacks were south of the stubbornly held city of Tula, directed north and north-west, with the twin aims of advancing on Moscow and encircling Tula from the rear. The 112th Infantry Division advanced along the trailing right flank of the 24th Panzer Korps, and by nightfall was close to the town of Uzlovaya. The troops went into bivouac, got as warm as they could and looked forward to a similar advance on the following day.

German reconnaissance had missed the presence of a newly detrained Siberian division in the area, and an accompanying armoured brigade with a full roster of the relatively new and highly manoeuvrable T-34s. The 112th Division, working on the assumption that any Red Army units in the area had been thoroughly scattered by the panzer advance, was in for a shock. Shortly before midnight, the forward sentries heard engines looming out of the night and soon made out the sloping shadows of around twenty T-34s. The alarm went up, but the division's ability to fight back was seriously limited. For one thing the German 37-millimetre anti-tank guns could take out a T-34 only at point-blank range; for another the gunners found that the packing grease on the shells had frozen solid and had to be scraped off before they would fit into the breech. And all this in darkness, fingers frozen and groggy from sleep, shells exploding amid and around them.

The regular infantry fared no better, their automatic weapons refusing to fire more than single shots. As the waves of Siberian infantry loomed into view behind the tanks, insultingly snug in their quilted white uniforms and felt-lined boots, racing forward and firing guns that actually worked the way they were supposed to, the denim-clad Germans broke and ran.

The panic, Guderian wrote, 'reached back as far as Bogorodisk', several miles to the rear. Earlier that evening, before hearing of the attack, the general had been writing a letter praising his 'brave troops', who were 'seizing all their advantages and are fighting with wonderful endurance despite all their handicaps'. But now perhaps they had reached their limits. The routing of the 112th Division was 'a warning that the combat ability of our infantry was at an end and that they should no longer be expected to perform difficult tasks'.[8]

Around 500 miles to the south of Tula – the German forces in the Soviet Union were now stretched along a 1,000-mile front – Army Group South's 1st Panzer Army had launched its attack across the Mius River that morning. Rostov, with its bridge across the wide River Don, was only forty miles away.

Both Field Marshal Gerd von Rundstedt, who commanded Army Group South, and General Ewald von Kleist, who commanded the 1st Panzer Army, had opposed this offensive. The worsening supply situation, the winter conditions, the general tiredness of soldiers and vehicles, all suggested failure. Rostov might be taken, but holding it would probably prove beyond them. And since the city mattered only as a stepping stone on the road to the Caucasus and its precious oil, its temporary seizure would be futile.

Back in East Prussia, things were seen differently. The oilfields seemed there for the taking, and stepping zones were for stepping on. Nazi Germany had only two major sources of the precious fluid that drove its tanks and planes – the Romanian fields around Ploesti and the synthetic oil plants at home – and they didn't produce enough. Like its future ally Japan, Nazi Germany was condemned to live with the permanent anxiety of running short. The oil of the Caucasus, which would dissolve this anxiety at a stroke, was worth almost any risk.

The first day of the German offensive proved successful enough. Von Kleist's two panzer divisions, with the SS *Leibstandarte* on their right, were almost halfway to Rostov by nightfall, leaving substantial Red Army units scattered behind them. So far so familiar, it seemed, until the news arrived of a Soviet attack that same day. Marshal Timoshenko, the commander of the Soviet South-Western Front, had been gathering reserves for this moment, and that morning the 9th, 18th and 37th Armies, supported by tank brigades, had launched an attack south-westwards, diagonally across the line of the intended German advance. The Soviets advanced ten miles that day, reducing the gap through which the Germans were now supplying their attack towards Rostov. If the city was taken, the takers might find themselves cut off.

At the northern end of the Eastern Front, Leningrad was into its third month of siege. The German Army Group North had cut the city's last rail link with the rest of Russia on 30 August, and its last road link on 9 September. This left the Soviets with only two ways of bringing in food and other much-needed supplies – by air, and by train via Tikhvin and Lednevo for shipping across nearby Lake Ladoga.

The soldiers of Army Group North had reached a point only seven miles from the Winter Palace in the second week of September, but shorn of Hoepner's 4th Panzer Group – transferred to Army Group Centre for Typhoon's assault on Moscow – they could advance no further. Hitler was not concerned. Remorseless aerial bombing and artillery bombardment would reduce the city to rubble; starvation and cold would claim its people. Determined to close every loophole, he ordered Field Marshal Wilhelm von Leeb to use his remaining armour in the taking of Tikhvin, another hundred miles to the east. On 8 November that city fell, and Leningrad's final lifeline with it.

Inside the city conditions rapidly deteriorated. As the temperature dropped, so fuel ran out, silencing the factories and immobilizing public transport. The bread ration had already been reduced three times, and on 13 November it was cut again, to 300 grammes a day – around 4 slices – for those still working, 150 grammes for those whose only occupation was keeping themselves warm. And even those grammes now contained twenty-five per cent of 'edible' cellulose. The city's daily consumption of flour had dropped by more than two-thirds in two months. Without a new lifeline Hitler would have his wish, and three million people would starve to death.

Lake Ladoga froze over every winter, and the idea of replacing the shipping route with a road laid across the ice had been discussed in October. The fall of Tikhvin, and the loss of rail connection which this involved, added another giant task to the Soviet list: the construction, in winter, of a 220-mile road through untamed forest and swamp to reach that section of the railway still in Soviet hands. While thousands were drafted in to pursue this project, others set to work building warehouses at either end of the projected ice road, and scientists in Leningrad puzzled over the details of travel on ice. How fast and how thick did water freeze at what temperatures? How many inches of ice were needed to support a fully loaded one-ton truck?

By the second full week of November the lake was beginning to freeze, and an hour before dawn on 17 November Lieutenant Leonid Sokolov led the roped-together members of the 88th Construction Battalion out across the ice from the lakeside town of Kokkorevo. Their destination was Kobona, twenty miles across the bay, at the eastern end of the intended 'road'. They were all wearing lifebelts and camouflage white, and carrying both weapons and ice tools.

It was a sunny day, but the wind was piercingly cold. The men ventured out across the creaking lake, leaving stakes with flags at hundred-metre intervals, making frequent stops to check the thickness of the ice. It was four inches thick in most places, enough, or so the scientists had told them, to support a riderless horse, but as they neared the halfway point it grew thinner and finally disappeared in a large circle of open water. They sloshed their way around its rim, until one man fell through the brittle perimeter and had to be pulled out. Dry clothes had been brought for such an eventuality, and the chain was soon edging gingerly onwards, first to the island of Zelenets, and then to the further shore, which was reached several hours after dark.

Sokolov radioed news of their arrival to Major Mozhayev, his superior in Kokkorevo. Mozhayev passed the good tidings on to Leningrad party headquarters and then, in a fit of glorious optimism, mounted his horse and followed the line of flags out across the frozen lake. Four hours later he, too, was in Kobona.

There might not be enough room on the available eastbound trains for the fuel, ammunition and winter clothing that the German troops desperately needed, but space was always found for the regime's favourite reading matter. The fortnightly *Das Reich* was considered, by its authors at least, essential for the maintenance of morale. How else would the troops know what they were killing and dying for?

The 16 November edition, which was now en route, featured an exhaustive explanation by Joseph Goebbels of the Jews' responsibility for the war. The Propaganda Minister began by reminding his readers of Hitler's prophecy in January 1939 – that if the Jews started another war the result would be 'the destruction of the Jewish race in Europe'. 'We are,' Goebbels added, 'seeing the fulfilment of the prophecy. The Jews are receiving a penalty that is certainly hard, but more than deserved.' Exactly what this penalty was he declined to say. The only punishment mentioned was the recent introduction of compulsory yellow stars for Jews still living in the Reich.

The numerousness of these stars had, Goebbels admitted, been a bit of a surprise to Berlin's non-Jewish citizens – the Jews had been so adept at concealing their presence. 'He had concealed himself, mimicked his surroundings, adopting the colour of the background, adjusted to the environment, in order to wait for the proper moment. Who among us had any idea that the enemy was beside him, that a silent or clever auditor was attending to conversations on the street, in the subway, or in the lines outside cigarette shops? There are Jews one cannot recognize by external signs. These are the most dangerous. It always happens that when we take some measure against the Jews, English or American newspapers report it the next day. Even today the Jews still have secret connections to our enemies abroad and use these not only in their own cause, but in all military matters of the Reich as well. The enemy is in our midst.'

For the moment there was little to worry about. But what would happen if Germany lost the war? These 'harmless-looking Jewish chaps would suddenly become raging wolves. They would attack our women and children to carry out revenge.'

The German people needed to keep reminding themselves that this could happen. Because 'if we Germans have a fateful flaw in our national character, it is forgetfulness. This failing speaks well of our human decency and generosity, but not always for our political wisdom or intelligence. We think everyone else is as good natured as we are. The French threatened to dismember the Reich during the winter of 1939/40, saying that we and our families would have to stand in lines before their field kitchens to get something warm to eat. Our army defeated France in six weeks, after which we saw German soldiers giving bread and sausages to hungry French women and children, and gasoline to refugees from Paris to enable them to return home as soon as possible, there to spread at least some of their hatred against the Reich. That's how we Germans are. Our national virtue is our national weakness.'

It was time to be hard, and not to be 'too good natured, since our enemies are not noble enough to overlook our mistakes'. Better by far 'an unforgiving, cold hardness against the destroyers of our people, against the instigators of the war'. The Jews were to blame for each and every German soldier who fell. 'They have him on their conscience, and must also pay for it.'[9]

Payment was being taken. Half a million Polish Jews had been imprisoned in the Warsaw ghetto for a little over a year, and the approach of a second winter was taking its toll on sick and mal-nourished bodies. 'The most fearful sight is that of the freezing children,' Emmanuel Ringelblum noted in mid-November. 'Little children with bare feet, bare knees and torn clothing stand dumbly in the street weeping.'[10]

On the night of 16–17 November eight Jews – two men and six women – had been caught outside the ghetto without permission and sentenced to death. Two of the women were under eighteen, another was a mother of three. Early that morning all were dragged from their cells, the women bound and blindfolded, by Jewish policemen, one of whom 'distinguished himself with his zeal'.[11] One of the two young women begged that her family be told she'd only been sent to a concentration camp; the other asked God to accept her in sacrifice for her people.

A small group of smiling SS officers, 'calmly smoking cigarettes and behaving cynically', looked on as the firing squad of drafted Polish policemen carried out the execution.[12]

On this same day 942 of Berlin's Jews were ordered to a railway yard in the city's south-eastern suburbs and were forced aboard a train of closed goods wagons. Wearing yellow stars was inadequate punishment for such enemies of the Reich. This particular trans-port, one of around thirty such trains which left Germany for the east between October and January, was bound for Riga in what is now Latvia. Many of its passengers, having received written instructions to prepare for a difficult winter, were carrying little heating stoves.

On the other side of the city, Generaloberst Ernst Udet was on his hotel room phone, very drunk and very distressed. 'They' were after him, he told his ex-girlfriend Inge. He announced his intention to kill himself, and almost immediately did so, holding the phone up so she would hear the shot. Someone called the police, who found scrawled messages on the wall and a suicide note.

Udet had been one of Germany's favourite sons for almost thirty years. A famous fighter ace in the First World War, he had spent the 1920s as a pilot for hire, working in movies, testing new planes for manufacturers, thrilling crowds around the world with his flying circus. He made a lot of money, had a lot of fun, and thoroughly earned his playboy image. Udet joined the Nazi Party in 1933, though not out of any ideological conviction. He was patriotic, liked the idea of developing a new German air force, and found his old comrade Göring hard to say no to.

Early on, he helped promote the Ju-87 dive-bomber, which so well complemented the panzer vehicles and tactics which Heinz Guderian was pushing at the same time. In 1936 he was given charge of the Reich Air Ministry's development wing, and three years later was made Chief of Armaments Procurement for the Luftwaffe. This was a crucial job, and one that was almost impossible to do well, given the feudal way in which Nazi Germany was organized, and the penchant of its barons for indulging in wishful thinking and deliberate ignorance. As long as the war went well, Udet's unsuitability for the post went unnoticed, but the moment things started going awry – as they did in the Battle of Britain – he proved the ideal scapegoat for his rival Erhard Milch and the habitually idle Hermann Göring.

By the summer of 1941 the Luftwaffe's shortcomings in both quantity and quality were being laid, with only partial justification, at Udet's door. He tried to resign, but Göring, only too aware of how that would look, refused him. Udet upped his drinking, smoking and eating to compensate, and complained of sleeplessness and depression. Inge Bleyle's desertion may have been the final straw, but Udet knew who deserved the blame: 'Iron Man' Göring was bitterly reproached in both the suicide note and the slogans scrawled in red across the headboard of the dead man's bed.

The 'Iron Man' heard the news around midday. He ordered the Air Ministry to issue a communiqué. 'While testing a new weapon on November 17, 1941,' it read, 'the director of air armament Colonel General Udet suffered such a grave accident that he died of his injuries.'[13]

The latest issue of the Amsterdam-published Nazi propaganda magazine *Das Europa-Kabel* came out with a new idea for solving the Reich's chronic shortage of funds. If those ex-Soviet enterprises now 'owned' by their conquerors were sold to German private business, then everyone would come out ahead. The buyers could hardly ask for a more business-friendly environment – both labour and resources were, after all, there for the exploitation – and the sellers could fund future conquests with the resulting windfalls.

The idea's proponents had clearly neither visited the western Soviet Union in recent months nor been told of the wholesale destruction of those industries not chosen for relocation. It would be another fifty years before their policy was put into practice, albeit under slightly less punitive circumstances.

Since the German invasion of their country in April 1940, many Norwegians had sought escape to Britain. The Germans set up control stations at all the ports in August 1941, and in late October the death penalty was introduced for leaving the country without permission. Boats had continued to vanish, however, and on this Monday the occupation authorities announced that henceforth all fishing craft would be confined to port between sunset and sunrise.

Two days earlier, the British submarines *Torbay* and *Talisman* had tried to land fifty-three British commandos on the North African shore of Cyrenaica, some two hundred miles behind Axis lines. Storm conditions had turned the disembarkation into a nightmare, with two men drowned and another twenty-three forced back to the *Talisman*. The original plan had involved half the commandos in disrupting enemy communications, but this element was now dropped. Three men were left behind to cover the re-embarkation, leaving twenty-eight to fulfil the mission's primary objective: the assassination of General Erwin Rommel, commander of the

German Panzergruppe Afrika. They moved inland for the planned rendezvous with Lieutenant-Colonel John Haselden, a member of the Long Range Desert Group who had been living undercover with the local Arabs. Haselden loaned them three guides and melted back into the desert like a clandestine Lawrence of Arabia. Thirty-six hours later the twenty-eight commandos were lined up on the crest of a dune overlooking Beda Littoria, peering through another storm-swept darkness at the dimly lit stone building that supposedly housed Rommel and his headquarters.

The mission had been planned in the office of Admiral Sir Roger Keyes, Director of Combined Operations, and was led by his eldest son, Lieutenant-Colonel Geoffrey Keyes. Much intelligence had been gathered from various sources, but, as later became apparent, the gathering process had been gravely compromised by a refusal to divulge the purpose for which the information was sought. Common sense was also in short supply – after two years of fighting the energetic Rommel in France and North Africa, the British should not have been expecting to find his HQ two hundred miles behind the front line.

The stone building in Beda Littoria was, in fact, the headquarters of *Afrikakorps* Quartermaster-General Schleusener. Both he and his deputy were currently in the Apollonia hospital, a few miles to the north, leaving Captain Weitz in command of the twenty-five-strong staff. All but two of these had taken to their camp beds in various rooms on the ground and first floors, leaving one sentry in the downstairs corridor, armed only with a bayonet.

Keyes' plan was to lead ten men in through the front entrance, while another three forced their way through the back door. The rest of the commando force was entrusted with the demolition of the Germans' electricity generator. At one minute to midnight, as the thunder rumbled across the desert, they started down the dune.

Erwin Rommel was asleep in Athens. He had just spent two happy weeks in Rome, staying with his wife Lucie at the Hotel Eden, taking in the sights of St Peter's. On 16 November a thunderstorm had diverted his plane to Belgrade, and then engine trouble had entailed an overnight layover in the Greek capital. Never a patient man, Rommel was more than usually irked by the delays. On 21 November his long-planned assault on the British-held enclave of Tobruk was due to begin, and he wanted time to personally check every last detail of the planned operation.

Keyes and his commandos were not the only British soldiers heading into action. Two hundred miles to the east of Beda Littoria, most of the 8th Army was in motion. Ever since the failure of General Wavell's 'Battleaxe' offensive the previous June, Churchill had been urging Wavell's successor, General Auchinleck, to mount another. It was intolerable, the British Prime Minister thought, for his troops to be sitting on their hands while Russia bled, and North Africa was the only theatre in which they could get to grips with a substantial enemy army. Auchinleck had wisely refused to be rushed but, with the German tide once more surging towards Moscow, had accepted the need to launch his attack with less-than-perfect preparation. The new offensive, code-named Crusader, was scheduled to begin that night.

The movement of troops and supplies behind the British lines had been under way for days, those on the coast road in daylight, those further inland – where the breakthrough was intended – under cover of darkness. 'Sunshields' of metal tubing and hessian had been fixed to the back of more than six hundred British tanks, in the hope that they would be mistaken, at least from the air, for three-ton lorries. Radio traffic was strictly limited, and those messages that needed sending were tagged with a false source.

The RAF pilots' main job was to keep the skies clear of prying German eyes, but the weather did it for them. The storms that swept across Cyrenaica between 16 and 18 November were of stunning intensity. Rain fell in sheets, drastically reducing visibility. Flash floods swept away bridges and immersed every Axis airfield. The Germans were grounded.

On the British side of the line the weather was better. Robert Crisp was one of the tank commanders moving up towards the front line on the evening of 17 November. It soon became 'so dark

that the drivers could only dimly discern the outlines of the tank or
lorry a foot or two in front of them', and someone at the front had
to dismount and lead them by foot. 'So we proceeded slowly
through the night, nose to tail, the desert filled with the low-
geared roaring of radials and the creaking protestations of hundreds
of springs and bogie wheels. To north and south of us the silence
of the empty sands was shattered by similar long, deadly snakes,
weaving forward for the strike.'[14] Like *Kido Butai*, like the
Wehrmacht on the Eastern Front, the British 8th Army was on the
move.

At the other end of Africa the British battleship *Prince of Wales* was
anchored in Cape Town harbour. She was on her way to
Singapore, there to serve as the flagship of the new Force Z.
Churchill had set up a meeting between the Force commander,
diminutive Vice-Admiral Sir Tom Phillips, and South African premier Jan Smuts, and the former was airborne, en route to Pretoria.
Churchill's purpose in arranging this meeting was unclear, but it
seems likely that he wanted Smuts' influential blessing for what
many considered a highly controversial mission.

Force Z had been conceived in Singapore. Worried by the constant bickering between the various political and military
authorities in Singapore, Churchill had sent out a junior minister,
Duff Cooper, to broker some sort of consensus. All the various parties – the commanders of the three services, the governor, the
British ambassadors to Thailand and China, an Australian Special
Representative – had met on 29 September and decided, among
other things, that the dispatch from home of a small squadron of
one or two capital ships would both encourage the locals and deter
the Japanese.

It would also, Churchill thought, show the United States that
Britain was willing to carry her weight in Far Eastern waters. A
'flying squad' of one battleship and one aircraft carrier would be
ideal.

The Admiralty was appalled. It had no capital ships to spare; only
two were available in home waters, for example, and there was no

knowing when the powerful German battleship *Tirpitz* might make a break for the North Atlantic. The navy top brass also feared that Churchill's proposed 'flying squad' might fall between two stools – too small to deter, too big to lose.

The Prime Minister, however, had the final say. He decreed that one of the two Home Fleet battleships, the *Prince of Wales*, should head east with the newly commissioned aircraft carrier *Indomitable*.

This force would certainly have offered a greater deterrent to the Japanese than the one which eventually arrived. Unfortunately for Phillips, now chosen to command Force Z, *Indomitable*'s trial run across the Atlantic ended ingloriously, the carrier running aground off Jamaica. And before any thought could be given to using *Ark Royal* instead, she was sunk by a U-boat in the Mediterranean. The *Prince of Wales* would have only the battlecruiser *Repulse* for company.

Arriving back from his meeting with Smuts, Phillips told his chief of staff that the South African premier was all for the mission and keen that it should be given the maximum publicity. Yet on the very next day Smuts would telegraph Churchill with a rather different take. He was worried, he said, about the division of naval strength in the Far East and Pacific. Force Z at Singapore and the US fleet at Pearl Harbor were far apart and 'separately inferior to the Japanese navy . . . If the Japanese are really nippy,' Smuts added, pun doubtless intended, there was every chance of 'a first-class disaster.'[15]

In Britain General Alan Brooke had just agreed to take over as Chief of the Imperial General Staff. Churchill had offered him the post at Chequers the previous evening, and 'nobody could be nicer than he was'. After walking Brooke to his bedroom door at two in the morning the Prime Minister had taken his new chief's hand, looked into his eyes and wished him the very best of luck. Brooke felt he would need it. 'We were faced with a possible invasion across the Channel, with increasing difficulties in the Middle East, a closed Mediterranean, dark clouds growing in the Far East and a failing Russia driven back to the very gates of Moscow. The horizon was black from end to end . . .' Though not an 'exceptionally religious person', Brooke decided prayer was an appropriate response.[16]

Most of His Majesty's forty-eight million subjects were rather less well informed. That morning's *Times* carried no hint of the offensive already under way in North Africa, and little to substantiate reports emanating from Singapore that matters were 'moving to a crisis' in the Far East.[17] Talk of a standstill on the Eastern Front was several days out of date, and the general air of complacency which pervaded coverage of the Eastern Front was exemplified by a cartoon in another paper, the *Daily Mirror*: a German soldier shivered in the snow above the tag line 'another frozen asset'.[18]

Better reasons for optimism were found in the *Times* small print – the reported German setbacks around Tikhvin and Tula, for instance – and, paradoxically, in a major article headlined RUSSIAN CITIES IN RUINS. This quoted neutral journalists whom the Germans had taken on a tour of the occupied east. One Swede had asked his hosts about the future of the Ukraine and been told that 'a certain degree of self-government' might be offered, but that an independent state was clearly not in German interests. In practice, or so it seemed to the foreign visitors, the Germans were going out of their way to antagonize all those who might have befriended them. The collective farms were not being broken up as the peasants wished, but simply handed over to highly paid German 'Commissars' who treated their new employees like plantation slaves. The cities really were mostly in ruins, but that hadn't stopped the Germans from renaming their streets after Hitler and Göring. Shops were bare, and many city dwellers could feed themselves only by making long foraging trips into the countryside. And despite all this the Soviet population appeared far from 'crushed by their fate'. They 'carried their heads high' and shot 'undaunted looks' at their foreign visitors. There was resistance in their eyes.[19]

The United States was not, as yet, officially at war, but its newspapers were dominated by coverage of the global conflict. The front-page headlines of the *New York Times* were split between this and a looming miners' strike, but the first seven pages were all war

news. There was prominent coverage of Japanese Prime Minister
Tojo's speech to Parliament earlier that day, and the 'three points' for
peace which it contained. 'Third powers' – by which he meant the
United States – were advised to (a) refrain from obstructing a successful conclusion of 'the China affair', (b) end the military
menacing and economic blockade of Japan and (c) make the utmost
effort to prevent the spread of war from Europe to Asia. Japan's
international behaviour was apparently not in need of adjustment.[20]

The *New York Times* had no fresh news of the senior Japanese
diplomat who had recently arrived from Tokyo. Saburo Kurusu had
reached Washington on the previous Saturday, with instructions to
help Ambassador Nomura find a peaceful way out of the growing
crisis between the two countries by 25 November. Neither diplomat knew the precise reason for their superiors' haste. Neither
knew that the First Air Fleet was already positioning itself for the
attack their probable failure would trigger.

At 10.30 that morning Secretary of State Cordell Hull received
Nomura and Kurusu in his office. Hull later claimed to have taken
an instant dislike to Kurusu – 'neither his appearance nor his attitude commanded confidence or respect' – and thought it
inconceivable that the new arrival 'did not know the plans of his
government and the role he was intended to play'.[21] This role, in
Hull's opinion, was a dual one – Kurusu had been sent to seal a
one-sided deal or, failing that, to distract the US leadership from
the real threat heading its way. That morning, however, the
Secretary of State was much more diplomatic. He complimented
Kurusu on the way in which he had handled himself since arriving,
and told him how much everyone liked and admired his new colleague Nomura. After twenty minutes or so, the three men set off
for their eleven o'clock appointment with President Roosevelt.
This was intended as an informal welcome for Kurusu, and though
the four men talked for an hour and a quarter they confined themselves to generalities.

What were the two sides thinking? The most recent diplomatic
initiative was Tokyo's so-called Proposal A, which had been presented to Hull on 7 November. It offered a Japanese withdrawal

from China after twenty-five years, and precious little else. Japanese troops would stay in Indo-China, and Japan would remain a member of the Tripartite Pact with Germany and Italy. In the event of its rejection, Nomura was instructed to offer the marginally more moderate Proposal B, which promised some Japanese withdrawals from Indo-China. The Americans had not accepted Proposal A, but, somewhat to Nomura's surprise, they had not definitively rejected it either. It seemed increasingly likely that they were simply playing for time, and time, as Nomura's superiors in Tokyo kept telling him, was not on Japan's side.

What the Japanese did not know was that the Americans had cracked their diplomatic code in August 1940, gaining full access to their diplomatic correspondence. Roosevelt and Hull already knew that Proposal B was waiting in the wings, and that it was as unacceptable as Proposal A. That diplomacy, in effect, was a dead-end street. But the Americans were also aware that their armed forces needed at least three months to prepare themselves for a Japanese onslaught, and that only diplomacy could fill the gap. Like the Japanese who faced them across the White House carpet, the American leaders harboured a faint residual hope that war between their two countries could be avoided – 'there is no last word between friends,' Roosevelt told his guests, quoting Williams Jennings Bryan.[22] But by this time both he and Hull were convinced of Japanese perfidy, and mostly concerned with where, when and in what circumstances the coming war would start.

Later would definitely be better, and that afternoon Roosevelt sketched out a possible six-month agreement for Hull to consider. The Japanese would be given 'some oil and rice now, more later', in return for a moratorium on military expansion and a de facto abandonment of the Tripartite Pact.[23] If, at the end of six months, the two sides were still unable to reach a lasting agreement, then nothing would have been lost, and the American armed forces would be in a much better position to fight a war.

TUESDAY 18 NOVEMBER

A few destroyers and one carrier were still in the Inland Sea, but most of the First Air Fleet's thirty-three ships were now working their way up the coastline off Honshu, spaced out over several hundred miles in ones and twos, beyond the range of shore-based eyes. The thousands of extra fuel cans and drums which occupied every spare space told the ships' crews that they were in for a long voyage, but few had any idea where this would take them. On previous occasions, their destinations had been south or south-west, and it was true that the usual supplies of tropical clothing had been loaded. But how to explain the foul-weather clothing and the weatherproof tarpaulins draped across the guns? Or the flaps and rudders of the carrier planes coated with anti-freeze grease? One thing was certain – it didn't feel like a training cruise. Both sailors and fliers had been ordered to leave all personal possessions behind, and the ships had been stripped of all flammable items not needed in combat.

Kido Butai had been given three I-class submarines for advanced reconnaissance, but a further twenty-seven would take the shorter, more southerly route. These, the biggest submarines in the world, could carry enough fuel for a round trip from Tokyo to San Francisco. The first group of three had left their Kure base a week ago, and a further nineteen had left Kure and Yokosuka in the intervening days. The five that remained had a special function to perform. They left Kure early that morning and sailed to nearby Kamekakubi to pick up their cargo – the five midget submarines and ten crewmen of the Special Naval Attack Unit.

The Japanese navy had toyed with the idea of such a unit since the late 1920s, when Captain Noriyoshi Yokou realized he could increase the accuracy of torpedoes by giving them human pilots. At that time the naval establishment was still unwilling to contemplate suicide weapons, but the potential of midget submarines was recognized, and future research went into developing a small craft that could fire unmanned torpedoes. By 1941 more than twenty of these midgets had been built. They were forty-one feet long, had an eight-hour battery life and could be carried piggyback on an I-class.

Earlier that year two enthusiastic lieutenants had championed the idea of using them in a surprise attack at the outbreak of a future war. Hearing of the Hawaiian plan, they worked out a plan for deploying the midgets inside Pearl Harbor. At first Yamamoto rejected the idea. Since the midgets could not be recovered, he argued, the mission would be suicidal. The two lieutenants were not so easily put off. If they could boost the range and improve the chances of recovery, would Yamamoto reconsider? He agreed that he would. Early that autumn they reported success, and the midgets were given a role in the Pearl Harbor attack plan.

The original plan had them infiltrating the American base ahead of the early-morning air attack, remaining submerged through the day, then launching their torpedoes at an enemy who thought the danger was past. But the ten volunteer crewmen objected to the long wait that this involved – their impatience, they claimed, would get the better of them. 'Some of us might become so excited we will give the game away,' their commander, Lieutenant Iwasa, admitted.[1] Somewhat astonishingly, this argument was accepted, and each midget commander was given leave to attack when he saw fit.

Yamamoto's dislike of suicide missions was not shared by these men, nor indeed by his chief of staff. Watching from the quarter-deck of the *Nagato* as the last of the midget-carrying submarines headed out towards the ocean, Matome Ugaki came to the nostalgic conclusion that nobility of spirit mattered more than mere effectiveness. 'How much damage they inflict is not the point,' he told his diary. 'The firm determination not to return alive on the part of those young lieutenants and ensigns who smilingly embarked on their ships cannot be praised too much. The spirit of self-sacrifice has not changed at all.'[2]

The Trans-Siberian railway was double track, and since mid-October trains had been heading for Moscow on both of them. Numerous infantry divisions and tank brigades were moving west, travelling mostly by night in packs of fifteen to twenty trains, an unseen avalanche of potentially decisive proportions.

On 14 September Richard Sorge, the leader of the Soviet spy ring in Tokyo, had signalled his employers in the Kremlin that Japan would only attack them if one of three conditions were met – the fall of Moscow, a three-to-one advantage in soldiers, or a civil war in Siberia. Three weeks later he had gone further and guaranteed that the Soviet Union was safe from Japanese attack for at least the duration of the winter.

But had he been believed? Sorge had given Stalin advanced warning of Barbarossa, a warning the Soviet leader had mocked and spurned. Perhaps Sorge's accuracy on that occasion had raised his credibility, perhaps his supportive evidence on this occasion – the signs of a Japanese move to the south, the immense difficulty of moving troops across the vast Siberian distances in Siberian winter conditions – was convincing corroboration. Or perhaps it was simply a case of necessity – if Moscow and the Caucasus fell, then what was the point of defending Irkutsk?

In Typhoon's opening fortnight, back in early October, around six hundred thousand Red Army troops had been encircled in two large pockets around Vyazma and Bryansk. Yet again the panzer spearheads had punched holes in the Soviet line, advanced into open country and wheeled in to link hands behind the Soviet armies. It was classic *blitzkrieg*, a faster, motorized version of the converging pincer tactics that Hannibal had used at Cannae over two thousand years earlier. In those grim days, as one Soviet observer put it, the Germans had advanced 'without even reconnoitring, without patrols, without flank guards, in comfort, riding in lorries . . .'[3]

But not any more. The Red Army was learning. Those who had escaped the encirclements, and those drafted in to fill the gaping holes where divisions had been, began fighting in a different way. With Moscow so close in the rear, the great temptation – one to which Stalin and Zhukov would occasionally succumb – was to defend every position to the last man, to contest each and every mile of the fifty that remained. The appropriate tactics, as pioneered by the 316th Division under General Panfilov and supported by his superior General Rokossovsky, were to make the best use of natural defences and fall back when necessary, but only after making the enemy pay the maximum price in blood and time.

Reinforcements were arriving from Siberia and Central Asia, but the Red Army in front of Moscow was still perilously thin on the ground – it was not uncommon for a battalion of seven hundred men to be covering a five-mile stretch of the front. In many locations, however, there was no need to spread them out. If the Germans had believed the old saying – that anywhere a deer can go a soldier can go, and anywhere a soldier can go an army can go – they now realized their mistake. Armies in 1941, particularly their own, could go only where a lorry could go. And such pathways were few and far between to the north and west of Moscow: the countryside was full of woods and forests, and remarkably short of usable roads. If the Germans chose to saw and axe their way to Moscow it would take them years; if they stuck to the roads the Soviets could concentrate against them. Crossroads in particular were heavily mined, overlooked by rifle trenches, covered by field and anti-tank guns. Eventually the Germans would bring up enough firepower to force their way through, but by then the

Soviet guns would have been pulled back, the men vanished into the trees, only to mount another ambush another mile down the road. Panfilov likened a series of these actions to a spring, cushioning the enemy advance, costing him days he didn't have.

It was a life of appalling discomfort, endless anxiety and occasional terror. 'At any moment everything might begin to roar, scream and howl . . . shells would streak overhead, tanks would rumble across the fields . . . men in field grey would come running out of the forest . . . men who were coming to kill us.' A silent forest would erupt, tracer bullets, like 'needles of fire', exploding through the snow-covered pines. At night, as the soldiers boiled water for tea and dried their clothes by a fire, German rocket flares would light the sky with their colour-coded messages, signalling who knew what, a show of beauty promising death.[4]

There were corpses everywhere. Mangled, crushed, lacking heads or limbs. Blown into trees, half-buried in snow, stretched out on a frozen stream. Friends and strangers, soldiers and civilians, their faces frozen in shock or fear. Each with a story cut short, a life bitten off. Just one body in Volokolamsk, noticed by one soldier: 'Amidst the ruins on the edge of the pavement lay a dead woman. A breeze stirred her dishevelled grey hair. But one lock of hair was glued to her head by fresh blood, still red and not yet congealed.'[5]

The dead had no interest in victory. Morale was critical now, and the Soviet leadership knew it. A ceaseless flood of propaganda reached the front lines, much of it read to the men by unit commissars. Much of it, of course, was true – the Germans *were* behaving like beasts to those they captured, the soldiers of the Red Army in front of Moscow *were* the rock on which the tide of evil might break. They had to stick together, and if the price of such solidarity was the execution of cowards and the use of NKVD blocking detachments to mow down unsanctioned retreats, then that was the way things had to be. Such toughness brought us victory, survivors would say in later years.

The charismatic Panfilov died that Tuesday, a stray mortar shell hitting his observation point near Siskino. His 316th Infantry Division was under attack by the 2nd and 11th Panzer Divisions and slowly giving ground. By nightfall the German spearhead had advanced seven miles, not much by summer standards, but a fair chunk of the remaining distance to Moscow. Further north, the 3rd Panzer Group was making even faster progress towards Klin, opening a dangerous gap between the 16th and 30th Armies. Fearing a major breakthrough and possible encirclement, Rokossovsky asked permission to withdraw the 16th Army to the line of the Istra River and Reservoir, almost half the way back to Moscow.

This was much too much for Zhukov, who forbade any voluntary retreat. He had been ordered to save Moscow, and he was going to do just that, with no attempt to cost or check the sacrifice involved. During these early days of the renewed Typhoon, unit after Red Army unit echoed the fate of the 44th Mongolian Cavalry, leaving carpets of bodies for the Germans to clamber over.

'There may be situations,' Rokossovsky wrote in his memoirs, 'when a decision to stand to the last man is the only possible one.' But he didn't think this was one of them. 'There were no troops behind the 16th Army, and if the defending units were smashed the road to Moscow would be open – which was just what the enemy had all the time been striving to achieve.'[6] He went over Zhukov's head, appealing the decision to Chief of the General Staff Marshal Boris Shaposhnikov. Agreement was forthcoming. 'Our spirits rose. Now, we reflected, the Germans would break their teeth on the Istra line.'[7]

The joy was short-lived. Shaposhnikov's decision had not been cleared with Zhukov, and an angry telegram reached Rokossovsky, reiterating the previous order. 'There was nothing I could do: an order is an order, and, being soldiers, we obeyed it. The results were unfortunate.'[8]

On the German side, at least to the west and north-west of Moscow, there was a sense of gathering momentum. The problem was to sustain it with the supply situation in crisis. The 87th Infantry Division, which had begun its advance that morning on the far right flank of Panzer Group 4, was in typically weakened condition. Numbers were down, and many that remained had been seriously disabled by frostbite. Ammunition was in short supply, and the winter clothing had still not arrived.

The 6th Infantry Division proved luckier than most, but not by much. Its winter clothing arrived that day – four heavy fur-lined greatcoats and four pairs of felt-lined boots for each company of two hundred men. Where was the rest of it? According to the Reich Press Chief's Order of the Day the Wehrmacht's winter clothing had been procured in the summer and was now waiting at the railheads for distribution. However, the transport situation was dire, and there might be some delay. 'For this reason,' he warned his journalistic subordinates, 'it would not be expedient to mention the troops' winter equipment at this time.'[9] It would be desirable to keep the population calm. On the basis of news in the press, the soldiers would write to their relatives that they had not yet received winter clothing. This might shake the public confidence in the German news service at a crucial time. For similar reasons, he advised that great care should be taken not to include pictures of German troops still in their summer uniforms. Shots of Soviet prisoners in overcoats, alongside German escorts without them, were particularly to be avoided.

On 18 November the troops were offered one slight compensation for the lack of winter clothing. After its sudden drop at the end of the previous week, the temperature edged back up. The soldiers welcomed the respite, however slight and temporary it might prove. Their better-clad generals were less impressed – rising temperatures often meant more snow.

In the south the 1st Panzer Army's advance on Rostov was slowed but not stopped by a 56th Army counter-attack, and by evening the Germans were less than fifteen miles from the city. The feeling that they were pushing at a revolving door persisted, however, as the Soviet 37th Army pressed its attack on the German's left flank. Around two hundred T-34s were involved, and Katyusha rockets were used for the first time against Army Group South. The SS Wiking Division was driven back in some disorder, the situation only restored, momentarily, by continuous Stuka attacks and the spending of precious reserves.

The capture of Rostov might prove straightforward, but the overall situation of Army Group South was growing more confused, with each German success matched by a Soviet counter, often in the same area. Around Grakovo, a hundred miles further north, the two armies were fighting what was an increasingly typical battle. The previous day two German regiments – one infantry, one artillery – had occupied a state farm. They soon came under attack, and the artillerymen were forced to abandon their guns and retreat to positions around Grakovo railway station. The infantrymen were soon compelled to follow, but that morning the artillerymen were able to reoccupy their firing positions. Again attacked, they opened fire on the Soviets at a hundred metres, holding them off for long enough to destroy their guns and retreat once more to the railway station. Two nights of bombardment followed, but the German infantry eventually managed to reoccupy the state farm.

Such rapid exchanges of territory were now commonplace, and often left units of the opposing armies dangerously intermingled across the vast battlefield. The long winter nights provided commanders with the chance to put things right, but like any blind shuffle also gave rise to a few surprises.

Some were even welcome. One group of teeth-chattering German soldiers was drawn to a large fire in the distance. Wearing woollen coats, felt boots and fur caps taken from a Red Army depot in captured Taganrog, they looked like Russians. After spending some time warming themselves by the fire – three blazing stacks of baled hay – they burrowed into some other straw bundles intent on sleep. 'Soon we noticed that there were more fur caps with Soviet stars around the fire. We knew these were genuine Russians. However, we were too weak and tired to think about it. We had been together for a surprisingly long time. Then we slept together peacefully. On the next morning, we gathered up our sleeping comrades, several dozen, and moved off to the west – homeward. Not a shot was fired, no hatred was displayed, no anger.

The cold made everyone equal. War can also be so human, so peaceful.'[10]

Or not. On that day the commander of the German 255th Infantry Division's artillery regiment reported on conditions in Transient POW Camp 231: 'The prisoners of war, who number at present about seven thousand, not counting the wounded, are accommodated in the shell of a factory building which gives protection only against the rain. On the other hand, the prisoners of war are exposed to the cold without any protection. The windows are several meters high and wide and without covering. There are no doors to the building. The prisoners who are thus kept practically in the open air are freezing to death by the hundreds daily – in addition to those who die continuously because of exhaustion . . .'[11]

These conditions were not the result of inefficiency, or of POW Camp 231 being run by an unusually sadistic commandant. They were the norm for Soviet prisoners, a reflection of Barbarossa's ultimate purpose, the wholesale reduction of a captive population.

Unlike, say, the German invasion of France, the German invasion of the Soviet Union was not undertaken in order to defeat and impose terms on a transient enemy. It was undertaken with a view to the permanent conquest of European Russia. The historical precedent that Hitler and the other Nazi leaders had in mind was the United States, and the American taming of the 'savage' West. The Volga, Hitler said, would be Germany's Mississippi.

Like America's 'Red Indians', the indigenous Slavs were considered sub-human. Hitler called them 'a rabbit family', intrinsically idle and disorganized.[12] All that they understood was 'the whip'. Goebbels spent a professional lifetime thinking up insulting phrases and drip-feeding them to the German people. The Bolsheviks were 'wild', 'depraved', essentially 'hostile to life', the Slavs stolid animals with a primitive tenacity, advancing from the Siberian tundra like 'a dark wave of filth'.[13] There was no point in treating them like fellow human beings.

So what was to be done with them? There was one big difference between the Native Americans and the Slavs – there were far too many of the latter to put in reservations. In Russia and Ukraine ethnic cleansing would be insufficient. The SS planners estimated that forty-five million people would have to be 'removed', but where could they be 'removed' to?

The logistics of the German military campaign clarified the issue. Food was needed for the 3 million soldiers and 600,000 horses now struggling eastwards. There was an overall shortage of food in German-occupied Europe, but even a surplus would have been undeliverable – the fuel and trains to carry it were simply not available. The Wehrmacht would have to live off the land, to consume the sub-human enemy's food. The Soviet cities were reduced to rationing and worse, the rural population to hiding, foraging and generally living off its local knowledge. And at the bottom of the pile, unable to forage, utterly and fatally dependent on an enemy who despised him, was the Soviet prisoner of war.

Many of those captured in the Bryansk encirclement were sent to DuLag-130, a purpose-built holding camp near Roslavl. No food was distributed during the seventy-mile march, and those who collapsed from exhaustion were shot where they fell. Conditions were little better at the camp itself, hunger, disease and exposure combining to kill around four per cent of the inmates each day. By early December around 8,500 had perished.

Further north, near Rzhev, 15,000 POWS and 5,000 civilians were incarcerated in unheated barracks. A steady diet of one frozen potato a day was topped up by rotten meat and bones, tossed through the barbed wire as if it was feeding time at the zoo. Those who grew too ill to work were shot.

Such facilities had sprung up all over the occupied territories. According to Wehrmacht statistics, over three million Soviet prisoners had been taken in the first five months of Barbarossa. By 18 November around two-thirds of them were dead. Six hundred thousand had been shot, the rest had succumbed to what passed for 'natural causes' in German-occupied Russia – hunger, exhaustion, exposure, ill-treatment of every description.

This was not only morally depraved but also utter idiocy. At the beginning of Barbarossa the men and women of the Red Army had assumed that surrender implied survival, but once they learned otherwise – that their real choice lay between a quick hero's death on the battlefield and a lingering death in captivity – there was no earthly reason for any Soviet soldier to throw in the towel.

It was a few seconds past midnight in Beda Littoria, thunder cracking as the rain sheeted. Keyes and his commandos crept towards Rommel's supposed front door, where a sentry was standing guard. Sergeant Terry had his knife ready, but the German saw him in time and managed to pull his assailant back inside the building. The sentry's shouts of alarm were drowned out by the storm, but his collision with a door woke the two men who were sleeping behind it. One yanked the door wide and opened fire, hitting Keyes in the thigh. At the same moment Keyes tossed a grenade past him, killing the other.

Upstairs, Lieutenant Kaufholz had grabbed his revolver and rushed towards the head of the stairs. Reaching it as the grenade flash illuminated the scene below, he exchanged shots with Keyes and his second in command, Captain Campbell. As Kaufholz killed Keyes with a shot through the chest, Campbell killed Kaufholz with a machine-gun burst, though not before Kaufholz had put a bullet in his shin.

Terry was now in effective command. More German voices could be heard upstairs, and machine-gun fire erupted outside. This was British commandos killing a German officer who had leaped into their midst, but Terry and his companions, fearing a trap, ran out through the door and headed for the desert, encountering and shooting another sentry as they went.

The commandos sent to the back door had been thwarted by paranoia – one of the Germans who slept in the back room liked to feel safe and insisted on blocking the unlockable door with a large receptacle of water and a filing cabinet. Unable to gain entry, startled by the machine-gun fire around the building's corner, these commandos also made a run for it.

Four Germans had died. Keyes was dead, Campbell wounded and captured. The Germans would apprehend all but two of their comrades within a few days, mostly by paying the local Arabs to betray them. According to Hitler's law, the British commandos should have been shot as partisans, but Rommel insisted that all were treated as prisoners of war.

After several advances and retreats, the front line in November 1941 – with the exception of the British-held enclave at Tobruk – was more or less where it had been when hostilities commenced in June 1940. The three-week battle now beginning would spread across a wide expanse of largely unpopulated desert, roughly equivalent in size to Connecticut or East Anglia. The topography consisted of a narrow coastal plain that rose in a series of steps or escarpments to a flattish desert plateau. The steps varied in width – the one housing the crucial Sidi Rezegh airstrip, for example, was around three miles wide – and the number of places where vehicles could climb or descend from one to another was seriously limited.

If this seemed, in some ways, the ideal place at which to hold a war, then appearances were deceptive. The virtual absence of civilians was certainly a bonus, but the terrain was hostile to both men and vehicles. It might be generally flat, but the main surface was uneven rock, with or without a coating of dust or sand. Both surface and particles were hard on vehicles, and the particles raised by the vehicles' passage made for poor visibility, particularly when augmented by the smoke of battle. The resulting navigational problems were further increased by the lack of obvious landmarks.

The British plan could hardly have been simpler. While XIII Corps (the 4th Indian and New Zealand Infantry Divisions) took on the Axis infantry manning the front line, XXX Corps (the 4th, 7th and 22nd Armoured Brigades, along with the 1st South African Infantry Division) would break through the undefended wire to the south and advance across the desert plateau in the direction of Tobruk, some hundred miles to the north-west. Forced to give battle, the Axis armour (*Afrikakorps*' 15th and 21st Panzer, the Italian *Ariete* Division) would be outnumbered and destroyed. The Axis troops on the frontier would be surrounded, Tobruk relieved.

First came the waiting. Much of the 8th Army suffered a sleep-less night; if the sappers blowing gaps in the front-line wire didn't keep them awake, then the cataclysmic thunderstorms did. The tank crews sat inside their vehicles, listening to the tattoo of rain on their 'sunshields', waiting for Tuesday's dawn and the order to move forward. When it came around seven, movement was slow, 'like a passage along Piccadilly in the rush hour' according to Robert Crisp.[14] It was ten before his tank reached the wire, its crew's enthusiasm dampened, like everyone else's, by the seemingly endless procession of stops and starts.

Once clear of the wire, however, the offensive got going, with the armoured units advancing in parallel columns like the ships of a fleet. Bedouin and camels occasionally loomed into view, but there was no sign of the enemy, either on the ground or in the air. During the afternoon the order went out to drop the 'sunshields', and the armada of lorries became an army of tanks. Crisp found his elation returning, and 'an immense curiosity'. What would happen to him? 'Not for one moment did I contemplate the possibility of anything unpleasant, and with that went the assumption that there was bound to be a violent encounter with the enemy, that it would end in our favour, and that if anything terrible were going to happen it would probably happen to other people but not to me.'[15]

By dusk Crisp had reached the austerely named Point 185, some sixty-five miles from his starting point that morning. He had seen no Germans or Italians, and in this he was far from alone. A few German vehicles had been sighted that morning to the north, but had swiftly disappeared. By nightfall the leading British units of the 7th Armoured Brigade had reached Gabr Saleh, around halfway to Tobruk, without encountering any resistance.

The British plan relied, more than a little foolishly, on drawing a particular response from the enemy. What if it was not forth-coming?

Rommel arrived back at his real headquarters that morning, intent on finalizing his army's preparations for the capture of Tobruk. The 15th Panzer was already in the area, the 21st Panzer moving west along the Trigh Capuzzo. Only two small reconnaissance units were active further south, in the seventy miles that separated Tobruk from the newly holed wire. It was one of these – Reconnaissance Battalion 33 – which almost ran into the right flank of the British advance early that morning.

Rommel received a report from this unit, and one from the front line reporting many explosions to the south during the previous night. But the Luftwaffe was still grounded by the weather conditions, and nothing could be checked. It was, Rommel decided, just a British reconnaissance-in-force. He would not be distracted.

There were no more scares until early evening. Shortly before sunset the other reconnaissance battalion reported an advance by '200 enemy tanks' but offered no explanatory details. At around the same time a British officer captured by the Italians was taken for questioning in Bardia. He not only revealed the overall British plan but claimed knowledge of Rommel's own plan to take Tobruk. The Germans decided he was a plant, intended to deceive them.

Rommel's refusal to believe that a major British offensive was under way proved as fortunate as it was wrong-headed. His failure to follow the British script left them alone on the desert stage, out of lines and forced to improvise. The mistakes were swift in coming.

An editorial in the morning's *New York Times* examined Tojo's 'three points' and found them seriously wanting. 'After the substantial discount is made for the fact that Premier Tojo was speaking for home consumption to a war-weary and disillusioned people, it is impossible to escape the conclusion that the Japanese terms are nonsense.'[16]

Hull agreed. That morning he, Nomura and Kurusu had another lengthy discussion at the State Department. The Secretary of State, still searching for a button that would eject Japan from the Tripartite Pact, suggested that a victorious Hitler would eventually 'get around to the Far East and double-cross Japan'. Kurusu, correctly interpreting this as an invitation to get Japan's betrayal in first, indignantly rejected it. Japan could not leave the Tripartite Pact, he said, but might render it irrelevant. A deal with America, he hinted, could 'outshine' the deal with Germany and Italy.

What sort of deal?, Hull wanted to know. A return to the situation existing in early July, Nomura suggested tentatively. A Japanese withdrawal from southern Indo-China in return for an end to the American embargoes, he added in explanation, ignoring Kurusu's questioning look. The two of them had no mandate from Tokyo to offer such a deal.

If Hull was interested, he didn't show it. What was to stop the Japanese using these troops somewhere else, he asked somewhat churlishly, before agreeing to pass the offer on to the British and Dutch. The United States had nothing to lose from such a deal, and something to gain. Time, at the very least.

Encouraged, Nomura and Kurusu sent off a series of messages to Tokyo. They also received one. Most Japanese residents in America who desired repatriation ahead of a possible war had already reached home – the liners *Tatuta Maru* and *Nitta Maru* had made cross-Pacific round trips for that purpose in October to November. The rest, Tokyo informed Nomura, would be collected several weeks hence. The *Tatuta Maru* would leave Tokyo for another round trip in early December, carrying Americans equally eager to reach their homeland.

This was a lie. The liner would certainly venture out into the Pacific, but not with any intention of crossing it. The Japanese were eager to give the impression that war was still some way off, that the time for vigilance had not yet arrived. The American passengers who eventually boarded the *Tatuta Maru* were taken in by the ruse, as was their government. So, too, were Nomura and Kurusu.

Japan's diplomats in Washington were kept in ignorance of their country's military preparations. Full knowledge, Tokyo believed, would put Nomura and Kurusu in an impossible position, and make a last-minute deal with the United States even less likely. This policy proved very beneficial to the Japanese cause, but not for the reasons intended. As already mentioned, American cryptologists had broken the Japanese diplomatic or 'Purple' code in August 1940 and were able to read all the briefings and instructions sent to the Washington embassy. If Nomura and Kurusu had been in the loop, the Americans would have been in it, too.

For communicating with the Japanese consulate in Hawaii, Tokyo used the J-19 code, not Purple. The Americans had also cracked this, and although the keys were changed on a daily basis it was theoretically possible to decode and translate a message in a matter of hours. In practice, it was hard to know which messages deserved priority, and the whole process was hamstrung by the decision to forward all messages by mail.

One such message that arrived for Consul General Nagao Kita in Honolulu on 18 November was finally translated in Washington on 5 December. It asked what seemed a fairly routine question – which American military vessels were anchored in which parts of Pearl Harbor? Unfortunately for the Americans, the more suspicious messages that reached Kita in late November and early December would be translated only once the need for warning was past.

WEDNESDAY 19 NOVEMBER

At sea, Great Britain was fighting what amounted to several different wars. The first was a simple struggle for control between surface fleets, and here the Royal Navy, through sheer weight of numbers, held the upper hand. Germany had started the war with seven capital ships either ready for service or in the pipeline. The pocket battleship *Graf Spee* had been scuttled by her captain off Montevideo in 1939, the battleship *Bismarck* hunted down and sunk in the North Atlantic the previous May. The battlecruisers *Scharnhorst* and *Gneisenau* had done some damage during a North Atlantic foray in April 1941 but had been holed up in Brest harbour ever since, repairing damage wrought by continuing bombing raids. *Bismarck*'s sister ship *Tirpitz* and the other two pocket battleships – *Admiral Scheer* and *Deutschland* – were, from spring 1941, confined to Baltic and Norwegian waters. They needed watching, but hardly constituted a major threat. Like suicide bombers, they might be used to dangerous effect, but were almost certain to perish in the act.

The Japanese fleet was another matter. Neither London nor Washington realized just how effective a fighting force the Imperial Japanese Navy had become, but they were aware of being outnumbered. For the moment both were relying on deterrence to keep the Japanese at bay, the Americans by building up their B-17 bomber force on the Philippines, the British by sending Force Z to Singapore.

Britain's other naval wars were all about supply. In the Atlantic, U-boats stalked the convoys, hoping to choke off Britain's supply line of food, fuel and weaponry. In the Mediterranean, opposing naval forces fought to prevent the supply and reinforcement of the other side's air and ground forces: on the one hand, Rommel's army in Africa, on the other, beleaguered Malta and besieged Tobruk. In the Arctic, a new convoy route had recently come into use for supplying Anglo-American aid to the Soviet Union, and on that morning the fourth outbound convoy, PQ4, left Iceland for Archangel. The Admiralty was worried about a possible intervention by the lurking *Tirpitz*, and with good cause – Admiral Raeder had suggested such a course four days earlier. But a shortage of boiler oil limited the battleship's range and sowed doubts in Hitler's mind. Unwilling to lose both his giant battleships in six months, he vetoed the idea.

The final battle at sea – a minor but strangely compelling contest – was being fought between the Royal Navy and eleven armed German merchantmen or 'auxiliary cruisers'. In November 1941 two of these were still waiting for their first ocean raid, and a further two would never get to see one. Of the other seven, *Pinguin* had been sunk in May of this year, while *Orion* and *Widder* had both been decommissioned. *Thor* was scheduled to leave Kiel in the next few days; *Komet* was off the coast of north-west Africa, on her way home to the same port. Only *Atlantis* and *Kormoran*, in the South Atlantic and Indian Ocean respectively, were still scouring the horizon for likely targets.

On that Wednesday *Kormoran* was running south about 200 miles off the coast of Western Australia, hoping to lay mines off the naval port of Fremantle. It was just before 16.00 hours when the foretop lookout reported another ship on the horizon, and only a few minutes later when the German raider's captain, Theodor Detmers, realized, with a sinking heart, what kind of ship she was.

'I just knew that I had to do my best, make every effort to increase our chances.'[1]

The thirty-nine-year-old Detmers had spent more than half his life in the navy. Given command of the *Kormoran* in June 1940, he had relished the chance to emulate his raider heroes of the previous war. His ship was the largest of the auxiliaries, with a displacement of 8,736 tons, a top speed of 18 knots and a crew of nearly 400 men. She had six 5.9-inch, two 37-millimetre and five 20-millimetre guns, all mounted out of sight below deck, and six torpedo tubes above and below the waterline.

Kormoran broke out into the North Atlantic in December 1940, and accounted for eight merchantmen in the mid- and South Atlantic during the first four months of 1942. The potential victim would appear over the horizon, and eventually realize that the ship heading innocently in its direction was not what she seemed. A chase would ensue, and the opposing captain would be given the chance to save himself and his crew by not using his radio. Most refused to oblige. They sent out their warning message, were fired on, and then surrendered. The Germans picked up what survivors they could, but once a message had been sent they could ill afford to hang around, because any encounter with an enemy naval vessel was likely to prove fatal.

In May *Kormoran* moved on into the Indian Ocean, where the pickings proved much thinner. Detmers and his men spent five months sailing to and fro across the eastern half of that ocean, hoping for victims, dreading a warship. 'Every wisp of smoke, every mast top could have spelled the end,' as Detmers put it.[2] He found only three more victims, and on 19 November he finally ran into the warship.

The Australian light cruiser *Sydney* was heading back towards Fremantle, having passed a Malaya-bound troopship on to its British escort. She was better armed than *Kormoran*, boasting eight six-inch and eight four-inch guns and four torpedo tubes, and was almost twice as fast. During Mediterranean duty in 1940–41 she had sunk three Italian warships, one cruiser and two destroyers. Sighting the apparent merchantman, *Sydney* altered course to intercept her.

Detmers knew that his only chance was to fight a battle at close range, where his weapons would be as effective as his opponent's. As the Australian ship drew closer, demanding that he identify himself, he played for time. Silence was his first response, then apparent incomprehension, finally a display of apparent incompetence. The Australian captain allowed himself to be suckered in, without even ensuring that all his guns were manned. With the two ships less than a mile apart, Detmers threw off the cloak. As the German battle flag went up, the merchantman metamorphosed into a warship in front of the Australians' eyes. Within seconds the guns were up and ranging, the torpedo tubes sliding out. One ranging shot was short, the second long, and then a three-shell salvo crashed into *Sydney*'s bridge and forward control tower. Another few seconds and the Australian cruiser had lost her catapult plane and both forward gun turrets.

The two rear turrets returned fire, one slamming shells into the *Kormoran* engine room and funnel. As *Sydney* turned to bring her four starboard torpedoes to bear, one of the forward turrets exploded into the air. The four torpedoes all missed, but the German ship's engine had been incapacitated by the earlier shellfire. *Kormoran* had offensive clout but no mobility, *Sydney* the reverse. Both ships were burning.

Sydney retreated southwards, pursued for a while by shells from the German guns. Hours later she was still a smudge of flame on the night horizon. By then Detmers knew that *Kormoran*'s engines were irreparable, and that flames were licking closer to the hundreds of mines stored below decks. At around midnight, shortly after two distant explosions seemed to signal the end of *Sydney*, the Germans took to their boats and moved away from the stricken *Kormoran*, then watched as the timed charges sent the mines towards heaven and their ship to the sea-floor. Detmers lost around sixty men in the action – twenty in the battle, another forty when one of the small boats capsized. *Sydney* and her 645-strong crew were never seen again.

★

Several thousand miles to the north, the myriad arms of the Japanese war machine were reaching out in all directions. As the widely spread components of *Kido Butai* and the Third Submarine Division headed north-east and east, other ships, naval and merchant, set off for the south and south-east.

For several days now the US Assistant Naval Attaché in Shanghai had been watching an intensification of port activity, with many Japanese ships arriving from the north and departing for the south. On 19 November he reported ten such transports. Some carried troops, others a variety of suspicious-looking cargoes. One ship he noticed was loaded with the sort of timber trestles an invasion force would need for constructing piers and bridges.

Masuda Reiji's freighter, the *Arizona Maru*, was hardly suited to modern-day naval operations, but like hundreds of others she had been drafted in to supplement Japan's overstretched naval resources. On 13 November she had crossed the Inland Sea to pick up 3,000 drums of fuel for the army division charged with invading the Philippines, and today she was leaving for Formosa. Over the next few weeks Reiji and his fellow crewmen would work overtime at keeping their old and overtaxed ship in working order. Steam hissed from crack after crack, and even at night they had to 'crawl all over the ship's boilers, candles in hand, desperately looking for leaks'.[3]

Back in Tokyo, the men in charge were still choosing to believe that Matome Ugaki's spirit of self-sacrifice would more than compensate for the thinness of the country's resources. Two important messages went out that Wednesday, both marking another deliberate step into the maelstrom. One was the 'winds-code' instruction, which was sent, in various versions, to several Japanese embassies around the world. The longer of the two versions sent to Washington warned Nomura and Kurusu that 'in case of emergency (danger of cutting off diplomatic relations), and the cutting off of international communications', certain key phrases would be included in the daily short-wave news broadcasts from Tokyo.[4] 'East wind rain' meant Japanese–American relations were in

danger; 'north wind cloudy' and 'west wind clear' implied a similar threat to Japanese–Soviet and Japanese–British relations.
Following receipt of such a message, embassy staff were to destroy
the appropriate code papers. There was, however, nothing in the
'winds-code' set-up to say that war would automatically follow a
broadcast warning, and certainly no indication of where the first
blow might fall.

The 'winds-code' messages were sent in the J-19 code, and not
processed until 26 November. The other message, instructing
Nomura and Kurusu to present Proposal B, went out in the Purple
code, and Hull probably read it before the Japanese diplomats.
Foreign Minister Togo, annoyed by his Washington representatives' ad-lib diplomacy on the previous day, laid down the law.
Nomura was told to present Proposal B on the following day, and
not to make any further concessions. If the US could not be persuaded to accept this final proposal, then 'the negotiations will
have to be broken off . . .'[5]

In mid-morning Halder picked up the phone in his Rastenburg
Forest office and called von Bock in Orsha. The chief of staff suggested that the 3rd Panzer Group's increasingly successful advance
towards Klin should soon be redirected south-eastwards towards
Moscow, and von Bock replied that he was already considering the
idea. He doubted, however, whether the forces available were
strong enough to carry it through. And in spite of all their efforts,
von Bock added, the advance might wither for lack of supplies.
'Strength of attack force is weak,' Halder noted in his diary.
'Impossible fuel use.'[6]

He was soon in his car, driving down the snow-cleared forest
roads to the Wolfsschanze. The 'Führer Conference' began at
13.00, and Hitler had his usual suggestions to make about moving
this division and that, the sort of matters which had always been the
responsibility of the army commanders on the spot. Where Army
Group Centre was concerned, he was keen to stress a more general
point – that the offensive must be conducted in such a way that the
Russian armies were eliminated, not simply pushed backwards.

The German forces should still be aiming for the line Vologda–Yaroslavl–Rybinsk, 'weather and supply permitting.'[7]

Halder had made notes for his presentation, the gist of which was that weather and supply would not be permitting. Seventy per cent of Germany's trucks were off the road, either dead or in need of major repair. Only sixteen supply trains were reaching Army Group Centre each day, against a minimum requirement of thirty-one. Most of Army Group South had been virtually immobilized by weather conditions and supply failures.

General Thomas, head of the Defence Economy and Armament Office, was also present, and his situation summary was even bleaker. German-controlled Europe was running short on food, fuel, metals and any residual goodwill on the part of the occupied. And there was no obvious way to rectify the situation.

Hitler refused to let this catalogue of gloom limit his military plans for the next few months. As if to encourage Thomas, he named the Caucasus and its oil as the primary objective for the coming spring. Further north, everything would depend on Typhoon's progress during the coming weeks, but German troops were still expected to advance at least 300 miles beyond Moscow. As for the rest, it would depend on the capacity of the railways.

But when it came to the wider geopolitical situation and the longer term, Hitler did seem markedly more cautious. A few weeks earlier the Russian war machine had been given its death rites, but now he seemed almost content with it needing 'a long time to recover'. And he was relying on 'internal social strains' to defeat the British, mostly, it seemed, because the chances of defeating her militarily were so remote.[8]

As he listened to this rambling exposition, Halder reached the conclusion that his Führer had accepted the impossibility of victory and was resigning himself to the possibility of a negotiated peace.

Given this gloomy background, that day's news from the Eastern Front was mainly positive. North-west of Moscow and south of the Volga Reservoir, Reinhardt's 3rd Panzer Group made more significant gains, with Rommel's old 7th Panzer Division leading the advance on Klin. If this small city on the Moscow–Leningrad road could be taken, the right flank of Rokossovsky's 16th Army would be exposed, and another giant encirclement might prove possible. In the meantime, the 16th Army had all its work cut out to resist the mounting pressure exerted by the 4th Panzer Group on its front. The line had been pushed back fifteen miles in three days, which didn't seem much but was still the sort of schedule which would get the Germans to Moscow in a fortnight. At some point in the not-too-distant future the Red Army had to do better than slow the advance, and actually halt it in its tracks.

When *Typhoon* got started at the end of September, Guderian's 2nd Panzer Army had been deployed some 250 miles south-east of Moscow. One major road led from the army's jumping-off area to the Soviet capital, and it passed through the towns of Orel, Mtsensk, Tula and Serpukhov. The leading panzers had advanced an astonishing hundred miles in the first five days; bursting into Orel on 3 October, they found themselves sharing the main street with still-running trams. The thirty mile stretch to Mtsensk proved much more testing. Realizing the danger, Stavka sent General Dmitri Lelyushenko to plug the road with a few batteries of the new Katyusha rockets and Colonel Mikhail Katukov's 1st Tank Brigade. Lelyushenko even stopped off in Tula to pick up some guns from the local artillery school, and had them towed to Mtsensk by town buses. This scratch force and the rapidly deteriorating road conditions kept the Germans busy for three weeks, the town not falling until 24 October.

Fuel was also short, but enough was found for one panzer brigade to advance on Tula, another eighty miles up the road, while the Red Army was still trying to mend its defences. Colonel Heinrich Eberbach's brigade reached the outskirts late in the afternoon of 29 October and decided against entering the town at night. By morning, however, the Soviets had blocked the highway with a formidable defence force of Workers' Militia, NKVD and

Anti-Aircraft units. Lacking artillery or air support, the Germans were unable to force their way into the city.

The rest of the 2nd Panzer Army moved slowly forward, until Tula stood like a tower in the front line's wall. From the second week of November growing German pressure north and south of the city was met by stiff resistance and occasional counter-attacks, but Guderian and Halder still hoped that the all-out effort scheduled for 18 November would bring the desired results. The 2nd Panzer Army's supposed objective in the renewed Typhoon was the area east of Moscow, and this involved a northerly advance across the Don at Serpukhov and Kashira. The 24th Panzer Korps was entrusted with this main thrust, and with swinging in behind Tula to cut the city off, deprive it of supplies and remove its capacity to hinder the main advance. Guderian's other panzer corps, the 47th, would advance on the 24th's right, protecting that corps' eastern flank and seeking to cut the vital Moscow–Ryazan railway link.

On 18 and 19 November the combined strength of the 3rd, 4th and 17th Panzer Divisions crashed into the line south of Tula, fragmenting the unfortunate Soviet infantry divisions that lay in their path. The speed of summer had gone, and the long hours of darkness offered greater hope of escape to those left stranded in the panzers' wake, but a breakthrough was a breakthrough. The 3rd and 4th Panzer Groups were already homing in on Moscow from the north-west; now the road from the south-west had been forced open.

Or so it seemed on the map tables of the distant Rastenburg Forest. Guderian, tirelessly moving from unit to unit, had more of a glass half-empty perspective. A breakthrough was indeed a breakthrough, but more Soviet units were arriving in the area, and flanks needed covering for advances to be sustainable. To his south, the 2nd Army was attacking westwards as ordered, opening a gap between itself and the 2nd Panzer Army. Given the ever-lengthening German front which an easterly advance dictated, such gaps were inevitable, but they still had to be plugged. The more successful 2nd Panzer Army's advance towards Moscow was, the more danger it would find itself in.

Guderian knew that his army was already running on empty. There were only 150 vehicles still running, and many of those were sitting around waiting for a fuel delivery. The winter clothing had still not arrived. The maximum distance his infantry could cover in a day was six miles. It seemed 'questionable whether my army was capable of carrying out the task assigned to it'.[9]

On 19 November the Soviet leadership was every bit as worried. The famous Guderian, his tanks adorned with their trademark 'G', had been at their heels since late June, and here he was again, punching another hole in the Red Army defences only a hundred miles from Moscow. Were the Soviet armies around the capital doomed to be his final victim? Zhukov was confident the centre could hold, but the threat emerging on the flanks was cause for serious concern. Klin in the north, Tula in the south – they had to be held, or the German panzers would be through into the Soviet rear.

The enemy had been at Tula's gates for three weeks now. A state of siege had been declared, a defence committee formed to coordinate its defence from party, NKVD and Red Army person-nel. Defensive plans had been drawn up, a Workers' Regiment and special tank-destroyer battalions raised, the latter armed only with grenades and Molotov cocktails. While the city's armament workers toiled around the clock, all other civilians were out in the cold, building new defences. Training in partisan and sabotage operations was given in case those defences failed.

The quality of those defence committees formed in late 1941 rested heavily on the calibre of the people involved, on individual intelligence and an ability to work together, on the courage to ignore instructions from Moscow which were inappropriate to the local situation. Tula was lucky in all these respects, and with each passing day it seemed more and more possible that the city might just be held.

It was still in danger of being bypassed, cut off, unconquered but unable to influence the wider picture. And the two Soviet armies – the 50th and 13th – which stood between Guderian and Moscow might not be able to hold him off. In recent weeks they had been reinforced by several Siberian divisions, one of which had given the 112th Infantry its salutary shock two days earlier, but these Siberians – many of whom actually came from Central Asia – were not supermen, and nor were they universally well equipped. Boris Godov, assigned to the 413th Infantry Division, found the soldiers well clothed and better fed than many, but lamentably prepared for actual combat with the Germans. They had nothing with which to fight off the German planes, and at least one artillery unit discovered it had been issued with the wrong size of shell for its guns. Their only anti-tank weapon was the grenade. Caught in the path of Guderian's panzer attack south of Tula on 18–19 November, it seems hardly surprising that these particular Siberians were simply overrun. According to Godov, only about 500 of the 15,000-strong division survived.

The Red Army was now having successes to balance such failures, but the one incontrovertible fact, as clear on Stalin's map table as it was on Hitler's, was the steady continuation of the German advance. In the south, von Kleist's panzers drew within five miles of Rostov, while the Soviet attacks on the German flank were halted by the Luftwaffe – almost four hundred sorties were flown on 19 November. The only negative news that Wednesday came from the north, where German-held Tikhvin was coming under threat.

Out on Lake Ladoga, beyond German eyes, a line of horse-drawn carts was inching across the creaking ice. The carts carried only a few sacks of flour, but each would save lives.

In Cyrenaica Robert Crisp and his 3rd Royal Tank Regiment colleagues were up before dawn. Sent north a few miles, they sat and watched an empty desert while enjoying a leisurely breakfast of bacon, biscuit, marmalade and tea. After two hours orders came through to intercept an enemy column to their east, and they set off, excitement mounting, 'eyes straining from the tops of turrets to the northern and eastern horizons for a glimpse of the significant silhouettes that would mean so much to each of us, one way or another'. Nothing turned up on this occasion, but another call-out a few hours later found the regiment lined up on a ridge above the Trigh Capuzzo, hungrily eyeing a long German supply column. 'It looked a piece of cake,' Crisp thought, 'with only a few armoured cars moving up and down the length of vehicles like shepherd dogs running beside a flock.'[10]

The Honey tanks charged down the slope, and the German column unravelled, lorries leaving the beaten-surface track and bumping away to north and north-east. Their minders – a posse of armoured cars and at least two Mark II tanks – accepted the unequal battle, and several were destroyed, but most of the 3rd Royal Tanks RTR were too caught up in the chase to notice. Plunging along in the wake of the faster but thinner-skinned lorries, Crisp soon found himself in sight of the blue Mediterranean, not to mention under fire from a distant artillery battery. Most of the other tanks in his unit had disappeared, and those that hadn't were running low on petrol. The sun was setting, and they couldn't raise their CO on the radio.

The 3rd RTR's gung-ho antics would draw a major mistake from the Germans on the following day, and inadvertently further the British cause, but other displays of unreasoning bravura would be punished more severely. The British army and corps generals who were running Crusader had all been taught that surprise was crucial in war, but by the evening of 18 November they were beginning to wonder if it might be overrated. In the words of the British plan: 'The approach march was unlikely to pass unobserved by the enemy; from his reactions we should know what the enemy meant to do; by the first evening [the 18th] his intentions would be known, and the decision [on operations for the 19th] could be taken.'[11] But the Germans had not reacted, and that decision now had to be taken in a vacuum.

It was not so much taken as allowed to take itself. Army commander General Cunningham prevaricated, and his equally in-the-dark subordinate, 30th Corps commander General Norrie, did little more than sanction reconnaissance missions towards Bir el Gubi and Sidi Rezegh requested by one of his subordinates, the 7th Armoured Division commander, General Gott. It was Gott, visiting the 22nd Armoured Brigade early on this morning, who recklessly abandoned Crusader's central plank. With no clear idea of Bir el Gubi's defences, and a lingering contempt for the Italian army as a whole, he sent the 22nd Armoured Brigade's inexperienced tank crews into battle with only minimal backup.

The Italian defences around Bir el Gubi were well constructed and well defended. Three battalions of infantry, ably supported by their own artillery and a further battalion of 105-millimetre guns, held three strongpoints. Behind them were *Ariete*'s 146 M-13 tanks and 7 truck-mounted 102-millimetre naval guns that fired armour-piercing shells. Soon after 11.00 the Italians saw a group of around forty British Crusader tanks approaching from the north-east at high speed, and sent sixteen M-13s out to engage them, rather in the manner of medieval knights sortieing out from a castle.

A ten-minute battle ensued, with tanks lost on both sides, and the thirteen surviving M-13s were eventually driven back by the arrival of the main British force. The 22nd Armoured Brigade boasted 158 brand-new Crusader tanks, and it now launched them in what one observer called 'the nearest thing to a cavalry charge with tanks seen during this war'.[12] The defences on the Italian left flank managed to channel the attack into the Italian centre, where the waiting artillery and M-13s took a heavy toll. This further deflected the British attackers towards the strongpoint on their left, whose defences were less complete, and whose infantry defenders were now overwhelmed. Many tried to surrender, but they fought on once they realized that there were no British infantry to take them prisoner.

In the meantime the leading British tanks had come under sustained artillery and anti-tank fire, and those following up found themselves in a minefield. Finally, and fatally for many, they ran into a line of innocent-looking lorries that turned out to be truck-mounted 102-millimetre naval guns. And as this attack on the southern perimeter fell back in some disarray, the *Ariete* commander launched his main tank strength against the enemy to the north, forcing a similar withdrawal. By 16.30 the British were back beyond the range of the Italian guns, and one Italian artillery commander was turning the battlefield into poetry: 'Here two tanks clashed with bows locked; they remained half suspended like rampant lions. Together they burned. One, two, three at a time, machine-gun rounds exploded with short sharp retorts, like bits of wood cracking in a fireplace. A few feet away another tank had its turret thrown off and lying to one side, like the top of an orange sliced off with a knife, and smoke slowly emerging from the damaged hole.'[13]

The Italians had lost over two hundred men, a dozen guns and thirty-four tanks, but they still held their threatening position on the left flank of the intended British advance on Tobruk. The 22nd Armoured Brigade, which had already lost more than thirty of the trouble-prone Crusaders to mechanical failure during the two-day advance, had seen a further fifty destroyed, halving its original strength. Gott's attack had proved a disaster for those directly involved, but that was not all. It had also set in motion the wholesale dispersal of the British armour.

The German airfields were still unusable, air reconnaissance impossible in the early hours. Despite the occasional alarming report, Rommel still couldn't *see* the British, and until late morning he clung to the convenient belief that they weren't there. His subordinates – particularly *Afrikakorps* commander General Ludwig Crüwell and the 21st Panzer Division commander, General Johann von Ravenstein – were more concerned. On the previous evening the latter had requested – and been refused – permission to mount an exploratory attack in the direction of Gabr Saleh. Around noon Rommel changed his mind. Reports of enemy armour north of the Trigh el Abd – the 3rd Royal Tanks' encounters with the 33rd Reconnaissance Battalion and the supply column – required further investigation. Von

Ravenstein quickly organized a battlegroup of a hundred and twenty tanks, four 88-millimetre and twelve 105-millimetre guns, commanded by the 5th Panzer Regiment's Lieutenant-Colonel Stephan. At around 14.30 he and Rommel watched it set off from just south of Gasr el Arid on the Trigh Capuzzo. Neither seems to have appreciated the enormous risk of sending this force into the unknown and a possible battle with the enemy's entire armoured strength.

Fortunately for the Germans, the British were proving even more adept at splitting their forces, and the 4th Armoured Brigade's three tank regiments were many miles apart. The 3rd Royals were still chasing lorries away to the north-east, and were not available for inclusion in any welcoming party for Battlegroup Stephan. The 11th Hussars and 5th Royals, for reasons best known to their brigade commander, were stationed ten miles apart, and it was the former that the Germans fell on in mid-afternoon. The latter managed to join the battle only in its final stages.

German planes, aloft at last, attacked the 4th Armoured Brigade HQ as Battlegroup Stephan closed in on the desperately deploying Hussars, tanks leading the charge, supporting artillery and anti-tank guns wide on each flank. The British returned fire, and war correspondent Alan Moorehead saw 'a line of grey shell-bursts' flare up. 'As the battle joined more closely these bursts grew together and made a continuous curtain of dust and smoke and blown sand.' The Hussars' Honeys drove into the curtain, 'weaving, zigzagging, making full use of their forty miles an hour to minimize themselves as targets . . . then they met and inter-mingled, and there was utter, indescribable confusion'. It was, in Moorehead's words, 'novel, reckless, unexpected, impetuous, and terrific'.[14]

For almost two hours the two sides traded blows in a literal fog of war. 'Tanks were duelling with tanks in running, almost hand-to-hand fights, firing nearly point-blank, twisting, dodging, sprinting with screaming treads and whining engines that rose to a shriek as they changed gear. As each new tank loomed up ahead gunners were swinging the muzzles of their guns automatically, eyes strained behind their goggles, fighting through the smoke and dust to discriminate friend from foe . . .'[15]

Given the closeness of combat, the final losses of eleven British and three German tanks seemed almost inadequate, and both sides claimed that the other had lost many more. The Honeys had done well, particularly when their lack of artillery support was taken into account – despite watching the Germans do it over and over again, the British couldn't seem to grasp the idea of coordinating tanks and guns. About an hour before sunset the panzers had hurried off the battlefield to refuel, and the German guns had stood sentry over the process, defying the poorly supported British tanks to come within range.

Gott's third armoured brigade was having a better time of it. By late morning Norrie and Cunningham had tired of waiting for the Germans and had convinced each other that a continuation of the advance to Tobruk had always been part of their plan. The 7th Armoured Brigade was ordered to seize the Italian airfield at Sidi Rezegh, some fifteen miles to the north-west and only fifteen short of Tobruk.

The advanced screen of South African armoured cars arrived on the ridge overlooking the airfield soon after 14.00. Their presence was detected an hour later, provoking a frantic rush to evacuate by the Italian ground staff and aircrews. Lacking tank or infantry support, the South Africans could only watch, wait and admire the distant view of the tomb that gave the airfield its name, a small white blob on the crest of the far escarpment, shining out over the dun-coloured landscape.

It was not until 16.30 that the tanks of the 6th Royals arrived, and they wasted no time, driving straight down the slope and on to the enemy airfield. It was the third charge of British armour that day, and the only one that faced minimal opposition. The airfield had been too far behind the lines to warrant a defence force, and the tank gunners gleefully shot up the Italian planes, some of them in the process of taking off.

Detachments of tanks and armoured cars were sent east and west to check out the far escarpment and ran into fire from German and Italian infantry. With no infantry of their own to exploit another breakthrough, the British and South Africans turned back, and by nightfall the leading elements of the 7th Armoured Brigade were leaguered on the airfield. The rest of the brigade's tanks were on their way to join them and would arrive by the following morning.

That evening neither Cunningham nor Rommel had a clear picture of what had happened during the day. Both were prone to underestimate the Italians, and neither appreciated what a sharp and painful shock *Ariete* had given the 22nd Armoured Brigade. Cunningham seems to have assumed the reverse and written the Italian armour out of his subsequent calculations. He had also misread the encounter between the 4th Armoured Brigade and Battlegroup Stephan, mistaking the latter for the bulk of Rommel's armour. In Cunningham's view the enemy was clearly on the defensive, quite possibly on the run. His own widely dispersed armoured forces had brought this situation about, and he saw no urgent need to re-concentrate them. On the contrary, he confirmed the dispersal, sending the 7th Armoured Support Group forward to Sidi Rezegh in support of the 7th Armoured Brigade, and the 1st South African Infantry Brigade towards Bir el Gubi in support of the 22nd Armoured Brigade. The 4th Armoured Brigade remained away to the east, around Gabr Saleh. The British, as Rommel's Intelligence Chief von Mellenthin later wrote, had been 'obliging enough to scatter the 7th Armoured Division all over the desert'.[16]

The Germans were almost as much in the dark but had a clearer grasp of essentials. 'When a situation is obscure,' von Mellenthin wrote, 'it is a good rule to concentrate and await further information.'[17] That evening von Ravenstein rang Crüwell and suggested bringing the two panzer divisions together. Crüwell's chief of staff Colonel Fritz Bayerlein took the matter to Rommel, who had finally grasped the scale of the British effort.

He agreed – a united *Afrikakorps* would try to pick off the British brigades one by one.

Always assuming they could find them. After their mad rush towards the coast, Crisp and his companions were slowly working their way back across the darkening desert. A chance encounter with some armoured cars set them on the right course, but they then ran out of petrol. The seven tank commanders conferred and decided on leaguering where they were: 'The blackness of night was upon us now, and we felt fairly secure in its impenetrability. I formed the tanks into a solid ring with guns facing outwards. My operator started yelling, and while I was still telling him not to make such a bloody row he shouted that he had got the C.O. on the air.'[18]

A petrol lorry was dispatched to their supposed location and eventually homed in on their signal – a burst of tracer bullets fired into the sky. 'It was well after midnight when we slunk into the battalion leaguer. The C.O. was still a bit peeved about our disappearance . . .'[19]

Back at OKH headquarters, Halder, for all his earlier gloom, pronounced himself satisfied. 'On the whole,' he wrote in his diary, 'this has been a good day.'[20]

Late into the night at the Wolfsschanze, the Führer regaled his cohorts with the usual mix of self-assertion and other-disparagement. The bourgeoisie were his particular target on this occasion. But for him, they would have overrun the party and spread the disastrous idea that people other than Germans might actually matter. The bourgeoisie were, of course, inherently hypocritical. They were snivelling now about the Jewish ejection from Germany, but had raised no objection when their own compatriots had been forced to emigrate. 'These Germans had no kinsfolk in various parts of the world; they were left to their own mercies, they went off into the unknown.' There was, of course, 'nothing of that sort for the Jews'. The rabbit-people had 'uncles, nephews, cousins everywhere'.

The absurdities tripped off his tongue. He claimed that his 'single aim' was to assert his own demands 'at all costs, come wind, come weather', yet insisted that 'things are as they are, and we can do nothing to change them'. If providence provided insufficient food for the population, that was all to the good, 'for it is the struggle for existence that produces the selection of the fittest'. But if providence filled the world with Jews and the party with 'waverers', then 'let them be expelled!'[21]

A troop train stood waiting in a siding close by Stuttgart Station. It was on its way from France to Russia, a journey that was likely to take weeks. Crossing western Germany, Henry Metelmann and his comrades had been struck by how well organized everything was, how clean and beautiful, and the woman in the Stuttgart yard was something of a reality check. Asked if they had any fat to sell, the soldiers said no, and innocently asked if supplies were short.

'Are you joking?' was the angry response. 'Everything is in short supply, no butter, no fat, no nothing – and the rich have got it all! Can you remember fat Hermann Göring, who was in charge of the war, making his bombastic speech to the Party Moguls and asking them whether they wanted butter or cannons – and all the idiots shouted cannons! Now *we* have got what *they* asked for, plenty of cannons' – she pointed at theirs on the wagon – 'and I have no butter to cook with!'[22]

Few men wielded more power in Hitler's Europe than Reinhard Heydrich. The thirty-seven-year-old SS *Obergruppenführer* had been making himself indispensable since 1932, when he had founded and assumed the leadership of the party's security service, the *Sicherheitsdienst*. In 1936 he had added the state's criminal (*Kripo*) and security (*Gestapo*) polices to his portfolio, and three years later all these organs of civil enforcement had been merged into a single organization, the RSHA or *Reichssicherheitshauptamt*. If Heydrich wanted something doing, he had the means.

In 1939 he became head of the Central Office for Jewish Emigration, with a remit that spoke for itself. The outbreak of war later that year hugely complicated his task, multiplying the Jews under German control by ten, dividing the number of places they could be sent by a similar number. Heydrich could hardly send four million Jews to the International Settlement in Shanghai.

The invasion of the Soviet Union both compounded the problem and brought it to a head. On 31 July Göring instructed Heydrich to 'carry out all the necessary preparations with regard to organizational and financial matters for bringing about a complete solution of the Jewish question in the German sphere of influence in Europe'.[23] Göring didn't spell it out, but he didn't need to. For someone like Heydrich, who knew what was already happening on an ad hoc basis in the occupied areas of the Soviet Union, the implication was clear. As Heydrich remarked to SS chief Himmler on the following day: 'It may be safely assumed that in the future there will be no more Jews in the annexed Eastern territories.'[24]

Questions remained, however. If the Jews were to be killed, then how? Shooting was time-consuming, not to mention hard on the shooters. Other methods needed investigating. And while the war continued, could the Reich afford to dispense with such a useful reserve of slave labour? The economists must be consulted. And as long as the military demanded every train for their own uses, how could the Jews be sent anywhere, whether for work or execution? Finalizing a solution would require study and eventual agreement among the various interested parties.

Heydrich had other calls on his time. In September he had been appointed Acting *Reichsprotektor* of what remained of pre-war Czechoslovakia, the Protectorate of Bohemia and Moravia, and on that day he stood, black-uniformed, in Prague's St Vitus Cathedral, receiving the seven keys to the Jewel Room from President Hácha. The vanished state's most prized possession, the Crown of St Wenceslas, was behind the locked door, and taking the keys into German hands seemed a suitably humiliating reminder of who called the shots in Europe's New Order.

★

In November 1941 the Czechoslovak resistance to Nazi rule was still gestating, but in also-dismembered Yugoslavia thousands had already died in armed strikes against the occupier and the consequent reprisals. By September the two main resistance groups – the Communists and Cetniks – had turned large areas of Serbia into no-go areas for the German occupiers, and Hitler had lost his patience. Three air-supported infantry divisions under General Böhme were sent in to sort the situation out, once and for all. By November the partisans had been ejected from the several small towns they controlled and driven south, but few had been captured, and there was little likelihood that the 100,000 German troops in the country could be redeployed in the foreseeable future.

In neighbouring Croatia and Montenegro, both of which lay in Mussolini's supposed sphere of Balkan influence, things were no better. Three hundred and fifty thousand Italian troops were stationed in the former Yugoslavia, more than those fighting the British in North Africa. On this particular morning the Duce and his Foreign Secretary, son-in-law Count Ciano, were presented with 'a rather discouraging account of the situation in Croatia'. Ciano put this down to the precarious position of the puppet fascist leader Pavelić, to 'domestic intrigues and growing German meddling'. The idea that any sort of occupation would stimulate resistance was not mentioned.[25]

And there were more important things to think about – Ciano was having his portrait painted by the famous Amerigo Bartoli. The painter was a bit of a scamp – his private cartoons of Mussolini were well known among Rome's cultural glitterati – but Ciano believed Bartoli to be 'a good patriot and a sincere fascist, even if he indulges in biting satire'.[26]

In Washington the usually mild-mannered Japanese ambassador was furious with Togo. Tomorrow was Thanksgiving, Nomura told his Foreign Minister – hardly the best day for testing American patience and resolve. He had not forgotten the 25 November deadline, but why was Togo in such a hurry to announce the sending of the evacuation ships? Didn't he realize how threatening it all seemed? Did he want to push the Americans over the edge?

Togo's haste was driven by the military's timetable, but he couldn't say so. Unable to let Nomura into the secret, he simply reiterated his previous instructions.

THURSDAY 20 NOVEMBER

A day ahead of *Kido Butai*, the gunboat *Kunajiri* reached Hitokappu Bay on the Pacific coast of Etorofu. The only village overlooking the six-mile-wide bay contained a concrete pier, three houses, a post office and a wireless station. The last two were closed down for an indefinite period, and village residents were forbidden from travelling.

The citizens of Rostov-on-Don had spent the last few weeks frantically working on their city's defences. Four belts of strongpoints had been planned, each around a mile and a half deep. Tank traps had been excavated, infantry trenches kept thin enough to allow the tanks to pass over them. Every crossroad had been sown with mines. Hundreds of machine guns and anti-tank guns in protective dugouts covered every inch of the prospective battlefields in interlocking fields of fire.

The preparations slowed the Germans, but they didn't stop them. Soon after dawn on that Thursday, the 13th and 14th Panzer Divisions broke through the last ring, then held back as the 60th and *Leibstandarte* Motorized Divisions fought their way down the main roads leading into the city. The former took the airfield around noon, and by 13.30 units of the latter had reached the station and city centre. There was mass panic and confusion, as Russian soldiers and civilians made for the still-standing bridge across the Don.

As the light faded in late afternoon the advance elements of *Leibstandarte* reached the near end of the bridge. At almost the same moment a train appeared, heading south full of Red Army troops and equipment. The Germans opened fire on the locomotive, puncturing the boiler and unleashing whistles of steam. 'This was the luck of war,' one German wrote in his diary, 'the enemy's confusion could not have been greater.' He and his comrades stormed out across the 500-metre-long bridge. 'A thick bundle of fuse at the bridge's foundation led to explosives, and it was skilfully cut by the engineers. On the two large bridge pillars was a large amount of dynamite, but the engineers simply ripped the detonator from the explosives.'[1] Though still under fire from the south bank of the river, the Germans managed to complete their seizure of the bridge and to establish a small bridgehead before nightfall.

Back in the city the almost continuous gunfire of myriad street battles was frequently punctuated by loud explosions. Rostov's streets and buildings had been liberally strewn with explosives. There were pressure mines under floors and stairs, hundreds of doors, windows, stoves and vehicles had been wired to explode, and entire city blocks primed for detonation by concealed radio operators. And as the bodies piled up, they, too, were turned into booby traps. Even the dead were fighting on.

At the other end of the Eastern Front, the people of Leningrad learned that their bread rations were being reduced again. The city had only five hundred and ten tons of flour per day to feed two and a half million people, which meant eight slices a day for the front-line troops, four for factory workers, two for everyone else. And bread was almost all there was. 'Edible' bark was being gathered, 'edible' sawdust produced, but luxuries like cat, crow and sparrow were becoming scarce.

Sergey Yezersky, asked to write the relevant editorial for the Leningrad *Pravda*, decided that honesty was the only option: 'So long as the blockade continues it is not possible to expect any improvement in the food situation. We must reduce the norms of rations in order to hold out as long as the enemy is not pushed back, as long as the circle of blockade is not broken. Difficult? Yes, difficult. But there is no choice. And this everyone must understand . . .'[2]

Moscow, meanwhile, waited and worried. The 3rd Panzer Group's spearheads were reaching either side of Klin, with the 6th Panzer on the Kalinin road to the north-west and the 7th Panzer crossing the Volokolamsk road to the west. The 4th Panzer Group squeezed Panfilov's old 316th Infantry division out of Novo-Petrovskoye, bringing it within fifteen miles of Istra and fifty of the Kremlin.

Despite the continuing advance, Army Commander von Bock was still hedging his bets, stressing his army's limitations to his superiors yet refusing to accept them as excuses from his subordinates. All movements, he told OKH, were contingent on the poor supply situation, and the latest directives from Hitler and Halder were based on 'inaccurate assumptions' of Army Group Centre's current state. Von Bock had no idea when fuel would be available for the advance beyond Moscow that his superiors were insisting on, but assumed it would be 'many weeks yet', by which time the weather would probably have ruled it out.[3]

Given such reservations, von Bock might have argued much more forcibly for a swift abandonment of Typhoon. So why didn't he? Any failure was hard to accept, particularly after two years of near-constant success, but von Bock could claim with some justification that the responsibility for this one would lie higher up the command structure. Success, on the other hand, might be unlikely, but any credit would be his to claim. And perhaps, deep down, he realized that failure outside Moscow would imply failure everywhere, and that any chance of success, no matter how remote, had to be pursued. Like Hitler and Halder, he could place his faith in the situation maps, where success was more visible than its ever-rising cost.

He and 4th Panzer Group Commander Hoepner leaned over

one that morning and blithely envisaged a 'double-sided envelopment' of the Soviet forces in front of Moscow. Later in the day, when a message arrived from Guderian requesting permission to suspend the 2nd Panzer Army's offensive operations, von Bock simply refused him. Typhoon would go on until Hitler or the enemy stopped it.

Guderian's reasons for wanting a halt were fourfold: threats to the flanks, chronic fuel shortages, high casualties and problems with his tanks. The last-named were of particular interest to the visitors he received that day at his Orel HQ – a team of weapons industrialists dispatched by Armaments Minister Fritz Todt to evaluate the state of Germany's war machine after five months of Barbarossa.

The key member of the deputation was Walter Rohland, the forty-three-year-old head of the National Committee for Tank Production. 'Panzer' Rohland had fought at Verdun as a teenager and actively resisted the French occupation of the Ruhr in 1923. When Hitler came to power in 1933, he was running the high-quality steel manufacturer *Deutsche Edelstahlwerke*, and soon thereafter became a principal player in the country's foremost steel corporation, the *Vereinigte Stahlwerke*. After joining the Nazi Party, Rohland brought his passions for nationalism and steel together and set about making Germany's tanks the best in the world. He joined one of the new panzer regiments as a reserve captain and made *Deutsche Edelstahlwerke* the world leader in armoured plate. When the National Committee for Tank Production was set up in autumn 1940 he was the obvious man to chair it.

Blitzkrieg – lightning war – was built around the tank, and the successes in Poland and the west ensured that sufficient supplies of steel, labour and manufacturing capacity were allocated for new production through 1940–41, mostly of the standard medium tank, the Panzer Mk III. The new tanks both replaced and augmented the increasingly inadequate Mk IIs, and effectively doubled the Wehrmacht's armoured clout for the Russian campaign. All seemed well until the Soviet T-34 appeared, confounding German assumptions of technical superiority. In autumn 1941 work was barely under way on designing the new, heavier German tanks which could take them on.

In the meantime the inherent weaknesses of the German war economy were beginning to make themselves felt. By the time Rohland and his colleagues travelled to Orel for their meeting with Guderian, there was insufficient fuel, steel and labour to satisfy the growing demands of Germany's armed forces. If, for example, the army was given the ammunition, tanks and petrol it said it needed, then the navy was doomed to sit idle in port and the already overstretched Luftwaffe could not be expanded to fight a forthcoming war with America. Things were tight all round, and Rohland was hardly expecting a glowing report from the men at the front. But he was not prepared for the almost unremitting gloom that awaited him.

There were shortages of virtually everything, from fuel to spades, radios to gloves. Those panzer troops not wearing stolen Russian clothing were still wearing threadbare summer uniforms. Not surprisingly, the shocked Rohland and his colleagues were even more concerned about the tanks these scarecrows were driving. In Russian winter conditions the Panzer IIIs and IVs were virtually useless. 'If the motors and gearboxes still worked,' Rohland wrote, 'the weapons failed due to freezing up.'[4] When they could move, the narrow tracks restricted their manoeuvrability in the snow, and the lack of caulk prevented them from climbing slippery slopes or crossing frozen waterways. Even in perfect weather, their guns and armour were markedly inferior to those of the nimble, wide-tracked T-34s and heavier KV-1s.

These were the tanks that Rohland and his Committee had put their faith in, had invested the Reich's resources in. These were the tanks that Germany's factories were designed to build, which they were still turning out in large numbers – tanks which to all intents and purposes were already obsolete.

While Rohland was lunching with Guderian, some 7,000 Jews were being shot by SS *Einsatzgruppen* near the village of Tuchinki, just outside Minsk. With 25,000 German Jews en route from the

Reich, the local authorities had decided to free up space in the city's overcrowded ghetto.

Minsk had been occupied for almost five months, having fallen on the sixth day of the campaign. A ghetto area had been cordoned off almost immediately, and filled to bursting point with Jews from the city and surrounding towns. Overwork, semi-starvation and sporadic ad hoc atrocities followed. Five thousand residents were taken out and shot in three August 'actions'; another twelve thousand perished outside Tuchinki on 7 November.

On 15 August a minor massacre of a hundred prisoners had been witnessed, at his own request, by SS leader Heinrich Himmler. Nauseated by the experience, and worried that the strain of such work might prove too much for his men, Himmler refused to sanction a similar fate for the inmates of the asylum he visited later that day. He had no doubt that they needed killing, but a less stressful method had to be found.

The *Einsatzgruppen* tried dynamite, but the results were even messier. Himmler, meanwhile, had begun wondering whether the main method of killing used in the recently abandoned T4 euthanasia programme might offer a tidier, less stressful solution. Seventy thousand so-called 'incurables' had been killed since 1939, the first few by lethal injection, the vast majority by poison gas. This killing rate was certainly slow by *Einsatzgruppen* standards, but it seemed probable that the process could be streamlined to accommodate the swifter dispatch of much larger numbers. There was no shortage of potential guinea pigs in the concentration and prisoner-of-war camps.

Experiments went on through the autumn. Someone had the idea of hooking up car exhausts to closed rooms, and someone else refined it by feeding a lorry's exhaust gas into its own rear. This seemed promising, and prototype vans of several sizes were commissioned, but too much fuel was needed to produce the carbon monoxide. Another gas was needed, and this had already been tested at the Auschwitz camp outside Cracow. On 3 September Zyklon B – or crystallized prussic acid – had been used to kill 600 Soviet prisoners of war and 300 Jews. The results were encouraging, more tests decreed.

Dr Fritz Mennecke was one of those involved in the selection of prospective victims. A veteran of the T4 programme, Mennecke had previously been instrumental in the killing of the mentally ill, physically handicapped and chronically sick. Now he was at Ravensbrück, deciding which Communists, Jews and other social misfits were worth preserving. 'The work goes quickly,' he wrote to his wife that day, 'because the answers to the questions have already been typed on the form, and I only have to record the diagnosis, main symptoms etc. I would prefer not to describe the composition of the patients in this letter, but will tell you later in person.' Buchenwald concentration camp was his next stop, Mennecke told her, before heaping praise on the Ravensbrück cafeteria. 'I feel marvellous,' he concluded.[5]

In later years, most of the Wehrmacht's prominent generals would claim ignorance of the crimes committed a few hundred miles behind their front line. They had been fighting the Russians, not the Jews.

Some facts suggest otherwise. Five weeks earlier, on 10 October, 6th Army commander Field Marshal Walther von Reichenau issued a directive to his troops. Conventional soldiering, he explained, was no longer enough. Each German soldier should consider himself 'the bearer of an inexorable national idea and the avenger of all bestialities inflicted upon the German people and its racial kin'. And just in case this all seemed a little abstract, von Reichenau spelled out the target: 'The soldier must have a full understanding for the necessity of a severe but just atonement on Jewish sub-humanity.'[6]

Von Reichenau, who died a few months later in an air crash, was more obviously in sympathy with Nazi race policies than most of his fellow commanders. His superior, Field Marshal von Rundstedt, was one of the old school, supposedly contemptuous of Hitler and his upstart Nazis, a soldier's soldier with a thoroughly professional outlook. Yet he approved von Reichenau's directive and sent copies to his other commanders, recommending that they issue it to their troops.

Field Marshal Erich von Manstein was one so urged. Now commanding the 11th Army in the Crimea, von Manstein had been the principal architect of the strategy that undid the French and British armies in 1940. In post-war years his military genius would be acclaimed by friends and former foes alike, his moral stature left mostly unchallenged. On that Thursday he issued the Reichenau order from his field headquarters in the Crimean city of Simferopol. Three weeks later, that city's 14,300 Jews would be gathered together and murdered.

In Copenhagen a German 'invitation' to join the Anti-Comintern Pact was delivered to the Danish government. Prime Minister Stauning thought it wise to accede, but a majority of his Cabinet ministers refused. Their German occupiers had promised to respect Danish neutrality, they argued, and such an arrangement would clearly breach it.

Hitler, back in Berlin for Udet's state funeral, was entertaining his entourage with the sort of insights which later generations would associate with recreational drugs. 'If the mental picture that Christians form of God were correct,' he explained, 'the god of the ants would be an ant, and similarly for the other animals.' Assorted 'wow!'s might have greeted this pronouncement, and encouraged the Führer into self-congratulatory mode: 'We Germans have that marvellous source of strength – the sense of duty – which other people do not possess. The conviction that, by obeying the voice of duty, one is working for the preservation of the species, helps one to take the gravest decisions.'

And as so often at moments like this, Hitler's thoughts turned in an utterly inappropriate direction, towards Mussolini. The Duce had dispelled the danger of Communism, had performed a service 'that must never be forgotten'. He was 'a man made to measure for the centuries. His place in history is reserved for him.'

Did Hitler really believe this nonsense any more? Ten years earlier his high opinion of Mussolini had been understandable, but now? If any single individual had doomed Barbarossa it was the

Duce, whose blunderings in the Balkans had cost the Wehrmacht five weeks of good campaigning weather. But Hitler couldn't, wouldn't, see it. Over the years Mussolini had become an alter ego. To praise the Duce was to praise himself, and the same was true when it came to criticism.[7]

In Rome the English offensive in Libya was under discussion. Some enemy successes were admitted, but Mussolini and Supreme Commander General Cavallero were not overly worried. Ciano, with rather more acumen, was concerned at the loss of supplies and the damage done to the Italian air force. His growing fears over the direction of the war went hand in hand with a lowering regard for Italy's principal ally. The Germans had already established a military headquarters at Frascati, just outside Rome, and now wanted to requisition the nearby College of Mondragone as a barracks. This would involve moving 500 Italian families, and would, Ciano thought, prove 'extremely unpopular'.[8]

Crusader was finally announced to the British public – WE ATTACK IN LIBYA: 50-MILE THRUST was the enthusiastic headline in Thursday's *Daily Mirror*.[9] But optimism was not confined to newspaper editors. 'The approach and deployment of our forces in Libya have been most successful,' Churchill wrote to Roosevelt, 'and the enemy taken by surprise. Only now does he realize the large scale of our operations against him. Heavy fighting between the armoured forces seems probable today. Orders have been given to press what is now begun to a decision at all costs. The chances do not seem to be unfavourable.'[10]

It was to be a day on which one mistake followed another with almost comic regularity. Rommel, still obsessing about his intended relief of Tobruk, had given Crüwell carte blanche to deal with whatever British intruders there were between the beleaguered port and the frontier wire. After sifting through the situation reports, Crüwell and his staff had decided that the British move towards Bardia posed the greatest threat – Crisp and Co.'s exploits had obviously grown in the telling. A re-concentrated 21st

Panzer – Battlegroup Knabe's infantry linking up with Battlegroup Stephan – was ordered to join the 15th Panzer in an eastward sortie down the Trigh Capuzzo and cut off the (non-existent) British thrust.

This was a bad mistake and, as von Mellenthin wrote later, a great opportunity missed. Cunningham had been 'obliging enough to scatter the 7th Armoured Division all over the desert', but his generosity was spurned.[11] If the two panzer divisions had combined that morning against either the 4th Armoured Brigade at Gabr Saleh or the 7th Armoured Brigade at Sidi Rezegh, they would likely have won a crushing victory, and quite possibly forced the British to abandon the whole offensive.

More mistakes followed. The refuelling trucks were late reaching Battlegroup Stephan, delaying its departure for the rendezvous with the rest of the 21st Panzer and making it harder for the panzers to disengage from their British opponents of the previous evening. A running battle ensued, costing more precious fuel. When the 21st Panzer was finally reunited that afternoon the tanks were virtually empty, the division stranded for the remaining daylight hours. The 15th Panzer, meanwhile, was off on its wild goose chase, cruising down the Trigh Capuzzo and finding nothing.

The armour was certainly being missed at Sidi Rezegh, where two early-morning attacks by the *Afrika* Infantry Division had failed to dislodge the unsupported tanks of the 7th Armoured Brigade from the airfield. Around 10.00 the 7th Armoured Support Group arrived from the south to solidify the British hold, and suffer the persistent but mostly ineffective attentions of German artillery and the Luftwaffe.

It was now the turn of the British to make a series of calamitous misjudgements. The Germans had made no real effort to dislodge their enemy from Sidi Rezegh's Italian airstrip, but the British command chose to see the 7th Armoured Brigade's holding of the position as a major success. In a similar manner, Battle Group Stephan's withdrawal from the Gabr Saleh area was misinterpreted as a victory for the 4th Armoured Brigade. The balloon of British self-confidence, already overblown, received another dose of inflation.

With the Germans in such dire straits, what was to stop the 7th Armoured Brigade pushing on towards Tobruk? And why should the garrison wait any longer to begin its breakout? Both Norrie and Gott thought this was the moment, and urged Cunningham to issue the appropriate orders for the next day.

Late in the morning Cunningham flew back from Norrie's HQ to his own in Egypt. Was this really the moment? The prospect was a seductive one – if the 7th Armoured Brigade joined hands with the Tobruk garrison, all the major German formations would be trapped in a huge British ring, with the sea at their backs. It would be an African Dunkirk, only better, with the Germans trapped on beaches and no boats coming to take them home.

It would also mean a final abandonment of the original plan, which had envisaged a breakout only after Rommel's armoured forces had been destroyed. Arriving back at Maddalena, Cunningham now received intelligence that large Axis forces had been seen heading west on the Trigh Capuzzo. Was Rommel pulling his army back from the frontier? Had Crusader done more damage than they had thought? If so, and the enemy truly was reeling, then why not go for the jugular? Cunningham made up his mind, and even the news that the 15th and 21st Panzer were now headed towards Gabr Saleh and the 4th Armoured Brigade failed to change it. Still unaware of the mauling that the 22nd Armoured Brigade had received at Bir el Gubi, he ordered it east to join the 4th Armoured Brigade at Gabr Saleh, on the reckless assumption that their combined strength would prove a match for two panzer divisions. And with the latter provisionally accounted for, Cunningham felt free to order a dawn start for the Tobruk garrison and the 7th Armoured Brigade.

Crüwell, meanwhile, had finally worked out what was really happening. The British thrust towards Bardia had been a figment of Italian imagination – the British armoured spearhead was actually at Sidi Rezegh, poised to advance on Tobruk, with another large armoured force guarding its flank at Gabr Saleh. Crüwell ordered the panzers south, with the intention of destroying the force at Gabr Saleh and cutting the supply line to the spearhead. The 15th

Panzer was able to comply, but the 21st Panzer was still waiting for the promised fuel trucks. Cunningham had apparently struck lucky.

So had Crüwell. The 22nd Armoured Brigade had to disengage, refuel and re-form before heading east, and darkness would be falling when it finally reached Gabr Saleh. The 15th Panzer, arriving at speed some ninety minutes earlier, had only the 4th Armoured Brigade to deal with. The British tanks were well sited, hull down on a slight rise with the sun behind them, but the arrival of the German artillery half an hour into the battle proved decisive. The British were slowly pushed down the opposite slope, and saved from total destruction only by the arrival of night and the remnants of the 22nd Armoured Brigade.

The British knew they had lost another twenty-six Honey tanks, but managed to convince themselves that thirty panzers had been destroyed. The true figure – once those disabled on the German-held battlefield had been recovered and repaired – was probably zero, but that's not what Cunningham was told. As far as he knew, his two armoured brigades had more than held their own, and he saw no reason to countermand his orders for the next day. If he, or his corps or brigade commanders, had talked to the tank crews, they might have learned something. By this point, as Crisp admitted, they had realized that the Honeys were no match for the Panzer IIIs and IVs. 'It was a simple proposition: our little cannons could not knock them out, and they could knock us out easily.'[12] And as for the German 88-millimetre guns, the very word 'eighty-eight' was 'invading the tank-crew vocabulary as a symbol of shattering mutilation. Within the week we were reckoning that it needed three Honeys to destroy one Mark IV.'[13] As Crusader unfolded, the experience of the British tank crews in Libya echoed that of the German tank crews in Russia: outgunned, under-armoured and needing a huge superiority in numbers to prevail. This was lost on Cunningham, just as it was lost on Hitler and Halder. Like them, he was far from the front line; like them, he was struck by the tiny expanse of map which his forces still had to cross.

Rommel, on the other hand, was used to leading from the front, and to having a better idea of what was actually happening than his opponent. Weather-restricted reconnaissance and his obsession with Tobruk had clouded his appreciation during the first few days of Crusader, but he finally had a grasp of the situation. After meeting Crüwell that evening, he issued orders for the destruction of the enemy force at Sidi Rezegh.

Five hundred miles to the north, four merchant ships carrying fuel, weaponry, ammunition and food for the German and Italian forces were preparing to cross the Mediterranean. The size of their escort – three heavy cruisers, two light cruisers and seven destroyers – suggested trouble, and with good reason.

Earlier in the year the Germans had threatened to dominate the entire area. The Luftwaffe had acquired airbases in Libya, Italy, Greece and Crete with which to threaten Malta, Alexandria and the British surface fleet. The forces on Malta had became almost impossible to supply, and in consequence had lost much of their ability to interdict the Axis supply route across the Mediterranean. But Barbarossa had changed everything. Most of the two Luftwaffe air corps in the Mediterranean theatre had been sent to Russia, leaving only two hundred operational planes to disrupt the Suez Canal, keep Malta quiet, bomb Tobruk, interdict the 8th Army supply route from Egypt, support Rommel's moves and fly shotgun for the Axis convoys. The Germans could have opted for doing one or two jobs well, but ended up doing all of them badly.

Malta, which had seemed down and out, climbed groggily back to its feet. Supply ships got through from Gibraltar and Alexandria, and a new strike force was laboriously put together. The submarine division, which had soldiered on alone through the first half of the year, was eventually joined by the surface ships of Force K and new squadrons of bombers – Blenheims and Swordfish at first, Albacores and radar-equipped Wellingtons from September – for a three-pronged assault on the Axis convoys. The results exceeded all expectations. Over the summer months the attacks grew in number and ferocity, and the tonnage reaching Rommel plummeted. The *Afrikakorps* needed a minimum of 50,000 tons per month, but by September it was getting only half that. The German command in

Italy described the situation as 'untenable', and begged OKH in vain for Luftwaffe reinforcements.[14] Ciano noted on 25 September that 'in responsible naval quarters they were seriously beginning to wonder whether we should not give up Libya voluntarily, rather than wait until we are forced to do so by the total lack of shipping'.[15]

There was worse to come. In October only thirty-seven per cent of the tonnage leaving Italy reached Africa. And the last convoy to reach Benghazi had docked on 18 October. No fresh supplies had reached Rommel for five weeks, and the chances of any arriving in the next few days were far from good.

Thanksgiving or not, Hull expressed his willingness to receive Nomura and Kurusu that Thursday morning. They duly handed over Proposal B, though probably more in hope than expectation. Both men knew only too well how little was being offered.

There were five parts to the Proposal. The first forbade both sides from making further aggressive moves in south-east Asia or the south-west Pacific. The second promised an immediate withdrawal of those Japanese forces now in southern French Indo-China, and a complete Japanese withdrawal from the rest of the country once the war in China was over. The third stipulated equal trading rights in the Dutch East Indies, the fourth an end to the American freezes and embargoes, and a full restoration of US–Japanese commercial relations. The fifth required the US to cease all support for Nationalist China.

It was, in Hull's later opinion, 'of so preposterous a character that no American official could ever have dreamed of accepting it'.[16] It effectively ratified past Japanese aggressions, offered the Japanese war economy a huge boost and left China utterly in the lurch. And for what – the (quite possibly temporary) relocation of one division and a few squadrons from one end of Indo-China to the other?

There were no last-minute surprises; it was the same Proposal B that Hull had received from the Purple translators more than a week before. That one, moreover, had come complete with Togo's insistence that this was the last chance, that Proposal B was, to all intents and purposes, an ultimatum. Nomura and Kurusu hadn't presented it as such, but Hull thought they knew just how much was at stake. And if he simply rejected the Proposal outright, who knew what the Japanese army and navy had up their military sleeves?

He hid his feelings as best he could, so as to 'avoid giving the Japanese any pretext to walk out of the conversations'.[17] The American army and navy had told him they needed time, and he promised Nomura and Kurusu he would give the Proposal 'sympathetic study'. He had to find some common ground, or at least some ground they might share for a few weeks or months. Once the two Japanese diplomats had gone, Hull started sketching out a counter-proposal, one he could sell to both Tokyo and the American people, one that avoided the taint of appeasement yet kept the Japanese talking.

FRIDAY 21 NOVEMBER

As the last submarines involved in the Hawaiian operation departed from Yokosuka on the Japanese mainland, three navy reconnaissance planes left two airbases on Formosa for the skies above the Philippines. Their mission was to confirm or deny the Japanese consul's alarming estimate of 1,200 American planes in the archipelago.

The K-15s had their rising suns painted out, and the officers on board had removed the rank insignia from their uniforms. Lieutenant Miza, charged with photographing the American Clark and Iba airfields from a height of around 7,000 metres, had been instructed to fly on south, to islands beyond the Philippines, if he was seen and pursued. Both he and his superiors knew, however, that he lacked the fuel to do so. The removal of the plane's machine gun had slightly extended its range, but only at the cost of making Miza feel more vulnerable.

He need not have worried. His pilot flew them over Clark Field without attracting attention. There were no American fighters aloft, causing the Japanese to assume they were all at lunch. A second flyover was noticed, but the American P-40s were soon left behind by the faster Japanese plane. Miza moved on to Iba, where no one on the ground noticed their presence. Back in Formosa, the photographs taken by all three reconnaissance craft were developed and studied. There were, it seemed, only 300 American planes in the Philippines.

As their self-imposed deadline for military action drew nearer, the Japanese grew increasingly concerned about the reaction of their Tripartite Pact allies. Would Germany join them in their war against the United States and, if so, at what price? Would Japan be expected to join Germany's war against the Soviet Union? In Tokyo that Friday morning the Japanese Foreign Ministry put the formal question to Ambassador Ott: would Germany promise not to make a separate peace should Japan become involved, for whatever reason, in a wider war?

Hitler was not obliged to say yes – a member of the Tripartite Pact was obliged to give military assistance only if a fellow signatory was attacked. This was the norm for twentieth-century alliances: no state, after all, wished to give another state a blank cheque on its own future. The Tripartite Pact, moreover, was weaker than most twentieth-century alliances. The German and Japanese governments had no joint economic strategy, and no agreement on the sharing of military technology. Their armed forces had no contingency plans for coordinated action, let alone a joint global strategy.

There were two main reasons for this. First and foremost, Nazi Germany and Imperial Japan were far from natural allies. The Nazis considered the Japanese an inferior race, and had not forgotten Tokyo's seizure of Germany's colonial possessions in the Pacific during the First World War. A telling remark by Hitler's military attaché in Thailand – that 'Germany would settle with Japan after she has won the war with Europe' – revealed an alliance resting solely on short-term expediency.[1]

The Japanese had less grandiose ambition, but no greater love of their allies. They thought of the Germans as white European colonialists with two, almost incidental, saving graces. The Germans had no colonies of their own in the Far East, and they were already at war with those who had.

The second reason for the lack of a joint strategy was the two sides' inability to decide what, if anything, they wanted from each other. Tokyo had fewer problems in this regard – Germany had either conquered or was still at war with all of Japan's European enemies, and the Japanese had no wish to see German armed forces in the Pacific. The one thing Tokyo knew it needed, as evidenced by the request to Ott, was Hitler's promise to keep fighting Britain and Russia until such time as Japan had secured its goals in Asia.

The Germans found it harder to decide what they wanted from their Japanese allies. When Foreign Minister Matsuoka visited Berlin in April 1941, Britain was still considered the principal enemy and Russia an easy conquest, so Hitler and Ribbentrop spent their time pressing for a Japanese attack on Singapore. Three weeks into the Russian campaign, they were not so sure, and Ribbentrop instructed Ott to advance the case for a Japanese attack on Siberia. Tokyo thought it over, dropped a few positive hints and then told the Germans on 19 August that they wouldn't be entering the war just yet. Ribbentrop had one more go at Ambassador Oshima on 23 August and was told that Japan was making preparations for both southward and northward advances, but had yet to decide a priority.

This sounded unhelpful, but there were ways in which a Japanese attack on the Soviet Union might prove detrimental to the German cause. If they were to attack Siberia, the Japanese would first need to reach some sort of agreement with the United States, and this would allow the Americans to concentrate their forces in the Atlantic and Europe. Further Japanese attacks in south-east Asia, on the other hand, would keep America busy in the Pacific. And the mere threat of an attack on Siberia would be enough to keep the Soviets from sending the troops stationed there to Europe.

By late November winter had overtaken Siberia, and no Japanese attack would be possible until the following spring. If the Japanese moved now, it would have to be southwards, against the British and perhaps the Americans. The Germans believed they could only gain from this fresh strain on Britain's military resources and the dispersion of American strength which it would also involve. If all the Japanese needed to get them in motion was a

German promise to avoid a separate peace, then they could have it. When the forwarded request reached Ribbentrop in Berlin, he was only too happy to sanction it.

The pressure on the Red Army forces defending the western and north-western approaches to the Soviet capital continued to build. While the 14th Motorized Division, advancing between the 6th and 7th Panzer Divisions, broke through the latest Soviet defences east of the Klin–Kalinin road, Hoepner's 2nd and 11th Panzer Divisions were approaching the same highway south of Klin. The northern half of the Soviet line in front of Moscow was being levered backwards, and seemed perilously close to breaking. Zhukov moved what reserves he had into each new gap, seeking to narrow the German blades, to render the wounds less serious.

A crisis − *the* crisis − was definitely brewing. Holding on to Solnechnogorsk and Klin were absolutely vital, Zhukov told Rokossovsky. The latter would supervise the defence of Solnechnogorsk, his commissar General Lobachev the defence of Klin. But by the time the two men arrived at their destinations, both towns were virtually surrounded.

South of Moscow, Tula seemed destined for a similar fate. Denied the suspension of operations their commander thought wise, Guderian's forces had resumed their advance to the east and north-east, sending more shivers up Stavka's collective spine.

There were few easy gains any longer, but the Germans were still pushing forward, still unaccustomed to the very idea of failure. The 87th Division's Kurt Gruman was south of Istra, close to the hinge of the German advance. 'Missiles are exploding in the trees,' he wrote in his diary, 'everyone is lying on the ground. Windows shook and their frames flew out. There are columns of dirt and smoke. Senior Lieutenant Tuemmler, Lieutenant Kanis and Lieutenant Mueller were wounded. The streets are filled with the moans and cries of the seriously wounded. We are advancing in the forest. My sergeant-major and a Spanish soldier died the death of heroes as a result of grenade fragments.'[2]

Higher up the chain of command, Army Group Centre commander von Bock spent the day visiting various corps commanders. The first described 'the pitiful state of his divisions, whose strength is spent', the second, whose corps was still making progress, thought his men would 'still get to the Moscow Canal, but then we're finished!' The whole attack, von Bock decided, was 'too thin and has no depth'. If one looked, as his superiors did, at the divisions spread out across the map table, 'the ratio of forces is no more unfavourable than before'. But 'in practice the reduced combat strengths – some companies have only twenty or thirty men left – the heavy officer losses and the overexertion of units in conjunction with the cold give a quite different picture.' Several enemy divisions might still be cut off and destroyed west of the Istra Reservoir, but that was about all.[3]

Guderian was having similar thoughts. He had spent three consecutive days up at the front 'in order to form a clear picture of the conditions there', and had been suitably appalled. 'The icy cold, the lack of shelter, the shortage of clothing, the heavy losses of men and equipment, the wretched state of our fuel supplies, all this makes the duties of a commander a misery, and the longer it goes on the more I am crushed by the enormous responsibility I have to bear . . .'[4]

Fifty miles west of beleaguered Tula, in Likhvin's central square, the corpse of sixteen-year-old Sasha Chekalin had been hanging from a gallows for fifteen days. Born in the nearby village of Peskovatskoye, Chekalin had joined the area's recently formed partisan detachment. Towards the end of October this detachment ambushed a German military column on the road running east from Likhvin, and Chekalin's accurately thrown grenade destroyed one of the vehicles along with its occupants. A few days later he fell seriously ill. Once confined to a bed in a local village, he was betrayed to the Germans, and the grenade he flung at the arrest squad failed to explode. He was taken to Likhvin, where he was tortured and hanged.

Chekalin, a posthumous Hero of the Soviet Union, was an early partisan martyr. The roots of the movement went back a long way, but the familiar Stalinist mixture of hubris and paranoia hindered its rapid development in the months following the German invasion. Partisan activity had played a large role in the civil war that followed the revolution, and the Soviet military establishment in the 1930s had allotted it a vital role in any future war with Germany: secret rear bases had been set up and much thought given to communication with them – through courier parachutists, for example – once they fell behind enemy lines. As the 1930s unfolded, however, Stalin decided that, for one thing, partisans might prove dangerously independent of central authority, and, for another, that a war with Germany would be fought on Polish and German, not Soviet, soil. Most of those responsible for the previous policy were purged, and those bases already prepared allowed to atrophy.

Once hostilities began, and spilled so extravagantly across the western Soviet Union, there was clearly need for a rethink. After only a week of campaigning, a secret directive was issued, calling for 'action with units of the enemy army, for kindling partisan war everywhere and anywhere, for blowing up bridges, roads, telephone and telegraph lines, destroying dumps and the like'.[5] Three weeks later the Central Committee outlined the organizational details, in particular the key role that local party organizations were supposed to play in setting up and controlling the partisan detachments.

In these early months those deliberately recruited and sent behind enemy lines were vastly outnumbered by those Red Army soldiers left stranded by the speed of the enemy advance. Since the Germans mostly kept to the roads, the scattered Soviet remnants were forced into the wide spaces that lay between them, a countryside of swamps and forests which offered ideal conditions for concealment. Groups of stragglers came together for survival and self-defence, armed themselves with weapons left lying on the growing number of abandoned battlefields, and, in most cases, eventually resumed their fight with the enemy.

During this period, before German plans for the occupied territories became appallingly apparent, many such groups were betrayed by the local population. Some people turned traitor because they hated the Soviet system, most because they feared German reprisals if they failed to report the presence of partisans. One party official, who found himself behind enemy lines after the Vyazma encirclement battles, heard the latter story in several villages. It would not change until the Soviets established an equally ruthless presence in the occupied areas, and provoked the Germans into such acts of repression as could only be counter-productive.

Aware of this, the party entrusted deliberate recruitment to the NKVD. Of the various organizations set up under its auspices, the Independent Motor-rifle Brigade for Special Tasks, or OMSBON, was one of the better known. Its early volunteers were given three months' training in partisan skills like sniping, explosives, parachuting and map-reading, then sent into Moscow to help quell the great mid-October panic. After that, they were ready for insertion behind enemy lines.

Vladimir Frolov, like Sasha Chekalin, was a village boy from the Tula region. A student at Moscow University when war broke out, he had quickly volunteered for OMSBON, done his training and then joined thousands of others working to strengthen the defence rings outside Moscow. On 21 November he was on his own, just outside the village of Davydkovo on the vital highway from Klin to Solnechnogorsk. The Red Army had fallen back to the east, and Frolov, having packed the drainage culvert that ran under the road with explosives, was nervously waiting for Germans to arrive.

Further to the west, in the town where Halder and the Army groups of staff had held their conference eight days earlier, Konstantin Zaslonov was signing on as an engineer at the locomotive depot. He and thirty other railwaymen from Smolensk and Orsha had left Moscow in early September. Picking up more comrades in Vyazma, they crossed the lines in early October and then spent over a month fighting off hunger, cold and German patrols. Finally, in mid-November, Zaslonov and a few others reached Orsha. The local party underground supplied him with the documentation he needed to apply for a job at his pre-war workplace, and the Germans, short of engineers and desperate to get the Russian railways in working order, gave him a job supervising the locomotive crews.

A resistance cell was born. Zaslonov lost no time in hiring his fellow partisans, and over the next three months, under the noses of their German masters, the group would turn the depot into a partisan stronghold. They manufactured mines and other explosives, and used them to blow up signal boxes, points, bridges and trains. Between mid-November 1941 and mid-February 1942 they caused ninety-eight derailments and incapacitated over two hundred locomotives and thousands of wagons. When his situation in Orsha finally grew too dangerous, Zaslonov left to form another detachment – eventually a 2,500-strong brigade – in the Vitebsk region. Killed in November 1942, he would also be a posthumous Hero of the Soviet Union.

In Moscow the local NKVD had set up two partisan schools, one in the southern part of the city, one at Kuntsevo in the western outskirts. Volunteers were given a brutal forecast of their likely fate – 'it's quite possible that most of you will be killed' – and then told that no one would blame them for choosing the slightly softer option of service in the regular army.[6] None did.

Eighteen-year-old Zoya Kosmodemyanskaya was one of the students at Kuntsevo. Training complete, she and eleven other members of Partisan-Reconnaissance Unit 9903 were sent through the lines in early November. Some were killed in a German ambush, but Zoya completed her mission and got back safely. On that Friday she was sent out again, this time with two male comrades, Vladimir Klubkov and Boris Krainov. They were charged with burning down buildings in Petrishchevo, a village just off the Mozhaisk highway, only ten miles behind the German front line.

In the Crimea, Field Marshal von Manstein was still hoping to seize the port of Sevastopol before the year's end. The city's ring of defences was well prepared, however, and he would be disappointed. One Soviet strongpoint that proved impossible to crack during these November weeks was the village of Mekenziya, seven miles east of the city centre. Among its defenders was Nina Onilova, whose fame was about to spread. On that day she slipped out of her trench and crawled twenty-five yards across open ground to destroy a German tank with two well-aimed Molotov cocktails. She was given instant promotion to sergeant and awarded the Order of the Red Banner.

Onilova had been born in a village outside Odessa and brought up in one of the city's orphanages. While working as a teenager at a textile factory she saw the civil war movie *Chapayev*, about a famous woman machine-gunner named 'Anka'. Inspired to emulate her new heroine, she took gunnery lessons at the factory's para-military club. After war broke out she volunteered as a medic, and it wasn't long before her gunnery skills came in useful. In the fighting outside Odessa her unit's machine gun jammed at a particularly inauspicious moment. Onilova not only cleared it but efficiently disposed of the Germans advancing towards them. Her comrades adopted her as their main gunner. Badly wounded in September, she refused to be invalided out and rejoined the unit as it fell back towards Sevastopol.

She was killed four months later, also in Mekenziya. Nina Onilova and Zoya Kosmodemyanskaya were two of the million Soviet women who served in the Red Army, Navy and Air Force, two of a hundred and fifty thousand who won awards for heroism. There were no women in Germany's front-line fighting forces, a point of contrast which said as much about the two regimes as the many other points of comparison.

In Copenhagen the German 'Plenipotentiary', former Ambassador von Renthe-Fink, told Foreign Minister Scavenius that the Reich was 'unable to comprehend' Denmark's refusal to join the Anti-Comintern Pact. As there were 'no political or other obligations' involved – Denmark was not expected to join the war against the Soviet Union – Renthe-Fink expected a reversal of the Danish decision that day.[7]

The Cabinet was called into session, and eventually agreed to join the pact if the Germans put Renthe-Fink's promise of no further obligations in writing and accepted other additions to the agreement – Denmark, for example, would remain neutral and restrict itself to internal police action only. This decision was relayed to Renthe-Fink, who forwarded it to Berlin for ratification.

Hitler had lunch with Albert Speer and then a three-hour conversation with Goebbels. The architect, busy redesigning what was now the capital of Europe, had put together a presentation in the new Chancellery's Model Room. The Führer was predictably entranced by the sheer size of the projected buildings. There was one problem, Speer admitted – he lacked a big enough workforce to materialize the dream. Hitler promised him 30,000 Russian prisoners of war.

Goebbels was obsessing about Berlin's Jews and eager for a decision on their removal. Hitler, though quick to sympathize, proved loath to take an actual decision. He agreed on the need for an 'energetic policy', but was eager to avoid 'unnecessary difficulties', and urged the Propaganda Minister to go easy on 'mixed marriages', particularly those in artistic circles.[8] Such unions were bound to die out over time. Berlin would be *Judenfrei* sooner or later, and there was little point in upsetting true Germans for the sake of a few years.

According to Goebbels, Hitler looked well, as if running a war agreed with him. And he was generally optimistic about the prospects. He wasn't expecting much from North Africa – the difficulties involved in supplying Rommel were immense – but it didn't really matter. Goebbels should be careful not to raise public expectations; perhaps he should stress how peripheral North Africa was. The war would be decided in the east, where things were going well. Now that the roads were frozen, the motorized units had regained their mobility, and favourable results could be expected. There were supply difficulties, but these occurred in every war. He reiterated his ultimate intention to raze Moscow and Leningrad, and hoped that the weather would hold long enough to allow the encirclement of the Soviet capital and its abandonment to hunger and devastation.

Goebbels asked him if he still believed in victory. Hitler answered that 'if he had believed in victory in 1918 when he lay without help as a half-blinded corporal in a Pomeranian military hospital, why should he not now believe in victory when he controlled the strongest armed forces in the world and almost the whole of Europe was prostrate at his feet?'[9]

Goebbels refrained from pointing out that the half-blinded corporal's belief had proved mistaken.

The planned breakout from Tobruk got under way at 08.00. During the night, paths had been cleared through the closest minefields, gaps cut in the wire and temporary bridges thrown across the anti-tank ditches. The tanks of the British 32nd Armoured Brigade moved off towards the enemy, hopeful of covering the eight miles that separated them from El Duda, and a link-up with the 7th Armoured Brigade, by the end of the day.

The first surprise was finding both Germans and Italians in front of them – Rommel had inserted a third of the *Afrika* Division into the Italian-held perimeter at the last moment. The second was how well Mussolini's troops fought – more Germans than Italians were taken prisoner during the morning, as the British battled their way through a two-mile breach in the perimeter defences. By noon they had driven a salient four miles into the Axis line, half the way to El Duda.

Three factors halted the advance. Enemy resistance was hardening, and led, with the usual energy, by Rommel himself. He had taken personal charge of four 88-millimetre guns and was wreaking havoc. The British had already suffered serious losses – over half their tanks and seventy-five per cent of the Black Watch infantrymen – and were willing to risk more only in a hopeful cause. The latter was now in doubt.

Following their orders of the previous evening, the 15th and 21st Panzer had started west at first light with hardly a parting shot at their desert neighbours, the 4th and 22nd Armoured Brigades. The latter, wrongly assuming a German retreat, compounded the error by taking their time getting started. By the time the British were under way, the German armour was halfway to Sidi Rezegh.

News of their approach reached the incumbents at 08.30, just as the infantrymen of the 7th Armoured Support Group were moving into battle. The original plan involved the Support Group infantry clearing and seizing the escarpment north of the airfield, with the entire 7th Armoured Brigade then pouring down the far slope to El Duda. This was now modified. The 6th Royal Tank Regiment would do the pouring, while the 7th Hussars and 2nd Royals would turn east to face the oncoming panzers. There was no great sense of risk – the Germans were, after all, in retreat.

A series of uneven battles ensued. The Support Group quickly dislodged the Axis troops on the ridge, but the 6th Royals, advancing over and down it, soon found themselves being picked off by Rommel's 88s. Away to the east, much worse befell the British. The 7th Hussars, ordered to 'locate and delay the advance of the enemy tanks', found them and were annihilated. The 2nd Royals were also mauled, and it took Support Group heroics, a fuel and ammunition crisis and belated pressure from the pursuing 4th and 22nd Armoured Brigades to keep the Germans off the airfield.

All of which produced a quite extraordinary situation: five alternating layers of forces, running from the Tobruk garrison in the north through the Bologna and *Afrika* Divisions, 7th Armoured Brigade and the *Afrikakorps* to the 4th and 22nd Armoured Brigades in the south. The three forces in the middle of this club sandwich were obliged to face two ways at once, a task that had already more or less done for the 7th Armoured Brigade. Anxious to avoid a similar fate, Crüwell pulled the *Afrikakorps* out of harm's way as soon as darkness fell. He intended to concentrate both divisions to the east, around Gambut, but at Rommel's insistence the 21st Panzer was moved to Belhamed, in that gap between Sidi Rezegh and Tobruk which the British were still hoping to close.

Cunningham, far away at Maddalena, had little idea of what was happening on the battlefield. That morning, after receiving news of the panzer divisions' 'retreat' from Gabr Saleh, he had set in motion the second half of the British plan – the envelopment of the bypassed Axis frontier positions by the New Zealand Division. This, as it turned out, would prove a good move, but not, as Cunningham imagined, because a British victory was looming. If anything, the New Zealanders would save the 8th Army from defeat.

It was not all Cunningham's fault. That evening he received two reports from the battlefield, and both seemed to justify the rampant optimism pervading his headquarters. A hundred and seventy German tanks had been 'hit', according to one, a further sixty were surrounded at Sidi Rezegh, according to the other. The armoured victory had apparently been won. In such a context, news of high British tank losses offered no real cause for alarm. No one had expected that the destruction of the *Afrikakorps* would come cheaply.

Somebody at Cunningham's HQ talked to the press. 'It is authoritatively stated,' one cable to Cairo read, 'that the Libyan battle, which was at its height this afternoon, is going extremely well. The proportion of Axis tank casualties to British is authoritatively put at three to one.'[10] Writing to Churchill, Cunningham's superior Auchinleck had the sense to restrain his optimism. 'It is very difficult,' he admitted, 'to arrive at a firm estimate of the enemy tank losses . . .'[11]

He and Cunningham should have been thinking about their own. The 7th Armoured Brigade had gone into battle at Sidi Rezegh that morning with 141 tanks, and by nightfall only 28 were in working order. When added to those suffered two days earlier by the 22nd Armoured Brigade at Bir el Gubi, these losses amounted to a severe weakening of the 7th Armoured Division. It could ill afford more 'victories' like this one.

The men, as usual, had a clearer sense of how the wind was blowing. For Robert Crisp, whose 4th Armoured Brigade missed out on the major battles, it was 'a confused day of constant skirmishing', one in which he actually saw two armoured shells fired by a Panzer II heading straight for himself and his tank, only to fall ten yards short. This gave him a better idea of the Panzer II's effective range, and showed that the Germans – who presumably knew how far their guns would fire – were just as afraid of getting too close. That was the day, he thought, when 'we shed our light-heartedness and eagerness. The sense of adventure had gone out of our lives, to be replaced by grimness and fear and a perpetual, mounting weariness of body and spirit.'[12]

Darkness had fallen in the Mediterranean. The Italian convoy had passed through the Strait of Messina and was now sailing down Sicily's eastern coast, prior to making its break across the open sea to Benghazi. The first sign of danger was the torpedo that ripped through the hull of the light cruiser *Duca degli Abruzzi*, courtesy of the submarine HMS *Utmost*. As the Italian destroyers quartered the area in search of the assailant, the *Duca degli Abruzzi* reversed course and limped, none too steadily, back towards Messina.

A few hours later the Malta-based RAF arrived on the scene. The radar-equipped Wellingtons found the convoy, called in the Albacore torpedo-bombers, and then lit up the ships with flares. Another Italian cruiser, the *Trieste*, was disabled by a torpedo strike, and the convoy commander decided enough was enough. He turned his ships back.

Writing his diary entry that Friday night, Halder was inclined to disregard the Eastern Front commanders' worries. He noted that von Bock had been 'profoundly affected by the severity of the fighting', and expressed his own shock that 'regiments with four hundred rifles are commanded by first lieutenants!', but the abiding impression was of satisfaction with the continuing advance. Guderian's troops might, as their commander reported, be 'on their last legs', but 'we may hope that they will be able to fight on'.[13]

His optimism spread to the situation in the south, where Rostov had fallen and the 6th Army was 'forging ahead slowly but surely'. Halder admitted that there was heavy fighting north of Rostov, but sensed 'no immediate danger'.[14] Nor did Hitler. If Rostov was taken, then Army Group South should move swiftly on, with a view to seizing the oilfields around Maikop. A new and dangerous habit of discounting failures and overvaluing successes was in the process of being established.

In Rostov itself, the idea of a further advance seemed ludicrous. The real decision lay between holding and retreating. All but one of the Don bridges was down, the supply situation was appalling and the Soviet attacks to the north of the city were beginning to drive a dangerous wedge between von Kleist's Panzer Group and the 17th Army. As his troops scoured the city for stragglers and saboteurs, von Kleist's conviction was growing that it couldn't be held.

At the other end of occupied Europe, not far from the Sorbonne on the Parisian Left Bank, an explosion ripped through a German propaganda bookstore. Since the beginning of September, seven German soldiers in France had been killed, and over a hundred and thirty French hostages had been executed in retaliation.

The Proposal B that Nomura and Kurusu had presented to Cordell Hull on the previous day made no attempt to resolve the two states' essential conflict of interests in eastern Asia. It was a modus vivendi, a Japanese take on how the ring might be peacefully held for a limited period. That the Japanese take would favour Japan — by ending both the oil embargo and American aid to China — hardly came as a surprise.

Hull and Roosevelt had been working on their own modus vivendi for several days, one that served American interests. They had three objectives in mind. The first, which both men knew was unlikely to be attained, was a Japanese change of course. The second, which assumed that war was inevitable, was to buy as much time as possible for the completion of American military preparations in the Philippines and western Pacific. The third was to show how interested the United States was in peace, and how determined the Japanese were for war. When the inevitable finally happened, Roosevelt and Hull wanted no one in any doubt as to where the blame lay.

Their modus vivendi, which Hull first showed to the military chiefs that afternoon, was initially intended to last for three months, subject to renewal by mutual agreement. Like Proposal B, it ruled out further advances by either party across international borders, included a Japanese withdrawal from southern Indo-China and agreed a mutual unfreezing of assets. Unlike Proposal B, it limited the Japanese to 25,000 troops in northern Indo-China and made no specific mention of renewed oil deliveries. Exports would remain subject to control measures imposed for reasons of national security, which might or might not imply a continued American reluctance to sell Japan anything that could be used for military purposes. On the question of China, the United States welcomed the opportunity to host Sino-Japanese peace talks in the Philippines, but made no mention of curtailing American aid to Chiang Kai-shek.

The military chiefs – Admiral Stark for the navy and Brigadier General Gerow (standing in for Army Chief of Staff Marshall) – were impressed with the modus vivendi. 'The adoption of its provisions,' Gerow wrote that evening to War Secretary Stimson, 'would attain one of our present objectives – the avoidance of war with Japan . . .'[15]

SATURDAY 22 NOVEMBER

In Tokyo Nomura's repeated requests for more time had finally been taken seriously. A few more days might make all the difference, the Foreign Office told the military leaders, who hummed and hawed and graciously acquiesced in a four-day postponement of the 25 November deadline. Military operations were, in any case, not scheduled to commence for another fifteen days.

Togo's message to Nomura and Kurusu made it abundantly clear that this was their final chance. There were 'reasons beyond your ability to guess' for the previous deadline, and it had been 'awfully hard' to change the date, but the two diplomats had been granted an extra four days. And no more. Any new agreement would have to be signed by the 29th. 'Let me write it out for you,' the Foreign Minister added somewhat gratuitously – 'twenty-ninth.' That was it. 'This time we mean it; that the deadline absolutely cannot be changed. After that things are going to happen automatically.'[1]

In 1941 the Kurile archipelago belonged to the Japanese. The largest island, Etorofu, had a population numbering only a few hundred, most of whom made their living from the rich fishing grounds off the Pacific shore. A few families had homes on Hitokappu Bay, a fifty-square-mile expanse of deep water shaped like a bear's head. Over the last few days they had watched their bay slowly fill with ships – oil tankers, destroyers, cruisers, battleships. Five of the empire's six large carriers were already there, vast marvels of modern engineering with pre-industrial names – *Akagi* (*Red Castle*), *Hiryu* (*Flying Dragon*), *Shokaku* (*Soaring Crane*), *Zuikaku* (*Happy Crane*) and *Soryu* (*Green Dragon*). The sixth, *Kaga* (*Increased Joy*), was expected early that evening.

The ring of snow-covered volcanoes, the patches of mist floating above the black waters, the pale grey armada spread across the wide bay – it was an awe-inspiring picture. Lieutenant-Commander Chigusa, whose destroyer *Akigumo* arrived early that afternoon, had no idea where this fleet was headed, but admitted to 'a feeling of great confidence'.[2] Masuda Shogo, a flight officer on the flagship carrier *Akagi*, felt like one of the forty-seven *ronin* (masterless samurai) in the famous *Chushingura* legend, as they gathered in the noodle shop before venturing forth in search of revenge.

Nagumo, meanwhile, had received the confirmatory signal from Yamamoto: 'The Task Force will move out from Hitokappu Bay on 26 November and proceed without being detected to rendezvous set for 3 December. X-Day [the day of the attack on Pearl Harbor] will be 8 December.'[3] That evening Nagumo summoned his key commanders to the cabin that housed the scale models of Oahu and Pearl Harbor. The main speaker was Lieutenant-Commander Suzuki, who passed round sketch maps and lists prepared by the consulate staff in Honolulu and reiterated what he had told the meeting in Tokyo. The American ships always came back at weekends, he said, so there was every chance of catching them in port. He detailed the American air presence – the airfields, the quality and numbers of the various types of plane. The numbers were actually wrong: the consul in Honolulu, like his opposite number in Manila, had come up with a gross overestimate. And these figures could not be checked from the air – the Japanese would go into this operation expecting greater resistance than that which they actually encountered.

There were regular American air patrols to the south and southwest of Oahu, Suzuki reported, but, as far as they had been able to find out, none to the north and north-west, the direction from which *Kido Butai* would approach. And even those to the south and south-west seemed to be scheduled around mealtimes, leaving after breakfast, returning for lunch, out again until dinner. There were, astonishing as it might seem, no patrols during the hours of darkness. If *Kido Butai* launched its planes at dawn they would be at least halfway to their targets before anyone saw them.

This all sounded good, almost too good to be true. The ever-anxious Nagumo had four major concerns. What if *Kido Butai* was seen en route? What if the Americans were alerted in advance, or were more alert as a matter of course than Suzuki had suggested? What if the American fleet wasn't in port? How strong would an American retaliatory blow against his fleet be?

Suzuki couldn't assuage these anxieties – no one could. And they gave rise to another – what if the American carriers were not in Pearl Harbor? The chance to destroy them at anchor would be lost, and the chance of an encounter at sea would have to be taken into consideration. In such circumstances, should *Kido Butai* move to the attack without Tokyo's permission? Genda and Fuchida believed it should. As far as they were concerned, once the fleet left Hitokappu Bay it was, to all intents and purposes, already at war.

Until September, Moscow's experience had been much like London's – the Germans might be coming but they were still a long way away, and more than a semblance of normality could be retained. Cinemas, theatres and concert halls remained open, even if performances were occasionally interrupted by air raids. The most valuable books in the Lenin Library might have been evacuated, but readers could access the rest. There was still enough food and power, if only just.

By late September things had begun to change. Now food really was running short, electricity and transport were increasingly rationed and the Germans were advancing through the Russian equivalents of Kent and Sussex. Guderian's sudden lunge in early October sounded the first great alarm. Moscow, it seemed, was actually under threat. The Soviet government took steps to alleviate the potential damage, ordering the evacuation of diplomats, scientific institutes, government departments, even Lenin's embalmed corpse. But old habits died hard, and the capital's ordinary citizens were left out of the loop. As rumours spread that the entire city had been wired for destruction, a general panic took hold.

It took four days to restore order. The NKVD shot anyone they could find who had planned on welcoming the Germans and used the opportunity to get rid of inconvenient prisoners. Stalin announced that he was staying in the capital, and the first phase of Typhoon faltered in the late-autumn mud. Things got back to what passed for normal.

Determined that they should remain so, Stalin insisted on celebrating the Anniversary of the Revolution on 7 November. His generals objected, but he was adamant – it would be a finger held up to the Nazis, an unmistakable declaration of confidence in the Soviets' ability to hold Moscow and continue the war. Extra fighters were brought in from other fronts to stiffen the city's air defences, Stalin gave a speech to the assembled party luminaries in the deepest Metro station and the usual parade was held on Red Square. The soldiers marched past the empty mausoleum, disappeared offstage and headed straight back to the front line.

Two weeks later the nearest Germans were less than forty miles from the Kremlin. Another morale boost was needed. The official news in Saturday's *Verchenyaya Moskva* included the announcement of a chess championship, to begin on the following Thursday. A long list of famous chess masters had been invited to compete in the tournament, which would be held in the capital's Physical Culture and Sports building. Moscow might be at serious risk, but that was no reason for dispensing with civilized pursuits.

The situation in front of the Soviet capital still provided grounds for German optimism. According to Halder, von Bock had taken personal charge of the battle from his 'advanced command post', and, 'with enormous energy', was driving forward 'everything that can be brought to bear'. Halder was also pleased with Guderian, who was 'again convinced he could continue the attack'.[4] The 2nd

Panzer Army infantry took Stalinogorsk that day, leaving the panzers to push north, aiming towards Moscow but also threatening a swing into Tula's rear. Halder noted with pleasure that recent Soviet communiqués were full of concern for that city's situation.

West of Moscow, the 4th Panzer Group and the northern wing of the 4th Army were still moving forward a few miles a day, the Red Army units struggling to maintain their coherence as they gave ground. In the German 35th Infantry Division's sector west of the Istra Reservoir the pressure was too much, and many Red Army soldiers either surrendered or deserted. South-west of Istra, Kurt Gruman's regiment had poured out of the forest and into the village of Surmino on the Istra–Zvenigorod road, only to find itself face to face with a T-34. The Germans opened fire with everything they had, and the Soviet tank crew turned this way and that, trying to crush them under its tracks. Its turret was jammed, and only the machine gun was working – eventually a shell fell into the exhaust pipe, and flames and smoke burst from the engine. The crew were still not done, and it took two more shells to tear off the tracks and finally halt the T-34. 'Surmino was in our hands,' Gruman reported triumphantly; 'the Istra–Zvenigorod highway had been cut.'[5]

Further north the German ring around Klin was virtually complete, leaving only a narrow corridor of escape for its Soviet defenders. Rokossovsky went to see for himself: 'the only conclusion we could draw was that the town could not be held.'[6] But how to stop the marauding panzers moving further east, towards Dmitrov, Yakhroma and the Moscow–Volga Canal? Rokossovsky requested more artillery support, and spent the night in the beleaguered city, hoping for, but hardly expecting, better news in the morning.

Five miles to the south, Vladimir Frolov had spent the hours of daylight hiding by the Moscow road, waiting for the moment to detonate the explosives he had placed in the culvert. It was fully dark when he heard German voices and tried in vain to ignite the fuse. Taking his life in his hands, he carefully worked his way

alongside the suddenly busy road, fixed a much shorter fuse, lit it
and ran.

He came round a few moments later, realized he was unharmed
and headed in the opposite direction from the cries of the
wounded. Finding shelter for the night in a nearby village, he
eventually reached Solnechnogorsk, only to suffer a second con-
cussion when the town's ammunition dump was hit by German
fire.

Halder's optimism over Army Group Centre's apparent new impe-
tus did not extend to the situation now confronting the other two
army groups. Rostov might be in German hands, but von
Reichenau's 6th Army was unable to get moving, and the Soviets
were transferring forces from that front to the Rostov area. Von
Kleist's 1st Panzer Army was in for a hard time, and the general was
already pleading with Army Group South commander von
Rundstedt to evacuate the city. Von Rundstedt was not yet convinced that such an unprecedented step was necessary.

In the north, von Leeb's forces in Tikhvin were out on a similar limb. After taking the town on 8 November, a further advance
to the north had briefly seemed possible, but a series of strong
Soviet counter-attacks soon put paid to that idea. The 39th Panzer
Korps, charged with holding the town, was also in for a tough few
weeks. Tikhvin, as von Leeb noted on 22 November, was 'more or
less encircled'.[7]

So was Leningrad, but the new 'road of life' offered hope. The
first major convoy set off across the frozen lake, sixty lorries carrying thirty-three tons of flour, sixty drivers anxiously following the
line of flags. Ivan Maximov was one of them. 'A dark and windy
night shrouded the lake. There was no snow yet and the black-
lined field of ice looked for all the world like open water. I must
admit that an icy fear gripped my heart. My hands shook, no
doubt from strain and also from weakness – we had been eating a
rusk a day for four days . . . but our column was fresh from
Leningrad and we had seen people starving to death. Salvation
was there on the western shore. And we knew we had to get there

at any cost.'[8] One lorry sank through the ice, but the rest reached the starving city in the early hours of the following day.

The train carrying 942 Jews from Berlin to Riga was stopped in Kovno (the current Lithuanian city Kaunas). The new 25,000-capacity concentration camp in Riga's outskirts, which Hitler and the SS had planned as a halfway halt on European Jewry's long journey to 'the East', was not ready.

The authorities in Kovno, asked to improvise a solution, needed no second bidding – they had been coming up with such solutions on a regular basis for several months. The 942 Berlin Jews were marched past the ghetto and along a three-kilometre road which, unknown to them, was known by the local Jews as the Via Dolorosa. Aaron Peretz watched the procession, and overheard one Berliner ask a guard if the camp was still far. 'We knew where the road led,' Peretz said later; 'it led to the Ninth Fort, to the prepared pits.'[9]

The Jews from Berlin saw only an old Tsarist fort, and the ice-lined cellars into which they were crammed without food or water. Most were still expecting to end up in a work camp, and found nothing sinister in their temporary accommodation. They had no way of knowing that two more trains were en route from Frankfurt-am-Main and Munich, or that the local *Einsatzkommandos* preferred one major massacre to several minor ones.

One of the first names on the Udet funeral invitation list was Werner Mölders, Germany's most successful fighter pilot. Born in 1913, Mölders had made his name in Spain with the Condor Legion, and added to that reputation in France and the Soviet Union. He matched von Richthofen's First World War score of eighty in the second week of Barbarossa, and became the first-ever pilot to make a hundred kills a fortnight later. Göring decided that Mölders was too valuable to risk in combat, and in August promoted him to Inspector General of Fighters, responsible for the development of the machines and the way they were used. Early in the morning of 22 November he left the Chaplinka airfield in the Crimea for Berlin.

The Heinkel 111 was flown by Oberleutnant Kolbe, an old comrade from the Condor Legion, with Mölders himself stretched out in the nose. Flying conditions were bad, and Kolbe landed at Lvov in the western Ukraine, intending to wait out the storm. Mölders insisted they fly on, despite reports of even worse weather to the west. As they approached Breslau, thunder and lightning cracking around them, one engine died. Kolbe brought the plane down through dense cloud and pelting rain, and was almost on the ground when a line of overhead cables suddenly loomed into view. As he wrenched back the stick, the plane stalled and plunged to the ground. Both he and Mölders were killed instantly.

In Berlin Udet's state funeral featured the usual Nazi trimmings – one leather-coated Führer, a forest of columns spouting flame, the Berlin Philharmonic playing Wagner's 'Twilight of the Gods'. Udet's coffin was borne by gun carriage through city streets lined with mourners to Invalidenfriedhof Cemetery, the obese Göring padding behind it in his self-designed uniform, clutching his field marshal's baton.

On that Saturday morning, a week after the relaunching of the Typhoon offensive, the German people were finally told that fighting had resumed in front of Moscow. On the maps carried by the newspapers, the hard-won gains of the previous seven days segued into one dramatic leap forward.

In Cyrenaica the two armies had suffered a wet night. As was fast becoming the ritual, they spent the morning distancing themselves from each other, trying to work out who was where, refuelling and replenishing their vehicles and weapons, and making their plans for the afternoon. The main British aim was to strengthen the 7th Armoured Division's grip on the Sidi Rezegh area and resume the march on Tobruk. To this end, the 22nd Armoured Brigade and the 1st South African Brigade were ordered north to join the 7th Armoured Brigade and the 7th Armoured Support Group at Sidi

Rezegh. The main German aim was to prevent any link-up between the garrison and the 7th Armoured Division, preferably by destroying the latter, but poor communications between Rommel and Crüwell that day resulted in two separate – and, as it turned out, mutually supportive – strategies for achieving this. Rommel blocked the intended British advance by moving the 21st Panzer Division into the gap between Sidi Rezegh and Tobruk, and the two generals then contrived a pincer movement as crushing as it was accidental.

Early in the afternoon Rommel ordered the 21st Panzer commander, von Ravenstein, to split his division, sending his infantry south against the mostly British-held ridge north of Sidi Rezegh and the panzer regiment several miles to the west, where it ascended an undefended stretch of the same escarpment ridge and turned back east in the direction of the airfield. Around two o'clock the first wave of panzers poured into the British position, just as the 22nd Armoured Brigade was arriving from the south. The German tanks were outnumbered, but the British tanks were outgunned, and the airfield was soon littered with the burning hulks of the latter.

The commander of the 4th Armoured Brigade, unsure of what was happening, sent a few tanks to find out. Crisp's was among them. When he arrived on the ridge overlooking the Sidi Rezegh airfield, a battle was already under way, and he found it almost impossible to tell friend from foe. A decision on what to do next was rendered unnecessary by the arrival of Brigadier Jock Campbell, the almost overly charismatic leader of the 7th Armoured Support Group. 'There's a Jerry tank attack coming in from the west,' he told Crisp from his standing position on the front seat of a small touring car. 'We need you. Follow me.'[10]

Crisp followed him, down the slope and through the British infantry and gunners spread across the airfield, Campbell standing straight in the bucking car, holding up a blue and white flag . 'The shells rained down and the flat surface was transformed into fountains of red and yellow earth and flying stones and lead through which the little car weaved and dodged and sometimes disappeared altogether in cascades of evil-smelling smoke. Miraculously it tore on and the arm that held the flag aloft never wavered.'[11]

They reached the far end of the airfield, whereupon Campbell looked at Crisp, waved his arm in a westerly direction and headed back the way he had come. Following the arm, Crisp's 'stomach turned over. Twelve hundred yards ahead of me stretched the array of dark brown shapes, sixty or seventy monsters in solid line abreast coming steadily towards the landing ground . . . towards me.'[12] A few highly fraught minutes followed, during which Crisp and his tank scored at least one hit. After a short period of playing dead among tanks destroyed earlier, they made a successful run back across the airfield. Looking back later from a position of relative safety, Crisp was surprised to see that the panzers had stopped at the edge of the airfield, despite the British rush to evacuate it. The Germans, as he discovered years later, had run out of fuel.

While the tanks and infantry of the 21st Panzer closed in from west and north, the 15th Panzer was slowly moving in from the east. Crüwell had ordered the advance on his own responsibility, but it was almost 15.30 before the panzers moved off, heading towards the sound of the distant battle. Ninety minutes later, with the light almost gone, the 15th Panzer enjoyed a wholly unexpected success, driving straight into the 4th Armoured Brigade as it settled down for the night. Most of the brigade's headquarter staff and fifty of its tanks were captured. The rest of the latter, racing out across the desert in all directions, would take more than a day to regather.

All three brigades of the 7th Armoured Division had been seriously weakened. At day's end the 7th and 22nd Armoured Brigades had ten and thirty-four runners respectively, the 4th Armoured Brigade only a handful available for the following day. The *Afrikakorps* had 173 tanks in running order, a huge advantage, but one that Rommel knew was bound to be temporary. Even as he congratulated von Ravenstein on the 21st Panzer's successful attack, Rommel was only too aware that fuel and ammunition shortages had once again hampered the full exploitation of a hard-won victory. As long as the British controlled the seas, they could replace and fuel their tanks and prevent him from replacing and fuelling his. He had to defeat them so completely that there would be nothing left to reinforce.

The next day was *Totensonntag*, the German Sunday of remembrance for their war dead. That evening Rommel and his staff devised a plan for trapping the remnants of the British armour between the massed tanks of *Ariete* and the two panzer divisions, and achieving what von Clausewitz called a *Schlacht ohne Morgen*, a 'battle without a morrow'.[13]

In the Mediterranean the pendulum was about to swing, albeit too late to influence the outcome of Crusader. Dismayed by the carnage of Rommel's supply ships, and overenthused by the U-boat sinking of the British carrier *Ark Royal* on 13 November, Hitler and his navy chief, Admiral Raeder, decided to move all their operational U-boats to that theatre. This shift of naval resources, when combined with an equivalent shift of air strength, would pay big dividends, but only for a while, and only in the area concerned.

When U-boat chief Admiral Dönitz received the order on 22 November he was appalled. 'The most important task of the German navy,' he wrote later, 'and therefore of the German U-boat arm, and the task which overshadowed in importance everything else, was the conduct of operations against shipping on Britain's vital lines of communication across the Atlantic . . . The number of U-boats transferred to the Mediterranean should have been kept down to a minimum, and to have denuded the Atlantic as we did and to put an end to operations there for something like seven weeks was, in my opinion, completely unjustifiable.'[14]

The problem for Germany was that both Hitler and Dönitz were right. More U-boats were needed in the Mediterranean if Rommel was to have any chance of defeating the 8th Army, and those same U-boats were needed in the Atlantic to stop the flow of British trade and American aid. There just weren't enough to go round.

Soon after first light, 200 or so miles north-east of Ascension Island in the South Atlantic, the German auxiliary cruiser *Atlantis* made a rendezvous with U-126. As ratings from the two crews saw to the trans-shipment of food, water and soap, and arranged the hoselines for refuelling the submarine, the U-boat captain and his senior officers settled down to a leisurely breakfast in the better-stocked *Atlantis* mess. The refuelling was still under way when they had finished, and the U-boat captain decided he had time for a proper bath.

He was mistaken. The auxiliary cruiser's only remaining seaplane had been damaged the previous day, so the first warning Captain Rogge had of the British County-class cruiser HMS *Devonshire* was the sighting of three telltale funnels from his foremast. The two German crews hurriedly disengaged their two craft, and U-126, bereft of its bathing captain, crash-dived. *Atlantis* turned her stern to the enemy, hoping to delay a definite identification by the British. If he could sucker the British captain in, and bring him within range of his own hidden guns or the vanished U-boat's torpedo tubes, then a miracle might be possible. It was, as Rogge wrote later, 'evident right from the start that our own chances were extraordinarily slim'.[15]

He had enjoyed a good long run. *Atlantis* had left Germany at the end of March 1940, and had been at sea for 600 days. During that time she had sunk nineteen enemy ships and captured another three in the Indian, Pacific and South Atlantic Oceans. And one of the former, the British cargo ship *Automedon*, had yielded the best prize of the auxiliaries' war, a slew of mailbags containing, among other things, details of Singapore's defences, new British codes, reports on British forces in the Far East, and British estimates of Japanese intentions. If anything could encourage a Japanese drive to the south, it was knowledge of how weak the British were, and how little they realized it. This was the kind of intelligence that might start a war, and perhaps even win it. Rogge sent the mailbags north to the German embassy in Tokyo, where his fellow countrymen demonstrated their commitment to the Tripartite Pact by bartering them for oil and a new seaplane.

Now time had run out for *Atlantis*. *Devonshire*'s Captain Oliver had no intention of closing to within the Germans' range. He launched his plane for a closer look and fired salvos either side of the raider. Rogge signalled that his ship was what its paintwork said it was, the Dutch merchantman *Polyphemus*, but it took the British only a few minutes to check that story and find it wanting. At 09.35 *Devonshire* opened fire in earnest, finding the range with her third salvo. As the Germans abandoned ship, thirty more salvos followed, killing seven of the crew and wounding more than twenty. The burning raider was scuttled at 10.16.

The British seaplane pilot had seen the German submarine, and Captain Oliver thought it wise to leave the area. U–126, which had mistaken the warning salvos for depth charges and gone deep, came up to find *Atlantis* gone and the ocean littered with small overpopulated boats. Only a few could be taken inside the submarine, so around fifty life-jacketed men rode up top. The rest were left where they were and taken in tow. *Atlantis* had gone, but her crew's adventure was far from over.

Over the last few days, while licking the American modus vivendi into shape, Cordell Hull had also produced a more comprehensive, longer-term plan for peace between Japan and the United States. This plan, which came to be known as the Ten Point Note, listed America's ultimate objectives, with no concern for their practicability. Hull claimed the ten points were only a starting point for future negotiations, but they also served as an implicit recognition that the time for negotiations was over. The Note offered Japan a full partnership in America's world, provided she play by America's rules. All troops would have to be withdrawn from both Indo-China and China. Japan would be required to back its current enemy Chiang Kai-shek and abandon its current friends in the Tripartite Pact.

That Saturday morning Hull met the British, Chinese, Dutch and Australian ambassadors. He described the Japanese Proposal B, and told them that rather than try to improve on it he had come up with short- and long-term proposals of his own. He then outlined the modus vivendi, and quickly ran through his ten points. No copies of the latter were handed out.

British Ambassador Lord Halifax expressed provisional support – a reduction of the Japanese force in southern Indo-China was certainly worth having, always assuming the Japanese were not given too much economic compensation in return. The Australian and Dutch representatives offered similar sentiments, but Chinese Ambassador Hu Shih was less effusive. He welcomed the troop reductions in Indo-China but was 'very reluctant' to see any reduction in the economic embargo.[16] He asked the Secretary of State whether the Japanese troops in China would be required to observe a ceasefire. They would not, Hull admitted.

The diplomats were left to contact their own governments. Later that day, Hull was brought the MAGIC-translated text of that day's message from Tokyo to Nomura and Kurusu. Time was clearly running out.

That evening the two Japanese diplomats visited Hull's apartment in hope of an answer to Proposal B. Energized by Tokyo's granting of four extra days, Nomura and Kurusu were sparing no effort to keep the talks going. Hull saw only perfidy. 'It was almost unreal,' he wrote in his memoirs, 'to see these representatives come to my home smiling, courteous, and outwardly friendly. It was a strain to talk to them in the same tone and on the same level, knowing what I did of Japan's nefarious plans from the intercepted messages, and knowing that Nomura and Kurusu had the same information.'[17]

He told his two visitors they would have their answer on Monday.

SUNDAY 23 NOVEMBER

'If the United States knew anything about the resolution of our empire,' Matome Ugaki noted in his diary, 'she might not keep quiet.' And since there was no possibility of that resolution weakening, the ball was very much in the opponent's court. If the Americans gave up trying to be 'the watchdog of the world' and accepted that they couldn't always have things their own way, then they would be 'spared much'. If they didn't, then it was on their own heads. 'Everything will be O.K. if our position is accepted and our demands met completely,' Ugaki continued. 'Nothing else will do.'[1]

Hopes of peace were fading fast, but Yamamoto was keen to give the diplomats every chance, and not to jump the gun. If negotiations with the United States proved successful, he told a meeting of army and navy leaders in Tokuyama, he would have no hesitation in recalling Nagumo and his ships, right up to 01.00 on the day of the attack. When some officers complained that such an order would be extremely difficult to carry out, Yamamoto lost his temper. 'The purpose of establishing and training armed forces for the past hundred years was only to maintain peace. If any officer here thinks he cannot obey, I order him here and now not to participate in this operation. And I demand that he resign at once.'[2]

★

In Hitokappu Bay the captains and senior officers of carrier divisions, support groups and individual ships attended a morning conference aboard *Akagi*. Some already knew that Pearl Harbor was the target, but many did not, and Nagumo's opening announcement had a suitably electrifying effect. Nothing was definite, he hastened to add – the negotiations between the United States might still prove successful – but he left the assembled company in no doubt of his own expectations.

Chief of Staff Kusaka laid out the possibilities. If *Kido Butai* was discovered in toto before X-Day, the day of the attack, then it would turn back. If only one or two ships were seen, they could still proceed. And if the enemy found them on X-Day itself, or attacked them at any time, then Japan would be at war, and the fleet would proceed with the attack if that was at all possible.

Senior Staff Officer Oishi took over, outlining how the fleet would be organized en route, what the route would be, the precautions to be taken against discovery. He passed out copies of Task Force Order No. 1, which Nagumo had signed that day, covering basic instructions for the voyage and strike. Commander Genda then spoke for half an hour, mostly about the planned attack. This would be concentrated on the American carriers, battleships and planes – Genda was keen to cause lasting damage to these few crucial targets, and was insistent that the Japanese pilots should not be diverted by the likely plethora of other tempting possibilities. The planes would attack in two waves – torpedo-, dive- and high-level horizontal bombers in the first, just dive- and horizontal bombers in the second. Both waves would have fighter protection.

Genda hoped that the attackers would have advanced knowledge of which ships were in harbour, and where exactly they were berthed. Current information from the consulate in Hawaii would be transmitted via the Naval General Staff on a regular basis, and Japanese submarines would be on watch in Hawaiian waters. On the morning of the attack, First Air Fleet would send its own reconnaissance planes – one each from the cruisers *Tone* and *Chikuma* – over the US fleet anchorages at Pearl and Lahaina

Roads. They would take off an hour before the bombers, and relay what information they gained by radio. During the attack the fleet would be protected by its own fighters, flying two-hour shifts at two different altitudes.

Communications Officer Ono then outlined the communication rules for the forthcoming voyage. *Kido Butai* would receive messages but not send them, a silence enforced by the sealing of transmission keys. The ships would communicate with each other by flag in the daylight hours, by narrow-beamed blinkers at night. All craft would observe a strict blackout.

Another meeting followed in the afternoon, with mainly the same speakers addressing all the flying officers. Genda enlarged on what he had said that morning, taking the fliers through the attack plan in some detail. He was challenged on two points. The hour gap between reconnaissance and attack flights seemed too long to the flying officers – if the former were spotted, the enemy would have enough time to prepare for the latter. Could the gap not be shortened to half an hour? The plan for lost or downed pilots to break radio silence was also vigorously opposed by one flight leader. At such a crucial moment, with the fate of the empire at stake, an individual's life was of no account. 'What about this?' he asked his colleagues. 'Why don't we die in silence if our engines conk out?' Approval of this sentiment was unanimous.[3]

At sea for four days with her cargo of fuel for the Philippine invasion force, the *Arizona Maru* docked in the Formosan port of Takao. Masuda Reiji found the wharves 'jammed with great piles of supplies – horses, men, trucks – all being moved back and forth as we loaded through the night'. He and his fellow crew members had their first taste of bananas and other tropical fruits, and 'after working all day in the scorching heat we told each other we'd never tasted anything so delicious. Maybe this, we thought, would be our final taste.'[4]

The German 4th Army had been the closest to Moscow when Typhoon resumed, but its infantry divisions had made little progress in the succeeding week. The centre and right wing had remained on the defensive for a number of reasons, some better than others. The Soviet units holding this part of the line were among the more experienced, and as long as the 4th Army pinned them where they were – and prevented Zhukov from moving them to more threatened sectors of the front – von Bock was happy. The 4th Army commander, Field Marshal Günther von Kluge, also claimed that his units had suffered more than most in recent weeks and were in no state to attack. Von Bock had not seen fit to challenge this highly dubious claim, but those in command of the panzer groups flanking von Kluge's army were growing increasingly exasperated by its inaction.

The 4th Army's left wing, fighting south-west of Istra, was certainly trying its hardest. After taking Surmino the previous day, Kurt Gruman's 87th Division took nearby Lukino, but the losses were heavy and neither village seemed really secure. A few miles further south, units of the 78th advanced along the Moskva valley and captured Lokotnya, but a similar distance to the north a regiment of the 252nd was ambushed in the forest near Kotovo.

Either side of 4th Army, the panzer groups made better progress. Having punched two major holes in the Soviet front south of Tula, Guderian's motorized divisions enjoyed a day of rapid progress. While the 17th Panzer motored north towards Venev, the 10th Motorized reached Mikhailov and severed another rail link connecting Moscow to the south and east. Guderian's spearheads were now fifty miles east of both Tula and Moscow.

Such successes were gratifying, but sustaining them was another matter. Guderian visited von Bock that afternoon, intent on getting his orders revised. He recited the familiar litany of difficulties – exhausted troops, lack of winter clothing, insufficient supplies, shortage of tanks and guns, the lack of support on his right flank, the steady stream of new Soviet units – and insisted that there was no way he could carry out his current orders. His army could probably reach and destroy the Moscow–Ryazan railway, but there was no way they could hold onto the area. They had to abandon such ludicrous objectives and go over to the defensive.

Von Bock told Guderian that his previous reports had been sent to OKH, and that the men in the Rastenburg Forest really did understand what conditions were like at the front. Realizing that Guderian was far from convinced, von Bock offered to call up Army Commander von Brauchitsch. With Guderian listening in through another earpiece, von Bock told von Brauchitsch what the 2nd Panzer army commander had told him. Von Brauchitsch, Guderian decided, was 'plainly not allowed to make a decision. In his answer he ignored the actual difficulties, refused to agree to my proposals and ordered the attack to continue.'[5] What Guderian should have said was that von Brauchitsch was not allowed to make the decision he wanted him to make.

His army was, after all, still moving forward. Further north, on the other side of the 4th Army, the 3rd Panzer Group's rate of advance was even more encouraging. North-west of Istra, on the centre-left of the German line, the 40th Panzer Korps was pushing the Soviet forces back towards the fifteen-mile-long reservoir. As its leading elements reached the western shore that evening, the spearhead of 46th Panzer Korps was advancing north of the reservoir, heading for Solnechnogorsk. Further north still, the 4th Panzer Group's 56th Panzer Korps reached the outskirts of Klin, and for several hours that morning the 7th Panzer and 14th Motorized Divisions fought a running battle with outnumbered Soviet tanks on the wide plain to the north and west of the city.

Rokossovsky was still inside it. Having already conceded that the town could not be held, he was still wondering how to check a further enemy advance towards the Moscow–Volga Canal when more devastating news arrived – Solnechnogorsk had fallen. In this situation, he decided, 'I could not remain on the flank any longer; we had to be at the centre of the army for the sake of better troop control and to prevent the front from being penetrated'. Repairing to the local post office, he reported in to Western Front Chief of Staff General Sokolovsky. The conversation was 'interrupted by a shell that hit the post office building and damaged the wires. Meanwhile enemy tanks enveloping Klin from the north broke into the town.'[6]

After leaving his deputy, General Zakharov, with instructions 'to resist the enemy advance towards Dmitrov and Yakhroma with every means at his disposal and thereby win the time needed for fresh forces to come up', Rokossovsky and his staff took the only safe road out of the burning town, the one running east to Rogachevo and Dmitrov. On several occasions their two cars attracted fire from German tanks, and as they crossed the frozen River Sestra one was hit by machine-gun fire. The Germans had obviously penetrated way beyond Klin, and who knew what waited among the trees, or behind the next snowdrift? There were several of them in the two cars, and they were kitted out like 1930s American gangsters: 'I had, beside my revolver, an excellent sub-machine gun presented to me by Tula workers and two hand grenades. We could stand up for ourselves if the worst came to the worst, but there was no sense falling into a German ambush in these woods . . .'[7]

Their circuitous route took them east, south and west, and it was almost midnight when they reached the Moscow–Leningrad road at Durykino, some fifteen miles south of newly captured Solnechnogorsk. 'There were no army units, only crowds of refugees from Solnechnogorsk, who said that the town had been taken by the Germans many hours ago. The situation appeared to be gloomy indeed.'[8]

Zhukov could only agree. 'It gets worse from hour to hour,' was his verdict on the fall of Klin.[9]

In the preceding fourteen days the 9th Army, on the far left flank of Army Group Centre, had received only one train-load of fuel. In earlier months such paucity might have been blamed on favouritism or bad luck, but by late November it was the norm.

It was also the result of misjudgements stretching back years. Hitler's love of the combustion engine had given the German army its cutting edge, but the price had been high. The capital invested in motorization had not been invested in the *Reichsbahn*, and over the last ten years the only form of transport which could run on the country's abundant reserves of coal had been badly neglected. By contrast, the new road-supplied army ate up fuel and rubber, two

commodities of which the Reich and occupied Europe were noto-
riously short. Sixteen hundred lorries, and considerably more
personnel, were required to replace the supply capacity of a double-
track railway line.

Vehicle numbers would always be a problem, even after Poland
and France had been scoured and looted, but German army logis-
ticians calculated that the existing fleet of vehicles could be fuelled
and maintained so long as the distance between supply depots and
fighting troops did not exceed 300 miles. In Poland and France that
stipulation was met, and in planning the Russian campaign the
general staff made the convenient assumption that the Red Army
would be destroyed west of the Dnieper–Dvina line. If, by some
terrible twist of fate, this did not occur, it was accepted that the
transport of adequate supplies to the men at the front would be
beyond the motorized services.

By the end of July the supply lines were 300 miles long, and it
was becoming painfully clear, first, that the railways would have to
play a larger-than-expected role in the continuance of the campaign, and, second, that they were ill-equipped to do so. The
Russian lines were few and far between, and built to a different
gauge. Both tracks and infrastructure were designed for the Soviet
locomotives that used them, and most of these had retreated eastwards with the Red Army. The German engines brought in to
replace them refused to run on the lower-grade Ukrainian coal;
they were also narrower with smaller water tanks, and generally
carried more weight on each axle. The German engineers could
not just change the track gauge – the lighter Soviet rails also needed
replacing, and new water towers were required at shorter intervals.

There were other enormous problems, even before the onset of
winter. The German and Polish railway administrations, asked to
staff the new military network in Russia and the Ukraine, tended
to see such postings as punishments, and sent their least reliable
workers. The retreating Soviets destroyed what they could of the
existing infrastructure, particularly water towers, bridges and
turntables, all of which took time to replace. The early partisans,
though few in number, quickly realized that long lonely stretches

of line through dark forests were easy and attainable targets. And then winter arrived, making matters even worse. Soviet engines, it transpired, were built with internal water pipes, which prevented them from freezing. German locomotives had outside pipes, most of which froze and burst.

In late November the German-adapted railway system in the western Soviet Union was utterly incapable of supplying Army Group Centre with those supplies deemed essential for a successful prosecution of the Moscow offensive.

In the Rastenburg Forest Halder presided over a Sunday meeting of the Eastern Front armies' administration and supply chiefs, and later that day summarized the discussion in his diary. He noted that England no longer possessed 'a continental dagger' and that an English blockade of Europe could be thwarted by German reorganization and 'harvesting' of the occupied territories. On the debit side, military operations and occupations were an enormous drain on Germany's military and economic resources: 'the means which are available to us for continuing the war are limited through use and the incredible strain imposed on our arms by the protected areas.' In a sentence guaranteed to lift the hearts of Germany's enemies, Halder admitted that 'the army, as it existed in June 1941, will not be available to us again'.

Although the list of resources in increasingly short supply – soldiers, armaments, labour, food and vehicles – could hardly be more comprehensive, a decisive military victory was still possible. If one failed to arrive, then, Halder surmised, in a very Hitlerish passage, the war might 'shift from the level of military success to the level of moral and economic endurance'. If such a shift occurred, then 'the demand for frugality in the employment of our forces and arms and ammunition will increase markedly. The use of the militarily conquered territories will be more significant.'

Halder conceded that the Soviet Union, though 'decisively battered', was 'not destroyed', and that, despite the Wehrmacht's 'extraordinary performance', such destruction was some way off. Indeed, he admitted, 'given the vastness of the country and inexhaustibleness of the people, we cannot be totally certain of success'. And then, once again, he lamented those halcyon summer days when 'major coordinated operations' were still possible. Now that resources were limited, the Wehrmacht must cut its cloth accordingly: 'We must reach our goals step by step and in various acts.'[10]

A new *Das Reich* hit the German bookstalls. In the previous edition Goebbels had endorsed Hitler's ludicrous assertion that the Jews were responsible for the war, but the intervening week had seen a change of heart – now it was Winston Churchill who had set the German military machine in motion: 'He prepared this war and incited it. In the fullest sense of the word, it is his war.'

'The Clay Giant' offered the usual sarcasm-strewn accumulation of accusations and insults. Churchill himself was 'a close friend of alcohol' and 'one of the world's best-known liars'. Lacking scruples or a political conscience, with a hide as 'thick as a rhinoceros', the British Prime Minister was 'wholly indifferent to the vast misery' that flowed from his successful warmongering. And to what end? Britain's situation was hopeless. She was losing the Battle of the Atlantic, losing the air war over Europe, and had miserably failed to create the much-touted second front in Europe. The British had 'nothing left but a bitter aftertaste', and were 'already on the road to defeat'.

Ordinary German readers might have wondered why Goebbels was choosing to write about Churchill and Britain when the German armed forces were fighting for their lives outside Moscow. Those higher up the Nazi hierarchy, particularly those involved with war production, discovered a rich vein of black humour – conscious or otherwise – in one particular passage. Goebbels generously conceded that British and American armaments industries were producing at full capacity, but implied that German factories were doing even better: 'We hardly believe that time is working in England's favour. We know exactly what England can and cannot do. We also know what we cannot do, and above all what we can do. We also have firm figures that give us a reliable grasp of our armaments capacities and those of the enemy.'[11]

The last sentence, depressingly for Goebbels and the Nazi project, was as close to a true statement as the article managed.

In Copenhagen all Danish hopes that the latest crisis in their relationship with Germany had been resolved were dispelled by a typically aggressive telephone call from Ribbentrop and a further abrasive meeting with Renthe-Fink. The Danish response to Germany's invitation to join the Anti-Comintern Pact was utterly unacceptable, both Germans insisted, and the Wehrmacht in Denmark was now on full alert. If the Danes didn't come to their senses, and put on an outward show of acceptance, then the promises of April 1940 would be revoked, and a territorially reduced Denmark would find itself joining the war under its own Nazi government. Five ministers, including Prime Minister Stauning and Foreign Minister Scavenius, thought Denmark should accede to these latest demands, but a majority held out for several more hours. It took another meeting to persuade them, in Stauning's words, of 'the danger of saying no'.[12]

The Cyrenaican desert was shrouded in heavy mists, an apt meteorological reflection of the military situation. The previous day Rommel had told his diary that the German signals network 'could hardly be worse. This is war the way the ancient Teutons used to fight it. I don't even know at this moment whether the *Afrikakorps* is on the attack or not.'[13] His opposite number Cunningham, ten times as far from the action at his Maddalena headquarters, was even more in the dark. He had not yet received a detailed rundown of the 7th Armoured Division's tank losses, but suspected that they had been heavy. It was time, he decided, for his infantry to take more of the strain.

While XXX Corps' tank battles around Sidi Rezegh had been claiming all the attention, XIII Corps' infantry had been steadily enveloping the Axis positions on the frontier and advancing along the Trigh Capuzzo in the direction of Tobruk. General Freyberg's New Zealand Division was leading the advance, and was now only thirty miles from Sidi Rezegh. Cunningham visited XIII Corps

HQ that morning, and told General Godwin-Austen that his corps, suitably reinforced by the transfer of XXX Corps' South African infantry, now had the primary responsibility for relieving Tobruk. Cunningham expressed uncertainty, however, over what to do with his remaining armour, and seemed, to both Godwin-Austen and his own staff, notably lacking in either confidence or resolve. He then drove back to Maddalena, where newly depressing estimates of yesterday's losses lay in wait.

Rommel's original plan for the *Afrikakorps'* day had been highly detailed, and, by the time Crüwell's staff decoded it, Crüwell had devised a better one. When, soon after dawn, his headquarters and communications staff were overrun by the New Zealanders, he had the excuse he needed for acting on his own initiative. In his plan, the panzer divisions would move south-west for a rendezvous with *Ariete*, then all three would turn north and trap the British between themselves and the German infantry.

Crüwell insisted on an early start. The 15th Panzer set off at 08.00, the tank regiment of the 21st Panzer struggling to catch up. They were seen and recognized by the crews of several South African armoured cars, but the latter's reports were not believed, and soon the panzers were crashing through the soft-skinned supply trains of the 5th South African Brigade and the 7th Support Group, picking off targets almost at will. Once again Campbell dashed hither and thither inspiring pockets of resistance, but desperate confusion was more the norm among the British and South African units. They were, the 15th Panzer commander, General Walther Neumann-Silkow, told Crüwell, there for the taking. He urged his superior to change plan and drive north-east through the disorientated enemy, but Crüwell insisted on collecting *Ariete*, and sticking to his original plan. 'There is no doubt we missed an opportunity here,' von Mellenthin wrote later, 'and that it would have been better to attack before the South Africans and British could coordinate their defence.'[14] As it was, they had six hours to prepare their positions.

Around noon the two panzer divisions rendezvoused with *Ariete*, and by three o'clock Crüwell had made his dispositions. The tanks were arranged in a long line – *Ariete* on the left, the 15th Panzer in the centre, the 21st Panzer on the right – like Indians lining a crest in a Hollywood Western. Lacking the time to bring up his infantry in the traditional fashion, Crüwell placed their thin-skinned lorries with the artillery and anti-tank guns close behind the armour, and set the whole lot in motion. It was, as von Mellenthin icily pointed out after the event, 'an innovation in German tactics'.[15]

The anvil of German-held Sidi Rezegh was twelve miles ahead of Crüwell's falling hammer, the South Africans and what remained of the 7th and 22nd Armoured Brigades suspended in between. 'The attack started well,' according to Fritz Bayerlein, 'but soon came up against a wide artillery and anti-tank screen.'[16] The South Africans had organized their defences well: unable to dig through the solid-rock surface, they had hidden their guns among vehicles knocked out earlier in the day. Several German and Italian tanks were destroyed, but much greater damage was done to the lorried infantry. An early casualty was the 115th Regiment commander, Lieutenant-Colonel Zintel, hit by machine-gun fire as he led his regiment's charge standing upright in his staff car. Most of the regiment's other officers and NCOs would be killed or wounded over the next hour.

Heinz Schmidt, also with the 115th, had seen Zintel drop from his car 'like a felled tree. Then I flashed past him. The Major was still ahead. I recognized infantry positions in front of me. There was a tall, thin fellow out in the open, running backwards as if impelled by a jet from a hose. I heard bursts behind me and followed the tracer as it whipped past me into the distance ahead. How slowly tracer seems to travel. The tall fellow dropped.' They were almost on the South African guns when the major's car turned over. 'I was alone out ahead in the inferno now. In front I saw nothing but belching guns.'[17]

The same terror gripped both charger and charged. Crisp, standing in his Honey turret a couple of miles east of the South African positions, watched the 'familiar battle formation – a solid, embattled column with the heavy panzers at the head of the battering ram in a ponderous phalanx of destruction – loom to the south. "Christ," I thought, "this is it; nothing can stop that lot. It's worse than yesterday. Yesterday I could at least run away.'" And then the relief of realizing that the panzers were heading for the South African leaguer, and not through him and his colleagues. 'It was a fleeting thought, but it lightened my darkness.' A minute later his tanks and the South African guns around them were firing on the Germans and receiving fire in return. As Crisp watched a nearby South African battery, 'the shield in front of the right-hand gun disintegrated in slivers of steel from a direct hit, and the man sitting behind it with his eye to the telescopic sight disintegrated in slivers of flesh. Men dragged away the mutilated body, and then went back to their job.'[18]

The guns that had slowed the German charge were destroyed, one by one, by the Germany artillery. The panzers moved forward again, punching holes in the sides of the two–mile–square defensive box that the South Africans had built around their leaguer, and 'tank duels of tremendous intensity developed deep in the battle-field. In fluctuating fighting, tank against tank, tank against gun or anti-tank nest, sometimes in frontal, sometimes in flanking assault, using every trick of mobile warfare and tank tactics, the enemy was finally forced into a confined area.'[19] The end came when the South African brigade HQ was suddenly and unexpectedly over-run at 16.15. The first intimation of disaster, according to the brigade's intelligence officer, 'was when one officer, peering round the wheel of the control vehicle where he was crouched with the telephone, saw the tanks about 300 yards away. Slowly, like monstrous black beetles, they advanced, spouting fire and smoke. The knowledge came as a thunderbolt from the blue. Inconceivable. But there they were, collecting prisoners as they lumbered on.'[20]

As night fell, the leading elements of the 15th Panzer made contact with the German infantry on the southern escarpment above Sidi Rezegh. The men of the 5th South African Brigade, and those of the 7th and 22nd Armoured Brigades who had fought alongside them after surviving the previous day's battle at Sidi Rezegh, had, almost to a man, been killed, wounded or captured.

All three brigades had been virtually destroyed as fighting forces. It looked like a stunning German victory.

But was it? Rommel, who had spent most of that Sunday in personal command of the infantry and gunners facing the advancing New Zealanders around Point 175, soon heard that a victory had been won, and, according to von Mellenthin, returned that evening to the Panzer Group HQ in 'a state of excited exultation'.[21] He had no details as yet, and according to Bayerlein it was 'long after midnight before we could get any sort of picture of the day's events, organize our force, count our losses and gains and form an appreciation of the general situation'.[22]

By that time, Rommel had given his orders for the following day, orders he stuck to despite the almost unanimous opposition of those around him. His intentions for the 24th, as he signalled Berlin at midnight, were to complete the destruction of the 7th Armoured Division and to advance with elements of forces – in fact, the entire *Afrikakorps* – 'towards Sidi Omar with a view to attacking enemy on Sollum front'. With the British armour, as he now believed, essentially destroyed, he would use his own to roll up the enemy forces on the old frontier, and to cut off the supply routes to those left between there and Tobruk. The 8th Army would be broken, the road to Egypt open.

Westphal, his operations chief, joined von Mellenthin in urging another course. The advancing New Zealanders offered both threat and opportunity – if left alone they might reach Tobruk, if left to the panzers they could share the same fate as the South Africans. Years later, von Mellenthin was still regretting the lost opportunity: 'If we kept the *Afrikakorps* in the Sidi Rezegh area, we would have won the Crusader battle. The 8th Army had a fatal practice of committing forces in succession, and we could have destroyed them one after another.'[23]

Rommel rejected his and Westphal's advice, and subsequent objections from von Ravenstein, Neumann–Silkow and Crüwell, who had a much better idea of what the day's victory had cost them. The last's tactics, whether necessary or not, had lost the

Afrikakorps 72 of 162 tanks and a large proportion of its experienced infantry officers. Neither were replaceable, but a huge number of crippled vehicles, German, British and South African, were still sitting on the battlefield, ripe for salvage, and Crüwell pleaded with Rommel for time to reclaim them. He was refused.

Rommel was after bigger game, an end to the campaign by the following evening, as he told von Ravenstein. And none of the other options promised the sort of decisive blow that the *Afrikakorps*, with its perilous supply situation, so desperately needed to inflict. It could not win a war of attrition – it had to be a knockout blow.

Rommel had reason for confidence. Six days into Crusader, the British had lost the initiative. Despite air superiority, despite having more tanks and more infantry, despite luck with the weather and – though it hurt to admit it – despite his own failure to appreciate the scale of their attack for several days, the British offensive had run into the sand. Their armour had been outfought and mostly destroyed; Tobruk had not been relieved. The British commander, Cunningham, clearly lacked the flexibility that desert warfare demanded, and Rommel knew in his heart that a display of boldness would unhinge him.

Early that afternoon, shortly after Cunningham left XIII Corps for Maddalena, several of his senior officers – Godwin-Austen, Brigadier Carver (representing XXX Corps commander Norrie) and Brigadier Galloway (Cunningham's BGS) – held an impromptu meeting. Galloway told the others how Cunningham was viewing the battle, and hinted that he was thinking of breaking it off. They were appalled, and Galloway returned to Maddalena convinced that his boss was in a minority of one.

Cunningham, meanwhile, had received more bad news – according to a latest, already outdated report, the 7th Armoured Brigade had lost all its tanks, the 22nd Armoured Brigade all but thirty. There was, it seemed, nothing to stop the panzers heading east, and no alternative to the abandonment of Crusader and a swift withdrawal behind the frontier. Unwilling to bear the sole responsibility for such a step, Cunningham got on the phone to Cairo and asked Auchinleck to fly up that evening. While waiting, he issued orders for moving himself and his headquarters back into Egypt. The returning Galloway did his best to slow up the execution. 'Some caravans and tents,' as one officer noticed, 'were taking an exceptionally long time to get packed up.'[24]

Auchinleck duly arrived, and took one of the war's more important decisions. He had been further from the fighting than Cunningham or Rommel, but had a less cluttered understanding of the overall situation. As long as the Axis supply line was broken, Rommel had to make do with finite forces. The British, whose supply lines were open, had only to continue the battle, and sooner or later their superiority in tanks, men, fuel and planes was bound to tell. Crusader would go on.

The last German auxiliary cruiser at large was *Komet*, otherwise known as *Schiff 45*. *Komet* had been at sea for 509 days, and had the unique distinction among German raiders of reaching tropical latitudes via the icy northern waters of the Soviet Union and the Bering Strait. The Soviets, then still at peace with the Germans, had supplied two pilots for this part of the voyage, and later sent the Germans a $130,000 bill for their services.

The return on all this time, effort and cash had been poor. In a year spent roaming the Pacific, *Komet* had sunk only six merchantmen and taken two. In October she had set off for home via Cape Horn and the Atlantic, and was now entering the Bay of Biscay disguised as the Portuguese freighter *S. Thome*. German aircraft had been sighted two days earlier, and *Kriegsmarine* minesweepers were on their way to meet her. Hamburg seemed almost within reach.

If Cordell Hull expected an immediate response to his proposals from Britain, China, Australia and the Dutch East Indies, he was disappointed. For one thing it was Sunday, for another America's putative allies were not at all sure what their response should be. The Dutch could be counted on to follow the consensus, but the British – whose lead the Australians would follow – were caught in a dilemma. Both Churchill and the Foreign Office were inclined to take a tough line with the Japanese, and Hull's modus vivendi had a whiff of appeasement about it. But the last thing the British wanted was to find themselves facing a Japanese onslaught without American help. Rather than accept or reject Hull's proposals, they would seek to beef them up, to make sure that Japan received economic concessions only if and when it removed all its forces from Indo-China and suspended operations in China itself. This would all have to be done with tact – Hull seemed rather sensitive to criticism of late – and at a suitably cautious pace.

The Chinese were simply furious, but, like the British, realized the peril of simply saying no. Rather than deliver an official response, they began an intense lobbying campaign, using their Washington and London ambassadors, press leaks in both capitals, and Chiang Kai-shek's sympathetic American adviser Owen Lattimore to spread their view that the modus vivendi was, in essence, an American betrayal of China.

MONDAY 24 NOVEMBER

In Hitokappu Bay the meetings continued aboard the ships of the First Air Fleet. Fuchida and Genda divided the fliers according to bomber type, and went through all the conceivable problems that each might encounter in a series of seminars, tutorials and one-on-one briefings. The fliers leaned over the relief models of the target, committing the topography to memory. By evening an icy gale was howling across the bay, making ship-to-ship movement extremely difficult, and most of the airmen remained aboard *Akagi*, drinking multiple toasts of sake to the success of the great endeavour.

General Walther Model had assumed command of the 41st Panzer Korps nine days earlier, when it was still employed in the defence of beleaguered Kalinin. Model had taken to the task with his usual energy, even starting up a winter clothing production line in one of the local textile factories, but on learning of Typhoon's resumption he had volunteered his panzers for a leading role in what might be Barbarossa's final scene. The 9th Army commander, General Strauss, proved reluctant to let his panzer corps go, and Model was left fretting for several days while his tanks were repaired and camouflaged for an advance they might never make. But on 20

November OKH had decided in his favour. Now, four days later, his panzers were bypassing conquered Klin to the north, the outer edge of the giant scythe swinging towards Moscow.

South of Solnechnogorsk, Rokossovsky spent Monday's daylight hours trying to work out where the greatest danger lay. The German advances north of Klin offered a potent threat, as did the growing pressure on the Istra line, south along the reservoir and river to the town of the same name. But the most immediate danger lay between these two, from the forces skirting the reservoir to the north, and their imminent link-up with those moving down the highway from Solnechnogorsk. Lacking reserves, Rokossovsky had no choice but to juggle his forces. Units were already on their way from the Istra sector to Klin, and these, he decided, would be better deployed south of Solnechnogorsk.

His main command post was moved to Lyalovo, a temporary one established only six miles down the road from Solnechnogorsk, in the village of Peshki. Rokossovsky arrived there in early evening, and received reports from the local commanders in one of the village buildings, a T-34 standing sentry outside. He was about to ask who was blocking the road when a solid-steel shell came through the wall, suggesting the proximity of panzers. Where was the Soviet armour? The tank commander had sent all but two of his tanks down the road to refuel. 'Are you quite sure those two tanks didn't go to refuel too?' Rokossovsky asked, causing the officer to flush. 'I had to tell him that at the front the practice was to bring the fuel to the tanks from the rear, not the other way round.'[1]

Rokossovsky told the man to get his tanks back. Moments later a liaison officer hurried in with news of German tanks. They were pushing into Peshki from the north, flanked by sub-machine-gun-firing infantry. Rokossovsky and his fellow officers rushed out to find shells 'exploding on all sides . . . The night was lit up by mortar-shell bursts and vari-coloured tracks left by tracer bullets. It was an impressive sight but the realization of danger blotted out all other thoughts.' Offered a ride to safety in the T-34, Rokossovsky sent it towards the Germans instead. He and the other officers made their way south through the village, found their cars and, 'realizing that it was no use wandering about under the enemy's nose', drove off to the new HQ at Lyalovo.[2]

Bad news was waiting. Rokossovsky's superiors had overruled him, and instead of deploying the reinforcements from the Istra in a defensive line south of Solnechnogorsk had used them in an ill-organized attempt to reverse the town's capture. The attackers, unable to sustain their initial successes, had eventually been thrown back with considerable losses.

As the German units in the Istra sector moved up to the river and reservoir, their commanders were scouting locations for crossing the ice. A few small bridgeheads had already been established across the river, which was only thirty yards wide. Soviet engineers opened a few locks, creating a wider barrier, but the dam was left intact.

South-west of Istra, Lieutenant Gruman's 87th Infantry Division was encountering fierce resistance from the Soviet 5th Army. Attacking fortified positions in the forest, they suffered huge losses. Over the last fortnight, the seventy men in his company had become forty, and the toll in officers had been even greater. The better ones, those who had 'set a personal example by leading their men forward', had been the first to go, and their replacements were rarely up to scratch: 'they had no conscience' and 'used every opportunity to move to the rear. Their favourite excuse was the necessity to remove the wounded.' Gruman's diary entry for the day listed the recent dead, and lamented the condition of those still alive – tired, disillusioned, 'frayed to the extreme'.[3]

As Guderian kept telling von Bock, his men were in much the same state, but they kept subverting his arguments with new successes. Though *Grossdeutschland* was still vainly beating at Tula's door, the motorized units advancing east and south-east of the city seemed to be gathering speed. The 29th Motorized made twenty-five miles that day, and the 17th Panzer, now entering Venev, pushed one combat group even further north, towards Kashira.

Guderian might think – might know – that these were the last flickers of the 2nd Panzer Army's fast-waning energy, but the pins in Zhukov's map were suddenly leaping closer to Moscow. Kashira, with its huge electricity generating station and railway ridge across the Oka, was clearly vital to Moscow's salvation – if it fell, the road to the Soviet capital was wide open. Zhukov ordered General Pavel Belov's Cavalry Corps to fill the yawning gap. This corps, then in the Serpukhov area, moved west as fast as the frozen roads and Luftwaffe allowed.

Rostov was now held by the *Leibstandarte* and the 60th Motorized divisions, the 13th and 14th Panzer having been withdrawn beyond the western outskirts to provide a mobile reserve against the expected Soviet counter-stroke. Sporadic fighting continued inside the city, but the real threat to a continued German occupation lay across the frozen Don, where the Soviet 56th Army was preparing to attack. The wider threat posed by the Soviet 37th Army to the entire German position east of the Mius River remained acute, and von Rundstedt was coming round to von Kleist's view that a strategic withdrawal from Rostov was necessary. Both men knew only too well that Hitler and OKH – who were still demanding a further advance into the Caucasus – would oppose such a decision.

Having, on the previous day, lamented the overall decline in the Wehrmacht's resources, Franz Halder was given fresh fuel for his anxieties. General Friedrich Fromm, who reported to him on that winter afternoon, had two interrelated jobs. As Chief of the Replacement Army, he was responsible for filling those spaces that death, injury or capture had created in the ranks; as director of the army's armament programme, he was responsible for providing the army with weapons of sufficient quality and quantity. Both jobs, as he now told Halder, were proving impossible. Armament output was declining rather than rising, and army establishments in the east would be 180,000 men short by April 1942. 'He thinks of the necessity to make peace!' Halder noted in his diary, the exclamation mark an accompanying yelp of dismay.[4]

Danish Foreign Minister Scavenius and German Plenipotentiary Renthe-Fink met again, this time in Berlin, where the Anti-Comintern gala was about to begin. The Germans, as Scavenius soon learned, had moved the goalposts yet again and were now insisting that even the secret protocols to Danish membership needed watering down. Scavenius told Renthe-Fink that he had no authority to sign an amended agreement, which gave Ribbentrop the excuse for more bullying. The German Foreign Minister considered having the Dane arrested, but the PR implications of such a move on the eve of the conference dissuaded him, and his subordinate von Weizsäcker was given the task of devising yet another compromise. After all this the elderly Scavenius looked, according to Ciano, like 'a fish out of water – a little old man in a morning coat who wondered why he was there . . .'[5]

In what had once been Czechoslovakia, a construction gang of 342 Jewish young men was dispatched from Prague to the old Austrian fortress town of Theresienstadt, some 40 miles to the north. The fortress had been used as a prison for over a century, and the German authorities had decided to use it as a multi-purpose ghetto, part-holding area, part-transit camp, part-showroom for the Third Reich's commitment to multi-culturalism. Thirty-two thousand Jews, most of them from Germany, Austria or Czechoslovakia, would eventually die within its refurbished walls. Many, many more would leave them for the death camps of Treblinka, Sobibor and Auschwitz. These latter included the 342 and their families, who had all been promised life in return for their labour.

At his meeting with Crüwell in the pre-dawn hours, Rommel laid out the situation as he understood it: 'The greater part of the enemy force aimed at Tobruk has been destroyed; now we will turn east and go for the New Zealanders and Indians before they can join up with the remains of their main force for a combined attack on Tobruk. At the same time we will take Habata and Maddalena and cut off their supplies. Speed is vital; we must make the most of the shock effect of the enemy's defeat and push forward immediately and as fast as we can with our entire force to Sidi Omar.'[6]

A dawn start was not possible – the armoured divisions were still refitting after the previous day's exertions – but Rommel had the 21st Panzer's 5th Panzer Regiment under way by 10.30 and set off hurriedly in its wake without realizing that his communications vehicle was stuck in a patch of soft sand. The consequences of this oversight would eventually prove severe, but no communication was necessary during the first few hours of what came to be known as 'Rommel's dash for the wire'. It was enough just to watch the enemy scatter. Striking out south-east from its night leaguers south of Sidi Rezegh, the *Afrikakorps* was soon ploughing through the headquarter and support areas of those units they had mauled the previous day: the XXX Corps, 7th Armoured Division, 1st South African Division, 7th Armoured Support Group and 7th Armoured Division.

Panic ensued, not least at 7th Armoured Division headquarters, where General Cunningham was discussing his plans for the day with Generals Norrie and Gott. Reports of Rommel's advance were quickly superseded by direct evidence in the form of shells, and Norrie ordered Brigadier Clifton, XXX Corps' chief engineer, to 'get General Cunningham off in his Blenheim at once!' The two men took off in Clifton's 'precious Ford utility . . . dodged through the thickening mob of runaways which hurtled across our course, urged on by occasional shell bursts or bouncing tracer . . . More by good luck than judgement, we hurtled down the strip to where the Blenheim was revved up, raring to go. The Army Commander and his staff climbed aboard, and off she bumped, clearing a crossing three-tonner by inches!'[7]

The narrowness of Cunningham's escape was unlikely to increase his morale, and the same was true of the many others caught up in what General Norrie sardonically termed the 'Matruh Stakes'. The journalist Alan Moorehead was at XXX Corps headquarters when the 5th Panzer Regiment came charging through, trailing a cloak of dust, pumping out a hail of shells and causing utter confusion. There was no time to issue orders; men just leaped into their vehicles and drove. 'All day for nine hours we ran,' Moorehead wrote. 'It was the contagion of bewilderment and fear and ignorance. Rumour spread at every halt, no man had orders. Everyone had some theory and no one any plan beyond the frantic desire to reach his unit.'[8]

Rommel's plan seemed to be working. As the long snake of *Afrikakorps* armour turned east on to the Trigh el Abd and headed for the frontier wire at Bir Sheferzen, he had no idea that two huge British supply depots lay, well camouflaged, only a few miles to the south, and that he had just missed one great chance to weaken his enemy. Rommel had his own narrow escape that afternoon, but, unlike Cunningham's, his was a confidence booster – after stopping to visit a field hospital, he belatedly realized that the wide-eyed patients were German and that a British officer was showing him around. 'I think we'd better get out of this,' he whispered to his aide, before heading back to his command vehicle at a suitably brisk pace. Fortunately for Rommel, the British had taken him for a Polish general and made no attempt to prevent his abrupt departure.[9] By 16.00 he had reached the gap in the wire at Bir Sheferzen, and was still brimming over with enthusiasm. He ordered von Ravenstein north-east into Egypt, towards the Halfaya Pass, with a view to encircling the British frontier forces from the rear. Von Ravenstein had only the command truck he was riding in, but Rommel promised to send 21st Panzer tanks and artillery on as soon as they arrived.

That might be some time. The *Afrikakorps* was now stretched out across fifty miles of desert, and paying for the haste that Rommel had demanded of it. The 5th Panzer Regiment had run out of fuel some way short of the frontier and was waiting for resupply. This might also prove a long wait, because Rommel's dash for the wire had effectively pushed the still-substantial remnants of XXX Corps to either side of what was now his supply line. Indeed, away to the west, one of these remnants – the 4th Armoured Brigade – had just come across an unprotected German supply and reinforcement column. Looking down across 2,000 yards, Bob Crisp could make out 'the dark, square shapes of the infantry lorries with heads peering curiously out of the open back, the hundreds of supply vehicles, the great, gaunt skeletons of a number of 88-millimetre guns on tow, and not a tank nor an armoured car in sight.' He and his fellow Honey commanders swept into the attack, causing the German vehicles to scatter in all directions. Ten minutes later the desert was littered with burning lorries, prisoners were being rounded up, and Crisp and his comrades were gazing awestruck at two captured 88s – 'we were staggered at the size of the things; no wonder they could blow our tanks to pieces at 3,000 yards!'[10]

With darkness falling, Rommel was joined at the frontier by Crüwell. He told the *Afrikakorps* commander that he had sent the 21st Panzer on towards the coast in the enemy's rear, and planned to send the 15th Panzer on a similar path to the west, thus trapping the XIII Corps' Indians and New Zealanders between them. Crüwell objected on a number of grounds: neither of them had a clear picture of where the enemy was (the New Zealanders, by this time, were close to Tobruk); the panzer attrition rate, already high, had grown still higher during the day; supply problems were escalating. The main aim of the manoeuvre, he concluded, had been to sow confusion in the enemy ranks, and, though this had apparently been achieved, it had left their own forces in a similar disarray.

Rommel heard Crüwell out but refused to change his plans, and the disgruntled *Afrikakorps* commander drove off into Egypt in search of von Ravenstein.

He wasn't the only general having a bad day. A shaken Cunningham had returned to his Maddalena headquarters late that morning, probably intent on advising retreat, but Auchinleck was waiting for him with a new, neatly written directive on the conduct of future operations. After acknowledging the two possibilities that Cunningham most feared – the complete destruction of the British armour, and the Germans getting their armour between the 8th Army and its Egyptian base – Auchinleck announced himself ready to accept the former and dismissive of the latter. After the battles of

the last few days, he wrote, 'it is most improbable that the enemy
will be able to stage a major advance for some time to come'. The
8th Army had two choices: either to break off the battle and abandon, for the moment, any attempt to relieve Tobruk, or to
continue with the offensive. The latter was 'the right and only
course'. Whatever the risks, Cunningham must 'continue to attack
the enemy relentlessly, using all your resources even to the last
tank'.[11]

Cunningham read and obeyed, though it seems unlikely he was
fully convinced. That afternoon, flying back from another visit to
XXX Corps, the sight of three columns of German lorries
trundling eastwards must have brought his doubts back to the surface. Auchinleck, though, was calmness personified. War
correspondent Eve Curie met him for the first time that evening,
and was struck by how little he said. But when he did speak, it was
with a confidence that Cunningham lacked. 'He is making a desperate effort,' Auchinleck said of Rommel and his advance, 'but he
will not get very far. That column of tanks simply cannot get supplies. I am sure of this.'[12]

Settling down for the night, Bob Crisp and his comrades had
come to a similar conclusion: 'It seemed to us as though Rommel
had gone clean off his bloody head.' They had, however, derived
a certain amusement from the day's events. 'We heard of the panic
in the headquarters and supply areas, and were unpatriotically
delighted at the thought of generals and staff officers fleeing for
Alexandria or wetting themselves in slit trenches . . . In this case
we reckoned that the top command was making a complete mess
of things anyway, and we could do just as well without them.'
Rommel might have scared Cunningham, but not Crisp and Co.:
'never for one moment, either on the night when we got the first
reports or at any time during the next few days when the crayoned
arrows prodded deeper and deeper until they penetrated Egypt,
did we have the slightest feeling of uneasiness about the situation
in our rear . . . We just assumed that the German commander had
made one hell of a blunder and in due course would get it in the
neck.'[13]

The German commander was still feeling restless enough to follow Crüwell through the wire, but his impromptu tour of the British rear was brought to an untimely end when his car broke down. Fortunately for Rommel, Crüwell's command vehicle eventually appeared out of the darkness and took the stranded army commander aboard. A vain search ensued for the hole in the wire, whereupon Rommel insisted on taking the wheel. But he couldn't find it either, and the wire proved resistant to a vehicular headbutt. There was nothing for it but to wait for morning.

Rommel's need of fuel was appreciated at OKW. The previous day two German tankers, *Maritza* and *Procida*, had left Athens for Benghazi, escorted by two Italian torpedo boats. They were loaded with vehicle and aviation fuel, bombs and ammunition for the Axis forces in Africa. The convoy's westerly course was beyond Malta's usual range, but the British had gleaned a good idea of where they were headed and when from recent Enigma intercepts. Force K (comprising light cruisers *Aurora* and *Penelope*, destroyers *Lance* and *Lively*) went out in search of probable prey, and found the convoy a hundred miles west of Crete. The torpedo boats did their best, *Cassiopeia* laying smoke and *Lupo* gallantly charging the British, but both tankers were sent to the bottom with all hands.

In the South Atlantic the savage dance of hunters and hunted continued. Almost forty-eight hours after scuttling the crippled *Atlantis*, the U-boat and small flotilla of boats carrying Rogge and his crew towards Brazil were met by the supply ship *Python*. Once on board, they learned that *Python* had just set up a rendezvous with several other submarines in need of restocking and refuelling.

This, as it turned out, was bad news for one of the three British cruisers sent to search the area for German raiders, supply ships and submarines. HMS *Devonshire* had accounted for *Atlantis*, and HMS *Dorsetshire* would eventually account for *Python*, but HMS *Dunedin* had the misfortune early that afternoon to sail across the path of U-124, en route to its rendezvous with the supply ship. The British spotted the telltale periscope, but then mistook the submarine's direction, and for over half an hour the two ships played an oceanic version of blind man's buff. Then, just as the encounter seemed over, Captain Jochen Mohr found himself with an almost impossible three-mile shot at the receding *Dunedin*. He fired a spread of three torpedoes, and two of them, through remarkable luck or judgement, struck the British cruiser amidships. She went down in 17 minutes, leaving 250 survivors scrambling after anything that might keep them afloat. Mohr circled the stricken men, but decided against helping them. Three days later, when an American merchantman arrived on the scene, injuries, exhaustion and sharks had reduced the number to seventy-two.

A July 1941 US War Department report on the overall strategic situation had mentioned in passing that the Netherlands government-in-exile might appreciate a temporary American occupation of its territories in the western hemisphere. The US government certainly liked the idea, and with good reason. Dutch Guiana provided sixty per cent of the bauxite for America's aluminium industry, and the health of that industry dictated how many planes the United States could build. A sabotage raid across the nearby border with Vichy-ruled French Guiana might seriously damage production at the all-important Moengo mine, and who knew what pressure the Nazis could put on those relatives of the mineworkers who were trapped in occupied Holland? A small military force had been dispatched, Washington announced. As of that day, Dutch Guiana was under American protection.

Irritated at the lack of a speedy response to his proposals, Hull summoned the Washington representatives of Britain, China, the Netherlands and Australia to a Monday-morning meeting at the State Department. Only the Dutch minister was able to communicate his government's approval; the other three were officially 'awaiting instructions'. That said, they had a number of questions for mere delivery men. When the Chinese ambassador innocently asked why five thousand Japanese soldiers would be allowed to remain in Indo-China, Hull told him, with some asperity, that General Marshall doubted whether five times as many would pose a real threat. The whole point of a modus vivendi was to gain time for the American military, who 'must be fully prepared to deal effectively with a possible outbreak by Japan'.[14]

More questions and objections followed, eroding Hull's thin reserve of patience. 'Each of your governments has a more direct interest in the defence of that area of the world than this country,' he eventually declared, ignoring both America's quasi-colonial position in the Philippines and its long insistence on keeping Asian markets open to American exports. 'But your governments,' he continued, 'through some preoccupation in other directions' – their national fights for survival, perhaps – 'do not seem to know anything about this matter under discussion. I am definitely disappointed at this unexpected development, at their lack of interest and lack of disposition to cooperate.'[15]

The representatives were dismissed, leaving Hull to simmer. He eventually passed the gist of the conversation on to Roosevelt, who promised to take matters up directly with Churchill. That afternoon the President sent a three-paragraph message to the British Prime Minister. The first two, penned by Hull, contained a detailed exposition of the modus vivendi; the third, written by Roosevelt, offered a pessimistic postscript: 'This seems to me a fair proposition for the Japanese but its acceptance or rejection is really a matter of internal Japanese politics. I am not very hopeful and we must all be prepared for real trouble, possibly soon.'[16]

The American military was experiencing the same premonition. Saturday's intercepted message to Nomura and Kurusu – that after the 29th 'things were automatically going to happen' – had started alarm bells ringing, at least in the upper echelons of the US navy, and Admiral Stark issued the first clear warning of war to the Pacific commands. 'Chances of favourable outcome of negotiations with Japan very doubtful,' it began. 'This situation coupled with [the] statements of Japanese Government and [the] movements [of] their naval and military forces indicate in our opinion that a surprise aggressive movement in any direction including attack on Philippines or Guam is a possibility.'[17] These two potential targets were the worst the navy could imagine. There was no thought, let alone mention, of Pearl Harbor.

TUESDAY 25 NOVEMBER

The First Air Fleet's final day in Hitokappu Bay saw a flurry of last-minute checks, adjustments and preparations. Fuchida and Genda continued their briefings on *Akagi*, the former now hoarse and barely audible after several days of almost continuous talking. There were also meetings on the other flagships, as the different parts of the fleet familiarized themselves with the details of their particular tasks. All the crews were busy checking the security of their communications and their weaponry.

The mood was upbeat verging on hysterical. 'An air attack on Hawaii! – a dream come true!' one seaman wrote. When the people at home heard the news they would be 'clapping their hands and shouting for joy . . . We would teach these arrogant Anglo-Saxon scoundrels a lesson.'[1] The senior officers were no less enthused. Admiral Yamaguchi, commanding the Carrier Division, gathered his flagship's crew on deck and gave them a parable. His sword was so sharp and so well tempered, his skill at wielding it so well honed by years of training, that he could cut a samurai helmet clean in half with a single sweep. The same was true of *Kido Butai*. It would 'cleave the enemy in two'.[2]

Only Chuichi Nagumo, commanding the operation he had so long opposed, seemed burdened with doubt. That night, unable to sleep, he summoned Suzuki to his cabin for another run-through of the intelligence they had received on Pearl Harbor. The special agent managed to dull the edge of Nagumo's anxieties, and the two officers in kimonos had a last glass of sake with each other – Suzuki was not going with the fleet.

Having sent Nagumo his orders to set sail on the following morning, Yamamoto headed off for a meeting with Chiyoko, his long-time geisha companion. With *Kido Butai* about to sail, and war looming at the end of the twelve-day voyage, he had arranged a final night together at their favourite inn on the nearby island of Itsukushima.

General Tomoyuki Yamashita's plane from Saigon arrived at Samah, the port on the Chinese island of Hainan where his 25th Army would embark for the invasion of Malaya. The fifty-six-year-old Yamashita had been chosen for this command less than a month ago, an excellent military record proving more important than his history of political differences with Prime Minister Tojo. Yamashita had no knowledge of the imminent attack on Pearl Harbor, and would have opposed it if he had. Returning from a military mission to Europe the previous spring, he had forcefully recommended that Japan avoid war with either the Soviet Union or the United States until its army had been fully modernized.

The Japanese 25th Army was, as it turned out, much better equipped for the task ahead than the British and Australian forces destined to face it. It was also better led, both militarily and politically. The British plans for the defence of Malaya were the product of long, unresolved wrangles between the Treasury and the armed forces, between the three branches of the armed forces, between a local strategy that made military sense and a global strategy predicated on not upsetting the Americans.

The contingency plan known as Matador was the classic case in point. The British expected a Japanese assault on Malaya to unfold in a certain way. Troops would be convoyed across the Gulf of

Siam, and bridgeheads would be secured in southern Thailand and probably northern Malaya, all under the protection of Japanese planes based in Indo-China. Once the bridgeheads were secure, the airbases would be moved across the Gulf, and the planes would be used to support the army's southerly advance through Malaya towards Singapore.

How could the British foil this plan? There was insufficient naval and air strength to prevent a crossing, but there seemed every possibility that the subsequent landings could be thwarted on the various beaches, if only the British could reach them first. The ones in Malaya were obviously covered, but the ones in southern Thailand were many hours away, and a British seizure would have to be pre-emptive. Thailand, of course, was a sovereign state, and a British invasion to thwart a future – if only by a few hours – Japanese invasion was unlikely to please the Thais. This in itself was of no importance – the problem was how such a move would play on Washington's Capitol Hill. Many in the British government feared that Congressional opponents of American belligerency would have a field day.

A fateful compromise was reached. The plan for pre-emptive action, code-named Matador, was adopted, but its execution was made subject to London's prior approval, which would rest on an assessment of the wider diplomatic situation. If this assessment was prolonged, then approval might arrive too late for the operation to be carried out. The C-in-C of Far East Command, General Brooke-Popham, who had only recently submitted a request for greater clarity in this matter, was now informed by Churchill that the decision on whether to implement Matador 'should reach you within thirty-six hours of receiving a report of any Japanese move'.[3] This was hardly reassuring: Brooke-Popham's army commanders believed that anything more than twenty-four would guarantee that the Japanese reached the beaches first.

Army Group South still held Rostov, but there was no obvious weakening of Soviet pressure on the surrounding fronts. The *Leibstandarte SS Adolf Hitler* and the 60th Motorized Divisions were deployed either side of the city along a thirty-mile stretch of the Don and shared responsibility for the city's waterfront, which over-looked the mile-wide frozen river and the distant plains of the northern Caucasus. *Leibstandarte's* reconnaissance battalion held the western sector of this waterfront, and its 300 men had done their best over the previous few days to improve their position, gouging what defences they could out of the frozen earth and cutting large blocks of ice for above-ground protection.

It was here, in the foggy dawn twilight, that the Red Army launched the first attack of a new offensive. With T-34s on the far bank offering supporting fire, the men of the 343rd Rifle Division charged across the ice, arms linked in suicidal solidarity, shouting 'hurrah!' at the top of their voices. The German machine and anti-tank guns took a terrible toll, leaving each successive wave of Red Army infantry with more dead and wounded to clamber across, but at the fourth time of asking the tide reached and breached the enemy lines. A German counter-attack finally forced the Soviets back across the river, leaving only artillery and tank fire to disturb the peace. The attack had been beaten off, but the Germans were under no illusions as to who now held the initiative. Their plans to cross the river were on indefinite hold; the Soviets could be expected to try again within hours.

No more forces could be brought in to stiffen Rostov's defences. The front to the north of the city had been quiet for a couple of days, but von Rundstedt and von Kleist were not expecting it to remain so. The taking of Rostov, and the advance north of the city which had accompanied it, had almost quadrupled the length of the line which the 1st Panzer and 17th Armies had to defend. That Tuesday's blow had fallen in Rostov, but the next could fall anywhere or everywhere along a 200-mile front.

Despite everything – the deepening cold, the exhaustion of men and machines, the sclerotic supply system – the German advance on Moscow continued to make progress. After two days of street fighting, the centre of Klin was finally secure, its crucial road junc-tions available to the supply columns feeding the further-advanced panzer and motorized spearheads. The 41st Panzer Korps took Rogachevo, halfway to the Moscow–Volga Canal at Yakhroma, and the 2nd Panzer Division fought its way into Peshki, the village on the Klin–Moscow road which Rokossovsky had prudently quit in the middle of the night. Peshki was defended by the Soviet 146th Tank Brigade, and the Germans found themselves face to face with early proof of Lend-Lease – a shipment of British-built Matilda II tanks which had arrived in Archangel at the end of October on the PQ2 convoy. Unlike the T-34s, they struggled against the German Mk IIIs and IVs, and three were left in the snow. Peshki fell in the afternoon, forcing the Soviets down the Moscow highway, their backs a little closer to the wall.

Fifteen miles to the south-west, the assault on Istra began. This town on the Volokolamsk–Moscow highway, with its famous New Jerusalem Monastery, was held by the 78th Infantry Division, which had arrived from Siberia in mid-October and was still almost at full strength. The Soviet divisions holding the river and reservoir lines to the north of the town were in considerably worse shape, and proved unable to hold even steep and forested shores. 'Corduroy' roads of parallel logs had been laid across the frozen reservoir overnight, and by afternoon the 11th and 5th Panzer had secured wide bridgeheads in the areas of Lopotovo and Rakovo. Closer to Istra, the 10th Panzer used the cover of a local blizzard to force two crossings of the river, before joining the SS *Das Reich* Motorized Division in a two-pronged assault against the town.

In the 2nd Panzer Army's sector the news was more mixed. Like Klin, Stalinogorsk refused to submit quietly, and several days of bitter conflict in and around the town's factories offered an early hint of the fate awaiting another German army in a similarly named city on the Volga. Closer to Moscow, Venev fell with hardly a whimper, and the 17th Panzer was close to winning its race with Belov's Cavalry Corps to seize Kashira. The Soviet commander in the threatened town sent out an anti-aircraft unit, with orders to use them, barrels fully depressed, on the approaching German tanks. The latter were stopped four miles short of the town, and

Belov had another twelve hours to get his forces astride the road to Moscow.

The Wehrmacht had been 600 miles from Moscow when it crossed the Soviet frontier on 22 June. Army Group Centre was now closing in from three sides – if von Bock had drawn a line on his headquarters table map connecting the flanking forces at Rogachevo and Kashira it would have passed through the Soviet capital. These flanking forces were, respectively, forty and sixty-five miles from the Kremlin, but they were moving faster than those forces on the Klin, Volokolamsk and Mozhaisk highways, all of which were a bare thirty miles from Stalin's desk.

To the German commanders, victory still seemed possible. Von Bock, summarizing the day's events, noted the problems but stressed the possibilities. The 3rd Panzer Group had gained ground in the north, the 4th Panzer Group was across the Istra, Guderian's tanks might still get across the Oka at Kashira. Further from the front, Halder was even more optimistic. Expected Red Army offensives against Army Groups South and North had not materialized, and Army Group Centre's advance continued. 'Guderian apparently now has freedom of movement in the direction of Kolomna,' Halder wrote, with the air of a magician whose wand had just been repaired. 'The enemy is desperately throwing in what troops he has left,' he added hopefully, knowing that his side already had.[4]

To the Soviet commanders, defeat still seemed possible. Zhukov rushed his forces from crisis point to crisis point, threatened his army commanders with everything from disgrace to a bullet in the head, and begged Stalin to release whatever reserves he was hoarding for a final battle. Such requests unnerved the Soviet leader, who demanded Zhukov's assurance 'truthfully, as a Communist', that the Soviet capital would be saved. 'We'll definitely hold Moscow,' Zhukov told him, 'but we'll need at least two more armies and another two hundred tanks.'[5]

In Leningrad a rumour that bread rations would end in a few days swiftly took hold. Crowds besieged the few stores with any food; at one, in Smolny, a huge queue failed to fully disperse even when the air-raid warning sounded. Bombs fell, killing and wounding several people, but the survivors refused to give up, and half an hour later the queue was again shuffling forward in pursuit of a life-giving hunk of bread.

At Kovno's Ninth Fort 942 Jews from Berlin, along with 991 from Frankfurt and 1,000 from Munich, were herded out into the open air.

Kovno's Ninth Fort had been used for mass murder as early as 26 June. Units of *Einsatzgruppen A*, arriving in the Lithuanian city hard on the heels of the army, dragged hundreds of Jews from their homes, took them out to the Ninth Fort and murdered them. Lithuanian militiamen, police and released convicts proved only too happy to help, and over the next few days staged their own series of sadistic killing sprees. It was not until the second week of July that the *Einsatzgruppen* adopted the more systematic approach of exterminating the smaller Jewish communities and ghettoizing the larger ones. On 15 August Kovno's 26,000 Jews were moved into a few sealed-off streets, allotted three square feet of living space each and forbidden to venture out.

The new ghetto offered no security. A few days after its sealing, an offer of clerical work persuaded 530 Jews to reveal their educational qualifications and guaranteed their immediate shooting. On 17 September several thousand more were led away and packed into a local synagogue while mass graves were dug for them in a nearby football pitch. On 26 September 1,628 were shot at Fourth Fort, on 4 October 1,500 at Ninth Fort, and on 28 October the entire ghetto was paraded in front of SS Sergeant Helmut Rauca for 'selection'. Nine thousand two hundred – more than a third of those present – were sent right by a flick of Rauca's wrist and marched out to the Ninth Fort, where pits fifteen metres wide and four metres deep had already been dug. A hundred were shot at a time, each group covering the last with chloride of lime before facing the drunken SS gunmen.

In the ghetto any residual hope that deportees really did end up in labour camps was soon dispelled – this latest massacre left a survivor. A twelve-year-old boy standing close to his mother was unhit, and was buried under only one thin layer of earth. He lay there until darkness, conscious of the hundreds buried alive still shifting the earth around him, and finally clambered his way out of the pit. Making his way back to the ghetto, he told his dreadful tale.

The Jews from Berlin, Frankfurt and Munich never heard it, and perhaps surprise was part of the reason for what followed. On that winter morning at the Ninth Fort, in the sudden realization of what their fellow Germans had in store for them, more than a few of these freezing, half-starved men, women and children fought back. There was no docile shedding of clothes on this occasion, no tidy sequence or neat symmetry to this slaughter. These Jews were buried in their clothes, and many of the *Einsatzkommandos* who killed them returned wounded and bleeding to their barracks.

At the Wolfsschanze, Hitler was picking at the past. If they had only started a month earlier, he told a clutch of generals that Tuesday afternoon, they could have taken Leningrad, captured the south and still been able to mount a successful pincer attack on Moscow. But, of course, they hadn't, and now that the winter weather was causing havoc 'time' had become 'his greatest nightmare'.[6]

There was no need for the German people to know that a mistake had been made, in this or any other matter. He telephoned Goebbels in Berlin, and urged him to be cautious in his winter clothing collection campaign. It was important to avoid any impression that the regime had neglected its responsibility to the troops.

In Berlin the delegates were arriving for the ceremonial renewal of the Anti-Comintern Pact. Twelve countries with varying degrees of independence – Japan, Italy, Hungary, Spain, Manchukuo (the Chinese region of Manchuria), Bulgaria, Croatia, Finland, Romania, Slovakia, Japanese-occupied China and Denmark – were represented, offering Ribbentrop a diplomatic minefield of challenging proportions. Hungary and Romania, for example, had to be kept apart, while minor hostilities existed between Hungary and Slovakia, Romania and Bulgaria, Croatia and Italy. The Italians and Spaniards had to be given absolutely equal treatment, lest one or the other take offence. The Danes and Finns were present only under duress, and needed either cheering up or bullying. All had Ribbentrop's speech and individual audiences with Hitler to look forward to over the coming days.

Ribbentrop and his staff mingled. The war in the east was won, he told a resigned Ciano. 'The Germans were playing master of the house,' the Italian wrote in his diary, 'and they made everyone feel it even though they were especially polite to us. There is no way out of it. Their European hegemony has been established. Whether this is good or bad is neither here nor there, but it does exist. Consequently, it is best to sit at the right hand of the master of the house. And we are at the right hand.'[7]

In Denmark news of the German bullying had leaked out to the general populace, and early in the afternoon several hundred students gathered outside the Royal Palace in Copenhagen. The reading of a protest resolution provoked a police assault, but this was broken up by the novel expedient of singing the national anthem. Demonstrations followed outside the local Nazi newspaper offices, Parliament House and Foreign Office.

The crowd was now several thousand strong, and the police lacked the power to disperse it. They managed to block the approach to the Hotel d'Angleterre, where the German occupation HQ was housed, but demonstrations multiplied, the singing of patriotic anthems – including that of occupied Norway – interspersed with shouts of 'Down with Scavenius' and 'Down with the traitors'. Truncheons were wielded and blanks were fired, but the mayhem lasted well into the evening. German windows were broken, and one member of the master race, drawn out on to his balcony by what he assumed was an anti-Communist demonstration, was greeted with a hail of missiles.

The city's journalists watched and listened, but knew better than to report. The only hint of breakdown in the following morning's newspapers concerned the tram service.

In Yugoslavia a foreign invasion had provoked a multilateral civil war – the same fate that Iraq would suffer sixty-two years later. On that morning two German divisions supported by Allied forces – Croatian fascists, Serbian fascists and Mihailovich's Cetnik partisans – attacked the small town of Užice in western Serbia. This was the culmination of a two-month drive against Tito's Communist partisans, and the liberated area which they called the 'Republic of Užice'.

The Communists had controlled this area, and a similar one around Krupanj a few miles to the north, since the summer. They manufactured weapons and published their newspaper *Borba* in Užice, but were under no illusions that they could hold this or any other town against a determined German attack.

It had taken the enemy almost two months to reach Užice itself, and many non-combatants had suffered in the process – the occupation authorities had decreed the execution of a hundred hostages for each German fatality, and fifty for a wounding. When ten were killed and twenty-six wounded in an ambush close to the town of Kragujevac the Germans scrupulously did their maths and carried out 2,300 executions.

Both Cetniks and Communists had taken part in that ambush, but by mid-November such cooperation was a fast-fading memory. Tito had tried to resolve the escalating dispute, but the ultra-Serb royalist Mihailovich had preferred collaboration with the Germans to cooperation with pan-ethnic republicans, and had even handed over 500 Communist prisoners. As Užice fell, and the Communists retreated to the safety of the mountains, the Cetniks joined in the German victory celebrations.

The following day the British and Soviet governments issued a joint statement urging the Cetniks and Communists to stop fighting each other and to unite under Mihailovich.

Late that afternoon the hydrophone operator aboard U-331, submerged off Alexandria, picked up the sound of turning screws.

Taking his U-boat up to periscope depth, twenty-eight-year-old *Kapitänleutnant* Tiesenhausen was treated to the sight of eleven British ships – three battleships escorted by eight destroyers – heading out into the central Mediterranean. With remarkable coolness he threaded his submarine between two of the flanking destroyers and brought it within barn door range of the middle battleship.

The Queen Elizabeth-class battleship *Barham* had enjoyed a tempestuous career. Launched in the second month of the Great War, she had taken shell hits at Jutland, delivered food in the General Strike, sunk a British destroyer in an accidental collision and suffered a wounding by torpedo in the Atlantic. Since fighting a minor skirmish with the Vichy French navy off Dakar in western Africa, *Barham* had served in the Mediterranean and was now en route to support an attack on Rommel's lifeline.

Tiesenhausen was less than a thousand yards away when he gave the order to fire all four torpedoes at the looming port side of the battleship. The sudden loss of weight tipped the submarine up, removed the target from view and brought the conning tower out of the water in plain view of the last battleship in line. This ship changed course, intent on ramming U-331, but Tiesenhausen and his crew managed, by the smallest of margins, to get their ship deep enough to slip under the approaching bows. While engaged in this little matter of life and death Tiesenhausen heard two loud explosions some while apart, and assumed that at least one torpedo had hits its mark.

Three had, and close enough together to create the first huge blast. As the battleship rolled over to port, her magazine exploded, and by the time the smoke cleared *Barham* had gone. Of the 1,258-strong crew, 862 went down with her.

U-331 had dived much deeper than her makers intended, yet lived to tell the tale. With the sea full of British sailors, the destroyers were unable to use their depth charges, and Tiesenhausen made good his escape. He had no certain knowledge of a sinking, and could only report that he had torpedoed an unidentified British battleship with uncertain effect. The British, intercepting his Enigma-coded message, decided on keeping quiet about the disaster.

It was several weeks before next of kin were informed, and several more before they were allowed to communicate their loss.

Some, however, were given premature notification. Holding a seance in Portsmouth only days after the sinking, the famous spiritualist Helen Duncan made contact with one of the battleship's dead sailors. A displeased Admiralty made every effort to discredit her, but the facts, when they did emerge, only added to her reputation. In the long run even the authorities must have decided she had the gift, because early in 1944 they arrested, tried and locked her up for nine months under the 1735 Witchcraft Act. Someone was afraid she would tell Hitler where and when the D-Day landings were scheduled to take place.

Over the first three days of the Crusader offensive, the British armoured divisions which made up the bulk of XXX Corps had almost achieved a link-up with the debouching Tobruk garrison, but over the following three days those armoured divisions had been almost destroyed. While this was going on, half of the British and Allied XIII Infantry Corps – the 2nd New Zealand Division – had followed XXX Corps around the desert end of the main frontier defences and struck out, albeit more slowly, in the same direction. By 25 November this force was promising the link-up with the Tobruk garrison which the armour had failed to deliver.

Rommel, though aware that the British armour had been largely destroyed, remained generally unaware of the threat posed by the New Zealanders. This threat was, however, becoming painfully obvious to Operations Officer Westphal, whom Rommel had left in charge of the Tobruk sector. Westphal's problem was compounded by the fact that Rommel, without his communications truck, was impossible to reach, and as the day progressed it seemed increasingly likely that, win or lose his battle of nerves with Cunningham on the frontier, Rommel would lose the battle for Tobruk.

As that Tuesday began, Rommel had several enticing options open to him – a search and destroy mission against the British supply dumps, an advance into Egypt across the British supply lines, or a concerted attack on the British forces still holding their positions on the frontier. But for once in his military career the German seemed incapable of concentrating his mind or his forces. He spent the day in a whirl, sending units in each and every direction, often in pursuit of wrong or non-existent objectives. The 15th Panzer ended the day with only a wrecked British tank repair shop to show for its fuel exhaustion, while the 21st Panzer's tank strength was halved by an ill-considered advance which led it through a German minefield and down the throat of the 7th Indian Brigade's dug-in artillery. It was, in von Mellenthin's words, 'a thoroughly unsatisfactory day in which we suffered heavy losses for little result'.

Many of the losses were incurred from the air. The German columns were subject to frequent attention from the RAF and received no assistance from the Luftwaffe. If Rommel, looking up at the enemy-dominated sky, wondered where the German fighters were, Westphal could have told him. The New Zealanders, advancing on Tobruk, had forced the Luftwaffe to evacuate its airstrip at Gambut, and the frontier sector was now beyond its operational range.

By afternoon the New Zealanders were approaching the trio of high points which dominated the area south-east of Tobruk, the Sidi Rezegh ridge and the hills of El Duda and Belhamed. Westphal, sensing both peril and opportunity – an armoured attack in the New Zealanders' rear might prove decisive – tried his best to contact Rommel, even sending out two reconnaissance planes with maps showing his version of the current situation. Both were shot down.

During the day the Tobruk garrison had renewed its assault on the Italian-manned perimeter, and, with the German *Afrika* Division fully occupied by the advancing New Zealanders, managed a two-mile advance. As evening fell, and the New Zealanders prepared for a night attack on the German-held hills, the gap between the two British forces was less than three miles.

Writing in his diary that evening, von Bock recorded the 'good news from Africa; the English are apparently taking a beating there'.[8] In Cairo the military situation was seen rather differently. 'I am convinced we only have to persist to win,' Auchinleck wrote in a letter to Churchill. 'The enemy is trying desperately to regain the initiative. In this he has succeeded in part, locally and temporarily only. So long as we can maintain our pressure towards Tobruk the real initiative is ours . . .'[9]

Cunningham had thought it advisable to cut and run, and Auchinleck's trust in him had been broken. Having 'reluctantly concluded that Cunningham, admirable as he has been up to date, has now begun to think defensively instead of offensively', Auchinleck took the decision to replace him with General Ritchie.[10]

When this news reached the troops, it was, in Bob Crisp's words, 'a shock to all of us, but not really a surprise. Even right down at the bottom of the ladder, it was impossible not to be aware of the absence of firm direction and purpose from above. Everybody welcomed the change as the beginning of an era of greater decisiveness.'[11]

When the news reached Rommel, he could only curse. Breaking Cunningham had cost him most of his irreplaceable armour, and got him nowhere.

In Washington the agonizing continued. Secretary of State Hull had his regular Tuesday-morning discussion of the international situation with War Secretary Stimson and Navy Secretary Knox. Shown the latest draft of the modus vivendi, the latter pair agreed that the US was giving nothing valuable away, but expressed doubts that the Japanese would accept a deal that offered them so little.

The mood was even more pessimistic at the weekly War Council, which also included the President, army chief General Marshall and navy chief Admiral Stark. Hull thought there was 'practically no possibility of an agreement', that the Japanese were likely 'to break out at any time'.[12] Roosevelt concurred, adding that the Japanese penchant for striking without warning might mean an attack as early as the following Monday. The important point, all agreed, was that Japan should bear the blame for any outbreak of hostilities. The key question, Stimson recorded in his diary, 'was how we should manoeuvre them into the position of firing the first shot without allowing too much danger to ourselves'.[13] Just as the British feared that Matador would lose them American support, so the American leadership feared that any kind of pre-emptive military action on their part would risk dividing Congress and the American public.

Returning to his own office, Stimson received news from G-2 (US Army Intelligence) that between forty and fifty Japanese transports had been sighted off Formosa heading south. This piece of intelligence, which had arrived via the British and the ONI (US Naval Intelligence) from separate sources in Shanghai, was now four days old. G-2 shrugged the Japanese movement off as normal, but the British were more concerned, and Stimson agreed with them. He immediately phoned Hull with the news, and sent off a written memo to the President.

Hull spent the afternoon and early evening in meetings with the allied representatives. Lord Halifax was first, bearing a message from Foreign Secretary Eden. The British government, while more than happy to leave such decisions in the hands of the Americans, inclined to the view that the Japanese should be asked for a lot – a complete withdrawal from Indo-China, a suspension of military activities in China – but given little, perhaps not even a resumption of oil shipments for civilian purposes. Hull reiterated the benefits of a temporary truce but gave no indication that he had made up his mind one way or the other.

The succeeding Dutch minister was more accommodating, but also questioned the wisdom of renewing oil shipments. Hu Shih, who came last, had an accusative message from Chiang Kai-shek: America was showing an inclination 'to appease Japan at the expense of China'. Chinese morale would be shaken, Hu said, and 'Chinese national trust in America would be undermined by reports of Japan's escaping military defeat by diplomatic victory'.[14] Hull went through the arguments in favour of the modus vivendi one more time – the removal of the immediate threat to Singapore, the Dutch East Indies and the Philippines, the weakening of the Japanese hold on Indo-China, the possibility of a negotiated end to the war in Hu's own country – but grew ever more exasperated by the Chinese ambassador's failure to appreciate them. If the US heeded Chinese objections and withdrew the proposal, the American added with some impatience, it was 'not to be charged with failure to send our fleet into the area near Indo-China and into Japanese waters, if by any chance Japan makes a military drive southward'.[15]

Once Hu had left, Hull sat down with his close colleagues to review the situation. He had kept nothing from the allies; he had explained why he was offering what he was, and what he expected to get in response. Each ambassador had insisted in his own way that Hull was offering the Japanese too much, when everyone knew that the Japanese would only settle for more. If Hull went ahead with the modus vivendi he could, as he wrote later, 'emphasize for all time that we were doing everything we could to avoid war'.[16] But at what cost? He could count on outright opposition from China, only lukewarm support from the other allies. There would be a difficult debate in his own country, and accusations of appeasement. Why create such difficulties for himself? Why make such an offer when rejection was already guaranteed?

ONI, though headquartered in Washington, had two field units in the Pacific, COM-14 in Hawaii and COM-16 in the Philippines. Their principal task was the tracking of the Japanese fleet, their principal method the analysis of radio messages that emanated from each ship. Only around ten per cent of the messages could be decrypted, but the American listeners got to know the 'signature' of the radio operators on certain Japanese ships, and, up until mid-November, Naval Intelligence was able to keep an intermittent track on the more important members of the enemy fleet. *Akagi* and two other carriers, for example, were correctly placed in home waters on 9 and 10 November.

Eight days later, Japan's six most powerful carriers were all observing radio silence on their journey to Hitokappu Bay. Not surprisingly, ONI in Washington still had them in home waters – *Akagi*, *Kaga*, *Soryu* and *Hiryu* were definitely in southern Kyushu, *Zuikaku* in Kure or Saebo, *Shokaku* perhaps in Formosa.

On 25 November COM-14 claimed to have located one unidentified carrier division in the Marshall Islands, but admitted to having no information on the others. COM-16 disagreed – correctly as it turned out – about the carriers in the Marshalls, but still placed the powerful First and Second Carrier Divisions in Japanese waters. This was not a ludicrous assumption on its part. As Lieutenant-Commodore Edwin Layton, Chief of Fleet Intelligence in Hawaii, wrote later, 'when carriers or other types of vessels go into home waters, home ports, home exercise areas, they use low power radio direct with shore stations. This is then handled normally on telegraphic land lines to prevent our direction finder stations and intercept stations from hearing their traffic.'[17] If the carriers were in home waters, then radio silence could be expected.

It was not a ludicrous assumption, but it was only an assumption. And if home waters normally implied radio silence, there was no reason why radio silence should necessarily imply home waters. The only evidence in support of COM-16's assumption was the lack of any evidence to the contrary.

WEDNESDAY 26 NOVEMBER

On lonely Etorofu the first light of day seeped through the lowering clouds as the Japanese crews readied their ships for departure. Shouted orders and the grind of anchor chains carried across the misty waters, and the anchors broke surface, streaming water and mud. Then a cable caught in the flagship's screws, pitching a sailor into the icy waters. It took a diver half an hour to free the propeller but no sign could be found of the missing man.

Around 07.00 the fleet began disgorging from the bay, and over the next few hours it slowly spread itself into a ring formation almost fifty miles long. The submarines scouted ahead, the destroyers rode shotgun on the perimeter. At the centre of the ring, ahead of the tankers, flanked by the cruisers and battleships, the two parallel lines of three flat-tops carried the First Air Fleet's real striking force – almost four hundred attack planes. It was, by some distance, the most powerful fleet that had ever sailed to war.

As Suzuki watched the ships grow smaller from the deck of the coastguard cutter *Kunashiri*, flight leader Fuchida was one of many gazing back at his receding homeland, wondering if he would ever see his wife and children again.

How had it come to this? Why was the Japanese fleet sailing to war with the world's greatest industrial power? For most of the last two decades the accepted wisdom in Tokyo was that Japan could not possibly win such a war. The long-dominant 'Treaty faction' in the Imperial Navy had based its entire strategic outlook on the acceptance of relative Japanese weakness, as enshrined in the Washington Naval Treaty of 1922. Japan not only lacked the industrial capacity to compete with the United States, but also relied heavily on America and British-controlled sources for its raw materials. Asked by Prime Minister Prince Konoye in September 1940 to evaluate the nation's prospects in a war with America, Yamamoto had replied: 'I can run wild for the first six months or a year, but I have utterly no confidence for the second or third year.'[1]

The fact that the question had even been asked was proof of Japan's desperation. The Japanese political and military establishment had found it easy to start their war in central China, but, after four years and over two hundred thousand Japanese deaths, an acceptable conclusion to hostilities remained beyond its reach. Convincing themselves, as so many invaders do, that only outside aid was keeping resistance alive, the Japanese did all they could to blockade their enemy. This failed to work, and also brought Japan into conflict with those supplying the outside aid, most notably the United States. There was no moral dilemma here – the Japanese believed they had just as much right to build an empire as the Europeans, and just as much right to conquer and 'civilize' other races as the Americans had – but there was a political and military dilemma of nation-breaking proportions. How could Japan win in China without losing to America?

The 1940 answer was to proceed slowly and carefully. More expansion was needed, particularly into areas rich in raw materials, but a combination of policies would be needed to deter American intervention. Japan should choose its battles and word its justifications carefully, so as not to provoke American action. A move into southern Indo-China, for example, would strengthen the Japanese position at minimal risk, particularly if Vichy France could be pressurized into legitimizing it. Japan should also strengthen its alliances, and give the Americans pause for thought about who and what they might be taking on. Signing the Tripartite Pact with Germany and Italy seemed, to the government in Tokyo, a judicious form of deterrence.

There was, however, always the possibility that the policy would fail, that the growing enmity between Japan and the United States would somehow explode into war. A strategic plan was needed, and since the army would have little part to play in such a conflict, at least during its opening phases, the navy would have to provide one. The prospects, as 1940 turned into 1941, were bleak – the industrial imbalance remained, and the passing of Roosevelt's 'Two Ocean Navy' bill in June 1940 ensured a steady deepening of the military imbalance. The Japanese navy believed it could fight a successful defensive war with a fleet half the size of its opponent's, which would be the situation in 1941–2. Over the next three years, however, Roosevelt's programme would reduce the ratio to 30:70. A long war was more unwinnable than it had ever been, and the traditional navy plan for such a war – attacking the Philippines and then waiting in ambush as the US fleet sailed to the rescue – involved surrendering both initiative and timing to the enemy. Something more proactive was needed.

The idea of an attack on Pearl Harbor – long the secondary Pacific naval base after San Diego, but now the US Pacific Fleet's principal home – was an old one, much beloved by Japanese novelists in the 1920s and occasionally tested in war games by both sides in the 1930s. It was no longer taken seriously by the US military – the Japanese, it was believed, had too far to come, would be seen long before they arrived, and could then be destroyed by the superior air and naval strength available to the commanders on Hawaii. And if by chance any Japanese planes got through, their attacks were bound to be ineffective – no air force could drop bombs with the accuracy needed to sink ships, and torpedoes were unusable in the Pearl's shallow waters.

These were all serious drawbacks, but the potential benefits were immense. Could the drawbacks be overcome? Yamamoto first

settled on the idea of opening the war with an attack on Pearl
Harbor in December 1940. His two-step premise – that the
enemy's main force could only be destroyed by a surprise attack,
and that such an attack was only possible at the outset of hostilities – was irrefutable, but left two essential questions unanswered.
Was such an attack possible? And, if successful, would it lead to a
wider victory? Over the next few months Yamamoto's staff spent a
lot of time answering the first question, but very little on the
second.

The more feasible the attack seemed, the more committed
Yamamoto became. In retrospect, it appealed to him for all the
wrong reasons. Throughout his career he had relished the big challenge, loved to gamble and championed the role of aviation in
ocean warfare; such an operation was made for him. Those who
opposed it were, in many cases, the same men who had always
opposed him, the cautious conservative types who still believed in
battleships. They argued that it wouldn't work, and Yamamoto set
out to prove them wrong.

If his opponents had chosen to argue that, work or not, the
attack would make no difference, Yamamoto would have had no
honest option but to hold up his hands. In January 1941 he wrote
that 'should hostilities break out between Japan and the United
States, it would not be enough that we take Guam and the
Philippines, nor even Hawaii and San Francisco. To make victory
certain, we would have to march into Washington and dictate the
terms of peace in the White House.'[2] And that, as he knew full
well, was never going to happen. As his friend Vice-Admiral
Shigeyoshi Inoue wrote in the same month, 'it would be impossible ... for Japan to defeat America and bring about its
capitulation'.[3] America had the military capacity to wipe out all the
Japanese forces in the field, and to occupy all of Japan, including
the capital. Japan, by contrast, wholly lacked the capacity to inflict
a similar defeat on the United States, and even as late as September
1941 this harsh fact was still being employed to argue against the
Pearl Harbor operation. 'If Japan could not bring America to its
knees,' Admiral Onishi said then, 'we must consider ways to bring

[a war] to an early end, which means in turn that at some point we'll have to reach a compromise. For that reason, whether we land in the Philippines or anywhere else, we should avoid anything like the Hawaii operation that would put America's back up too badly.'[4]

Yamamoto knew all this, knew that whatever the short-term benefits of a successful raid on Pearl Harbor might be, the best he could hope for was an eighteen-month postponement of the inevitable. As he himself admitted to Navy Minister Shimada at the end of October: 'my plan is one conceived in desperation, on account of my own imperfectly developed abilities . . . if there is some other suitable person to take over, I am ready to withdraw, gladly and without hesitation.'[5] Shimada didn't take him up on the offer, and Yamamoto, for reasons best known to himself, decided against resignation, preferring to hone his plan in the hope that it would never be used.

That hope grew increasingly forlorn. If Yamamoto, who understood the odds only too well, was willing to contemplate war, it came as no surprise to find that other, less incisive minds welcomed the chance to settle things once and for all with the overbearing Americans. After all, Japan had a history of beating the big teams – China in 1894, Russia in 1905 – and what did numbers matter, of soldiers or ships, when the national spirit of self-sacrifice burned so brightly? How else were they going to solve the problem of China? The Americans had effectively offered them a choice between withdrawal and war, which was really no choice at all. The only real question was one of timing, and opportunity would never knock louder than it did in late 1941, with America's potential allies Britain and Russia fully engaged elsewhere. As the Two Ocean Navy programme kicked in, America would get stronger; as the American oil embargo kicked in, Japan would get weaker. If one could somehow disregard the inevitability of eventual defeat, it sounded like a no-brainer.

As it turned out, one could. The conventional wisdom – that going to war with America was a particularly painful way of committing national suicide – was indeed forgotten, ignored, disregarded. One Colonel Iwakuro, speaking to a government

liaison conference in August 1941, rolled out the unflattering statistics – the US produced twenty times as much steel as Japan, ten
times as much oil, five times as many planes, twice as many ships.
Against such odds, Japan had no chance of winning. Prime
Minister Tojo asked for it all in writing, and then shipped Iwakuro
out to recently occupied Cambodia.

Having opted out of the argument over 'whether', Yamamoto
concentrated all his efforts on the 'how'. It was, as he admitted, 'a
strange position' he found himself in, 'having to pursue with full
determination a course of action which is diametrically opposed to
my best judgement and firmest conviction'.[6]

The 'hows' of an attack on Pearl Harbor broke down into two basic
categories: those concerned with reaching it undetected and those
concerned with achieving the destruction required to cripple the
American Pacific Fleet. The naval general staff had done all they
could to answer the former set of questions, but only the actual
voyage could offer proof of success. When it came to the latter set
of questions, Yamamoto could be surer of knowing the answers,
because a long process of innovation and testing had already taken
place.

The Japanese had three types of bomber they could use: dive,
torpedo and high-level horizontal. Dive-bombing was the most
accurate, and could be used with devastating effect against airfields,
planes, anti-aircraft guns and installations. It could not, however, be
used against capital ships – the armour plating was too thick for the
payload and speed of delivery. Torpedo-bombers could sink capital ships, but the torpedoes were likely to hit bottom if dropped in
less than sixty feet of water, and Pearl Harbor had only twenty.
Added to which, the American habit of berthing their battleships
in pairs meant that only half of them were vulnerable to side-on
attacks. High-level bombers could, theoretically, drop payloads at
sufficient speed to pierce American naval armour plating, but in
early 1941 the Japanese lacked both the bombs and the accuracy of
delivery required.

By November, however, all these problems had been solved.

The torpedo-bomber pilots had driven the citizens of Kagoshima mad with their constant practice, but had acquired the necessary contour-flying skills. After many experiments, the scientists at Yokosuka had come up with a torpedo that these low-flying hot-shots could successfully drop into twenty feet of water, and a race had got under way to manufacture enough for the operation. *Kaga*'s belated arrival at Hitokappu Bay had been caused by her wait for the final delivery.

The high-level bombing crews had worked as hard as their tor-pedo colleagues, and, with pilots playing a bigger role in the aiming process, accuracy had risen threefold. They, too, had received their reward from the boffins – bombs converted from naval shells that would cut through armour plating if dropped from over 9,000 feet.

In the Formosan port of Takao, Masuda Reiji and his fellow mer-chant seamen welcomed 1,300 infantrymen aboard their ship. Sailors and soldiers eagerly asked each other when and where they were going, but neither knew.

Japanese shipping movements were now stretched out across the eastern Pacific and China seas, with convoys carrying men and sup-plies towards Malaya and the Philippines strung out along China's eastern seaboard. As *Kido Butai* headed out across the northern Pacific, submarine I-26 was in Alaskan waters and approaching Kiska harbour in the Aleutian Islands. Sensing no danger, Captain Minoru Yokota took his submarine right into the harbour and surveyed the scene through his periscope. American preparations for the coming conflict seemed 'very inadequate'.[7]

In the Philippines General Brereton returned from his mission to Australia. His B-17 touched down at Clark Field just before sunset, and the reception committee were given no opportunity for pleas-antries. 'Gentlemen, I have just seen this field from the air,' the angry Brereton began. 'Fortunately for you and all who depend on us, I was not leading a hostile bombing fleet. If I had been, I could have blasted the entire heavy bomber strength of the Philippines off the map in one smash.'[8]

Behind him on the field, the 19th Bombing Group's other thirty-four B-17s had been lined up with suicidal precision. 'Do you call that dispersal?' Brereton asked. 'It's wrong, completely wrong. And wrong places will have no place in the functioning of this field, or any other field under this command. You will rectify the condition at once. And you'll never permit it to occur again. Do we understand each other, gentlemen?'[9]

His subordinates signalled their assent, and refrained from adding what would have been a reasonable caveat. There was certainly no need for the ranks of B-17s to present quite such a perfect target, but the size and topography of Clark Field – in particular the softness of the surrounding ground – prohibited the sort of dispersal Brereton had in mind. Short of commissioning lengthy and costly engineering works, there was little the airfield commander could do to protect the heavy bombers, other than ensure that they were off the ground in the event of an attack.

Kido Butai had been at sea for around six hours when the first dim light of day reflected off the Russian and Ukrainian snowfields. Along the thousand-mile line that snaked south-eastwards from the Gulf of Leningrad to the Sea of Azov, several million men of the Wehrmacht and Red Army were locked in a vicious embrace.

The German soldiers emerged from whatever warmth they had found, lit fires under their tanks to start the motors and checked their own extremities for frostbite by the light of torches or vehicle headlights. They gulped down their fast-cooling *ersatz* coffee, chewed on what the supply company had managed to deliver and stuffed what fresh insulation they could find inside their thin boots and denim uniforms. Another day of wondering if the winter clothing and winter oil would arrive, another day of hammering at Moscow's door.

Army Group Centre seemed to be playing 'creeping up on Stalin', taking a quick careful step here, daring lunge there, whenever the opportunity presented itself. And every now and then the Soviet leader would catch them at it and send them back a few miles.

South of the capital, Guderian's leap towards Kashira had been seen in time. Restarting their advance on the Oka River town that morning, the 17th Panzer found General Belov's 1st Guard Cavalry Corps, the 112th Tank Division and the Red Air Force ready and waiting for them. The panzers were driven back several miles, suffering serious losses in the process.

Tula, which Guderian was rapidly coming to believe constituted the 2nd Panzer Army's last hope of a major success before Hitler or the snow called a halt to offensive operations, was almost encircled. Attacking from the west, the 3rd Panzer, 4th Panzer and the *Grossdeutschland* Infantry Brigade had severed the city's last remaining rail and road links, and were waiting for the 43rd Infantry Korps to seal the ring from the east.

In the meantime, the pressure on Guderian's other, widely stretched forces was still mounting. German reconnaissance reported heavy rail traffic to the east, and one Soviet division – the 239th Siberian Rifles – was caught detraining rather too close to the enemy and instantly trapped between two German divisions. When night fell the Germans sought shelter from the plummeting temperature, leaving a line of telephone-linked outposts with straw beacons to warn them of an enemy attack. Shortly before midnight the Soviet division's motorized headquarters unit penetrated the line without raising any alarm, but was then heard, seen and destroyed by the guns of the German defensive line. In the early hours of the following morning the division's foot soldiers would prove more successful.

Further north, the Red Army continued to give ground. As the 10th Panzer, pummelled by repeated Katyusha attacks, fought its way into the northern outskirts of Istra, *Das Reich* and the 78th Siberian Rifles bitterly contested the woods to the west and south of the town. Casualties were high on both sides, but by nightfall on that Wednesday the SS infantry had taken the fortress that commanded the western approaches and were clearing the first barricaded streets. Istra, it seemed, was falling.

Solnechnogorsk had already fallen, and the ill-organized attempt to recapture it had proved a costly failure. Now, as Zhukov later

noted, 'an alarming situation evolved'. Stavka was hurrying units to
this sector, but for the moment 'our frontage curved dangerously,
forming weak spots here and there. The irreparable seemed likely
to happen at any moment.'[10]

Returning to his army HQ at Lyalovo, Rokossovsky found himself reliving the Peshki experience. German tanks suddenly
appeared in the outskirts of the village, and 'everyone rushed into
the fight, including officers from the army headquarters'. A battalion of 85-millimetre anti-tank guns covered the necessary
evacuation: 'shells whined overhead and blasts shook the ground as
we made our way out of Lyalovo and headed for Kryukovo.' They
were now twenty-five miles from the Kremlin, and Rokossovsky's
defences 'were spread so thin that they threatened to burst'.[11]

Fortunately for the Red Army, the German offensive was
becoming equally attenuated. The 3rd Panzer Group was making
good progress towards the Moscow–Volga Canal, but there was no
longer any chance of hooking it round behind the Soviet capital –
the 4th Panzer Group was simply too weak to defend both its
lengthening flanks and continue the advance down the Klin highway towards Moscow. That evening von Bock ordered the 3rd
Panzer Group to establish defensive bridgeheads across the
Moscow–Volga Canal and turn its main forces south in support of
the 4th Panzer Group. The Wehrmacht would bludgeon its way to
the Soviet capital – the brutal elegance of encirclement was now
beyond them.

In Berlin the assembled luminaries of the newly expanded Anti-
Comintern alliance listened to Ribbentrop's much-revised speech.
So, via the wonder of radio, did a large proportion of the German
people. Those unfortunate or careless enough to miss the broadcast
were able to read it in the following morning's newspapers, where
it was spreadeagled over three pages of extremely small type.

With the New Europe temporarily on hold outside Moscow,
Ribbentrop concentrated on Britain, which 'must be kept out of
Europe once and for all'. The British, of course, had started the
war, as they had so many before. Every European knew that 'the

British would like nothing better than to see the old Europe collapse and be engulfed by a Bolshevik catastrophe, in the hope that they could remain safe on their island'.[12] Somewhere amid this lengthy diatribe, Ribbentrop took time to deny one particular accusation, that in convincing Hitler of Britain's unwillingness to fight for Poland he had himself set the whole ghastly show on the road. He was, he said, happy to let history be the judge.

Speech delivered, Ribbentrop rushed off to find out what Hitler, listening in far-off East Prussia, had thought of it. The luminaries were left with each other and Göring, who was in sparkling form. In Russia, he told Ciano, the prisoners were so hungry that marching columns no longer needed guards. A camp kitchen sufficed at the head of each column, the smell of cooking food pulling the prisoners in its wake. In several prison camps, he added, the Russians had resorted to cannibalism, and had even eaten a Germany sentry.

Ciano found this 'impressive', and thought the tears filling Göring's eyes at the mention of Udet and Mölders proof of the *Reichsmarschall*'s 'kind-heartedness'. A Spanish story from the Russian front was rather more amusing. The soldiers of the Spanish Blue Legion, whom Franco had obligingly volunteered for Barbarossa, had sought the solace of female company. 'Anti-erotic pills, which work so well on the Germans, do not have the least effect on them. After many protested, the German command authorized them to visit a brothel and had contraceptives distributed among them. Then came a countermanding order: no contact with Polish women. The Spaniards in protest inflated the contraceptives and tied them on the ends of their guns. Thus one day in Warsaw one saw a parade of 15,000 contraceptives displayed by Spanish legionnaires.'[13]

In Cyrenaica two separate battles were being fought out at either end of the fifty-mile-wide battlefield. At the eastern end, amid and around the Axis defensive positions on the Libya–Egypt frontier, elements of the *Afrikakorps* were trying to encircle and destroy those British and Allied forces still in the area. At the western end, two brigades of the New Zealand Division and the Tobruk Garrison were trying to squeeze out those Axis forces which still held them apart. This second battle revolved around a series of important physical features – the heights at El Duda and Belhamed on the nearest escarpment to the coast and the ridge of the Sidi Rezegh escarpment a few miles further inland.

Wednesday began with the New Zealanders in precarious charge of Belhamed, the Axis troops in equally precarious charge of El Duda and the Sidi Rezegh ridge. A morning attack by the German infantry on Belhamed was beaten back with some difficulty, but early in the afternoon the Tobruk Garrison's 70th Division seized El Duda with relative ease. The New Zealanders' General Freyberg decided to continue the battle after darkness, sending part of the 4th Brigade to forge the link with the 70th Division at El Duda and the 6th Brigade against the Italians and Germans on the Sidi Rezegh ridge. The former was accomplished without too much difficulty at around 22.15, but the latter proved a hard and bloody slog. According to anti-tank gunner W. E. Murphy, 'a significant feature was the sight of many men who had been hit by solid shot of anti-tank guns fired at point-blank range. These projectiles had torn large portions of flesh from the bodies of their unfortunate victims, and it would be hard to imagine a more unpleasant sight or a more heavily contested battlefield.'[14] The Italian *Bersaglieri* fought with particular courage: 'the numbers of their dead and the posi-tions in which they lay showed that they had kept their guns in action to the last. Indeed, it was reported from several of our men that the first to break under our onslaught were the German troops . . .'[15]

Away to the east, the battle around the frontier had produced an occasional spark but few real flames. Rommel, still out of contact with his headquarters, dashed from unit to unit cajoling men and vehicles into motion, but to no clear or coherent purpose. Ordered south, the 15th Panzer soon headed north to Bardia for replenish-ment and refuelling. Ordered to prepare for an eastward attack into Egypt, the 21st Panzer headed west, fought its way through the stretch of frontier defences held by the 5th New Zealand

Brigade and also reached Bardia. When von Ravenstein reported his breakthrough to Rommel, the latter shouted 'why are you here?' at him. And when the 21st Panzer commander explained that he'd received orders to head back towards Tobruk, Rommel jumped to the immediate conclusion that the British had broken their code and sent out a false message.

It had, in fact, come from Westphal. Unable to contact either Rommel or Crüwell, and only too aware of the defeat unfolding south of Tobruk, he had taken the risky course of summoning the only German division he could actually reach – the 21st Panzer. As the New Zealanders prepared that evening for their successful link-up with the 70th Division, Rommel's 'dash for the wire' was at risk of descending into farce.

Komet, the last German auxiliary cruiser at sea, crept into Cherbourg, guns manned, crew in lifejackets, boats ready for low-ering. After spending the daylight hours anchored behind the French port's inner mole, the cruiser set off up the Channel, accompanied by a posse of E-boats, grateful for the cover of dark-ness.

If Cordell Hull, waking that morning, had already decided to aban-don the modus vivendi, then the overnight telegram from Churchill which awaited him could only confirm the decision. The British Prime Minister left no doubt of his misgivings. 'Of course it is for you to handle this business,' he began diplomatically, 'and we certainly do not want an additional war. There is only one point that disquiets us. What about Chiang Kai-shek? Is he not having a very thin diet? Our anxiety is about China. If they col-lapse, our joint danger would enormously increase. We are sure that the regard of the USA for the Chinese cause will govern your action. We feel that the Japanese are most unsure of themselves.'[16]

This last sentence struck a chord with Hull, echoing as it did the opinion of his own Special Adviser on Far Eastern Affairs, Stanley Hornbeck. If Churchill and Hornbeck were right, then a hard line might even stop the Japanese. There were certainly no signs that the modus vivendi would do so, and, in Hull's opinion, the 'slight prospect' of Japan's agreeing to it 'did not warrant assuming the risks involved. . . especially the risk of collapse of Chinese morale and resistance . . .'[17]

Arriving at the White House to inform Roosevelt of his decision, Hull found a receptive audience. Depressed by the latest news from the Russian Front (it was 'awful', he told Treasury Secretary Henry Morgenthau that morning; Moscow was 'falling') and rendered almost incandescent by the reported sighting off Formosa of the southbound Japanese fleet, the President was also inclined to take a hard line with Tokyo.[18] The modus vivendi was ditched.

But what other reply could they offer to Proposal B? There was only Hull's American wish list, the ultra-combative Ten Points.

'Yes, but not yet' was the military response. The War Plans Division, under the general supervision of the army and navy chiefs, was working on another memo to the President. Like its 5 November predecessor, this memo stressed the American military's need for time – three months at least to bring the ground and air defences on the Philippines up to a level that could see off a Japanese attack. Not that the service chiefs actually expected an attack on MacArthur's archipelago. If the Japanese really did attack US, British or Dutch territory, then the service chiefs assumed that the US would fight, but such a move was considered improbable. So was a Japanese move against the far eastern territories of the Soviet Union. In the US military's view, the Japanese were much more likely to attack the Burma Road or Thailand, in the hope of improving their position in China without provoking a wider war. If they did the former, or merely attacked eastern and central Thailand, the memo advised against US military involvement. If they attacked Thailand's Kra Isthmus, which offered routes into both Burma and Malaya, that should be an American casus belli, and the Japanese should be apprised of that fact.

At 16.45 Hull received Nomura and Kurusu at the State Department for what turned into a two-hour meeting. No, he told them, the United States government could not accept Japan's Proposal B. In its place, Hull told the two diplomats, he was offering – purely as a basis for discussion – the outline of a possible long-term agreement between their two countries. He handed over the Ten Points.

Nomura and Kurusu read through the document, exchanging looks of despair. Their nation was being asked to pull all its troops out of China, to abandon the Tripartite Pact. These were ridiculous demands, far beyond anything that was politically possible for their government in Tokyo. Surely Hull understood this. They could not report such an offer, the diplomats protested; their government would just 'throw up its hands'.[19]

Look at the economic advantages, Hull responded – the most favoured nation status, the unfreezing of funds, the chance to make Japan rich. The two diplomats looked at him as if he was talking in tongues – did he think sacrifice and honour could be measured in money?

Later that evening a depressed Kurusu told Tokyo that he had 'made all efforts, but they will not yield'.[20]

THURSDAY 27 NOVEMBER

The official American response to Proposal B reached Tokyo in mid-morning, was hurriedly decoded and rushed across town to the Liaison Conference then under way at the Imperial Palace. These conferences, which performed the same function as the American War Council meetings, were attended by the Prime Minister, Foreign Minister, armed forces ministers and chiefs of staff, but not by the Emperor himself.

Prime Minister Tojo read the American reply aloud. The stunned silence that followed was broken by a single voice expressing what everyone felt – 'this is an ultimatum!'[1]

Some were less pleased than others. Foreign Minister Togo, who had carried on hoping for big American concessions, was shocked into stuttering disbelief. The army men had we-told-you-so smiles on their faces, but those from the navy looked sombre, as if they had only just realized the enormity of what was happening.

No one considered the American reply in any way reasonable. The Japanese were being asked to evacuate China. This was a big enough ask in itself, even bigger if the American definition of China included Manchukuo, and there was nothing in the Ten Points to suggest otherwise. The Japanese government was being asked to give up everything their nation had gained through ten long years of bloody sacrifice.

How could the Americans ask such a thing and expect to be taken seriously? They knew such demands could only be refused, so why were they making them? There could be only one reason – to prolong the negotiations, to gain time for their own rearmament and the dwindling of Japanese oil stocks, before striking out themselves.

There was nothing else to try. The moment had finally arrived. The fleets would not be recalled.

A final decision on *Kido Butai*'s route to the target had been made only a few weeks before the fleet set out. The chosen route had to satisfy two basic conditions: it had to be navigable in winter and it had to offer the prospect of invisibility. Of these, the latter took priority – the outcome the Japanese dreaded most was an American sighting of *Kido Butai* before it could launch its attack.

When Kusaka was put in charge of turning Yamamoto's idea into a plan, his first instinct was to go for a northern route. The chances of detection would be greatly reduced, and the difficulties of navigation and refuelling could, he hoped, be minimized by innovation and practice. He set up an in-depth study of the Pacific Ocean, its sea and weather conditions and its shipping routes, and handed the results to Flight Officer Genda with instructions to furnish options.

Genda came up with five. The first two headed south-east from the Inland Sea to the Japanese-owned Marshall Islands, where they could refuel. From there, one route led straight to a launch-point 250 miles south of Oahu, the other hooked around Christmas Island to attack from the south-east. The two routes offered the advantages of calm seas and convenient fuelling, but such an approach, under blue skies and through a known American training ground, seemed unlikely to escape detection.

Genda's third route – south-east from the Inland Sea, then north-east past American-garrisoned Midway to a position north of Oahu – was even worse: refuelling would be more of a problem, detection just as likely. The fourth and fifth routes followed the rough line of the 42nd parallel eastwards, the fourth stopping north of Oahu, the fifth proceeding further to swing around from the north-east. These seas would be rough, but the records showed that no merchant shipping used them in November and December, while fog and low cloud would offer further insurance against discovery.

Presented with these options, Kusaka followed his original instinct and went for a northern route, choosing the fourth rather than the fifth to eliminate the chance of encountering shipping traffic between Hawaii and North America.

Nagumo had contested this decision, arguing that the difficulties of navigation and refuelling would prove insurmountable, but he had been overruled. He and the *Akagi* navigator, Commander Gishiro Miura, were now charged with surmounting those difficulties, guiding their large blacked-out, radio-silenced fleet through heavy seas and pitch-black nights. Miura certainly took the job seriously. Known among his fellow officers as a happy-go-lucky personality, he now peered out from the bridge at the dim-dark world and prayed that morning would find the fleet still in some sort of formation. As *Kido Butai* plunged on, word spread around the ship that Miura had even forsaken his usual carpet slippers for a proper pair of shoes.

In Moscow the chess championship began. Eight of the Soviet Union's finest players had been chosen to contest the thrice-weekly matches, which were held at various locations in the capital. They were given wide coverage in the press and on the radio, and people from all over the country avidly followed each twist and turn. Several early games were interrupted by air-raid alerts, but the eight men soon decided they would rather carry on playing than let the Germans decide the timing of their moves. The eventual winner, Lieutenant Mazel, overcame one formidable handicap – he was serving with a unit just outside Moscow, and spent the weeks of the championship in a near-permanent commute between the city and the fighting.

★

In the northern seas the Soviet Union's allies were increasing the flow of material assistance. Two convoys left that Thursday morning, the full PQ5 leaving Iceland, the empty PQ3 departing Archangel. PQ4 had left Iceland eight days later than PQ3 but had eventually caught the slower convoy up, and the fifteen heavily laden merchant ships were now entering the Gulf of Dvina. Before leaving Seydisfjordur, PQ3's cruiser escort, HMS *Kenya*, had celebrated the anniversary of Lenin's revolution by hoisting the Soviet flag, a gesture much appreciated by the staff of the Soviet military mission she was carrying home.

Guderian, visiting the 29th Motorized that morning, found a division in shock. Around two in the morning a horde of white-smocked, white-gunned Siberian infantry had suddenly loomed out of the night and broken through the German defence lines, leaving confusion and casualties in their wake. Guderian was initially inclined to blame sloppy reconnaissance and security arrangements, but he soon discovered otherwise: 'the great number of dead, all in uniform and with their weapons in their hands, were grim proof that the troops had done their duty and had been simply overwhelmed by numerical superiority.'[2] He did his best to encourage the survivors.

His day did not improve. Reports arrived of further reverses – the 17th Panzer was withdrawing towards Venev, the ring around Tula could not be closed. Perhaps the latter could yet be taken, if all his strength was concentrated to that end, but any wider objectives had receded beyond reach. Guderian drove on through the gathering dusk, intent on spending the night at the 24th Panzer Korps headquarters. The Russian elements and German supply system had defeated him: 'only he who saw the endless expanse of Russian snow during this winter of our misery and felt the icy wind that blew across it, burying in snow every object in its path: who drove for hour after hour through that no-man's-land only at last to find too thin shelter with insufficiently clothed, half-starved men: and who also saw by contrast the well-fed, warmly clad and fresh Siberians fully equipped for winter fighting: only a man who knew all that can truly judge the events which now occurred.'[3]

The battle for Istra continued, General Afanasy Beloborodov's Siberian 78th Rifle Division contesting each street as if it was the last. For many it was, and by evening enough of the town was in German hands for the Red Air Force to unleash its bombers. Over two thousand bombs were dropped over the next twenty-four hours, shattering houses and churches, denying the victorious Germans shelter.

North of Moscow, a 7th Panzer combat group was only a few miles short of the Moscow–Volga Canal. Captain Hans von Luck was summoned to division HQ and given his orders for the following day: to 'take, intact, the bridge over the canal at Yakhroma, form a bridgehead on the east bank and wait for the bulk of the division to arrive.'[4]

Between Istra and Yakhroma, along the axis of the Klin road, Hoepner's 4th Panzer Group was still pushing Rokossovsky's 16th Army back towards Moscow. On the left wing of this advance one small German unit almost reached Krasnaya Polyana, which was within artillery range of the capital. A counter-attack drove this particular unit back, but elsewhere it was the Red Army in retreat, falling back towards Rokossovsky's new headquarters at Kryukovo. His 16th Army, 'bled white and still bleeding from countless wounds, clung desperately to every inch of ground, resisting the enemy with dogged tenacity, retreating a step and coming back again and again, gradually sapping the enemy's strength. We could not halt him completely, but neither did he succeed in breaching our defences.'[5]

Hoepner's advance was slowing down, and he thought he knew why – the new Soviet formations which kept appearing in his path were being transferred from the front line south of Istra. Von Kluge's refusal to set the 4th Army's right wing in motion was allowing the Soviets to redeploy his immediate opponents, and putting the whole offensive in jeopardy.

Von Kluge's reluctance to attack had now lasted almost five

weeks, since his army moved up to the line of the Nara River in late October and dug itself in. It had certainly been counter-attacked, but on nothing like the scale which he claimed, and was in no worse shape – casualty or supply wise – than any other part of Army Group Centre. When Typhoon resumed, von Bock had been sufficiently convinced – or conned – into giving von Kluge the essentially passive role of pinning the Soviet centre, but over the last few days the pins had clearly fallen out.

According to von Kluge's chief of staff, General Günther von Blumentritt, the two of them spent these late-November evenings agonizing over their own immobility: 'night after night von Kluge and I sat up late discussing whether it would be wise or not to agree to [Hoepner's] insistence [that they attack].'[6] And now, at last, the time had come. XX Corps would launch its attack on 29 November, von Kluge informed von Bock.

In the Crimea severe weather caused the postponement of Manstein's 'final' assault on Sevastopol. Given time to strengthen the town's defences, the Red Army would prove capable of retaining this last foothold on the peninsula for another seven months, tying down large numbers of enemy troops and ruling out a thorough German exploitation of the Crimean route into the Caucasus.

Further east, along the Rivers Don and Tuslov, Marshal Semyon Timoshenko's armies went over to the attack, hammering at the edges of the salient occupied by the 1st Panzer Army. The Red Air Force was much in evidence, the Luftwaffe conspicuous by its absence – Army Group Centre's needs were deemed more pressing.

In and around Rostov the Soviet 56th Army sent wave after wave of singing, vodka-fuelled infantry across the frozen Don. Each wave crested and fell back, adding to the mounds of snow-covered corpses on the ice, draining the resources and straining the will of the increasingly desperate German defenders. Darkness fell with no let-up, and by midnight the Soviet 33rd Motorized Infantry and two battalions of the Rostov militia had seized and secured a bridgehead around Theatre Square and the nearby cement factory.

Boris Krainov, Vladimir Klubkov and Zoya Kosmodemyanskaya spent that Thursday hidden in woods not far from the village of Petrishchevo, some fifteen miles behind the German lines. Late in the evening they set off, their bags full of Molotov cocktails. Each had their assigned targets: houses billeting German soldiers in the central and northern parts of the straggling village for Krainov and Klubkov, three houses and a stable in the southern section for Kosmodemyanskaya. Since the Germans were bound to be alerted by the first tongues of flame, it was important that the three partisans synchronized their attacks.

Krainov and Kosmodemyanskaya managed as much, but eighteen-year-old Klubkov was still fiddling with his matches when some Germans caught sight of him. He tried running for the safety of the forest, but only ran into two German sentries. Threatened with shooting, he gave up the number and names of his co-arsonists. Krainov got away, but Kosmodemyanskaya did not. Brought back to the village, she denied any involvement. Confronted with Klubkov, she told her German captors that they might as well kill her – she would tell them nothing.

Travelling overnight from East Prussia, Hitler reached Berlin in mid-morning. His first meeting of the day was with Finnish Foreign Minister Rolf Witting, who seemed in need of ideological instruction. 'One should be clear about the fact that the entire world Jewry stood on the side of Bolshevism,' Hitler told the Finn. And as these same Jews controlled the press and public opinion in countries like England, then that press was bound to be pro-Bolshevik. 'The entire national intelligentsia of England should be *against* the war,' Hitler insisted, 'as even victory could not achieve anything for England. It was the Bolshevist and Jewish forces which kept the English from pursuing a reasonable policy.'[7]

Further meetings with the Hungarian, Bulgarian, Danish and Croatian Foreign Ministers followed, keeping the Führer busy until nine in the evening. By the time he saw Danish Foreign Minister Scavenius, the endless parade of minor nations was giving him cause to doubt the potency of his own. 'On this point I am icily cold,' he told the long-suffering Dane: 'If one day the German nation is no longer sufficiently strong or sufficiently ready for sacrifice to stake its blood for its existence, then let it perish and be annihilated by some other strong power. They are no longer worthy of the place they have won for themselves.' He would, he said, 'shed no tears for the German nation'.[8]

Further down the Wilhelmstrasse, Ribbentrop had just received a report from Hans Thomsen, the German chargé d'affaires in Washington DC. The Americans had apparently given the Japanese what amounted to an ultimatum, which Thomsen thought 'bound to result in the immediate breakdown of the talks'.[9] Buoyed by the obvious advantages of a Japanese entry into the war, and seemingly oblivious to the equally obvious disadvantages of an American entry, Ribbentrop told his staff to arrange an early meeting with Japanese Ambassador Oshima.

In Ethiopia the surrender of Gondar, the last Italian garrison, to General Fowkes' multi-ethnic army of Scots, Indians and Africans offered a suitably ironic counterpoint to the celebrations in Berlin. During the 17-month campaign 230,000 poorly motivated Italian and Ethiopian soldiers had succumbed to British-led forces of fewer than half that number.

A corridor of British-occupied desert now connected Tobruk to Egypt and the rest of the empire – the garrison had been relieved. But what came next? What were the British to do with their success? The architects of Crusader had assumed that the relief of Tobruk would follow the destruction of the *Afrikakorps*, but in the event it had been achieved in the panzers' absence. And that afternoon, as the British discovered from an intercepted message, the German armour was on its way back.

The good news was that XXX Corps had been given several precious days in which to recover from its maulings around Sidi

Rezegh. The 7th Armoured Brigade was too far gone, and would eventually be reconstituted for service in Burma, but the 22nd and 4th Armoured Brigades had been rested, replenished and resupplied with new tanks. The two brigades now boasted 119 runners between them, a steep reduction from the division's 600 on 17 November, but still more than the *Afrikakorps* could put into the field.

General Ritchie had some reason for optimism, but not nearly as much as he thought. On hearing that afternoon that the panzers were moving towards Tobruk, he came to the wholly erroneous conclusion that they were 'escaping westwards'.[10] Fortunately for Ritchie, his decision to attack them with the 4th and 22nd Armoured Brigades also made sense in the real world, foiling as it did an immediate German assault on the New Zealanders' rear.

Rommel had abandoned his dreams of a frontier victory and ordered his panzers west, but only in the manner of a surly teenager. The 21st Panzer was allowed to take the straighter, supposedly safer route along the coast, but the 15th Panzer was sent south to take another hopeful swipe at the 5th New Zealand Brigade before turning west on to the Trigh Capuzzo. More by luck than judgement, the swipe fell on the 5th Brigade HQ, causing 100 casualties and netting 700 prisoners. Having received something for its three days of flailing, the 15th Panzer headed out in the direction of Tobruk, and duly ran into the waiting British armour three miles east of Bir el Chleta.

The British had more tanks but fewer guns, and less idea of what to do with either. As usual, their units proved incapable of coordinating their attacks, and the 4th Armoured Brigade arrived only towards the end of the four-hour battle. The 22nd Armoured Brigade had brought the 15th Panzer to a halt, but the real possibility of inflicting terminal damage on the German division had been lost. And when the British followed their usual practice of a night withdrawal into leaguer, the Germans were able to occupy the very positions which battle had denied them.

By nightfall Rommel was on his way back to El Adem, his HQ

south of Tobruk. Still sulking a little over the failure of his frontier move, he refrained from balling out Westphal, and had the grace to commend him the following morning. That evening he wrote to Lucie. It was their twenty-fifth wedding anniversary, and he thanked her for 'all the love and kindness through the years which have passed so quickly'. He told her he had just spent 'four days in a desert counter-attack with nothing to wash with. We had a splendid success.'[11]

The last sentence was questionable, but the battle was certainly far from over. Later that night he and Crüwell argued over how they should break the New Zealanders, Rommel favouring an attack that would cut them off from Tobruk, his subordinate an attack that would force them into the town. The Battle of Sidi Rezegh, which the two men had won so thoroughly four days earlier, was about to be resumed, in, as von Mellenthin wrote, 'conditions that were far less propitious . . . The New Zealanders had made a firm junction with the Tobruk garrison, and our forces in that quarter were gravely weakened. The *Afrikakorps* had accomplished nothing decisive on the frontier and was only a fraction of the magnificent force which had entered the battle on the 18th.' The British, by contrast, had been reinforced, and their air force 'dominated the battlefield'.[12]

Komet docked at Le Havre at 09.15 and set off for another eastward dash at 17.30, this time accompanied by eleven lightly armed minesweepers and three torpedo boats.

Early that morning Stimson called Hull to ask how the meeting with Nomura and Kurusu had gone. Badly, Hull told him – all the diplomatic options had been exhausted. It was now up to Stimson and the men who joined him in his office an hour or so later – Knox, Admiral Stark and Marshall's deputy, General Gerow (Marshall himself was attending army manoeuvres in North Carolina).

The four men went over their memo to the President one last time, agreed that it had not yet been overtaken by events and sent it off to the White House. If Hull's hard line worked, and they were granted the months they needed, then fine. If it failed, if the Japanese proved more reckless than reasonable, then war was imminent, and new warnings had to be issued to the Pacific commands. The army and navy had both been working on drafts, which Stark and Gerow now presented to Stimson and Knox for amendment and approval.

Both warnings went out later that day, reaching Hawaii that evening and the Philippines the following morning. 'This dispatch is to be considered a war warning,' the navy version began. Negotiations with Japan had 'ceased', and an aggressive move by Japan was 'expected within the next few days'. Possible targets included the Philippines, Borneo and Thailand. The recipients of the warning were asked to 'execute an appropriate defensive deployment' before proceeding with the moves already agreed for an outbreak of war.[13]

The army version lacked the navy's dramatic opening sentence, and was less categorical in writing off the negotiations. It twice stressed the importance of Japan striking the first blow, but told commanders that 'this policy should not, repeat not, be construed as restricting you to a course of action that might jeopardize your defence'.[14] A stepping-up of reconnaissance activities was advised, but not at the cost of alarming the civilian population. Commanders were told that only a minimum number of 'essential officers' should be apprised of the warning itself.

The army memo was not the only important document to land on Roosevelt's desk that day. The British Maud Committee, set up the previous year to investigate the possibility of a uranium bomb, had issued a series of reports in the summer of 1941. These had been sent to the US scientific authorities, but the conclusions reached – that a bomb could probably be manufactured before the war ended, and that the Germans were probably trying to manufacture one – were only fully shared with President Roosevelt on 9 October. The latter's first and last instinct was to make sure that leadership of the research and development programme should be given to the government and military. The scientists would make the bomb but would have no say in whether or how it was used.

The Office of Scientific Research and Development, headed by Vannevar Bush, took three weeks to produce a draft American equivalent of the Maud Report. Its authors thought that a significant quantity of fission bombs could and should be produced 'within three or four years'. Whether or not they helped to defeat the Germans, the possession of such weapons would be crucial in any post-war world: 'Adequate care for our national defence seems to demand urgent development of this programme.'[15]

Receiving the report that Thursday, Roosevelt could only agree.

Hull, meanwhile, was asking his State Department advisers for something positive to offer the Japanese at that afternoon's meeting with Roosevelt. No one could think of anything, and one man, Special Far Eastern Adviser Stanley Hornbeck, was particularly adamant that nothing should be offered, that a firm line should be adhered to. If the Japanese were foolish enough to start a war, then Hornbeck was sure the United States would win a quick and easy victory. He was, however, equally certain that the Japanese lacked the nerve. In a memo written that afternoon he made a forecast that would soon be famous: 'Were it a matter of placing bets,' he said, he would 'give odds of five to one that the United States will not be at "war" on or before December 15 . . .'[16] There was, in short, no danger of an imminent war.

At the White House, Nomura and Kurusu had their requested meeting with the President, who merely repeated what Hull had told them the day before. The Ten Points should be seen as a basis for discussion, an opportunity rather than a threat.

Shortly before midnight Kurusu called Kumaichi Yamamoto, the head of the American bureau in Japan. His latest report hadn't yet reached Tokyo, and Yamamoto wanted to know how the meeting with the President had gone. Kurusu told him, using the code he'd been assigned, the sort of code that a five-year-old would have no trouble understanding. The wedding (a US–Japanese agreement) was still officially on, and Yamamoto was keen for the negotiations to continue, even though the birth of a child (military action) was now imminent, and Tokugawa (the army) was 'really champing at the bit'.

'That's why I doubt if anything can be done,' Kurusu added.

'Well, we can't sell a mountain,' Yamamoto told him. Japan could not simply yield.[17]

The army warning reached General Short in Hawaii some time in the afternoon. He went over it word for word, but managed to miss the significance of the whole. The invitation to step up reconnaissance was ignored, because Short mistakenly assumed that the writer had mistakenly assumed that the army on Hawaii shared such duties with the navy, as it did in the Philippines. But when it came to avoiding civilian alarm and limiting the number of those in the know, Short went way too far. There were three stages of alert open to him, but the second and third – which were invoked under threat of an outside attack – seemed incompatible with these instructions. Only Alert No. 1 – which was invoked against domestic sabotage and subversion – would allow him to keep the population calm and restrict dissemination of the warning.

This seemed sensible to Short, who thought an outside attack highly improbable, yet had a bee in his bonnet about sabotage. The planes under his command were deployed accordingly, unarmed and closely grouped for easier defence against saboteurs.

The naval warning reached Admiral Kimmel later that evening, but its first sentence failed to deliver the intended jolt – as Kimmel said later, he took it to mean that a Japanese attack somewhere in south-east Asia or the Pacific was probably imminent. This was hardly a revelation, and the list of possible targets did not include Hawaii. Kimmel was left pondering the gnomic 'appropriate defensive deployments' – what exactly would they be? He decided that he already had them in place, at least insofar as his ships were concerned. The concept of defending Pearl Harbor itself escaped him, and with it the idea of extending the inadequate reconnaissance which his planes were carrying out.

One man not shown the war warning was Rear-Admiral Patrick Bellinger, in charge of the naval patrols. Nine months earlier Bellinger and his army opposite number, General Martin, had looked into the possibility of an enemy attack on Pearl Harbor, and decided that a surprise assault, launched from one or more carriers less than 300 miles offshore, was definitely feasible. The only defence against such an attack was greatly increased reconnaissance, with planes 'as far as possible to seaward through 360°'.[18] Bellinger and Martin had accepted that a shortage of pilots and planes prohibited the setting up of permanent patrols, but saw no reason why they should not be undertaken in a crisis. A crisis had apparently arrived, but Bellinger had no way of judging how serious it was. His only sources of information at this juncture, as he later testified, were the Honolulu newspapers.

Rather than worry about Japanese intentions, Kimmel concentrated on doing his bit for the grand strategic plan. The reinforcement of the Philippines – both now, with the onward dispatch of B-17s, and later, if hostilities broke out, with the sending of the Pacific Fleet to south-east Asian waters – was central to that plan, and Kimmel decided to strengthen the staging posts that lay between himself and MacArthur. Over the next week he would use his two carriers to deliver additional planes to the airbases on Wake and Midway.

This move came with a collateral bonus, but not the one that Kimmel expected. Sending the carriers to Wake and Midway would, he knew, allow a big expansion of aerial reconnaissance over Hawaii's south-western approaches, and render a surprise Japanese attack from that direction almost impossible. As things turned out, sending the carriers away from Pearl Harbor would save them from the real surprise, which would soon be swarming in from the north.

FRIDAY 28 NOVEMBER

It was a moment that many had dreaded – the first refuelling in the rolling Pacific swell. The potential problems of the process had been exercising minds since the Pearl Harbor plan was first mooted. Not all the Japanese ships needed top-ups — the three largest carriers, two battleships and two heavy cruisers could carry all they needed – but most needed some, and the destroyers needed a daily intake. Working out how much oil was needed for which speeds and distances, and how many tankers would be needed to carry it, was a fairly straightforward task, but the mechanics of transfer from tanker to warship in heavy northern seas were likely to prove problematic. Nagumo had initially been set against the northern route for that very reason.

Practice sessions had been held. Refuelling had been tried in several positions, the umbilically connected tankers sailing ahead, behind and alongside the warships. It had not, however, been possible to simulate such operations in the kind of seas which *Kido Butai* was likely to encounter en route to Hawaii, and this first refuelling was a fraught affair. As ships rose, fell and violently tilted this way and that, hoses flexed and viciously snaked, sweeping several unfortunates overboard. None was rescued, but the

fuelling was eventually completed, and one major doubt had been
laid to rest.

The message containing Hull's Ten Points was far from the last that
Foreign Minister Togo received from his men in Washington.
Nomura sent several requests for more time, and even went over
the Foreign Minister's head with appeals to Tojo and the Lord
Privy Seal. His answer, dispatched from Tokyo that morning, was
definitive: 'With the report of the views of the Imperial
Government that will be sent to you in two or three days, talks will
be de facto ruptured. This is inevitable. However, I do not wish
you to give the impression that the negotiations are broken off.'[1]
From this day forth Nomura and Kurusu were not so much diplomats as actors, and Togo expected a convincing performance.

The official 'war warning' reached the Philippines in the early
hours of 28 November, and MacArthur sent back promises of an
immediate response. Air reconnaissance would be 'extended and
intensified', ground security improved. 'Everything,' he wrote to
Marshall, 'is in readiness for the conduct of a successful defence.'[2]
When, later that morning, he shared the news with Brereton,
MacArthur was quick to accept his subordinate's recommendation
that the air force be put on a war footing. All personnel were confined to bases, planes armed and dispersed to the fullest possible
extent. Half the B-17s would be moved to Del Monte airfield on
Mindanao when sufficient supplies had been stockpiled.
    Marshall could hardly have asked for more, and there was noth-
ing to indicate that MacArthur's reading of the warning was any
different from that which the writer had intended. But it was.
MacArthur, as it subsequently transpired, was over-impressed by his
government's insistence that Japan should 'commit the first overt
act'. Against what, he wondered. US soil? If that was the intention,
did the Philippines count as US soil? And what level of US reconnaissance would constitute an 'overt act' on his part?
    He didn't ask. Seeking clarification might be construed as weak-
ness, and there was, in any case, no cause for immediate concern.

Only the previous day he had told American High Commissioner Sayre and Admiral Hart that 'it would be impossible for the Japanese to attack the Philippines before the following April'.[3]

Since his receipt, three days earlier, of London's less-than-satisfactory ruling on the possible implementation of Matador, General Brooke-Popham had been left in less-than-blissful ignorance by his Whitehall masters. What exactly was happening in Washington? 'We ourselves are completely in the dark,' he signalled London reproachfully. 'You will realize how important this matter is to us, especially if the breakdown stage is approaching.'[4]

Though lacking in heavy weapons – the ice on the Don was too thin to support tanks or artillery – the Soviets were still holding their Rostov bridgehead when dawn brought reinforcements. Von Kleist, by contrast, had no reserves to deploy – the 1st Panzer Army's resources were already stretched to the limit and beyond, with panzer divisions down to twenty tanks or fewer, infantry companies of only fifty men. It looked very much as if Rostov was going to be the first city surrendered by the Germans in the Second World War.

Yakhroma was a small textile town on the western side of the Moscow–Volga Canal, thirty-nine miles due north of the Kremlin. The German attack began shortly before midnight on the 27th, von Luck's reconnaissance group feeling its way through the woods north of the town to reach the Moscow–Volga Canal at around four in the morning. Moving quickly southwards along the western bank, it managed to seize the only bridge from a surprised forty-strong Soviet security detail, and set up camp on the far bank. The 3rd Panzer Group's General Reinhardt had what he called his 'springboard to the East'.

The rest of Colonel Hasso von Manteuffel's 7th Panzer assault group – the 6th Rifle Regiment and part of the 25th Panzer Regiment – now moved forward, and those Red Army units to the west of the town, caught between two German forces, escaped as best they could. In the hours straddling the dawn, German infantry cleared the town of enemy forces and seized the line of higher ground a half-kilometre or so beyond the canal.

They were soon challenged. At around 07.30 several T-26 tanks and an armoured train advanced along the tracks on the eastern side of the canal and almost succeeded in reaching the bridge before a counter-attack by the 25th Panzer Regiment's Mk IIIs and IVs crippled the locomotive and forced the tanks to retreat. The German armour was then withdrawn across the bridge while the infantry enlarged the bridgehead, forming a defence perimeter around two miles long and one mile wide. Reinhardt called von Bock in the early afternoon with the happy news, and suggested that the entire panzer group continued its advance to the east. Bock was tempted – 'its execution might bring about the collapse of Moscow's entire north-eastern front'.[5]

Similar visions haunted the Kremlin. When news of von Manteuffel's bridgehead reached Moscow, the alarm was intense. Were the pincers reaching out again – could the Germans still get behind them? Stalin was quickly on the phone to Zhukov, demanding a counter-attack and, for once, offering fresh reserves for that purpose. By noon two of the recently formed 1st Shock Army's tank brigades were on their way to Yakhroma, and thousands of militia and civilians were stiffening the defences along the entire eastern bank of the canal.

As Friday unfolded von Manteuffel's force came under increasing pressure from Soviet infantry, artillery and air attacks. A combined infantry and Katyusha assault from the north-east was repulsed only with difficulty in mid-afternoon, and by early evening Reinhardt – far from considering further advances – was asking von Bock whether the bridgehead had to be held 'at all costs'. 'Yes and no, no unnecessary casualties!' was von Bock's less-than-helpful reply.[6]

After dark the newly arrived Soviet tank brigades launched a further assault, fighting their way south along the canal towards the bridge. Their T-34s proved, as usual, more than a match for the

German Mk IIIs and IVs, and by 21.30 the German-held bridge was under fire.

From Yakhroma, the boundary between the two warring armies stretched in a wavy line to the south-west. Those forces moving south-east and east on either side of the Leningrad and Volokolamsk highways were less than thirty miles from the centre of Moscow, and still pushing a few miles closer with each exhausting day. The 4th Army, moreover, was due to resume its long-delayed advance on the following day, threatening Moscow from a new direction and relieving the strain on Hoepner's and Reinhardt's overstretched panzer groups.

The 4th Army commander, von Kluge, however, was having second thoughts. Staring at his office map, clutching his well-thumbed copy of Caulaincourt's famous account of Napoleon's Russian comeuppance, the time just didn't seem ripe. He was leaning towards a postponement, the 4th Army commander told von Bock that evening, and von Bock, for reasons best known to himself, agreed that 'the moment' had not yet come.[7]

Earlier in the day he had acquiesced in Guderian's more justified shrinking of ambition. The long-range objectives assigned to the 2nd Panzer Army would be indefinitely postponed in favour of one, last, thoroughly prepared attempt to seize Tula.

In Petrishchevo Zoya Kosmodemyanskaya was stripped and beaten so badly with rubber truncheons that two German soldiers went in search of other shelter from the cold. The ones who stayed amused themselves by parading her half-naked in the snow and beating her some more. The only thing she told them was that her name was Tanya.

Later in the day two women whose houses had been torched on the previous night were ushered in, and invited to abuse Zoya in whatever way they saw fit. One threw a bowl of cold washing-up water over her.

A gallows was under construction in the village square.

★

While Zoya's fate would remain unpublicized for another two months, a group of earlier victims received the full treatment in that Friday's edition of *Red Star*. In a piece entitled THE TESTIMONY OF THE TWENTY-EIGHT FALLEN HEROES, A. Krivitsky told the story of an anti-tank platoon from Panfilov's 316th Division. On 16 November, armed only with rifles and Molotov cocktails, Krivitsky's twenty-eight had fought and held fifty German tanks at Dubosekovo Halt on the Volokolamsk highway, and perished in the process. 'Not a step back!' their leader, Political Commissar Klochkov had told them. 'Russia is vast, but there is nowhere to retreat, for Moscow is behind us!' 'At their critical moment', Krivitsky wrote, 'the heroes, though only a handful, were not alone. With them were the heroes of old, who refused to submit to foreign invaders . . . They died, but they didn't let the enemy through.'[8]

The story of the Panfilov Heroes was, of course, too good to be completely true. The sharp reader wondered how, in the absence of survivors, Klochkov's inspiring words had been preserved for posterity, and over the coming weeks doubts over where, when and how many seeped to the surface. It was a good story, though, and one that touched a real chord. Millions of less-feted Soviet citizens were, as Krivitsky wrote of the twenty-eight, laying 'their lives on the altar of the Motherland'.[9]

In Riga the German occupation authorities announced the imminent liquidation of the Jewish ghetto. At dawn on the following day working-age males would be moved to a fenced camp elsewhere in the city; on Sunday the women, children and elderly would be transported to a special camp at an undisclosed location. Each adult was allowed one suitcase with a maximum weight of twenty kilogrammes, and most spent the night agonizing over what to take and what to leave behind.

Years later, Frida Michelson described that night, 'the last night before parting with the loved ones – the relatives – fathers, sons, brothers, husbands. The feeling was that this was parting for ever. Nobody slept, nobody ate, few words were spoken.

By morning no more tears were left to shed and hopelessness set in.'[10]

It was a day of many meetings in Berlin, some crucial to the German war effort, some resembling ill-written scenes from a Marx Brothers movie. Hitler's first guest was another veteran of the anti-Jewish struggle, Palestinian nationalist Hajj Muhammad Amin al Husseini. The British authorities in Palestine had once sentenced Husseini to fifteen years, but decided on reflection that appointing him chief religious judge, or Grand Mufti, of Jerusalem would reflect better on their mandate. Husseini took the job but not the hint, and continued organizing opposition to Jewish immigration. He played a large role in the Arab Revolt of 1936, fled the country the following year and eventually gravitated to Berlin, where he paid homage to his fellow anti-Semite.

What he wanted, Husseini said, was German backing for Arab, and particularly Palestinian, independence. He knew the Führer would be sympathetic to these aims and their natural corollary, an end to the appalling notion of a Jewish National Home on Arab soil. In return the Mufti offered military help – an appeal by himself 'to the Arab countries and the prisoners of Arab, Algerian, Tunisian and Moroccan nationality in Germany would produce a great number of volunteers eager to fight'. Hitler only had to say the word – in public, of course – to 'rouse the Arabs from their momentary lethargy and give them new courage'.

Hitler hummed, hawed and generalized. No one doubted his 'fundamental attitude on these questions', or that he 'stood for uncompromising war against the Jews'. Indeed, he and Germany were currently 'engaged in a life-and-death struggle with two citadels of Jewish power: Great Britain and Soviet Russia', and it 'went without saying that they would furnish positive and practical aid to the Arabs involved in the same struggle', because 'platonic promises were useless in a war for survival or destruction in which the Jews were able to mobilize all of England's power for their ends'.

But – and he was sure the Mufti would understand this – he had

to consider the big picture. If he declared himself for Syrian independence, then de Gaulle's supporters in France would gain
strength, and German troops needed in the east would have to be
deployed in the west. When the war in the east was won, and the
German armies reached 'the southern exit from Caucasia', he
would have no hesitation in telling the Arabs that their 'hour of liberation' was at hand. When that hour arrived the Mufti would be
'the most authoritative spokesman for the Arab world', but until
that moment – still, regrettably, some months in the future – he
would have to wait for his public declaration.

The Mufti expressed his confidence in Hitler's reading of the
future, and understood his reluctance to make a public statement at
this time. But could the Führer give him and his Arabs a confidential declaration?

He just had, Hitler told him.[11]

Returning from his mid-November tour of the Eastern Front,
Walter Rohland shared his sense of crisis in a Ruhr meeting with
Germany's other leading steel barons, *Vereinigte Stahlwerke*'s Albert
Voegler and *Bochumer Verein*'s Walter Borbet. The threesome travelled to Berlin and met Armaments Minister Fritz Todt on that day,
intent on convincing him of how critical things were. They need
not have bothered – Todt's tales of war industry woe were every bit
as gloomy as their own. All agreed that the war against Russia
could no longer be won, but who was going to tell the Führer?

Having seen off the Mufti, Hitler had a brief audience with King
Michael of Romania and his mother, before reviving his anti-
Jewish tirade for Romanian Foreign Secretary Mihail Antonescu.
The last listened patiently and said little. He was, in Ciano's words,
'a novice in foreign politics' who 'does a pretty good job' but
'remains a Romanian and looks shady'.[12]

The Führer 'spoke at length', and seemed to be feeling a little
sorry for himself; he complained that the Jews, Slavs and Anglo-
Saxons who were fighting Germany and its allies owned most of
the fertile land and raw materials. The Jews, he told Antonescu,

had a 'certain destructive tendency, which found expression in the fight of Bolshevism and Pan-Slavism'.[13]

The latter was flavour of the moment in the Berlin press, thanks to the sudden rediscovery – it had first caused a sensation almost forty years earlier – of Peter the Great's alleged last testament by a Belgian newspaper. The testament was known to be a forgery, but that didn't worry Hitler or Ribbentrop, who liked to portray Russian foreign policy in the same expansionist light. 'It didn't matter,' as Hitler's aide Schmidt wrote to Ribbentrop, 'what some professor or other had discovered with regard to this testament of Peter the Great. What mattered rather was that history had demonstrated that Russian policy was conducted according to these principles . . .'[14] The *Volkischer Beobachter* followed government instructions to point out this historical continuity, noting that 'Peter the Great has become very popular among Bolshevists, who call him "the first Bolshevist"'.[15]

The German press was also keen to counter enemy descriptions of the Anti-Comintern Conference as a puppet show. According to the *Borsen Zeitung*, the foreign ministers who had put their signatures to the renewed Pact had 'acted on behalf of nations who, without exception, have already clearly proved their determination to destroy Bolshevism by participating in the east front military conflict or by repressive measures at home'.[16] The *Volkischer Beobachter* invited its readers to imagine a Europe in which England had been victorious over the last two years: instead of being able to face the world united, having at its centre a Reich immeasurably greater in power and potentialities, Europe would now be split into fragments consisting of nothing more than a small heap of non-organic separated parts . . .'[17]

The *Deutsche Allegemeine Zeitung* thought a Reich-victorious future would unite Europe as never before. The League of Nations, after all, had been destroyed by the Jew-carried Bolshevik plague, which brought democracy, uncertainty and division in its wake. The states of the New Europe, by contrast, 'standing shoulder to shoulder in the Anti-Comintern Pact are homogeneous and resolved, for there is no going back, no vacillation'.[18] Sounding like a time traveller from the 1990s, the *Frankfurter Zeitung* argued that the demand for 'European fusion' had grown ever stronger, and that 'not even the British have been able to deny this. This feeling has taken possession of Ministers, deputies, and all the millions of human beings in various countries and is now seeking visible form . . . Common development will acquire the inherent force of acquired habit. The peoples of west and south Europe will learn from direct daily experience to feel the unity of the Continent as something natural. What Anglo-Saxon states do to tear Europe apart will only cement Europe together . . .'[19]

The 'East' was another matter. The *Schwarzes Korps* noted, in terms that only chill with hindsight, that the occupiers' task was 'not merely to create order from chaos, [but] to mobilize the forces and resources of this space for the sake of the independence of Europe'.[20]

The most consequential meeting of that Friday took place at the Foreign Ministry. The Belgian surrealist René Magritte painted a picture of two people kissing with bags over their heads and called it 'The Lovers'; had he followed it up with two men similarly attired on either side of a desk and dubbed it 'The Diplomats' he would have captured the essence of that evening's meeting between Ribbentrop and Japanese Ambassador General Oshima. Neither man knew that the Japanese First Air Fleet was en route to Pearl Harbor, and Oshima had not yet been informed of the breakdown in Japanese–American negotiations. Ribbentrop, who had summoned the other man at – and with – Hitler's instructions, seemed remarkably uncertain of what he wanted to say.

He began by insisting that the war against the Soviet Union had taken 'definite shape', that the outcome could be 'unerringly foretold'. Given which, it was hard to imagine a more propitious time for Japan to enter the fray. If Oshima's masters in Tokyo hesitated, 'all the military might of Britain and the United States will be concentrated against Japan'. This was a strange opening, suggesting, as it did, that at some point in the future Germany would either lose or withdraw from the war, leaving its Tripartite Pact allies in the lurch. Perhaps noting a quizzical look on Oshima's face, the German inserted one of his master's mysterious generalizations: 'as Hitler said today, there are fundamental differences in the very right to exist between Germany and Japan and the United States.'

This statement clearly needed no explanation, and Ribbentrop ploughed on, informing the general that the negotiations in Washington had effectively come to nothing: 'If this is indeed the case, and if Japan reaches a decision to fight Britain and the United States, I am confident that that not only will be in the interests of Germany and Japan jointly, but would bring out favourable results for Japan herself.'

What, Oshima wondered, was Ribbentrop saying? 'Is Your Excellency,' he asked carefully, 'indicating that a state of actual war is to be established between Germany and the United States?'

Ribbentrop wasn't sure what he meant, as his reply made clear: 'Roosevelt is a fanatic, so it is impossible to tell what he would do.' Oshima had thought that Ribbentrop was promising automatic German entry into a Japanese–American war, but the German Foreign Minister now seemed to be implying that a German–American war would need to be started by the United States. Which was it?

As Oshima wondered, Ribbentrop headed for firmer ground. The Führer, he said, was now determined 'to crush the Soviet Union to an even greater extent than he had planned at first'. It was, in fact, almost done, and most of the German troops would soon be coming home. Further advances to the Urals and into the Caucasus would follow in spring, and Stalin would be chased deep into Siberia. As for the British, they were about to be evicted from Africa, Gibraltar, the Middle East and the Mediterranean. There were plans for an invasion of Britain itself, but Ribbentrop doubted one would be necessary – the British government was riven by splits, and public order was breaking down.

Oshima listened, believed, but was not distracted. As the meeting came to an end, the Japanese ambassador felt obliged to revive the crucial question – what would Germany do if Japan became involved in a war with 'countries which have been aiding Britain'.

And this time, much to his surprise, there was no evasion. 'Germany, of course, would join the war immediately,' Ribbentrop replied, as if astonished by the mere possibility of doubt. 'There is absolutely no possibility of Germany's entering into a separate peace with the United States under such circumstances. The Führer is determined on that point.' Oshima could hardly believe it: his government had been given the blank cheque it hoped for, but hardly expected to receive.[21]

To say, as the British and their desert allies were saying, that Tobruk had been relieved was something of an overstatement. It would probably be more accurate to say that the perimeter had been expanded to include the area, around nine miles long and four miles wide, now occupied by the 2nd New Zealand Division. The four corners of this rectangle roughly corresponded to the heights of Belhamed, Zaafran, Point 175 and the Sidi Rezegh escarpment. The connections between this 'enlarged Tobruk' and the rest of the British forces – the 7th Armoured Brigade away to the south and south-east, the rest of XIII Corps on the frontier – remained tenuous, and gave the Axis forces the chance of either re-establishing the 'smaller Tobruk' with the New Zealanders inside (Crüwell's preference) or isolating the New Zealanders from both Tobruk and the rest of the British forces (Rommel's preference).

The twenty-eighth of November was, for the Germans and Italians, a day of preparation, of fuelling and replenishing their units and moving them into position for coordinated attacks on the following day. In the process, they enjoyed one major piece of luck: the 15th Panzer overrunning a New Zealand dressing station – taking many British prisoners and releasing many of its own men – in the dusk half-light as it moved west towards the following morning's jump-off point.

There were no major armoured battles during the day, but the New Zealander and German infantry both enjoyed successes against the other in isolated exchanges. At command level the British largely wasted the day. Although it was generally realized that the New Zealanders badly needed support, no urgency was applied to the task of bringing up the 1st South African Infantry Brigade, which was currently based twelve or so miles south of Sidi Rezegh. The 7th Armoured Division, which could and should have also been moved north to exert pressure on the German armour, restricted itself to occasional and limited side-swipes.

There was one obvious reason for this excessive caution. The commanders of both South African infantry and British armour had been almost traumatized by the whirling bloody dance of the last ten days, and were unlikely to make any sort of decisive move without orders of unignorable clarity. Their superiors knew what was probably coming – as XIII Corps' decision that evening to move its HQ inside the old Tobruk perimeter made clear – but took precious few other measures to avert or even soften the expected blow.

Off Boulogne and Calais *Komet* and her escort fought a running battle with Dover-based British motor torpedo boats during the early hours. With both sides suffering similar damage and casualties, and *Komet* herself reaching the safety of Dunkirk harbour before dawn, the encounter could be seen as a relative victory, but the German captain could only reflect that slipping in and out of home waters had become a much more difficult proposition.

In London *The Times* reported that after eleven nights of poor flying weather the RAF had finally managed to dispatch a large force of bombers against Germany. The targets were not mentioned, but the chances of hitting them had recently been much improved, by the simple expedient of vastly expanding the bull's-eye. Hitting particular buildings or bridges was out, hitting towns was in.

The change of policy went back to August's Butt Report, which revealed, among many other devastating findings, that only a third of bombs dropped fell within five miles of their intended target. Another related fact, not in the Butt Report, was that one bomber was being lost for every ten tons of bombs dropped. That scale of losses in pursuit of that level of inaccuracy was not sustainable.

Navigational and bomb-aiming technology was improving all the time, and the precision bombing campaign could have been scaled down or suspended until it became a realistic proposition. The temporarily unemployed bombers would certainly have been welcome in the Atlantic and North African theatres. But neither Bomber Command nor the British government was inclined to wait. By late November 1941 the decision had been taken to target Germany's cities, and the Cherwell Report of March 1942 offered only a post-facto rationalization for what was now under way. The intention was to destroy a third of Germany's urban housing: 'Investigation', Lord Cherwell wrote, 'seems to show that having one's house demolished is most damaging to morale. People seem to mind it more than having their friends or relatives killed.' In the British city of Hull, 'signs of strains' had been evident when a tenth of the houses were destroyed, and Cherwell envisaged doing 'ten times as much harm' to Germany's fifty-eight largest towns. 'There seems little doubt,' he concluded, that 'this would break the spirit of the people.'[22]

Cherwell was mistaken, as Hitler and Göring had been in 1940. The carpet-bombing of cities killed lots of people but was more likely to stiffen than lower the morale of survivors. It was also terrorism by any reasoned definition, and a serious blow to the Allied claim of moral superiority. The British government realized as much – the War Cabinet had already taken the decision not to tell the British people about this change in bombing policy.

In mid-morning Stimson received an updated G-2 report on the Japanese convoy in the South China Sea, the reported sighting of which had so upset Roosevelt on 26 November. The author went beyond reporting the facts, speculating at length on where the 25,000 or so soldiers on board might be landed. They could, of course, be reinforcements for already-occupied southern Indo-China, but the Philippines, Dutch East Indies, Thailand and Singapore seemed equally feasible destinations.

Stimson thought the report 'a formidable statement of dangerous possibilities', and made sure Roosevelt had time to peruse it before the noon session of the War Council.[23] It wasn't the only paper on the President's desk – he had also received another pre-emptive memo from his service chiefs begging for time and cautioning against any action that might provoke an immediate Japanese attack.

Once the others – Stimson, Knox, Stark and Marshall – had arrived, Hull opened the proceedings by reiterating his belief that 'the Japanese were likely to break out any time . . . and might make the element of surprise a central point in their strategy and also might attack at various points simultaneously . . .'[24] The President then went to the G-2 report, listing the convoy's possible landfalls and adding one of his own – a landing on the Kra Isthmus. This would open the way to Rangoon, and allow the throttling of China's Burma Road supply line at source.

The six men still found it hard to believe that Japan would attack the Philippines. Why, after all, would the Japanese deliberately pull America into a war before they absolutely had to? From Tokyo's perspective it surely made better sense to attack a neutral country like Thailand, a country which Congress and the American voter might well refuse to fight for.

'It was now the opinion of everyone,' Stimson wrote, 'that if this expedition was allowed to get around the southern point of Indo-China and to go off and land in the Gulf of Siam, either at Bangkok or further west, it would be a terrific blow at all of the three powers, Britain at Singapore, the Netherlands, and ourselves in the Philippines. It was the consensus of everyone that this must not be allowed.'[25]

But how to stop it? The US could neither launch a pre-emptive military strike against the convoy nor simply allow it to proceed – the only remaining option was to draw a line across the ocean and warn the Japanese that crossing it would constitute a casus belli. Roosevelt suggested including such a warning in a personal telegram to the Emperor, but Stimson opposed that idea: for one thing, 'one does not warn an Emperor'; for another, 'it would not indicate to the people of the United States what the real nature of the danger was'.[26] It would be better, he thought, to deliver the warning in an address to Congress, and to send a separate, more tactful appeal to the Emperor. The others agreed, and Stimson, Knox and Hull were given the job of preparing drafts.

The President was heading off to his home in Warm Springs, Georgia, for the weekend, and some of the urgency seemed to go with him. The feeling that an attack was possible on Monday had vanished – the position of the threatening convoy, still some days from the Gulf of Siam, and that evening's interception of Tokyo's 'de facto ruptured' message, which promised a diplomatic interval of several days, both pointed to a crisis some time in the following week.

At 08.00 the ships of Admiral Halsey's task force – the carrier *Enterprise*, three battleships, three heavy cruisers and nine destroyers – began threading their way out of Pearl Harbor. The battleships were not going on Halsey's aircraft-delivery mission to Wake, and set off for their usual exercise area soon after – they had only been included in the departure to give the appearance of a routine mission.

With yesterday's war warning fresh in his mind, the admiral was half expecting an encounter with the Japanese. 'How far do you want me to go?' he had asked Kimmel before leaving, and received in return 'the finest orders that were ever given to a man' – 'Goddammit, use your common sense!'[27]

Like Nagumo, Halsey thought himself already at war. His ships were told to arm their torpedoes and stand by their guns. Any submarine or plane whose bona fides were at all in doubt should be sunk or shot down.

SATURDAY 29 NOVEMBER

In mid–October the Japanese Emperor Hirohito had stuck a spoke in the accelerating military wheel. He had let it be understood through his Lord Privy Seal, Marquis Koichi Kido, that he would only accept Tojo as his new Prime Minister if the latter agreed to conduct a thorough review of Japan's situation and the decisions which had shaped it.

Tojo had done so, but neither he nor his fellow military leaders could find any faults in their previous reasoning, and the war machine had been allowed to gather speed once more. In this last week of November the Emperor tried once more to apply the brakes, or at least reassure himself that they still worked. The semi-formalized grouping of former Prime Ministers known as the *jushin* still retained a degree of autonomy from the ruling military-political complex, and Hirohito asked that it be summoned to take stock of the current situation.

The meeting began at 09.30. Tojo and four fellow Cabinet ministers were on hand to answer questions from the eight former Prime Ministers, and the going was hard from the outset. Foreign Minister Togo's blithe acceptance of imminent military action was immediately challenged by Baron Reijiro Wakatsuki, who thought a period of *gashin-shotan* (hard times) would be preferable to war.

And when General Teiichi Suzuki, the Head of the Cabinet Planning Board, argued that Japan would have no chance of winning a war once it settled for *gashin-shotan*, Wakatsuki saw it as an admission that Japan's resources were stretched alarmingly thin. Tojo tried to reassure him: they could get enough oil from southeast Asia and could 'somehow manage' when it came to aviation fuel.[1]

Former Prime Minister Admiral Okada asked about the European war and its relevance to Japan, and Tojo seized the opportunity to paint a positive picture. Japan would crush Britain's forces in eastern Asia and move west to link up with the Germans, taking India en route. Okada was not impressed. He steered the discussion back to the awkward topic of resources, and received another of Tojo's bland reassurances: 'I think we can get along. Please trust us.'[2]

Okada cut to the chase – was the Imperial Navy strong enough to beat America? Tojo avoided a direct answer. He insisted, quite rightly, that the navy was preparing for a long war, but was unable to claim that its commander-in-chief had any confidence in the final outcome. Seeing Okada's sceptical expression, and aware of how unconvincing he sounded, Tojo fell back on his default position: 'Suppose we don't fight. What would be the result? We can't just bow to England and the United States. We've lost one hundred and sixty thousand lives so far in the China Incident. Now more than two million people are suffering. No more suffering! If we go on like this for a few years, we'll lose our chance to fight.'[3]

Or lose their chance to lose. After two and a half hours of discussion, the conference adjourned to the palace, where lunch with the Emperor was followed by another non-meeting of minds. Invited to state their views, the former Prime Ministers obliged. Wakatsuki and Okada were not alone in preferring hard times to war. Prince Konoye supported them, and so did Admiral Yonai, who saw only two alternatives: hard times or ruin.

Tojo held his ground, claiming with some truth that he and his colleagues had thoroughly explored the question of whether Japan could supply itself through a long war, and carefully omitting the crucial fact that no positive answer had been forthcoming. He also implied that they knew how to end such a war, but all he could actually suggest was mediation by the Soviet Union or the Vatican.

It didn't matter – the *jushin* were powerless, the Emperor suspended above the fray. The audience over, Tojo convened another liaison conference. Germany and Italy, he said, should be warned that war was coming. But on which day? Togo and Finance Minister Kaya needed to know, the former to alert his diplomats, the latter to organize a soft landing for the stock market.

The Navy Chief of Staff, Admiral Osami Nagano, was reluctant to tell them, but he realized he had no choice. It was 8 December, he admitted. Togo, wondering why Nagano didn't want the diplomats in Washington to know, finally extracted an admission that the Imperial Navy was planning a surprise attack.

There would have to be some sort of advance notification, Togo insisted. Anything else would be 'entirely impermissible . . . hurtful to national honour and prestige'.[4]

The whole nation, someone else replied, would have to resemble Kuranosuke Oishi, the samurai leader in *Chushingura* who feigned drunkenness to disarm the suspicions of his enemy.

Not amused, Togo left the meeting to compose the warning cables Tojo had requested. Ambassador Oshima was instructed to tell Hitler and Ribbentrop that 'lately England and the United States have taken a provocative attitude, both of them . . . that they are planning to move military forces into various places in East Asia and that we will inevitably have to counter by also moving troops. Say very secretly to them that there is extreme danger that war may suddenly break out between the Anglo-Saxon nations and Japan through some clash of arms and that the time of the breaking out of this war may come quicker than anyone dreams.'[5]

If there was one thing that Operation Z's supporters and opponents agreed on, it was that the First Air Fleet's arrival in Hawaiian waters had to be a complete surprise. Anything else, and there was a high chance of utter catastrophe, as the plan's opponents had been only too keen to stress. Nagumo had been one of them, and he was now doing everything in his power to ensure that his fleet passed in secrecy.

The ships burned only the highest-grade fuel to minimize smoke, and at night the whole fleet was blacked out, with only a few blinker lights dimmed to the edge of invisibility. At Hitokappu Bay the fleet's rubbish had been taken ashore and burned, and now it was being bagged and stored in whatever spaces could be found. The rapidly accumulating empty oil drums were being crushed and stacked on the decks. Nothing was going overboard to leave a telltale trail.

Radio silence was essential, as the Japanese had learned in the previous summer. After Yamaguchi's Second Carrier Division had taken part in the occupation of southern Indo-China, it was learned that the British had followed its movements through the carriers' radio transmissions, and a repeat performance had to be avoided at all costs. The ships of *Kido Butai* were strictly forbidden to send, and many radio officers disabled their equipment to prevent an accidental transmission – one even slept with a key component under his pillow.

Silence might hide the fleet, but it was also suspicious, so messages purporting to come from the fleet's ships were being regularly transmitted by other ships in the Inland Sea, with the intention of convincing any listeners that the carriers in particular were still in home waters.

It was equally essential that *Kido Butai* should be capable of receiving messages, especially one calling it home in the unlikely event of a diplomatic breakthrough. If, as most expected, the attack went ahead, then Nagumo and Genda needed up-to-date information, the former on weather conditions, the latter on which ships were in Pearl Harbor. Reports on both were regularly sent, most on navy wavebands, some attached to innocent-sounding broadcasts from Radio Tokyo. The battleship *Hiei* had the strongest reception, and incoming messages were often relayed to *Akagi* by signals.

An emergency procedure had been agreed. If something utterly unforeseen occurred, Nagumo, posing as a merchantman, was allowed one signal home. Tokyo would get back to him.

The 1st Panzer Army's ambitions, which had once included the early seizure of Maikop and its oil, no longer stretched to the retention of Rostov. The order to evacuate the city had been issued during the night, and that morning the infantry of *Leibstandarte* and the 60th Motorized scuttled their way westwards down a shrinking panzer-held corridor. By dusk on Saturday the smoking, booby-trapped city was once more in Soviet hands.

Outgunned and almost out of ammunition, von Manteuffel's force in the Yakhroma bridgehead was in imminent danger of being overwhelmed. At 00.20 an order was issued to begin evacuation at 05.00; by 07.00 the Germans were back on the west bank of the Moscow–Volga Canal, a partially destroyed bridge protecting them from Soviet pursuit.

Losing Reinhardt's 'springboard to the East' mattered only if a further advance was possible or wise, and neither was the case – the Germans no longer had the strength to encircle Moscow. But extending their hold on the west bank south from Yakhroma would open up a more realistic opportunity – a defensive line along the canal would offer the perfect shield for a direct advance on the Soviet capital. So the 7th Panzer was left around Yakhroma and the 23rd Infantry Division moved up on its right, leaving the 6th and 1st Panzer Divisions to drive south through the wide stretch of wooded dacha country which lay between the canal and the Leningrad highway.

The 6th Panzer had advanced about seventy miles since 15 November, and another thirty-five still separated it from Moscow. When fuel permitted, the spearheads pushed forward through the abbreviated hours of daylight, using roads where they existed, but bypassing blocking positions wherever that was possible. Around mid-afternoon they would start looking for their night lodgings, preferably a few buildings in a wide clearing. Once a central command post had been set up, the tanks would form up in a circle, guns trained on the facing stretch of trees. Infantry positions would be placed ahead of the tanks, in ditches or behind low embankments where these existed, in laboriously dug foxholes where they did not. Ahead of them, carefully sited outposts and constant patrolling would offer a first line of defence. According to the 6th Panzer commander, Erhard Raus, 'the Russians recognized the strength of these protective measures . . . and resigned themselves to harassing the hedgehog area with tank and machine-gun fire and a few rounds of artillery shells'.[6]

A thousand miles from home, cold beyond their previous imaginings, his troops watched the anti-aircraft light show over distant Moscow, and listened to Lale Anderson sing 'Lili Marlene' on forces radio, three short minutes of melancholy warmth to set against the long hours of paralysing frost.

Von Bock found reasons for both hope and concern in the southerly advance. If the Soviet defences north-west of Moscow collapsed in the next few days, then fine. If they did not, then von Bock feared a Great War-style battle of attrition, a 'soulless head-on clash with an opponent who apparently commands very large reserves of men and material, a second Verdun'.[7]

If any Soviet location qualified for this dubious honour, it was likely to be Kryukovo. Rokossovsky had his headquarters in this small town, which lay astride the Moscow–Leningrad railway, and a few miles south-west of the equivalent highway. Stavka had also recognized its importance: 'Kryukovo is the final point of withdrawal: there can be no further falling back. There is nowhere else to fall back to. All and any measures must be taken quickly to win a breathing space, to stop the retreat.'[8]

General Momysh-Uly's 316th Division had been fighting and retreating for almost two months, and he was running out of map – both Kryukovo and Moscow, he discovered on 29 November, were on the last fold. Looking at the map, he imagined 'overturned trams and trolleybuses, dangling telegraph wires, dead soldiers and civilians lying in the streets, and German lieutenants in dress uniform, with white gloves, canes and everything, strolling about with the insolent smirks of victors on their faces'. It was too much. Taking a penknife from a subordinate, Momysh-Uly cut away the last section of the map. The subordinate gasped, and then realized – 'we would not need to find our way about among the roads, streams and villages or anything else that lay behind Kryukovo . . . we'd either beat the Germans back or die at Kryukovo.'[9]

It was going to be a close-run thing. Rokossovsky's last head-quarters at Lyalovo had fallen on the previous day, and the German 46th Panzer Korps was rapidly closing on the still-forming Soviet defensive line which ran through Barancevo, Kryukovo, Matushkino and Klushino. With the 11th and 2nd Panzer Divisions moving forward on either side of the Moscow-Leningrad road and railway, and the 35th Infantry Division following close behind, the Soviet defenders were hard pressed. 'We threw all we had into the battle,' Rokossovsky remembered, 'but even so the Army Command Post in Kryukovo was in trouble. With mortar and gun shells exploding in the streets, our troops resisting enemy panzers in the northern outskirts and enemy planes strafing the defenders, we had to move it out of range of the enemy.'[10]

One good sign was the number of Red Air Force sorties now being flown. Rokossovsky believed that the Germans still enjoyed numerical superiority, but this view was not shared by his imme-diate opponent, the 4th Panzer Group commander, Hoepner, who warned von Bock that day that Soviet superiority – both on the ground and in the air – might soon halt the German advance. Further success, in Hoepner's opinion, depended on the 4th Army finally entering the battle and taking some pressure off the north-ern wing.

Von Kluge had rescheduled his planned offensive for 1 December, but only under protest. He would set the bulk of the 4th Army in motion for two reasons: because the enemy in front of him was withdrawing, and because 'the Supreme Command insists on the continuation of the offensive even if it means risking the last strength of our troops completely'.[11] He clearly hoped for a reprieve, telling von Bock that he would attack only 'if he wasn't forbidden to do so', but the Army Group Centre commander declined the implied invitation. Von Kluge gave him one last chance that evening, but von Bock 'saw no reason not to attack'.[12]

Hoepner's northern wing was not the only force in need of relief – the 4th Panzer Group's southern wing, advancing eastwards from Istra, and von Kluge's own northern wing, slogging its way through the woods north of the Moscow River, were both struggling to make headway against stiffening resistance. Lieutenant Gruman, whose 87th Infantry Division was part of the latter force, had reluctantly concluded that his unit would be denied 'the glory of reaching Moscow first', but was still hoping, rather less realistically, that others would win this accolade – either 'the SS formations' on the Istra road or 'Guderian's tank units' to the south.[13]

Wishful thinking was not confined to lieutenants. At Army Group Centre headquarters in Orsha, von Bock surveyed the changing position maps in the manner of a football manager entering the final ten minutes. His side was a goal down; a draw was less than useful, a victory most unlikely. But still possible, still worth taking risks for.

Verdun was not the only battle on von Bock's mind that day. Like most German generals of his generation, he was also haunted by another earlier failure. The Battle of the Marne in September 1914 – and, by implication, the Great War – had been lost, or so much of the German military establishment believed, when the High Command refused to risk its last reserves at the crucial moment. Von Bock, a man most conscious of his reputation, did not want to be remembered as the maker of a similar, war-changing error. If one last push, one last sacrifice, would do the trick, then how could he call a halt?

Neither Halder nor Hitler was going to stop him. They would spend the next few days obsessing over the situation in the south, while the German advance around Moscow slowly bled to a halt.

Around midday Zoya Kosmodemyanskaya was led through Petrishchevo to the site of her execution. Bare-footed, smeared with her own blood, she showed no sign of fear. The word 'arson-ist' had been crudely scrawled on the placard that hung from her neck.

The villagers, summoned by their German occupiers and forced to wait several hours in the sub-zero temperature, watched in silence as the rope was placed around Zoya's bruised neck. 'You can't hang us all,' she told her executioners, as those of them with cameras carefully lined up their shots.[14]

As the day dawned in Riga, all able-bodied Jewish men were ordered out on to the street, formed up in columns and told to wait. Four hours later they were marched into the barbed wire enclosure which had been built inside the ghetto. 'It is hard to describe the terror, the confusion this new order created,' Frida Michelson wrote later. 'Men were running to say their last good-byes . . . Everybody thought that it was the men who would be liquidated.'[15]

The women, children and elderly remained in their rooms, packing and repacking, wondering about the shots they could hear in the distance. As evening fell these grew more frequent, and around seven o'clock everyone was ordered outside by the Latvian police auxiliaries, and drawn up once more in marching columns. For two hours they stood there, carrying their most precious pos-sessions, inching closer together for warmth, listening to the almost continuous volleys of distant gunfire, almost out of their minds with fear.

And then the police disappeared. Frida and her friends sneaked back inside, but kept their coats on for the eventual summons. Hours passed, exhaustion took over, and everybody went to sleep 'in whatever position they happened to be'.[16]

In Kovno two more trains arrived from the Reich. One had left Vienna on 23 November with exactly a thousand Jews on board; the other had departed Breslau on the same day with a thousand and five. All were marched from the station to Ninth Fort, where new pits were waiting. Over several hours 693 men, 1,155 women and 152 children were shot at, the lucky ones killed outright. All were buried between layers of quicklime.

Another train was nearing Riga, this one with a thousand Jews from Berlin. Were they to be killed on arrival, as those arriving in Kovno had been killed? Were all Jews now being killed as a matter of course? The *Einsatzgruppen* had shown themselves willing to kill whoever was put in front of them, oblivious to the lack of any clear-cut directive, but the Reich Commissars for the occupied territories of *Ostland* and *Belorussia*, Hinrich Lohse and Wilhelm Kube, were not so sanguine. The lack of clarity in official Jewish policy was not only making their life harder, but also taking a political and economic toll on the Reich and its war effort.

They had brought their concerns to SS *Reichsführer* Heinrich Himmler's attention in mid-November. Lohse's main problem – one shared by the Wehrmacht – was the potential loss of much-needed skilled labour – should he be killing Jews who could still be economically useful? Kube was more interested in distinguishing between Jews. Surely those from the Reich, from 'our own cultural sphere', were more worthy of life than the 'native brutish hordes' of Poland and Russia?[17] And surely Reich Jews with war decorations, Aryan partners or some Aryan blood were more worthy than those without?

Until now Hitler's government had taken no steps to implement a coordinated plan for genocide; it had written punitive laws and set a murderous tone, leaving its various minions to ship some here, kill some there. The *Einsatzgruppen* had been let off their leash since July, and the number killed had come, in Russia at least, to vastly exceed the number shipped, but no blanket death penalty had yet been issued. Hitler and Himmler might assume that an ultimate aim of killing each and every Jew was self-evident, but for men like Lohse and Kube, gouging away at genocide's coalface, it clearly was not. They needed a line to be drawn, if only to separate immediate victims from later ones.

It was clarification which Reinhard Heydrich had in mind when he sent out invitations, on that day, to a gathering in the Berlin suburb of Wannsee. On 9 December a select coterie of SS and government officials would meet to agree and authorize that clear and definitive Jewish policy which the Reich so badly needed.

In the meantime the thousand Jews on the train approaching Riga included several recipients of the Iron Cross First Class from the Great War. Remembering Kube's arguments, and confident that Heydrich's forthcoming conference would soon be ruling on such unfortunate anomalies, Himmler decided to stay the execution of this particular shipment. He sent a message, via Reinhard Heydrich, to the local *Einsatzgruppen* commander in Riga: 'Jewish transports from Berlin – no liquidation.'[18]

Henry Metelmann's troop train had reached Lvov, or Lemberg as it was now called. It was the first time he and his comrades had been let off the train since leaving France, and coffee and cakes seemed the least they deserved. Sitting in the restaurant window, they found their enjoyment somewhat compromised by their pavement audience – a group of yellow-starred urchins with hollow eyes and hungry stares. There were Jews everywhere. 'Many of us had seen the odd Jew wearing the yellow star in a German city; but this was all so different, so incomparable in scale, and seeing them walking around in their abject misery we did not know any more whether we should hate these people or feel pity for them.'

Back at the station, another train had pulled in beside theirs. 'We then noticed that there were people in the wagon, most of which had small window openings about six feet above floor level, and from them we were met by staring eyes. Looking closer, we could make out that they were mainly faces of older people, with younger women amongst them – and then we also heard the voices of children. One woman opposite our window quietly said "bread", and managed to push her hand out. Then two SS guards came walking along the train, each of them carrying a rifle and a pistol in loose fashion over their greatcoats. They looked fed up and ill-tempered, and when we asked them whether we should give the woman any bread, one said: "To hell, you won't! They are Jews, lousy Jews, and they had their bellies filled to the rim only

yesterday!" So we did nothing, just tilted our heads in a half-apolo-
getic fashion to the woman and left it at that. When the train later
pulled away from us and we saw the eerie, staring eyes from every
one of the passing openings, many of us felt uncomfortable, if not
guilty, but none of us said anything about the encounter.'[19]

It was the last day of Hitler's visit to Berlin, and the break from the
gloomy Wolfsschanze seemed to have lifted his spirits. When Albert
Speer suggested that work be halted on the new Berlin until victory was assured, the Führer quickly set him right: 'The building
must begin even while this war is going on. I am not going to let
the war keep me from accomplishing my plans.'[20]

Goebbels also noted Hitler's confident mood. A lesser leader
might have brooded over the setback at Rostov, but his saw it as
opportunity – once von Kleist had pulled out of the city, the
Luftwaffe could bomb it into rubble. Large cities, after all, were
more trouble than they were worth – all those women and children
who needed feeding.

He admitted that the planned encirclement of Moscow was no
longer possible, but still expected the Soviet capital to fall. And
when it did, it, too, would be left in ruins. A rather better future
beckoned for the Crimea, which would be repopulated by
Germans, turned into a province of the Reich and named after
their ancestors, the Ostrogoths. Despite all the trials and tribulations, the Eastern project was alive, and 'what cannot be achieved
now will be achieved in the coming summer'. Nineteen forty-two
might be difficult, but by 1943 the Caucasus and Ukraine would be
supplying the oil and food which the Reich needed, and 'our victory can no longer be endangered'. The position of the Western
'plutocracies' was 'hopeless'.[21]

Hitler may have believed what he told Goebbels – if one chose to
ignore the crippling constraints of the German war economy, the
military situation still *looked* manageable – or he may have decided
that a brave front would motivate his Propaganda Minister. If he did
believe a German victory was still possible, the next meeting must

have given him pause for thought. The lengthy afternoon War Council featured his top military leaders – army commander Brauchitsch, OKW chief Field Marshal Wilhelm Keitel and operations chief General Alfred Jodl – and selected movers and shakers from the war economy, most notably Fritz Todt and Walter Rohland.

It was Rohland who put the cat among the pigeons with a long and clinical account of what was going wrong. He took the meeting through his recent experiences in Russia, and his distressing realization that the Red Army, not the Wehrmacht, now had the better weaponry and equipment. Reluctantly twisting the knife, he then used his knowledge and long experience of American industry to get across the sheer enormity of what the Reich would face in the event of a transatlantic war. The implication could not have been clearer: once the United States joined Britain and the Soviets, it was all over.

If Hitler and his generals expected any compensatory good news from Todt, they were disappointed. German armament production, bedevilled by poor planning and shortages of labour and raw materials, was chaotic and inadequate. 'This war,' Todt concluded, 'can no longer be won by military means.'

'How, then, shall I end it?' Hitler asked with remarkable calmness.

'It can only be ended politically,' Todt told him in similar tone.

Hitler neither shouted nor wept, merely admitted that he had no idea how such an ending might be contrived.[22]

Further down the Wilhelmstrasse, Foreign Minister Ribbentrop was receiving Subhas Chandra Bose, self-styled leader of the exiled, non-Congress opposition to British rule in India. The forty-four-year-old Bose had served two terms as Congress President but had finally broken with Gandhi over the issue of violence. The British, having jailed him eleven times, were unwilling to let him out of India while the war continued, but Bose managed to escape, travelling across Afghanistan disguised as a deaf-mute tribesman. When the Soviets, still at peace, refused him help, he moved on to Berlin, where Ribbentrop gave him a hotel suite, salary and the chance to raise a 'legion' from the Indians taken prisoner in North Africa. What the Germans refused to do was publicly commit themselves to Indian independence. Like the equally hopeful Mufti, Bose was told to wait for the right moment.

That moment never seemed to come. Bose had arrived in April, and this was only his second audience with Ribbentrop – Hitler still hadn't found a space in his diary. And the Indian had a particular bee in his bonnet. In *Mein Kampf* the Fuhrer had written that 'in spite of everything' he would 'rather see India under English rule than any other'. This was insulting to all Indians, and Bose wanted an immediate correction.

He eventually got the meeting with Hitler, but never the correction. Like Husseini, Bose never quite grasped the depth of his Nazi hosts' racism, and the lie it gave to the old idea of a mutual enemy sparking friendship.[23]

Hitler and Ribbentrop both took the train for East Prussia that Saturday evening, and the Foreign Minister, still obsessing over his final words to Oshima, took the chance to double-check. What, he asked Hitler, would Germany do if Japan attacked the United States? The Tripartite Pact, after all, only committed the two nations to declare war in the event of one being attacked.

That didn't matter, was Hitler's reply. If Germany failed to support Japan, the Tripartite Pact was worthless. 'The Americans are already shooting at us,' he added, 'so we are already at war with them.'[24]

Another winter day in the desert. The two sides had now been slugging it out for almost a fortnight, and most of the men, like most of the vehicles, were running on empty. The bitter cold didn't help: 'we bedded down at night under four blankets and, although we were fully dressed and wearing greatcoats and balaclava helmets, the icy wind swept right through us.'[25] There was insufficient water for drinking, let alone bathing, and food supplies could never be relied on. The New Zealanders, in particular, were running short of everything.

But if doom awaited them, it would not be for want of supplies. After dark on the previous day, XXX Corps' chief engineer, Brigadier Clifton, had put together a column of 260 vehicles, loaded them up with ammunition, food and water, and led them north-west from the frontier, eschewing known tracks on the assumption that he must eventually come across the Trigh Capuzzo. The positions of the German and Italian leaguers in his path were, as usual, illuminated by flare patterns, and Clifton steered his enormous convoy around and between them, before finally pouring his vehicles down the escarpment – few vehicles or drivers, it was said, were ever the same again – and on to the sought-after highway. A few more miles and a welcoming barrage from both sides' artillery later, and the convoy rumbled its way into the area held by the New Zealanders.

Less than an hour later, New Zealanders manning an outpost near Point 175 received an equally welcome visitor – General von Ravenstein. The 21st Panzer commander was on his way to a meeting with Crüwell, and his driver had stopped to ask the wrong people for directions. Von Ravenstein initially claimed his name was Schmidt, but then blurted out his real name by accident when he was introduced to General Freyberg. His division was supposed to attack the New Zealanders around Zaafran from the east, but instead spent most of the day rearranging its command structure

The Italian *Ariete* Division, whose allotted task for the day was to hold the southern edge of the New Zealander rectangle while the Germans bashed in its sides, had a much more productive day, getting the better of a typical desert war comedy of errors. Mistakenly believing that Point 175 had fallen to the 21st Panzer, *Ariete* drove up to the New Zealander-held height with berets waving, and the New Zealanders, warned to expect help from the 1st South African Brigade that afternoon, waved right back. By the time the two sides realized who the other was, it was the Italian armour that held the whip hand.

Twelve miles to the west, and three beyond the western end of the rectangle, units that until recently had formed part of the Tobruk garrison began the day in occupation of the El Duda heights. Their dislodgement was the task allotted to Rommel's strongest remaining force, the 15th Panzer. Crüwell started the division off in a northerly direction from west of the Sidi Rezegh airfield, following his own preference for forcing the defenders back towards Tobruk, but around midday Rommel shifted the armour around to the south-west and launched it towards El Duda in a north-easterly direction, thus following his more ambitious preference for severing the link between the New Zealanders and the garrison. The ensuing battle was indecisive. The Germans took precarious control of El Duda late in the afternoon, but would lose it to an Australian counter-attack in the early hours.

It had been a frustrating day for Rommel and Crüwell. Though lacking assistance and virtually encircled, the New Zealanders had fought on, losing only Point 175 and taking a further toll on the Germans' rapidly diminishing resources. Crüwell in particular was growing increasingly pessimistic, and if the British and South African forces to the south had joined the battle – instead of finding ever-more roundabout reasons for keeping out of it – the Axis troops would have been hard pressed to continue.

Komet had set out again after dark, and continued on through the day up the Belgian and Dutch coasts. The captain allowed his Dutch prisoners to listen to their national radio, but the woman who had been giving knitting instructions when they sailed several months earlier was still in full flow. Lulled by this or the nearness to home, the sailor on watch failed to spot the approach of a low-flying British Blenheim, which dropped four bombs. Three missed, and the fourth passed through the railing of the bridge deck without exploding, leaving one young German officer staring in happy disbelief at the broken-off tail section it had left behind.

Believing they had at least a weekend's grace, the US government's big four had gone their separate ways. Hull had remained in the capital, on the watch for the 'sudden breakout' he feared, Roosevelt had gone to Warm Springs, and Stimson and Knox had taken the morning train to Philadelphia, intent on supporting their

respective teams in the army–navy football game. The match programme contained a picture of a battleship with a caption reading:
'A bow-on view of the USS *Arizona* as she ploughs into a huge
swell. It is significant that despite the claims of air enthusiasts no
battleship has yet been sunk by bombs.'[26] The enthusiasts had only
eight days to wait.

Given the circumstances, the G-2 estimate released that day
sounded rather complacent. The report's authors believed a
Japanese attack was imminent but thought the Japanese armed
forces incapable of concentrating against any of the likely objectives
with any assurance of success. The economic blockade and the
threat posed by the American Pacific Fleet were the 'primary
deterrents against Japanese all-out entry in the war as an Axis part-
ner'. Once the US was drawn into war, its Philippine-based naval
and air forces could launch 'a serious offensive' against Japan.[27]

If this was obvious to G-2, would it not also be obvious to the
Japanese? If the US Pacific Fleet and the US forces on the
Philippines were the main obstacles in Japan's expansionist path,
would the Japanese not seek to remove them at the outset of hostilities, through surprise attacks? The connection was not made. A
possible attack on the Philippines was mentioned only in passing,
Hawaii not mentioned at all.

On Oahu a slender Japanese man with longish hair was shown into
Nagao Kita's office. The rest of the consulate staff knew him as
Tadashi Morimura, a junior diplomat who did little apparent work,
but his real name was Takeo Yoshikawa, and he worked for Naval
Intelligence. It was the second time in two days that Kita had sum-
moned him – things were hotting up.

The previous day Tokyo had requested reports on 'the entrance
or departure of capital ships and the length of time they remain at
anchor, from the time of entry into port until the departure'.[28] This
was routine stuff, the sort of information that any naval power
would seek to gain about a possible enemy. Today's request,
though, was different. 'We have been receiving reports from you on
ship movements, but in future will you also report even when

there are no movements.'[29] Kita passed on the message without comment, but both men were jolted by the implication – that their masters in Tokyo were taking an unusual interest in berthed and anchored American warships.

Yoshikawa had been in Hawaii since late March. He was something of a renaissance man: a champion swimmer, kendo devotee and Zen scholar with a serious fondness for geishas and alcohol. Health problems arising from the last had cut short a promising career in the regular navy, but a man of such talents was too good to waste, and his superiors found him a niche in Naval Intelligence. When Yamamoto decided, in February 1941, to push for the Pearl Harbor attack, he asked for a suitable spy on Hawaii, and the fluent English speaker Yoshikawa seemed the ideal choice.

His knowledge of the US navy, as Kita soon realized, was encyclopaedic – when Yoshikawa saw something, he generally knew what it was, and the significance of it being there. And he made every effort to see all he could. Starting with tours of all the islands, he satisfied himself that Pearl was the only naval installation of any significance, and concentrated on finding a number of vantage points overlooking the harbour and the nearby airfields. As the weeks went by, he began supplementing his twice-weekly tours of the military sights with occasional excursions by boat and aeroplane. He never carried a camera and used a telescope only in one location – the second-floor room of his local geisha house and restaurant, which featured a panoramic view of the harbour.

Yoshikawa began to notice patterns in American military activity, and two in particular seemed significant: the Americans liked their weekends, and most of the fleet could be observed at anchor on Saturday and Sunday; their planes often flew out to sea, but almost never in a northerly direction.

Neither he nor Kita had been told of a possible attack, but both were offered clues. On 24 September Tokyo asked that future reports of American ships in Pearl Harbor port should be broken down geographically, with each ship located in one of five sub-areas. This message could be interpreted – and was by its American interceptors – as an exercise in thoroughness, simplification or both, but the potential relevance of such information to attackers was clear enough. Suzuki's visit and questionnaire in early November offered further grounds for suspicion, as did the doubling of reports demanded on 15 November. Now that ships which failed to move were interesting Tokyo, Yoshikawa could be forgiven the odd flight of fancy – a carrier force, perhaps, heading for Hawaii.

Admiral Isoroku Yamamoto, Commander-in-Chief of the Imperial Japanese Navy, who insisted on opening his country's war on America with the attack on Pearl Harbor

Advance!

Striding into Russia – a German assault troop leader in 1941

A German all-arms unit
drives Red Army soldiers
from their positions in a
fortified village

German engineers re-gauge
a Soviet railway line in the
autumn of 1941

Resist!

Red Army cavalry charging across the snow during the battles in front of Moscow

Muscovite women digging tank-traps outside the Soviet capital, October 1941

'Let's fight for Moscow'
– a Soviet poster from
autumn 1941

ОТСТОИМ МОСКВУ!

A truck crosses frozen
Lake Ladoga with
supplies for besieged
Leningrad. The driver
has his door open, ready
for a quick exit should
the ice road give way

North Africa

Rommel in his element, the irrepressible Desert Fox

A British column on the move during the Crusader battles

British gunners blast a distant enemy

KMS *Schiff* 16, aka the
German auxiliary
cruiser *Atlantis*

Japanese Ambassador
Kichisaburo Nomura, US
Secretary of State Cordell
Hull and Japanese Special
Envoy Saburo Kurusu take
a stroll in the White House
gardens

B-17s under construction at
the Boeing plant in Seattle

The new battleship *Indiana* is
launched at Newport News,
21 November 1941

Crimes against Humanity

A mass murder of Ukrainian Jews by German *Einsatzgruppen*, autumn 1941

Zoya Kosmodemyanskaya, hanged in the village of Petrishchevo on 29 November 1941

Yugoslav patriots hanged by the German occupation forces

Chinese civilians
executed by Japanese
occupation forces

Infantrymen of the New Zealand Division wait the order to advance

Afrikakorps in retreat – two British soldiers watch German vehicles burn

The men caught napping in Malaya – (left to right) RAF commander
Air Marshal Pulford, Army commander General Percival and theatre
commander Air Chief Marshal Brooke-Popham

The men caught napping in the Philippines – General Douglas MacArthur (left)
and his Chief of Staff, General Richard Sutherland

Pearl Harbor

Japanese sailors cheer off the Pearl Harbor-bound airmen, early on the morning of 7 December . . .

Destruction on Pearl Harbor's Battleship Row, as *Arizona* succumbs to the Japanese onslaught

The beginning of the end – a Soviet T-34 swishes past a frozen German corpse

SUNDAY 30 NOVEMBER

Togo's 'quicker than anyone dreams' message had gone off to Berlin in the early hours, and the Japanese military leaders, aware that peace had another seven days to run, were expecting a Sunday off. They reckoned without the Emperor, who couldn't quite grasp why his navy had spent so much time and energy planning for a war it wished to avoid.

Prime Minister Tojo, Navy Minister Shimada and Naval Chief of Staff Nagano were summoned to provide clarification.

Were they ready for war with America? Hirohito asked the two navy men.

They told him that adequate preparations had been made, and refrained from adding that even perfect preparations were unlikely to produce a victory.

Noting their 'considerable confidence', the Emperor told Tojo to 'proceed as prearranged'.[1]

The twenty thousand men under Nagumo's command were given no let-up. A quarter of the sailors remained at battle stations – a figure that would double after *Kido Butai* passed the halfway point – and six fighters on each of the six carriers were kept armed and ready for an emergency launch. The sharpest-eyed men on every ship spent hours scanning the empty sea for the sight they feared most – the periscope of an American submarine.

Aboard the destroyer *Akigumo*, executive officer Chigusa recorded a typical twenty-four hours in his diary: 'Through the night we operated searchlights and deck lights because of the heavy fog to guard against collision . . . This afternoon I navigated the ship and we refuelled astern very slowly. The towing line broke. Very dangerous but fortunately no injuries. We tried again to refuel but it became dark and we gave up . . .'[2]

The fliers continued their training, poring over models and maps, familiarizing themselves with approach routes, playing identification games with flashed-up silhouettes of American ships. They warmed up their engines and checked the controls, some more thoroughly than others – one pilot on *Soryu* wore his flying jacket throughout the trip and spent several hours each morning and afternoon in the cockpit of his plane. The only bored fliers were those who had drawn the short straw and been given the job of flying sentry over the fleet while their comrades grabbed the glory over Pearl Harbor.

It was cold in the northern Pacific. The men were warmly enough dressed, but cold baths were the norm – hot water was available only on *Shokaku* and *Zuikaku*, the new carriers with the higher fuel capacity. The engine room crews dined at work, the mess hall attendants carrying the rice balls and pickled plums down to their sauna-like realm, but most sailors and fliers ate in the mess halls. The same tables hosted frequent games of *go* and *shogi*, while those more interested in individual pursuits could draw, paint or write in whatever personal space they could lay claim to.

On the bridge and in their own better-appointed cabins, the men entrusted with all these lives went about their business, Nagumo continually fretting over this and that potential difficulty, Kusaka in equally endless pursuit of a countervailing Zen-like calm, Genda obsessively shuffling the pieces of his attack plan in a frantic search for perfection.

Off Fiji, the Japanese submarine I-10 launched her float plane for a night reconnaissance flight over Suva Bay. The submarine had left

Yokosuka in Japan on 16 November, and this was her first scheduled stop in a scouting voyage that would take in Samoa, Christmas
Island and – once the Pearl Harbor attacks had been launched –
that stretch of ocean east of Hawaii which any crippled American
ships would have to traverse en route for San Diego.

The pilot of the float plane reported no enemy ships in Suva Bay,
and thereafter disappeared. I-10 searched the area for several days
but found no trace of the plane. Either the British had shot it
down – and fired the first shot of the Pacific War – or the plane had
crashed into jungle or sea.

The main body of the Combined Fleet remained in the Inland Sea,
ready to move in whatever direction events dictated, but the rest of
the Japanese navy was now at sea. Over the last ten days invasion
fleets for Guam, the Philippines, Thailand and Malaya had all left
the Inland Sea for their jump-off points in the Bonin Islands,
Pescadores and Palau Islands. While the Fifth Fleet guarded the
eastern approaches to Japan itself, the Second and Fourth Fleets
headed south and south-east, the former to cover the planned inva-
sions of Malaya, the Philippines and the Dutch East Indies, the
latter to support the capture of Guam and provide any necessary
support to the First Air Fleet. The lack of any attempt to conceal
these movements was deliberate – they held the enemy's eyes,
blinding him to the blow that mattered most.

In Tokyo Ambassador Oshima's report of his meeting with
Ribbentrop was well received. The Germans were winning their
wars with Britain and the Soviets and were willing to join the
Japanese in theirs against the British and Americans. The government decision to open hostilities was clearly the right one. It
would, however, be good to get something in writing.

At Clark Field in the Philippines, the 19th Bomb Group officers
were addressed by their commanding officer, Lieutenant-Colonel
Eubank. He passed on the gist of what Far East Air Force commander General Brereton had told him and other key officers the

previous day, that the situation was serious and that all units were expected to maintain a high level of alertness and security in the days ahead. As far as the 19th Bomb Group was concerned, the primary need was to camouflage their B-17s and B-18s and make sure that they were armed and ready to fly at all times. When Eubank asked for questions, no one thought to raise one well-known problem – that there was nowhere near enough green paint to camouflage the bombers.

This job was allowed to lapse, a victim of circumstance and the more culpable confusing of internal and external threats. Like Kimmel and Short on Oahu, MacArthur and Brereton had received war warnings from Washington which overemphasized the former and underemphasized the latter. In some cases the measures needed to meet the internal threat – like concentrating planes in a small area – actually made it harder to meet the external threat, but even where this was not the case an overemphasis on the former was bound to distract attention from the latter.

The 1st Panzer Army, now in full retreat from Rostov, was still in danger of envelopment by the Soviet 37th Army. Field Marshal von Rundstedt and General von Kleist, commanding Army Group South and the 1st Panzer Army respectively, had opposed the Rostov venture for weeks, arguing that their forces were too weakened by losses, supply problems and the weather conditions to sustain an offensive. They had been right, but it hardly paid to advertise the fact, and when von Rundstedt approved a single-stage withdrawal by von Kleist's army to the Mius River that morning, he did so without seeking advance approval from OKH or the Führer.

According to Halder, Hitler had been in a 'state of extreme agitation' over the Rostov situation since returning from Berlin, and he was in no mood to accept von Rundstedt's fait accompli. He decided that the 1st Panzer Army should be halted further east – 'these people have no conception of the state of our troops,' Halder noted acidly – and called in Army Commander von Brauchitsch to tell him so.[3] It was not a convivial meeting. The Führer did all the talking, 'pouring out reproaches and abuse, and shouting orders as fast as they came into his head'. Suitably cowed, von Brauchitsch issued the appropriate orders.

Over several hours and phone calls, von Rundstedt's staff argued in vain for those orders to be rescinded. Finally, as evening wore on, the field-marshal upped the stakes. 'Should confidence in my leadership no longer exist,' he wrote to von Brauchitsch, 'I beg to request that someone be substituted who enjoys the necessary confidence of the Supreme Command.'[4]

Halder saw the reply and made his own feelings clear in his diary: 'only the commander on the spot can have a complete picture, and his decision must be trusted.'[5] He also noted, more ominously, that the Führer had reserved the decision for himself.

In the early hours of that Sunday morning the Soviet military leaders – Stalin, Chief of Staff Shaposhnikov and his deputy General Alexander Vasilevsky, Zhukov and others – gathered in the blacked-out Kremlin for a long-desired discussion. On the table in front of them was a map festooned with westward-pointing arrows. Over the last terrible weeks, waiting and hoping for the German advance to finally run out of blood and steam, Shaposhnikov and his staff had been writing and rewriting their plan for the first great Soviet counter-offensive.

Assaults would be launched on the centre of the German line, but only in order to pin it. The principal attacks, which were scheduled to commence on 3 and 4 December, would be directed against the wings of Army Group Centre, one aimed through Solnechnogorsk and Istra towards Volokolamsk and Klin, the other at the gap between Guderian's 2nd Panzer Army and the 2nd Army in the Yefremov area. Most of the new tanks and planes which Stalin had hoarded for this moment would be used in these sectors, where advances of over fifty miles were hoped for. According to Zhukov, the aim 'was to smash up the striking forces of Army Group Centre . . . to throw the enemy as far away from Moscow as we could, causing him maximum casualties'.[6]

★

Von Bock was still pushing his subordinates towards Moscow, fretting, on this particular day, about the 3rd Panzer Group's lack of southerly progress. A radio message emphasizing 'the importance of a rapid advance' went unanswered, so he phoned Reinhardt. 'It was,' Bock wrote that evening, 'surprisingly difficult to convince him of the necessity.'[7]

Reinhardt's panzers did, in fact, make steady progress through a day of heavy snowfalls. The 6th Panzer reached the Moscow–Volga Canal south of Yakhroma to take up its holding duties, and the 1st Panzer, though required to spend much of the day rescuing the almost-surrounded 23rd Infantry Division south of Fyodorovka, was well on its way to occupying the stretch beyond. On their right, the 4th Panzer Group's 2nd Panzer made astonishing progress, reaching and taking the town of Krasnaya Polyana, just over twenty miles from Red Square, that afternoon. While small combat groups fought their way into nearby Pushki and Katyushki, one motorcycle patrol unit from the engineer battalion blithely advanced down an invitingly empty road, across the site of the future Moscow International Airport, to the outer suburb of Khimki. These men watched the locals flee for cover, stared at the snow-covered tram lines pointing south and realized, perhaps, how far out on a very thin limb they were. They headed back northwards, having come within twelve miles of the Kremlin.

This fleeting presence of a few motorcyclists offered no threat, but the strong German forces now gathering around Krasnaya Polyana were another matter. Their sudden proximity came as a shock, particularly for men still deeply imbued with the heady optimism of their projected counter-offensive. Once again the cry went up – city in peril! As tankmen drove new T-34s off suburban assembly lines and into the latest battle, all available sources of motor transport – trains, buses, lorries, taxis, even commandeered official cars – were deployed to carry another ragbag army of Siberian professionals, local militia and barely trained Komsomol youths towards the looming danger.

West of Moscow, other Siberian units were playing a crucial role. Though defeated at Istra and Vysokovo, Beloborodov's Siberians had taken, and continued to take, a heavy toll on the German divisions – 5th Panzer, *Das Reich* and 10th Panzer – fighting their way eastwards on either side of the Volokolamsk highway. So had the conditions. 'It is icy cold,' one officer of the SS *Deutschland* Regiment wrote, 'and this when there is poor shelter and insufficient supply for the fighting troops. The supply problems mount. They are the main cause of our plight.'[8] By this time his lice-ridden comrades looked like Russians, with their stolen coats and fur caps, but neither insulated them sufficiently from the cold. The breeches would seize in their automatic weapons, the fuel and water freeze in their vehicles. Engines could be started only by lighting fires under the oil pan. 'The day is coming,' the officer wrote, 'when the troops will not only be at the end of their strength, but the companies will completely lose their combat strength due to the loss of numerous wounded, frozen and dead.'[9]

That day had not quite come. His regiment's running battle with the Siberians had now reached the village of Lenino, two miles west of the town of Dedovsk. Both battalion commanders were seriously wounded during the course of the day, but by nightfall the troops had managed to take half the village and all of the hill overlooking it. 'But at night we had to give it all up again,' another officer reported, 'in order to defend ourselves against the continuous Russian counter-attacks. We only needed another eight miles to get the capital within gun range – but we just could not make it.'[10]

A little further to the south, other Siberians were deployed against Lieutenant Gruman's 87th Infantry Division. Muscovite Natalya Kravchenko, staying at the family dacha in Nikolina Gora, met them on their way to the front. Hearing a strange noise, she left the house in search of an explanation, only to find the road lined with snoring Siberian troops on a sleep break. 'It's difficult to imagine the speed at which the Siberian troops were moving forward,' she said. 'They used to only sleep two or three hours a day.'[11]

On the other side of the line, an 87th Division officer went over the sleeping choices facing its lightly clad soldiers: 'The casualties from exposure in the cold are accumulating so fast that company commanders are frequently compelled to say that the risk of artillery fire on an overcrowded house is worth taking . . .' Unsurprisingly, 'the emotional strength of the men had noticeably diminished'.[12]

Das Reich had not taken Lenino, let alone Dedovsk, but Stalin was told otherwise. He phoned Zhukov: 'Do you know that Dedovsk has been captured?'

Zhukov did not.

'A commanding general should know what's happening on his front,' Stalin told him. He ordered Zhukov and Rokossovsky, the relevant army commander, to personally organize a counter-attack.

Zhukov suggested that leaving his headquarters at such a difficult time would be 'rather ill-advised', but Stalin was having none of it. 'We'll manage,' he insisted.

Zhukov rang Rokossovsky, who reassured him that Dedovsk was still in Soviet hands. It was the village of Dedovo, some four miles to the north-west, which had been partially occupied by the Germans.

So far so good. Zhukov rang Stalin with the good news, only to be told that he and Rokossovsky should now supervise the recapture of Dedovo. And not only that – they should enlist artillery specialist General Govorov – now commanding the 5th Army in the critical Moscow River valley area – to organize the supporting fire.

'Under the circumstances,' Zhukov wrote later, 'there was no sense in arguing,' and when Govorov tried, he told him as much. The three generals proceeded to the 78th Division HQ, where a 'not especially overjoyed' General Beloborodov explained the situation in Dedovo. The Germans had captured a few houses on one side of a deep gully, and recapturing them would be 'tactically inexpedient.'

Unwilling to tell his subordinate why, in this particular case, he was 'not guided by tactical considerations', Zhukov simply told Beloborodov to take the houses back and headed back to his own headquarters. On arrival he found several messages from Stalin asking where he had got to.[13]

Zhukov's opposite number also had an unstable dictator to deal with, albeit at one remove. That afternoon von Bock spoke to his master's voice in Rastenburg, the army C–in–C Field Marshal Walter von Brauchitsch. Hitler had raised von Brauchitsch to this pre-eminence in early 1938 as part of his campaign to destroy the army's traditional autonomy, and quickly ensured that any residual flickers of dissent were browbeaten out of him. Since the start of the war von Brauchitsch had operated as a reasonably efficient transmission belt for the Führer's queries, desires and orders.

His message to von Bock on that particular day was clear enough: 'The Führer is convinced that the Russians are on the verge of complete collapse. He desires a definite commitment from you, Field Marshal von Bock, as to when this collapse will become a reality.'

Von Bock, who had opened the conversation with a description of his Army Group's weakness – one unit, he told von Brauchitsch, had recently been repulsed by Russians bearing shovels and hammers – returned once again to this basic truth. His troops, deprived of winter clothing and supplies, no longer had the strength to force a decision.

'But the winter supplies have been delivered,' von Brauchitsch insisted.

Oh no they hadn't, von Bock told him, and the fact that they hadn't was 'the best indication that higher headquarters are not aware of the true situation here'.

Von Brauchitsch refused to believe it – the winter supplies had been on their way since October.

'Statistics will show,' von Bock went on, 'that the necessary winter supplies for my Army Group are safely ensconced in storage areas and warehouses far behind the front. That is, if they exist at all. I repeat, Field Marshal Brauchitsch, a gross miscalculation has been made. Army High Command, and the Führer as well, have unfortunately overestimated the situation . . . Brauchitsch, are you still there? Hello! Has the connection been cut? Brauchitsch, are you still listening?'

The commander-in-chief of the German army was hearing what he wanted to hear, and nothing more. 'Yes, I am listening,' he said. 'The Führer wishes to know when Moscow will fall.'

Later that Sunday evening, noting this conversation in his diary, von Bock could only conclude, with masterly understatement, that 'something isn't right there'.[14]

If the winter supplies really were 'in storage areas and warehouses far behind the front', it was because there were hardly any trains to carry them forward. Seventy per cent of locomotives were now out of action, most crippled by the cold, some by sabotage. Those still running were often delayed for days on end by partisan demolition of tracks and bridges. Since the resumption of Typhoon on 15 November, 9th Army had received only one fuel train. The 4th Panzer Group had received no supplies from the rear whatsoever.

The shortage of fuel was offset only by the growing shortage of vehicles. Reinhardt's 3rd Panzer Group was down from 259 tanks on 16 October to 77 on 30 November, and one of its divisions, the 6th Panzer, was now defending a long stretch of the Moscow–Volga Canal with only 4. Guderian's Group Eberbach spearhead, which had fielded 110 tanks on 18 November, now had fewer than 30. Overall, Army Group Centre had lost over 300 tanks in a fortnight.

In the same period, it had suffered 33,295 casualties, and total German losses in Barbarossa now exceeded three-quarters of a million.

Could such numbers be replaced? Not according to General Walter Buhle, Chief of the OKH Organization Branch, who reported to Halder that morning. After noting that the army in Russia was now 340,000 men short of its nominal strength, he confessed that only 33,000 were available to fill the spaces and that 'the bulk of the replacements are not yet broken in to the front-line routine and so have limited combat value'.[15] Only sixty per cent of trucks were serviceable, and it would take six months to bring the all-important panzer divisions back to strength. Fewer than half of the motorcycle losses were replaceable. Some new equipment was coming through, but at an exceedingly slow pace. Only one infantry division could be converted into a motorized division in the foreseeable future.

Fresh from asserting his authority over Army Groups South and Centre, Hitler spent a pleasant evening remembering the good old days, and particularly the definitive Nazi demonstration at Coburg in October 1922. He had taken 800 Bavarian storm troopers with him on the train from Munich, including Eduard – now General – Dietl, one of his guests at the Wolfsschanze on this particular evening. The enemy had put in an early appearance at Nuremberg Station: 'Our train, which was beflagged, was not to the taste of some Jews installed in a train halted beside ours. Schreck leaped into the midst of them and started laying about him.'

The tone was set. On reaching Coburg, Hitler went on, he had discovered that his local supporters had made a deal with the local Left – there would be no marching in ranks, no flags or music out front. This was intolerable. He had formed his procession, complete with banners and band, and put himself at its head.

Off they had gone, surrounded by jeers, to the beer hall hired for their lodging. Once inside, they had been forbidden to leave – the police could not guarantee their protection. Unsurprisingly, Hitler had announced that he and his men were capable of looking after themselves, and ordered the gate reopened. 'Once we were outside, we gave them such a thrashing that in ten minutes' time the street was cleared. All our weapons came in useful: our musicians' trumpets came out of the affray twisted and dented.

'We slept on straw,' the Führer continued, in case anyone doubted his credentials as a man of the people. And during the night, learning of attacks on a few of his supporters, he had sent out a rescue party. 'Three Reds were brought back to me – three Reds whose faces were no longer human. It was at this moment that a policeman confided to me: "You can't imagine how we suffer under the domination of these dogs. If only we'd known that you'd settle their hash like that!"' Next day, Hitler and his men had broken up a counter-demonstration with similar ferocity, and Coburg's 'citizens were rejoicing at the thought that the devil's fangs had been drawn'.

Not completely, however – the railway unions had refused to provide a driver for their return train. '"Very well," I said to their delegates, "I'll start by taking you as hostages, and I'll have a round-up of all your people who fall into our hands. I have locomotive drivers amongst my men; and they'll drive us. And I'll take you all on board with us. If anything at all happens, you'll accompany us into the Other World!" Thereupon I had them all rounded up, and half an hour later the "proletariat" decided to let us go.'

These early days in Coburg, he added with great satisfaction, had marked 'the beginning of a new era'.[16]

In the hour before dawn the inhabitants of the Riga ghetto were ordered back on to the street and formed up once more into columns five abreast. There were, apparently, too many of them for what the authorities had in mind, and Latvian police scurried down the ranks explaining which street's inhabitants would go and which could return to their homes. Frida Michelson, in the latter group, watched from the window as the former were led off. 'Suddenly, in front of our window, a German SS man started firing with an automatic gun point blank into the crowd. People were mowed down by the shots, and fell on the cobblestones. There was confusion in the column. People were trampling over those who had fallen, they were pushing forward, away from the wildly shooting SS man . . . The Latvian police were shouting "Faster! Faster!" and lashing whips over the heads of the crowd.' Michelson heard herself screaming: 'They shoot the Jews! They shoot the Jews! Come see the nightmare!'[17]

Others joined her, then tried to pull her away from the window before she became a target. Michelson resisted. Determined to bear witness, she watched as the columns went by, moving at a half run, trampling any who could not sustain the pace. And when the street was finally still, she stared down at the bloodied bodies that lay scattered across the cobblestones. In the hours that followed these were collected – 700 of them, Michelson heard – and buried in a single grave in the old Jewish cemetery. None of the Jews left behind knew what had happened to the thousands who had been led away.

They, and the thousand Berliner Jews who had arrived that morning, had been marched out of the city on the Moscow road and led in batches to the chosen killing site, a clearing in the nearby Rumbula Forest. This site had been chosen with customary thoroughness – it was close enough for walking, far enough for secrecy, and blessed with soil that was easy to excavate. The staggered arrivals were ordered to strip, then hustled through a gauntlet of kicks and blows to one of three pits, where a dozen schnapps-fuelled marksmen were working in shifts, forcing each new batch to lie face down on the bleeding bodies of its predecessor and dispatching each new victim with a single bullet from their Russian automatics.

It took twelve hours to kill twelve thousand, but Himmler's message ordering clemency still arrived several hours too late.

The refurbished multi-purpose ghetto at Theresienstadt received its first intake – a shipment of Jewish children, women and old men from Prague. A second would arrive from Brno three days later. Of the 144,000 Jews who eventually passed through the ghetto gates, 17,500 would survive the war.

On the previous evening Rommel had written to his wife that he was 'full of confidence', and the events of the next thirty-six hours would bear this out.[18] His plan for 30 November was to launch the 15th Panzer against the 6th New Zealand Brigade's positions on the Sidi Rezegh escarpment, with the 21st Panzer and *Ariete* in a dual supportive role, exerting pressure on the New Zealanders from the east and holding off the British forces to the south. The 15th Panzer had taken more than a few knocks during its unsuccessful battle for El Duda, but Rommel was in no mood for a postponement, and by early afternoon the division was ready to go. A ferocious artillery bombardment was launched, which 'smothered everything under a heavy pall of dust and smoke'.[19] The Germans, having survived an RAF attack and worked out a way through the minefields, sent in the tanks and infantry. Above them, the New Zealanders watched the approaching armour with dismay. 'Infantry were crossing down the southern escarpment and moving northward through the wadis. The 25-pounders had practically ceased firing . . . One by one the anti-tank guns were knocked out. Two more sent up by Brigade HQ suffered a similar fate after they had fired a few shots . . . Enemy infantry moved in from the south. As they neared the sector and crossed the ridges the tanks opened fire . . . Firing as they came, the enemy armour breasted the escarpment and fanned out across the lower ground. The 24th Battalion was overrun . . . A few men made a break and escaped.'[20]

As the attackers swept along the ridge towards Point 175 and down towards the Trigh Capuzzo, over 600 of the 6th New Zealand Brigade's 855 men were taken prisoner. The 4th New Zealand Brigade still held Belhamed and Zaafran – now the only heights in Kiwi hands – and the 6th Brigade's escaping survivors were sent to the former, despite their commander's request that they be allowed to retire into Tobruk. The South Africans were still supposedly riding to the rescue, and XIII Corps had not given up hope of reversing its perilous situation.

Where were the South Africans? Where was the 7th Armoured Division? Both had finally got moving that morning, but like particularly shy suitors seemed prone to lose heart at the slightest setback. Challenged south of Sidi Rezegh, the 7th Armoured decided on a new course – they would swing eastwards around the apparent block, attack and take Point 175, and thus free the way for the South Africans to move west along the Trigh Capuzzo and relieve the New Zealanders. Unfortunately, the 7th Armoured proved incapable of wresting Point 175 from the numerically inferior *Ariete*, and the South Africans debouched on to the Trigh Capuzzo seven miles further west, only to fall back after a single skirmish. The South Africans were now further away from the desperate New Zealanders than they had been that morning. That evening their commander, General Pienaar, received a bitterly clear message from General Freyberg: 'Our position is untenable unless you can capture [Sidi Rezegh] before dawn on 1 December. You will therefore carry out this task at once.'[21]

The bitterness was appropriate, the clarity both welcome and rare, but the order itself was impossible to fulfil. Pienaar, having done nothing for several days, was now being asked to march through *Ariete* and the 21st Panzer in a matter of hours, a task that even General Norrie realized was beyond the South Africans. He told Pienaar not to move before first light.

Rommel could hardly have asked for more, but he knew, as well as Auchinleck, that there was less to this than met the eye. The *Afrikakorps* had entered Crusader with 244 tanks, and that morning only 60 remained in running order. More had been lost during the day, and more would be lost in tomorrow's planned assault on Belhamed. During that day's battle Rommel had discussed the supply situation with his nominal superior, General Bastico, and they had sent a joint plea for more guns, trucks and tanks to their political bosses. If these failed to arrive, it would not matter who held Sidi Rezegh or Belhamed – British reinforcements would simply overwhelm the shrinking Axis army.

'This evening we are going to try and get a convoy of five steamships through by breaking the blockade,' Ciano wrote in his diary. 'How many will make it?'[22]

Soon after 11.00 the homecoming *Komet* and departing *Thor* drew up alongside each other in the mouth of the Elbe estuary. The captains talked shop for an hour or so before going their separate ways, *Komet* moving upriver towards Hamburg on the last leg of a voyage that had lasted 515 days, *Thor* setting off on a 17-day coastal journey to the Gironde estuary in south-west France. After bad weather and enemy activity had detained her for several weeks, *Thor* would begin her second epic journey on 17 January. It would last eight months, account for ten enemy merchantmen and end in a ball of fire – the raider succumbing to an accidental explosion in Yokohama Harbour.

Unknown to Brooke-Popham in Singapore, London's agonizing over Matador had been sub-contracted to the Dominions. The replies coming in reflected the divisions within the British politico-military establishment over the wisdom of pre-emptive action. The Australians were all for going ahead, with or without US support; the New Zealanders were more cautious, recommending such action only if the Americans were 'in general agreement and . . . willing to offer such assurances of assistance as [their] constitutional situation allows'.[23] The South Africans were confident of US support, the Canadians, whose answer arrived early on the following day, were opposed. 'So long as there is uncertainty about the degree and immediacy of US support,' the latter's submission read, 'it would be a terrible mistake to commit any course of action which might result in war between Japan and the British Commonwealth of Nations.'[24]

The British chiefs of staff agreed with the Canadians.

In Washington British intelligence of an imminent Japanese attack on Thailand – including the Kra Isthmus – reached Hull's desk. The Sunday edition of the *New York Times*, which lay beside it, featured excerpts from a recent and particularly belligerent speech by Tojo. The intelligence was faulty, the speech neither Tojo's nor accurately translated, but both seemed credible enough to Hull. He phoned Roosevelt at Warm Springs and urged an immediate return to Washington.

MONDAY 1 DECEMBER

Kido Butai was keeping Japanese hours, and it was only 01.34 when the sun went down behind Nagumo's ships. Shortly thereafter the fleet crossed the International Date Line and found itself briefly returned to November. It was now halfway to the intended launch-point north of Oahu.

Aboard *Akagi*, Chuichi Nagumo's anxieties showed no sign of abating. The fifty-four-year-old vice-admiral had enjoyed a long and varied career in the navy, with many years at sea, a few with the general staff, and one studying other navies in Europe and the US. But he had no experience of naval aviation, and it was seniority, not aptitude, which had seen him appointed commander of the First Air Fleet seven months earlier. His immediate subordinates – Kusaka, Genda and Fuchida – had the experience he lacked, and Nagumo had been professional enough to give them their heads, but his instinctive distrust of the Pearl Harbor operation persisted, and when push came to shove the First Air Fleet's 20,000 lives were his responsibility.

Nagumo was popular with both officers and men, but Fuchida's first impression had been one of conservatism. Not even its author had denied that this was a risky operation, and Nagumo was more averse to risk than most. When one of the September game table trials had seen two of his carriers sunk and two damaged for insignificant American losses, he had taken it as confirmation of his doubts. When the other had proved successful, he had pointed out that real seas were rougher. If the moment ever came when circumstances dictated a choice between upping the stakes and scooping a modest pot, there was little doubt which way Nagumo would jump. He might be stuck with a gambler's plan, but he was not a gambler.

In Tokyo an Imperial Conference opened at 14.05 in Room One East of the Imperial Palace, Emperor Hirohito perched on his dais above the political and military leaders. There were two inter-related items on the agenda: the failure of the negotiations with the United States and the government's desire for a declaration of war on the United States, Great Britain and the Netherlands.

Prime Minister Tojo kicked off proceedings with a general statement of the position. The United States, he said, had refused to make concessions, and had even added fresh demands – most notably a complete withdrawal from China and a de facto Japanese abandonment of the Tripartite Pact. 'This not only belittled the dignity of our empire,' he continued, 'and made it impossible to harvest the fruits of the China Incident, but also threatened the very existence of our empire.' Diplomacy had failed, and time was running out for the military. 'Under the circumstances, our empire has no alternative but to begin war . . .'[1]

Foreign Minister Togo took over, offering a more detailed account of the negotiations. The Americans had stuck to their principles without stopping to consider how relevant these were to the 'actual situation' in eastern Asia, and without showing any 'indication of a willingness to compromise'. On the contrary, their proposal of 26 November had represented a 'conspicuous retrogression'. If Japan were to accept it, 'the international position of our empire would be reduced to a status lower than it was prior to the Manchurian Incident, and our very survival would inevitably be at stake'.[2]

After Chief of Staff Nagano had announced the navy's readiness to begin operations, Tojo stressed the people's support for their government, then somewhat spoiled the effect by calling for 'stringent' security measures against Communists, nationalist extremists, foreigners, rumour-mongers and ordinary people who expressed any concern over where their next meal was coming from.[3]

Finance Minister Kaya thought the domestic economy would cope, but admitted that other countries caught up in the empire's struggle for survival might have something to worry about. The soon-to-be-invaded countries of south-east Asia were big importers, and would suffer when their economic lifelines were cut. Japan did not have enough reserve capacity to make up the difference, Kaya said, before adding, in a chilling echo of the Nazi debate which preceded the invasion of the Soviet Union, that 'for quite a long time it will not be possible for us to be concerned with the livelihood of the peoples in these areas'.[4] Compounding the intended crime, Agriculture Minister Ino stressed that Japan itself would need to import more rice from these countries.

A question and answer session followed, with Yoshimichi Hara, President of the Privy Council, asking the questions on the Emperor's behalf. Did the American definition of China include Manchuria? No one seemed to know. Were the US and Britain too powerful for Japan? Not at all. Had preparations been made to deal with the inevitable air raids? It was hoped that those burned out of their homes would find refuge either 'elsewhere' or in yet-to-be-constructed 'simple shelters'. This last answer – which exemplified the ludicrously improvisational nature of the entire project – gave even Hara pause for thought: 'It is not enough merely to have given thought to the matter,' he said sternly. 'Your plans are inadequate.'[5]

As, on so many levels, they were. But like everyone else in Room One East, Hara was too busy revelling in national hubris – 'our nation . . . is, from a spiritual point of view, certainly unsurpassed in all the world' – to really concern himself with the interests of ordinary people, Japanese or otherwise. The United States was being 'utterly conceited, obstinate and disrespectful', he said, and such an attitude could not be tolerated 'If we were to give in, we would give up, in one stroke, not only our gains in the Sino-Japanese and Russo-Japanese wars, but also the benefits of the Manchurian Incident. This we cannot do.'[6]

War was indeed inevitable, and a long-term war at that. Hara thought it important to 'bring about an early settlement', to 'start thinking now about how to end the war.' Tojo agreed. Though Japan was 'fully prepared for a long war', he was just as keen to see 'an early conclusion'. But like Hara, like all his stiff-backed colleagues in Room One East, he had no idea how this might be achieved, only a reckless hope that some stroke of outrageous fortune would confound the unfavourable odds. The vehicle would be set in motion, the lack of brakes left for later consideration. And all in the cause of 'putting His Majesty's mind at ease'.[7]

Aboard *Nagato*, Yamamoto took a call from the Imperial Palace – the Emperor wished to see him at 10.45 on Wednesday morning. As most Japanese knew, it was traditional for Emperors to wish their commanders well on the eve of war, and Yamamoto, not wishing to alarm his public, boarded the 16.00 train from Iwakuni in civilian clothes. If the news was as he expected, his staff would send the prepared message to Nagumo.

In the Philippines there was a sighting of unidentified, presumably Japanese aircraft over Clark Field. Over the next two days there would be several more sightings, causing the leader of Brereton's interceptors to remark: 'They've got all they need now. The next time they won't play. They'll come in without knocking.'[8]

The planes were most likely coming from Formosa, which raised the question of US reconnaissance. Shouldn't their planes be over-flying the Japanese airfields on that island? Brereton thought so, and requested permission from MacArthur to mount 'high-altitude photo missions of southern Formosa, particularly in the region of Takao, a large Japanese base from which the first signs of action were anticipated'.[9]

MacArthur rejected the request. The war warning had forbidden any 'overt acts' against the Japanese, and he feared that such missions might fall into that category.

At 01.00 von Rundstedt received notification that his resignation had been accepted. His replacement, the 6th Army commander, Field Marshal von Reichenau, was given orders to halt the retreat of the 1st Panzer Army on a line some six miles short of the Mius. When these were passed on, chaos ensued, with motorized units which had already reached the river turning back into the path of those which had not.

Von Kleist was adamant he could not defend Hitler's chosen line and continued to press the case for the Mius line. He had the support of General Georg von Sodenstern, the Army Group South chief of staff, but not his new superior – von Reichenau actually broke in on a telephone conversation between Halder and von Sodenstern to confirm his agreement with Hitler's orders. Halder then talked to von Kleist's chief of staff, Colonel Zeitzler, and was given more evidence in support of the opposing view. The 1st Panzer Army's divisions were so under-strength that two commanders had suffered complete nervous breakdowns, Zeitzler said, and on Hitler's chosen defence line the infantry would have no choice but to 'lie without cover on the hard-frozen ground'.[10] Most of the artillery was now back on the Mius line, where substantial defensive positions already existed. Neither Zeitzler nor von Kleist could understand why their troops 'should stand here and have the enemy punch through their line when nine kilometres in back of them there is a much better position'.[11]

After hearing from von Sodenstern that von Reichenau was showing 'no inclination to endorse the arguments advanced', Halder took the matter to Jodl and asked him to 'present the facts' to the Führer.[12] Jodl passed the poison chalice to von Brauchitsch, who entered Hitler's presence with some trepidation. But on this occasion luck was with the army commander. Before he could broach the subject, a telephone call came in from von Reichenau – Soviet forces had punched a hole in that part of the new line held by the SS *Leibstandarte* 'Adolf Hitler' Division, and he wanted permission to fall back on the Mius line. Hitler had no choice but to agree. 'Now we are where we could have been last night,' Halder noted. 'It was a senseless waste of strength and time, and to top it we have lost von Rundstedt.'[13]

Twenty miles north of Moscow the German juggernaut had finally stuck, wheels spinning wildly in an icy vacuum. Krasnaya Polyana, Pushki, Gorki and Katyushki had been occupied with the usual ferocious abruptness, the railway at nearby Lobnya blown up by a raiding group, but already the Soviets were hitting back with their appallingly effective T-34s and seemingly inexhaustible infantry. Katyushki, the southernmost of these villages, changed hands more than once in the course of the day, and none of the newly occupied towns felt even remotely secure. Further advance, for the moment at least, was out of the question.

It was the same along the Moscow–Volga Canal, where repeated attacks by the 1st Shock Army were stretching the 3rd Panzer Group to the limit. Only five days after seizing his 'springboard to the East', Reinhardt was telling Bock that further advances were impossible, and urging the need to occupy a defensible line.

It was the same on the Moscow–Leningrad axis, where Hoepner's other panzer corps, after taking Klushino, Matushkino and the Kryukovo terminus of a Moscow suburban rail line, suddenly discovered they could take no more.

It was the same on the Volokolamsk highway, where the SS soldiers of the *Das Reich* Division spent that Monday in another vain and bloody attempt to prise Beloborodov's Siberians out of Lenino.

The only German successes came further south. Several villages were taken in small infantry advances north of the Moscow River, and the 4th Army's long-deferred offensive was launched, albeit by only a single army corps. The four divisions involved different fortunes. While the 292nd Infantry broke through to Akulovo, on the opposite flank the 183rd Infantry made little progress. Between them, the 3rd Motorized pushed through and out the other side of Naro-Fominsk, and the 258th Infantry took a giant stride towards Moscow, advancing over ten miles before nightfall. Reaching the village of Yushkovo, a mile or so north of the Kiev highway, the leading detachment sought shelter from the cold in a line of concrete pillboxes. They were thirty miles from the Kremlin.

As von Bock reported during the day, only 'local successes' were now possible. And just in case von Brauchitsch, Halder and Hitler hadn't yet got the message – a more than reasonable supposition given his conversation with von Brauchitsch on the previous day – he also sent off a confirmatory telegram. The current attacks might 'result in modest gains' but would 'scarcely have a strategic effect'. As the fighting of the past fortnight had shown, any notion of a Soviet collapse was a wild dream. Stuck where they were, at the gates of the Russian transport hub, his armies were bound to find themselves fighting a defensive battle against much greater numbers. 'The forces of this army group,' von Bock insisted, were not equal to this, 'even for a limited time.' Supposing 'the improbable should become possible' and Moscow was reached, his 'forces would not nearly be sufficient to encircle Moscow and seal it off to the south-east, east and north-east'. As such, 'the attack appears to be without sense or purpose . . .'[14]

In Orsha the pfennig had finally dropped, but not in Rastenburg. During the afternoon, Hitler was on the phone to von Bock, demanding to know why those 4th Army units that had broken through the Soviet line were now advancing towards Moscow, rather than swinging east to encircle the Soviet units that had been in front of them. Von Bock wearily explained that he and von Kluge no longer had the numbers to pull off such encirclements, and thanked his lucky stars that Hitler was too busy obsessing over Rostov to pursue the matter.

The Führer was not the only one clinging to wild dreams. Halder was still extolling the 'last reserves' argument, first in a telephone conversation with von Bock, then to himself in his diary: 'An effort must be made to bring the enemy to his knees by applying the last ounce of strength. Once it is conclusively shown that this is impossible, we shall make new decisions.'[15] He was, of course, 'concerned about the human sacrifice' but showed no sign of losing any sleep over it. Or, indeed, over the possibility of a Soviet counter-offensive. How could they possibly mount one? As both he and von Brauchitsch pointed out that day, the Red Army had no significant reserves.

If von Bock and Halder had been men prone to metaphor, they might have likened the situation in front of Moscow to a pair of boxers expending their last reserves of energy prior to collapsing where they stood. The Russian writer Konstantin Simonov saw things differently – in his view the energy expended in each German blow was being transferred to the recipient, lending weight to an inevitable counter-attack. The Germans might be running out of energy, but their Soviet opponents 'were beginning to feel like a spring that is compressed by a terrific force, but however tightly compressed will always preserve enough tensility to spring back. It was precisely this feeling of both moral and physical vigour, this innermost conviction that they could stand up to any ordeal and hit back at the first opportunity, that animated the men . . .'[16]

    Von Clausewitz would have agreed with Simonov. An invader who suddenly found himself forced on to the defensive had reached 'the culmination point.' Beyond it was 'the turnaround, the rebound', the power of which was 'usually much greater than the force of the thrust'.[17]

In Leningrad a particular sight and sound was becoming familiar: a brightly coloured children's sled loaded with a sheet-swathed corpse, its runners squeaking and squealing on the icy ground. Over 11,000 of the city's inhabitants had now died of starvation, and winter was only just beginning.

The tanks of the 15th Panzer set off at 04.00, reaching the southern slopes of Belhamed as darkness segued into a misty dawn. The divisional artillery opened up on the slopes above, shrouding the whole battlefield in falling clouds of dust and blinding the enemy gunners. The losses and stress of the last few days had disorganized the New Zealanders, and the mines brought by Clifton's convoy had not been laid. Some of the infantry were still brewing their breakfast cuppa, others burying yesterday's dead, when the German tanks loomed out of the half-light. Those few guns that were pointed in the right direction had time only for a round or two before their gunners fell within range of the panzer machine guns.

Belhamed overrun, the panzers swept on towards the New Zealanders' divisional HQ, where Freyberg was desperately trying to reach Norrie on the radio. As his gunners surrendered only 200 yards away, Freyberg got Norrie's promise that the South Africans would keep *Ariete* and the 21st Panzer busy while the 4th Armoured Brigade helped cover the New Zealanders' withdrawal.

The 4th Armoured Brigade was already on the way, Crisp and his comrades having been woken before dawn with the news that the New Zealanders were in danger of being overrun. 'It was a shock to us,' he wrote later, 'to discover that our complete ignorance of the course the battle was taking, except in our limited vicinity, was concealing a setback of such magnitude.'[18]

The attempt to save something substantial from the disaster was as badly handled by the British and allied commanders as everything else in these few days, the 4th Armoured Brigade clearing a safe route to the south as the New Zealanders headed east towards Zaafran. Fortunately for the latter, *Ariete* and the 21st Panzer ignored a direct order to stay where they were – an anvil to the 15th Panzer's hammer – and headed west towards Sidi Rezegh, thereby opening an easterly escape route for Freyberg and his fellow survivors.

There were precious few of them, and all were evacuated to the frontier. Two and a half thousand men, forty-five guns and a mountain of equipment had fallen into German hands – in three days of fighting the division had been all but destroyed. El Duda remained in British hands, but only as an outpost of a re-isolated Tobruk. The Germans were in control of Sidi Rezegh and the principal heights to the north and west, the British licking their wounds in the distant desert. It looked, as the first battle of Sidi Rezegh had looked, like a decisive victory.

But the cumulative cost had been far too high, and the Germans, from corps commander to private, knew it well. Crisp, watching the German victors through his binoculars from the Sidi Rezegh ridge, thought he had 'never seen such a jaded, dispirited lot of men. Many of them were capless, and the slanting rays of the early sun revealed starkly the dirt and dishevelment, the weariness of the spirit reflected in those weary faces . . . If the enemy had just won another Sidi Rezegh battle, those blokes didn't know it.'[19]

A German officer who spoke to the captured New Zealander General Kippenberger was quite clear: 'We have taken Belhamed and our eastern and western forces have joined hands. But it is no use. We have lost the battle. Our losses are too heavy.'[20] Von Mellenthin was equally succinct: 'On paper we seemed to have won the Crusader battle. But the price was too heavy; the Panzergruppe had been worn down . . .'[21]

The Axis troops were in desperate need of rest and resupply. They would get neither.

The Italian navy was still trying, and still failing, to resupply Rommel. Alerted by an intelligence intercept, four light cruisers and three destroyers of Force K had left Malta late on 30 November. Around 03.30 on 1 December they found and sank the *Adriatico*, a merchant ship carrying military supplies, and a few hours later, some sixty miles north of Tripoli, they caught and sank the tanker *Iridio Mantovani* and the destroyer *Alvise da Mosto*.

This was 'not brilliant', Ciano conceded. Nor were the photographs of Italian prisoners playing football and attending concerts in Egypt, which had appeared in a Vatican newspaper. An annoyed Mussolini had insisted on a formal protest. The Duce considered it a well-known fact that his troops were 'inclined to let themselves be taken prisoner. If they see that their comrades are having such a good time over there, who can hold them back?'[22]

And Italy's grip on the further-flung provinces of the new Roman Empire was not as firm as it should be. Ciano's meeting in

Zagreb with the Croatian leader Pavelić had been postponed – the local police could not guarantee his security.

Hitler's Monday ended with another philosophical discussion about the Jews. When one aide suggested that Aryan women divorcing their Jewish husbands after 1933 had been guilty of a less than creditable conformism, and another argued that in making the original marriage the woman had already displayed a lamentable lack of racial instinct, Hitler interjected that before the Nazi takeover 'our intellectual class hadn't the least idea what a Jew was'. This was why he had introduced his race laws.

He allowed that 'there are Jews in Germany who have behaved correctly – in the sense that they've invariably refrained from doing injury to the German idea'. The problem, of course, was that these Jews had failed to take issue with their more destructive co-religionists. Hitler conceded that most Jews were unaware of 'the destructive power they represent', but still refused to excuse them: 'He who destroys life is himself risking death. That's the secret of what is happening to the Jews.'

That said, the Jew certainly played a useful role. Nature had made him 'the ferment that causes peoples to decay, thus providing these peoples with an opportunity for a healthy reaction'. Powerful and destructive Jews – men like St Paul and Trotsky – were really the Aryan's best friends: 'by the fact of their presence, they provoke the defensive reaction of the attacked organism.'[23]

Hermann Göring remained Hitler's successor and leader of the Luftwaffe, with further ill-defined responsibilities for running the German war economy. As potentially decisive battles raged outside Moscow and Tobruk, he took the short ride from Paris to Saint-Florentin for a meeting with the French collaborationist leader Marshal Pétain. The two men had a straightforward deal to sign – German use of French naval facilities in North Africa in return for the freeing of French POWs – and Göring was hoping that twenty minutes would suffice. He angrily emerged three hours later. The deal had been duly signed, but Pétain had apparently forgotten that his was the defeated nation, and presented Göring with a list of French conditions for future collaboration. When Göring had refused it, the Frenchman had reached out and slid it into the German's breast pocket.

The *Reichsmarschall* returned to Paris, where real work awaited him. A lengthy sojourn in the Jeu de Paume, and shorter visits to several smaller galleries, resulted in a large shipment of paintings leaving next day for his Karinhall estate. Far from sated, Göring and his private train moved on to Antwerp, The Hague and Amsterdam, where virgin galleries awaited. A few more days and he was back in Paris, shopping for his wife at her favourite couturier, seemingly oblivious of the turn his party's war had taken.

Ambassador Oshima had also been enjoying the arts – a Mozart festival in Austria – when his staff summoned him back to Berlin. His employers in Tokyo wanted Germany's promise of a declaration of war in writing, and they wanted it immediately.

Ribbentrop, whom Oshima managed to see late that evening, was his usual infuriating self. Though personally eager to oblige, he could not possibly sign a formal agreement without first consulting the Führer. Tomorrow would have to do.

In London the War Cabinet debated the Soviet demand for British declarations of war on Finland, Romania and Hungary. There was no enthusiasm for such a step, but, as far as the latter two countries were concerned, little in the way of reluctance – both had unpleasantly fascistic regimes and had volunteered their soldiers for Barbarossa.

Finland was another matter. Churchill had spoken for much of the English-speaking world when he described the Finns' fierce resistance to the Soviet invasion of November 1939 as 'heroic, nay, sublime', and some of this sympathy had survived their later joining of the Barbarossa bandwagon.[24] Churchill had been angry enough to demand the Finns' subjection to 'every inconvenience in our power', but understanding enough not to push matters any further.[25]

Inconvenience was not enough for Stalin – he wanted British declarations of war on all three countries, and particularly on Finland. Churchill argued that these were both unnecessary – 'our extreme blockade is already against them'[26] – and counterproductive: such declarations would lock the three countries more firmly into their alliances with Germany and, in Finland's case, upset their American sympathizers. 'Do not pray suppose,' Churchill wrote to Stalin, 'it is any want of zeal or comradeship that makes us doubt the advantage of this step.'[27]

The Soviet leader was unimpressed; the continuing British failure to declare war on Finland was 'intolerable'.[28] Churchill reiterated his arguments on 21 November, but accompanied this final appeal with a promise to declare war if the Finns refused to stop fighting in the next fortnight. On 28 November he wrote to the Finnish leader, Marshal Mannerheim, urging him to do just that. Churchill said he was 'deeply grieved at what I see coming', adding that 'it would be most painful to the many friends of your country in England if Finland found herself in the dock with the defeated Nazis'.[29]

No reply had arrived when the War Cabinet met on 1 December, and a decision was taken: the Finns would be given five days to withdraw their troops from Soviet soil. An answer arrived within one: 'I am sure you will realize,' Mannerheim wrote to Churchill, 'that it is impossible for me to cease my present military operations before my troops have reached positions which in my opinion would give us the security required.' It was, he added, 'very kind of you to send me a personal message in these trying days'.[30]

This was the first War Cabinet meeting for General Alan Brooke, the new Chief of the Imperial General Staff. He had spent the day familiarizing himself with the current situation. Crusader still seemed in the balance, the Russian situation, Rostov aside, only a hair's breadth from disaster. The Japanese threat was looming, and Brooke's predecessor Dill had, as he freely admitted, 'done practically nothing' to meet it.[31]

At this same meeting Churchill made reference to Auchinleck's dismissal of Cunningham five days earlier. 'It was doubtful,' he added, 'whether this action was in General Auchinleck's competence.' Nobody seemed to mind.[32]

Eight days had passed since the sinking of *Atlantis*, five since the crew's transfer to the relative comfort of the supply ship *Python*. The latter had been scheduled to refuel and replenish three U-boats on the previous day, but only one, U-68, had turned up. Another, U-A, arrived that day and was taking on fuel when the alarm sounded. For the watching members of the *Atlantis* crew, the sudden appearance of a three-funnelled ship on the horizon offered déjà vu at its most depressing.

The Germans sprang into action. U-A was quickly cut loose, but U-68, which had been taking on torpedoes through open deck hatches, took an interminable time to free herself. *Python*'s boats, meanwhile, were being readied – the supply ship, with no means of defending herself, was a lost cause.

Aware that there were U-boats in the area, and keen to avoid *Dunedin*'s fate, the *Dorsetshire* captain advanced on an oblique course without cutting his speed. His signals went unanswered, but warning shots had the desired effect – the Germans hurried to scuttle and abandon the doomed *Python*. *Dorsetshire* went on her way, unaware that U-A had missed with five torpedoes.

Once the British had fully departed, the two U-boats surfaced once more, and a hundred or so men from the *Atlantis* and *Python* crews were crammed aboard each, leaving the rest to ride in a flotilla of open boats. Other U-boats and four Italian submarines would eventually share in the chore of ferrying them all the way back to France.

A message from Churchill was waiting for the returning Roosevelt, long on courtesy, long on suggestions. 'It seems to me that one important method remains unused in averting war between Japan and our two countries,' the British Prime Minister wrote, 'namely a plain declaration, secret or public as may be thought best, that any further act of aggression by Japan will lead immediately to the gravest consequences. I realize your constitutional difficulties . . . Forgive me, my dear friend, for presuming to press such a course upon you, but I am convinced that it might make all the difference and prevent a melancholy extension of the war.'[33] Of course, the extension would only prove melancholic if America was not pulled into a British–Japanese war – hence Churchill's interest in a joint ultimatum. Roosevelt was not personally averse to such a step, but the 'constitutional difficulties' which Churchill alluded to – his inability to taken certain steps without Congressional approval – were real enough.

Across town Nomura and Kurusu were meeting Hull at the State Department. The discussion ran along familiar lines – the three of them were only going through the motions, and they knew it. Hull then talked the whole situation over with Roosevelt at the White House. Both saw some advantage in a direct appeal to the Emperor, but Hull, who had actually prepared a couple of drafts, still considered this a tactic of last resort. Churchill's idea of a final warning was also put on hold.

That Monday afternoon Roosevelt entertained British Ambassador Lord Halifax, and Hull's absence – the Secretary was feeling unwell – may have reduced the President's political inhibitions. The two men discussed numerous hypothetical situations involving Japanese aggression, and the President as good as promised American support for British counter-action against any of them. 'In the case of any direct attack on ourselves or the Dutch,' Halifax reported the President as saying, 'we should obviously all be together.'[34] In seeking American approval for Matador, Halifax mistakenly informed Roosevelt that only pre-emptive *naval* action was planned against a Japanese landing on the Kra Isthmus, and the President reiterated that the British could count on US support.

Alarm bells were ringing louder. An updated ONI report stated that US-Japanese relations had broken down, and implied that war was imminent. ONI was still unwilling to guess which way the Japanese would jump, but the evidence presented in the report all pointed to the south. A huge build-up of troops in Indo-China and Formosa was noted, along with an appropriate redeployment of naval and merchant shipping. The Japanese carriers were all, allegedly, in home waters or the south-eastern Pacific. Japanese nationals were being evacuated from Hong Kong, the Philippines, the Dutch East Indies, Singapore and India.

The head of ONI's Far Eastern desk, Commander McCollum, felt sufficiently alarmed to write an accompanying memo, expanding on the evidence and adding detail. At a meeting that morning he read it aloud to Admiral Stark and other naval leaders. Knowing nothing of the war warnings which had gone out on 27 November, McCollum anxiously asked whether his superiors believed the Pacific Fleet had been sufficiently alerted. They assured him it had.

Two other events offered confirmation of McCollum's fears. In Washington Togo's 'war will come quicker than anyone dreams' message to Oshima was decoded and translated. And in Hawaii Rochefort's enemy fleet-tracking unit realized with a shock that the Japanese had changed their call-signs again, after only one month. This had never happened before. It represented, as the unit's daily summary put it, 'an additional progressive step in preparing for active operations on a large scale'.[35]

TUESDAY 2 DECEMBER

Admiral Nagano and General Sugiyama, the two Japanese chiefs of staff, arrived at the Imperial Palace late in the morning. The Emperor, who had already approved the decision for war, was now informed that hostilities were scheduled to commence on 8 December – 7 December in Hawaii. It was a Sunday, Nagano explained, and most of the American warships should be in port. The moon would be up until sunrise, which would help the launch. Asking no questions, the Emperor gave his sanction.

Back at his headquarters, Sugiyama sent a two-word message – *Hinode Yamagata* – to Japan's Southern Army commander, General Terauchi. This, a prearranged code, confirmed the 8 December date for launching the war, and, by implication, every other date and time in the Army's lengthy calendar of preparations.

At Yamashita's HQ in Samah, the struggle to get everything ready in time was already trying the nerves of his staff. Six days hence his troops were supposed to be fighting their way on to Thai and Malayan beaches, and the fleet he needed to get them there, a fleet scrounged from ports all over east Asia, was still arriving in dribs and drabs. Those boats that had arrived were being loaded in laborious fashion – Samah had no jetty, and all the supplies had to be transferred from shore to ship by lighter. There were also disputes over what to take: the Third Air Group, apparently oblivious to the one-trunk-per-two-officers rule, had been happily loading 'iron beds, bathtubs and sofas'.[1] This was too much for Shipping Officer Kera, who announced, with a loud bang on his table, that all inessential baggage would be thrown overboard.

Aboard *Nagato*, Yamamoto's Chief of Staff Matome Ugaki received the naval go-ahead from Nagano's deputy, Vice-Admiral Ito. At 17.30 he sent *Kido Butai* a simple, prearranged instruction – *Niitaka-yama nobore* (Climb Mt. Niitaka) 1208. The ever-pessimistic Nagumo was being asked to scale the highest mountain in the Japanese Empire.

Not that his immediate boss was feeling particularly sanguine about the operation now in progress, as a private conversation at the Navy Ministry made clear. 'Considering how I opposed the war, I ought, properly speaking, to have resigned,' Yamamoto told Takei Daisuke that Tuesday afternoon. 'But it wasn't possible. One thing we could do now is disperse as many subs as possible around the southern Pacific so as to make the other side feel they've been set on by a swarm of hornets. If the hornets around it buzz loudly enough, even a hefty animal like a horse or cow will get worried, at least. American public opinion has always been very changeable, so the only hope is to make them feel as soon as possible that it's no use tackling a swarm of lethal stingers.'[2]

This was wishful thinking, and Yamamoto knew it.

Over at the Foreign Office, the usual pre-war instructions to destroy codes and related machinery were being sent out. Japanese embassies and consulates in London, Hong Kong, Singapore, Djakarta and Manila had already received theirs, and now it was the western hemisphere's turn. Staff at the Washington embassy were told to destroy all but a few designated codes and one of the two coding machines; those in provincial Havana, Panama, Vancouver, Ottawa, Portland, Seattle, Los Angeles and Honolulu were also warned 'not to arouse the suspicion of those on the outside'. An 'emergency situation' was expected, and all of Tokyo's employees were urged to 'remain calm'.[3]

Deception was rife. In Yokohama Harbour the Japanese liner *Tatuta Maru* set sail across the Pacific, with the apparent intention of returning expatriate Americans to their homeland and bringing back expatriate Japanese. The voyage had been heavily advertised in both America and Japan; its itinerary took in San Francisco, Manzanillo in Mexico and Balboa in Panama, with a scheduled return in early January.

The liner's captain had no idea that *Kido Butai* would beat him to Hawaii, but he knew something was up. He had been told to expect special instructions on 8 December, and given a large box to open when they arrived. The instructions were to turn back, and the box was full of pistols for quelling the potential passenger mutiny.

In the Philippines Brereton's newly appointed supply officer, Major Gregg, was making a series of unwelcome discoveries. There was insufficient capacity for overhauling the engines of those planes currently in the Philippines, let alone those needed and expected as reinforcement. There was a shortage of ammunition for the fighter pilots to practise with, and nowhere near enough for fighting the Japanese – only a sixth of the required estimate. And there was a shortage of bombs, particularly of those incendiaries needed for fulfilling's Marshall's stated intention of setting Japan's paper cities on fire.

The estimated delivery dates for the ammunition and bombs was March 1942, which would be cutting it fine even if the Japanese proved MacArthur right and deferred their attack until April. And this seemed increasingly unlikely to many of his subordinates, who noted the growing frequency of Japanese reconnaissance flights over Luzon and pressed for reconnaissance missions of their own over Formosa. MacArthur, however, refused to budge.

The battleship *Prince of Wales* and battlecruiser *Repulse* dropped their majestic anchors in Singapore's Sembawang naval base – salvation had arrived. 'The Japanese are caught in a trap of their own making,' the *Malaya Tribune* trumpeted: 'Neither by land nor sea nor in the air do they have even a glimmer of a chance of victory.'[4] This prognosis was widely shared. 'Everyone was told that the Japanese fleet was absolutely useless,' Richard Smith, a young rating on *Repulse* remembered; 'it was just a lot of ricepaper and string. We would go up there and knock them about and cause havoc – it would be a walkover and we would enjoy ourselves. This was the whole mentality when we were lying in the harbour with all the lights on. Everybody was ashore wining and dining and all the colonials we saw were making merry and having a wonderful time. The Fleet had arrived and Japan would not now enter the war.'[5]

Like MacArthur in the Philippines, the British military in Malaya were expecting a Japanese attack at some time in the future. And like him, they grossly underestimated Japanese readiness and military capability, as the latest draft of Matador made only too clear. Asking themselves the pertinent question – how long would it take the British forces to reach the relevant Thai beaches? – they came up with a detailed answer: twelve hours to detect an invasion fleet and request the go-ahead, the already-agreed thirty-six hours for London to authorize it, six hours to order the advance, forty-eight hours to reach the beaches and a final twenty-four to dig in – or more than five days altogether. What wasn't explained was how they would get there ahead of the enemy, who was only four days' sailing away. Or how the British troops would cope if they were still en route when the Japanese landed and were forced to fight an encounter battle on unprepared ground.

The situation in the south and the thwarting of his wishes by generals and fate were still playing on Hitler's mind. With the crucial battles around Moscow still teetering in the balance, he took the extraordinary decision to drop in on the 1st Panzer Army, which had, to all intents and purposes, abandoned operations for the duration of the winter. Three flights conveyed him, via Kiev and Poltava, to Zhdanov, where General von Kleist and the *Leibstandarte* commander SS General Sepp Dietrich were waiting for him.

Hitler was more than willing to disbelieve von Kleist – these regular army people always stuck up for each other – but the *Leibstandarte* commander was another matter. Dietrich had commanded his personal bodyguard as long ago as 1928, had toured Germany with him when power was just a dream. If anyone could be trusted, he could. Dietrich backed up von Kleist, and so did the pile of warning reports that the 1st Panzer Army had issued since mid-November, and which the Führer had not seen. Hitler ate humble pie and set off for home.

The weather had other ideas, grounding him overnight at Army Group South's Poltava HQ, where von Sodenstern was on hand to solve the mystery of the unseen reports. They had, it seemed, been passed on to Jodl and Keitel, along with many similar warnings of a verbal nature. Hitler then asked to see von Rundstedt, who was waiting in another room. As the field marshal told von Sodenstern immediately afterwards, 'a scene of reconciliation took place, in which Hitler excused himself on the grounds of a "misunderstanding", begged the field marshal to see that his health was restored by a period of sick leave and then once more place his incomparable services at his disposal'.[6]

Von Rundstedt was not reinstated. A private apology was one thing, a public admission of error something altogether different.

North and north-west of Moscow, the Soviet 16th, 20th and 1st Shock Armies had fought the German 3rd and 4th Panzer Groups to a virtual standstill. Battles still raged along the Moscow–Volga Canal, along the line from Krasnaya Polyana through Kryukovo to Lenino, but only insignificant stretches of snow-covered ground were changing hands. A 4th Panzer Group report on the 10th Panzer claimed it was no longer fit to attack – 'the men are so torpid that nothing can be done with them'.[7] These German forces were only going to reach Moscow if a breakthrough further south drew away the Soviet forces in front of them.

There was still movement. Further south, von Kluge's 9th and 20th Infantry Korps made inroads on either side of the Soviet 5th Army, the former advancing in a south-easterly direction towards the confluence of the Istra and Moscow Rivers, the latter in a north-easterly direction between the Kiev and Mozhaisk highways. If these two pincers could close with any strength, then the encirclement and destruction of the 5th Army seemed possible.

Having spent a freezing night in Yushkovo's concrete pillboxes – thirty men reported frostbitten fingers and toes when morning came – the leading detachment of the 20th Korps' 258th Infantry Division pushed on across the Golitsyno–Petrovskoye road, where the smoking chimneys of another village promised life-giving warmth. Burcevo was taken with little difficulty, allowing its occupiers the chance to warm themselves and their weapons.

They didn't have long to sit by the stoves. Their advance on the previous day had elicited the usual firefighter's response from Zhukov, and reserve units of the Soviet 33rd and 43rd Armies were already on their way to douse these particular flames. Soon after dark a brigade of T-34s supported by artillery and a single anti-aircraft gun drove the German infantry back across the road and into the dubious shelter of an already-burning Yushkovo.

Further south still, Guderian's latest attempt to encircle Tula was under way. Starting from a position around twelve miles north-east of the city, the 3rd and 4th Panzer attacked in a westerly direction, and succeeded, despite the minus 30°C conditions, in breaking through the Soviet forces defending Tula's road and railway lines. Once the railway had been reached and blown up at Revyakino, the 4th Panzer Reconnaissance Battalion pushed on to the road, some six miles further to the west. Assailed by Soviet forces and lacking support, it was forced to retreat. The armour behind it and the other arm of the intended encirclement were already bogged down by growing Soviet resistance.

Von Bock found the initial advance encouraging and was still seeking crumbs of comfort wherever he could find them. That evening he told all his corps commanders that 'the undoubtedly serious moment of crisis that the Russian defenders are facing must be exploited wherever the opportunity presents itself', but then privately admitted to his diary that he doubted whether any of his 'exhausted units' were capable of doing so.[8]

Earlier in the day a group representing the city of Smolensk had presented him with a certificate of thanks for their liberation from Bolshevism.

Numb-toed soldiers at Yushkovo had not taken their boots off, knowing full well the skin would come off with them. At the end of sentry duty men didn't dare lie down, because their foreheads were already sore and keeping warm was all that would keep the frostbite at bay. Soldiers who knelt in the snow found their knees frozen to the ground, while those who lay full length found ice forming between their tunic and coat. The hands of the gloveless froze to their rifles, causing strips of skin to pull away, revealing quick-freezing blood.

The cold also dehumanized. Deprived of winter clothing by the incompetence of their superiors, the German troops stole from the Russians. 'We pulled the boots off old men and women on the street if ours were wanting,' Willy Reese remembered. 'The torture of the marches embittered us to the point that we became impervious to the sufferings of others.' With the chronic supply situation, hunger was another constant companion, another reason to behave badly. Reese and his comrades 'weren't bothered by tears, hand-wringings and curses. We were the victors. War excused our thefts, encouraged cruelty, and the need to survive didn't go around getting permission from conscience.' In a farmhouse outside Schigry in the 2nd Army's sector, Reese saw one fellow soldier wolf down a proffered meal of bread and milk, only to demand honey, flour and lard. 'The farmer beseeched him, his wife cried, and in their fear of starving the couple tried to wrest his booty away from him. The soldier smashed in the farmer's skull, shot the farmer's wife and furiously torched the place.'[9]

One morning three weeks earlier, the citizens of Warsaw had emerged from their homes to find the slogan 'Poland will live! Poland will conquer!' scrawled or daubed across hundreds of walls and buildings, fences and pavements. The German authorities had reacted swiftly, promising serious punishment for both the artists and the owners of the surfaces in question. The Poles decided that action would speak louder than words. On that Tuesday a large number of factories in the Tarnow district of southern Poland suddenly found themselves without power – a huge explosion in the early hours had destroyed several buildings and furnaces of the local electricity generating station.

The Poles were far from alone. In Germany's ally Bulgaria, troops ordered west to fight the rebellious Serbs refused to go, and incidents of sabotage inside the country were increasing – three oil trains blown up in September, four German aircraft set ablaze in October, an oil refinery attacked in November. In allied Romania, production at the Ploesti oilfields – Germany's only major source of crude – had declined sharply through November after several successful acts of sabotage by the local workforce. In Greece near-famine conditions were feeding the nascent Communist resistance, and in Yugoslavia the Germans already had a full-scale war on their hands. Eastern Europe, a substantial part of that occupied realm which Hitler hoped to organize for victory, was showing all the signs of a resistance epidemic.

In Cyrenaica the two armies spent a day of dull skies and intermittent rain adjusting to another largely pyrrhic German victory. On the previous evening Auchinleck had descended on his army commander's HQ, just as he had after the last near-destruction of an Allied brigade on *Totensonntag*. There the similarity ended, however: Auchinleck had detected no desire on Ritchie's part to cut and run, and there was general agreement that the routing of the New Zealanders had not fundamentally changed the strategic situation. After two weeks of Crusader, the 8th Army was still deeply ensconced in territory previously held by the enemy, and the British hold on Tobruk now looked stronger than the Axis hold on their frontier defences.

Auchinleck had news of further reinforcements. The rest of the 1st Armoured Division – the 2nd Armoured Brigade with 166 tanks, the divisional artillery and an armoured car regiment – were soon to be sent forward, along with infantry brigades from Cyprus and India, more armoured cars from Syria and a reconnaissance battalion from Palestine. In the meantime the 11th Indian Brigade would advance into the area south of Sidi Rezegh, in the first move of a series that would see the 4th Indian Division substituted for the vanquished New Zealanders.

Ritchie's latest plan was strikingly similar to Cunningham's original. After forty-eight hours of regrouping, repositioning and replenishment, his intentions were, as Cunningham's had been, the destruction of the German armour and the relief of Tobruk. The 11th Indian Brigade would take Bir el Gubi – still held by the Italians eleven days after the first abortive attack by the South Africans – and secure the left flank of an advance on El Adem, due south of Tobruk, by the 4th Armoured Brigade. This advance would draw Rommel's panzers south and west, and free the way for XIII Corps' to establish a new corridor into Tobruk.

Rommel had no reinforcements to play with, only those forces, now exhausted and much reduced, with which he had started the battle. But he had just won a victory, and his first instinct was to exploit it. There was also the problem of the frontier garrisons, which were now essentially isolated. Another 'dash for the wire' would kill two birds with one stone, offering succour to the garrisons while keeping the British off-balance. Battalion groups from each panzer division would head off at first light on 3 December along the Via Balbia and Trigh Capuzzo towards Bardia and Sidi Azeiz, with tanks following behind as soon as they were ready. In the meantime a thorough reimposition of the siege would require a strengthening of the perimeter forces and the recapture of El Duda. And the British forces south of Sidi Rezegh still needed watching, and might well need stopping, which would take more than a couple of armoured cars.

Rommel's subordinates were appalled. He seemed intent on repeating his mistake of 24 November in committing, as Crüwell put it, 'the error of giving up to the enemy a battlefield on which *Afrikakorps* has won a victory and undertaking another operation some distance away, instead of destroying the enemy utterly'.[10]

Crüwell added that if Rommel was intent on another 'dash for the wire', he should commit all his forces to it, rather than disperse them, Cunningham-style, in several different directions. His own preference was to concentrate on the capture of El Duda.

Both Rommel and Crüwell were wrong, and for one simple reason – the Axis forces at their disposal were no longer strong enough to force a favourable decision in this battle. They could probably muster the strength to take El Duda, as Crüwell urged, but a local success like that would have no lasting significance. Rommel's plan did offer the possibility of a real strategic break-through, but only if the resources were there to implement it, and they were not.

In Italy Mussolini was wondering how to feed his population over the next few months. He could probably borrow the necessary half a million tons of grain from Germany, and pay it all back when the Italian harvest arrived in July, but asking Hitler for help in this regard would be somewhat humiliating. But then so, of course, would be food riots.

For Britons the news of von Kleist's expulsion from Rostov had provided the first welcome chink of light at the end of their ally's seemingly endless tunnel. Tuesday's *Daily Mirror* carried a celebra-tory cartoon: a slogan-plastered Goebbels – 'All Russian soldiers are now dead! The East Front war is over!' – in headlong flight from a looming Russian giant.[11]

The British War Cabinet was finally shown Hull's Ten Points and found them to be suitably harsh. It was then given even better news – Roosevelt had promised American support against a Japanese attack. 'In the light of this assurance,' Churchill said, 'we can now say to the Dutch that if any attack was made on them by Japan, we should at once come to their aid, and that we had every confidence that the United States would do so also.'[12]

In Washington it proved a quiet day on the diplomatic front, as if Roosevelt and Hull were still recovering from their fit of rashness in effectively guaranteeing the British and Dutch Empires in south-east Asia. The lead editorial in the *New York Times* concerned the Monroe Doctrine.[13] At first glance this seemed a strange choice of subject matter, but the paper's reasons soon became clear. The Doctrine, as defined by the newspaper – 'that the United States would oppose with all its force any extension of non-American sovereignty in the Western Hemisphere, and equally oppose the transfer of any part of the Western Hemisphere from one non-American power to another' – was clearly relevant to the current situation, not least in its clear rejection of any possible transfer of French Guiana to German control.

This, however, was not the main point: the paper was much more exercised by the cheek of the Japanese in claiming that their Greater East Asia Co-prosperity Sphere was essentially 'a Monroe Doctrine for Asia'. The very essence of the American version, the *New York Times* thundered, was 'the right of self-determination – that is, the right of every nation living in this hemisphere to decide its future for itself'. The Japanese intention, by contrast, was 'to stake out an area from which the influence of all other powers is barred and within which they can rule and plunder as they please'. And just in case the reader had somehow missed the difference, the writer spelled it out once more: the American Monroe Doctrine 'demands, and receives, scrupulous respect for the rights of every one of the American republics, great and small alike'.

This would have raised an eyebrow or two south of the Rio Grande.

Across town at the Waldorf-Astoria that Tuesday evening, another America was on display. Eleven hundred guests turned up to honour CBS's chief European correspondent, Ed Murrow, who, more than any other journalist, had brought the reality of the European war home to Americans. Murrow talked about the war, this new and terrible kind of war, 'twisting and tearing the social, political and economic fabric of the world', from which America still stood aside. Britain and Russia had no chance of winning the war on their own, Murrow said, no matter how much material aid they received from the United States. He understood the common British wish that America accept its responsibilities as the world's greatest power and enter the fray. 'No one who has lived and worked in London for the last three years can doubt,' he said, 'that the important decision, perhaps the final decision, that will determine the course of human affairs will be made not in front of Moscow, not on the sands of Libya, but along the banks of the Potomac.'[14]

Murrow was not to know that the decision had already been taken, and in Tokyo rather than Washington.

The instruction to destroy codes was not the only one Consul Kita received that day. 'In view of the present situation,' Tokyo informed him, 'the presence in port of warships, aircraft carriers and cruisers is of utmost importance. Hereafter, to the utmost of your ability, let me know, day by day. Wire me in each case whether or not there are observation balloons above Pearl Harbor or if there are any indications that they will be sent up. Also advise me whether or not the warships are provided with anti-torpedo nets.'[15]

There was no mistaking the significance of this message – only would-be attackers with bombs and torpedoes needed to know about balloons and nets – and it was duly intercepted by American intelligence. But four weeks later, when this clearest of warnings was finally translated, it was some way past its use-by date.

Yesterday's unexpected call-sign change had worried Kimmel and his intelligence chiefs, particularly as it coincided with a marked lessening of Japanese fleet radio traffic. If the former, along with the obvious diplomatic ructions, suggested the imminence of war, the latter suggested an enemy navy already at sea.

But where exactly? Kimmel had asked Layton to liaise with his opposite number at Cavite and produce a current location map for the Imperial Navy, and now, twenty-four hours later, he had it in front of him. The Japanese First and Second Carrier Divisions were nowhere to be seen. Didn't Layton know where they were?

Layton admitted he did not. 'I think they're in home waters, but I don't *know* where they are.'

'Do you mean to say they could be rounding Diamond Head and you wouldn't know it?' Kimmel asked.

'I hope they would be sighted by now,' was the best Layton could offer.[16]

Having crossed the International Date Line, Nagumo actually received the order to Climb Mount Niitaka on the day before it was sent – at 20.00 on 1 December. *Kido Butai*, however, was still keeping Tokyo time, and the fleet's calendars showed a less disorientating 2 December. The hour was more problematic, as each day's easterly progress took clocks further out of synch with the sun. On *Kido Butai*'s 2 December the latter set at 13.01, which seemed a trifle early.

By evening all the crews had been mustered and told, and every man in the fleet knew where it was headed. Masuda Shogo, the *Akagi* flight officer who had compared himself to one of the forty-seven *ronin* in Hitokappu Bay, recorded in his diary that 'everything is decided; there is neither here nor there, neither sorrow nor rejoicing'.[17]

WEDNESDAY 3 DECEMBER

At 10.45 the uniformed Yamamoto took part in a formalized exchange with his Emperor, bowed and took his leave, clutching the imperial rescript which allowed him to start a war. The Emperor, as Yamamoto told Ugaki two days later, seemed 'serene after fully realizing the inevitability of going to war'.[1]

Ugaki himself was getting excited. *Kido Butai* was encountering unusually calm seas, which had to be some sort of sign. Roosevelt and his military leaders were having their meetings, but they had no idea what was bearing down on them, 'that the biggest hand will be at their throat in four days to come'.[2]

In Samah Yamashita addressed his troops, and 'there was not even a cough to be heard' as he read out his army's orders. 'It infused new life into our death-defying resolution,' the watching Masanobu Tsuji wrote: 'It was a scene of deep emotion. Officers and men alike gave way to tears.'[3]

Similar scenes took place in Japanese bases across eastern Asia and the south-western Pacific. At Tainan Air Base on Formosa the pilots were briefly told of the decision for war, then given a stirring address by their deputy leader, Commander Kozono. Japan, he said, was facing 'the most serious threat ever to its existence . . . encircled by the ABCD powers, led by the Americans and British,

who are cutting off our supply of raw materials'. The oil embargo
was crippling Japan, and there was only one answer: 'if they don't
sell it to us, we must go and take it by force!'[4]

Hitler detected an unusual level of hostility during his sleepover at
Poltava, and told his valet Heinz Linge that he would never again
forsake his HQ for direct contact with his army commanders. The
paranoia spilled over into the subsequent flight. 'I'm glad you're sitting behind me,' he told the faithful Linge, 'instead of a
Gruppenführer who could shoot me in the back!'[5]

Outside Moscow the scales were beginning to tip. The 3rd Panzer
Group, which Bock was still hoping might help the 4th Panzer
Group forward, was at the end of its collective tether – the 6th
Panzer reported eighty cases of soldiers collapsing from exhaustion
in forty-eight hours. At the 4th Panzer Group HQ, Hoepner uni-
laterally called it a day. The reasons given, according to a divisional
battle diary, were 'physical and emotional over-exertion, unacceptable losses, and inadequate winter shelter'.[6]

The army and panzer group commanders might know it was all
over, but many of their long-suffering troops were finding it hard
to make the adjustment. The men of one SS regiment still
believed they could 'count the days on one hand until they
entered Moscow', and many of the less ideologically driven were
hoping that the current setbacks were only temporary, that a
simple transfusion of fuel and winter clothing could once again
transform the situation.[7] A report on the 11th Panzer's situation
exemplified this state of mind. After listing everything that the
Soviets were throwing at his division in Kryukovo – 'five new
enemy batteries and Stalin Organs which fire the dreaded rocket
salvos . . . several heavy tanks' – the writer happily assumed that
'the original line can be re-established with a counter-attack'. He
then went on to explain how he and his friends were burying their
fallen comrades – by digging a small hole in the frozen ground,
inserting a hand grenade and blowing out a shallow grave. 'That is
all we can do for them here.'[8]

Further south, the last spasms of Barbarossa were expiring in a similar mix of bravado and pathos. North of Tula, in a raging blizzard, Guderian's 24th Panzer Korps found itself low on fuel, unable to make any further progress and in danger of being cut off by strong Soviet attacks from the north. The 43rd Infantry Korps made no progress at all. First the road, then the rail link, were recaptured by the Red Army. Tula was not going to fall.

As units of his division reached the edge of a forest east of Maslovo, close to where the Istra flowed into the Moscow River, the 87th Division's Combat Diarist recorded an imaginary climax. They were only twenty kilometres from Moscow, he wrote, and the towers of the city were visible in the distance. This dubious sighting – they were actually thirty kilometres away – was apparently sufficient. The men could now 'boast with pride, along with all other German soldiers, that in the Second World War the capital of the Russian Empire was theirs!'[9]

In Yushkovo they were too busy fighting to search the eastern horizon for golden domes. The battle had continued through the night, and though the Germans had fought off the T-34s – six of which were still smouldering in front of them – any possibility of continuing the advance had vanished. When the order arrived to fall back, the dead were left unburied, the morphine-dosed casualties loaded aboard horse-drawn carts and makeshift sledges. To one participant, it all seemed a little too reminiscent of a Napoleon-in-Russia movie.

Soon after they left Yushkovo, the Soviets began shelling the column, first with artillery from behind, then with tanks from the flank. Two horses were hit and their carts blown over, tipping out their human cargo, and panic was averted only by a doctor drawing his gun and overseeing the reloading of the carts. A dozen of the fitter men took the place of each horse, and trotted the carts into the shelter of the nearest trees.

Von Kluge had also had enough. First he withdrew his spearhead, then asked von Bock for permission to withdraw the whole of the 20th Korps back to their starting line behind the Nara River. Von Bock asked for a few hours to think it over, but von Kluge went ahead anyway, claiming that new Soviet attacks on the 20th Korps' left wing were threatening to cut off his advanced units. The 4th Army's offensive, so long in the making, had lasted less than three days.

It was von Bock's sixty-first birthday, and all he had to cheer him was a telegram from the Führer. Later that Wednesday evening he spoke to Halder on the phone and told him that the troops were almost at the end of their strength. Halder pointed out 'what changing to the defensive would involve. The disadvantages of that policy,' he added, 'were one of the reasons why we stuck to the offensive.'[10]

German reconnaissance remained poor. New Soviet concentrations were noted — only the previous day the third Panzer Group had seen 'evidence of increased concentrations of motorized and horse-drawn vehicles' in the woods east of the Moscow–Volga Canal — but wrongly interpreted.[11] Everything had to fit OKH's distorted bigger picture: since the Soviets lacked substantial reserves, any new concentrations must reflect the movement of troops from one part of the front to another. There was no growing threat.

The Soviets were proving rather more successful at guessing the current strength of their enemy. Over the last few days, since taking the decision to begin their counter-offensive, they had been sending out patrols with the specific purpose of taking prisoners. The subsequent interrogations had made it abundantly clear that the German soldier outside Moscow was dangerously close to the end of his tether.

Like Rostov in the south, Tikhvin in the north was proving a step too far. Since von Leeb's admission on 22 November that the city was 'more or less encircled', Soviet pressure and German casualties had continued to grow. As elsewhere, the slight Soviet superiority in numbers was less critical than the German failure to supply their troops with adequate food, fuel, winter clothing or vehicles and weapons that worked in sub-zero conditions. Tikhvin could no longer be held, the 39th Panzer Korps reported, but no one seemed to be listening. The situation, Halder decided, was 'not yet quite clear'.[12]

Henry Metelmann's troop train had crossed the Dnieper, travelled on east and ended up in a small marshalling yard in the Donbass region. 'As soon as we arrived we knew that something had gone drastically wrong . . . soldiers, officers and all, were running around in a panic, and our Company Commander had to report to the headquarters at once.' The men sat silently in their compartment, depressingly aware that they would soon have to leave it. 'Someone outside said that the Red Army had broken through somewhere and was coming for us. It was not a pleasant thought.'[13]

In Berlin Ambassador Oshima again asked Ribbentrop to put his previous promises of German support in writing, and was again told that the Führer, who alone could sanction such a deal, remained incommunicado.

Mussolini was not. Granted an audience, Rome's Japanese ambassador ventured forth on a long and detailed history of his country's attempts to secure a negotiated settlement with the United States – attempts that had, alas, ended in failure. Hostilities would soon begin and, when they did, his government hoped and expected that its Tripartite Pact allies would first declare war on America and then pledge themselves not to make a separate peace.

The Tripartite Pact required its members to support each other only in the event of an attack, but Mussolini tactfully refrained from pointing this out. He would need to consult the Germans, he said, but he did not foresee any problems. And once the ambassador had left, his ego took over: 'So now we come to the war between continents, which I have predicted since September 1939.'

Ciano was more concerned at the likely implications of the war's globalization. Roosevelt, he believed, was manipulating the Japanese into attacking America because that was the only way he could get his own country into the European war. And American intervention in Europe meant a very long war. 'Who will have the most stamina?' Ciano asked himself, before noting, almost in passing, the success of the 'unexpected Soviet offensive' around Rostov.[14]

NAZIS AGAIN CUT TOBRUK OFF – WE LOSE REZEGH ran the outdated headline in Wednesday's *Daily Mirror*, but underneath, in smaller type, the editor demonstrated a confidence that Auchinleck would have appreciated: 'It may,' the subsidiary headline read, 'delay the final issue for a few days longer.'[15]

Battlegroups Geissler and Knabe, heading east down the Via Balbia and Trigh Capuzzo to relieve the Axis frontier garrisons, were both spotted from the air. Suitable receptions were organized, Battle Group Geissler falling victim to a New Zealander ambush ten miles short of Bardia, Battlegroup Knabe running into a strong force of British armour and artillery. Both were pulled back twenty miles or so, having suffered significant losses for no gain. Away to the west, the planned German attack on El Duda was postponed until the following day. According to its commander, General Sümmermann, the 90th Infantry Division (the *Afrika* Division until 27 November) was 'no longer in a fit condition to attack'.[16]

The British, meanwhile, completed their preparations for Ritchie's planned advance on El Adem. The 4th Armoured Brigade moved forward from Bir Berraneb to a blocking position astride the road from El Adem to Bir el Gubi, while the 11th Indian Brigade began a forty-seven-mile night march towards the now-isolated Bir el Gubi, intent on a dawn attack.

In London the War Cabinet and Defence Committee met to discuss further British aid to the Soviet Union. Tanks, aircraft and two full divisions for the defence of the Caucasus were suggested, but all shared the same drawback – they were needed in North Africa.

The Soviet situation certainly seemed critical, and the implications for Britain of a Soviet collapse were all too evident – a German army and air force refuelled from the Caucasus oilfields, the Middle East under attack from another direction, large German forces freed to mount an invasion of the British Isles. Churchill was inclined to weaken the British forces in North Africa if that was the only way in which he could help Stalin.

General Brooke, who had only started work as the new Chief of the Imperial General Staff on the previous Monday, disagreed. He thought 'the conception was a wild one' and foresaw enormous administrative difficulties. His own plans for Britain's forces were much more focused than those of his political boss. If two divisions were sent to Stalin, Auchinleck would have to shut down Crusader, and Brooke was convinced that an early defeat of Rommel was vital: 'It was plain to me that we must clear North Africa to open the Mediterranean, and until we had done so we should never have enough shipping to stage major operations.'[17]

Churchill was not convinced, and the decision was deferred until the next day.

In Washington Nomura and Kurusu had apparently decided that Hull was the main stumbling block in their negotiations. The previous day Kurusu had contacted Roosevelt's friend Bernard Baruch through a third party, and asked if Baruch could arrange a private meeting with Roosevelt. The President refused this, but asked Baruch to find out what Kurusu had in mind. The latter claimed that he, the Emperor and the Japanese people were being railroaded into war by the military-dominated government, and that the only solution was for Roosevelt to appeal directly to the Emperor.

Roosevelt received the same message from another source, the famous Methodist missionary Dr Stanley Jones. When the President told his White House guest that he had refrained from contacting Hirohito directly for fear of putting the Japanese envoys in an impossible position, Jones told him that Nomura and Kurusu were all in favour: 'They asked me to ask you to send a cable. But they also said there could be no record, for if it were known that they had gone over the heads of the Japanese government to the Emperor, their own heads wouldn't be worth much.'[18]

Roosevelt decided he could bypass Tojo and his colleagues by sending the cable to his ambassador in Tokyo. Grew could then pass it on to the Emperor.

Hull was against it. An appeal to Hirohito was still, in his mind, a last resort. The man was only a figurehead, after all. Ignoring the real government would definitely be seen as an insult, and quite possibly as a sign of weakness.

Roosevelt agreed to wait. At a further meeting with Lord Halifax that afternoon he used the idea of a direct appeal to deflect the ambassador's renewed suggestion of a final warning to Japan, but declined to fix a date. He was, he said, still waiting for a formal Japanese reply to Hull's Ten Points.

Halifax was mostly concerned with confirming his interpretation of what the President had told him two days earlier. 'All being together' did mean American *military* support, did it not? The President assured him that it did.

The message intercepted on 15 November requesting the consulate in Honolulu to make twice-weekly reports on the warships in Pearl Harbor was finally translated, and interpreted, quite reasonably, as a stepping-up of Japanese efforts to track the location of all American naval units in the Pacific area.

Such messages told the Americans that war was coming, but offered no clue as to where the Japanese might strike. If, as seemed most likely, their primary targets lay to the south, the whereabouts of Kimmel's fleet was a vital concern. Warships that were in Pearl Harbor could not be in Cavite.

The previous day's message ordering Japan's Washington embassy to destroy codes and a code machine was also translated, and a G-2 officer was dispatched for a quick look over the wall. Unsurprisingly, he saw staff stuffing papers into a fire.

In Honolulu evidence of similar activity was verified by the FBI wiretap on the cook's quarters in the Japanese consulate. The consul was burning his papers, the cook happily told a Japanese friend elsewhere on the island. The Rising Sun was obviously going to war in the very near future, but there was no real fear of that war ever reaching Hawaii. According to that day's *Advertiser*, there was no need to fear, full stop. Japan was 'the most vulnerable nation in the world to attack and blockade. She is without natural resources. Four years of war already have left deep scars. She has a navy, but no air arm to support it.'[19] Fuchida's planes would come as something of a surprise to *Advertiser* readers.

Kido Butai was around 1,500 miles north–north–west of Oahu. At 04.00 the latest intelligence from Yoshikawa reached *Akagi* via Tokyo: six battleships, eleven cruisers, eighteen destroyers, four submarines and one carrier – the *Lexington* – had been in Pearl Harbor on the previous Saturday.

THURSDAY 4 DECEMBER

Having taken the decision for war, the Japanese government was forced to consider the manner in which hostilities would be announced. In 1904 the Imperial Navy had used the simple expedient of attacking the Russian fleet at its Port Arthur anchorage to announce a state of war, and had been praised for its boldness by at least one American newspaper, but the current government was strangely reluctant to follow its predecessor's example. Though fully bent on an aggressive war, they wished to convey at least an impression of respect for international standards. Some sort of notice would have to be given.

But exactly how much? The longer the notice, the greater the respect; the shorter the notice, the harder it would be for the Americans to mount an effective response. As was usual in Imperial Japan, the needs of the military trumped the needs of the politicians. Admiral Ito told the meeting that the announcement should be delivered in Washington at 12.30 p.m. (Hawaii at 7.30 a.m.) on 7 December. In Tokyo, the Philippines and Malaya that would be on 8 December, at 2 a.m., 1 a.m. and 12.10 a.m. respectively. Would that be before the attacks?, Tojo and Togo wanted to know. Ito assured them that it would, before adding that the need for operational secrecy precluded him from revealing the length of the interval.

The nature of the announcement was also discussed. Only Togo favoured a formal declaration of war; the others saw no reason to go beyond a regretful recognition that the negotiations had failed. The Americans could deduce the probable consequences in whatever time Ito had left them for such musings.

Having spent a rare night at his family home, Yamamoto enjoyed a morning send-off party at the Navy Ministry and lunch with Chiyoko before boarding the 15.00 train at Ginza Station. He would arrive at Miyajima before dawn on the following day and be back aboard *Nagato* in time for a late breakfast. The next sixty-seven hours would be spent waiting and hoping, as the myriad arms of the assault he had plotted inched across the operations map towards their prospective targets.

The bulk of Yamashita's Malaya invasion force set sail from Samah at dawn. According to Masanobu Tsuji it was a beautiful morning, the rising sun and sinking moon scattering gold and silver ripples across the harbour. As he watched the eighteen merchant ships and their cruiser/destroyer escorts head out into the open sea, Tsuji was caught up in thoughts of the family he had left behind, and a similar introspection seemed widespread: 'The convoy sailed in silence. Not a voice was heard from the two thousand officers and men aboard the ship. All was peaceful.'[1]

This fleet was scheduled to rendezvous with two smaller convoys – one from Vung Tau, south of Saigon, the other from Phu Quoc Island, off the Cambodian coast – over the next two days. The three convoys would then sail as one to a position in the Gulf of Siam just over two hundred miles north of Khota Baru, before dispersing in the direction of three major and three minor targets.

Any movement of military forces on this scale would look suspicious, but observers of the main convoy during the first two days of its voyage could not be certain that this particular movement amounted to anything more than a major reinforcement of Japanese forces in southern Indo-China. The further it sailed into the Gulf of Siam, however, the less credible that destination became, and the more certain an observer could be that this was an invasion force bound for Thailand and/or Malaya. The route had been set to keep the enemy guessing until the last possible moment, but Vice-Admiral Ozawa, the man responsible for the fleet and its 27,000 passengers, had not given up hope that his fleet could reach its destinations without being seen at all. The local climate at this time of year promised leaden skies, frequent downpours and low visibility.

As Ozawa knew, getting the troops safely ashore would be more than half the battle won. These Japanese army units had much more experience of war than the men they would be fighting: the 5th Division, tasked with the capture of Singora and Patani on the Kra Isthmus, had been in China since 1937; Takumi Force, given the job of capturing Khota Baru in Malaya, was part of the 18th Division, which had also seen extensive service in the Sino-Japanese War. They were also better trained and equipped for jungle warfare, better armed and better supported. Yamashita was taking 230 medium and light tanks to Malaya, where the British had none; he had 534 modern planes at his beck and call, against the RAF's 158 mostly obsolescent types. Tsuji's expectation of victory was well founded.

On each of the last four nights Interceptor Command on the Philippines had picked up small formations of bombers flying down from Formosa to the Lingayen Gulf area, some hundred miles north of Manila. 'Presumably,' Brereton wrote in his diary, 'they were making trial navigational flights to familiarize themselves with the air route.'[2]

Outside Moscow the weather took a further turn for the worse, the temperature plummeting to minus 35°C. Vehicles and radios were increasingly unlikely to function, cases of frostbite multiplied and the lice that plagued the ordinary soldier seemed ever more insistent. Applying hot irons to garment seams offered a partial antidote, but the issue was only one iron per regiment.

Army Group Centre enjoyed one success, when the 134th

Infantry Division finally broke into the railway junction town of Yelets, over 200 miles south of Moscow. North and South of Yelets, however, the wings of the 2nd Army were coming under increasing pressure, and there was an obvious risk of the Germans burrowing themselves into a closing bag.

Elsewhere, the news was of resistance and retreat. Von Bock noted the growing pressure on the 3rd Panzer Group's Moscow Canal defence line, and the 4th Panzer Group's 2nd Panzer Division, still struggling for control of the villages around Krasnaya Polyana, experienced 'a whole day of repeated systematic attacks from the south and south-west'.[3] The whole of the 4th Army was now back behind the Nara.

Guderian had one last try at encircling Tula, launching an attack from the west by the 31st Infantry Division. High combat casualties and even higher losses from exposure soon forced its abandonment. He drove to the divisional HQ, and then on to the battalion where he had started his career for a lengthy conversation with company commanders. Their willingness to try again was encouraging, which was more than could be said for the journey back. This was rudely interrupted when his command tank tumbled into a deep ditch and left the 2nd Panzer Army commander in need of a lift from a passing signals truck.

The OKH War Diary entry for that Thursday was full of enemy attacks repulsed, turned back, warded off, with hardly a mention of German attacks, successful or otherwise, but both OKH and Army Group Centre remained reluctant to call the whole thing off. Von Bock was still claiming that 'the obvious weakness of the enemy would have to be exploited by pushing German forces to the limit', and in a phone conversation with Halder his chief of staff, General von Greiffenberg, said he expected the 3rd and 4th Panzer Groups to resume their offensives on 6 December, and saw no reason for Guderian to call off his offensive against Tula.[4] Halder, for his part, had no objections.

Neither he nor von Bock expressed any hint of alarm in their respective diary entries for the day. And why should they? According to Army Group Centre, the Soviets' fighting strength was 'not thought to be so great that they can mount any great counter-offensive with their forces facing the army group front'.[5] OKH's Foreign Armies East Section concurred: the Soviets 'were completely drained and now incapable of mounting counter-attacks'; there was no possibility of the enemy mounting 'a large-scale offensive at this time without a substantial increase in reinforcements'.[6]

That morning Rommel's staff presented him with an update on German losses during Crusader. Around 3,800 men had been killed or seriously wounded, including 16 commanding officers, and 142 tanks, 25 armoured cars, 390 lorries, 8 88s and 34 anti-tank guns had been destroyed. The lorries had mostly been replaced by captured enemy vehicles, although the fuel to move them was running out. Everything else was irreplaceable, and would remain so until Malta's grip on Rommel's Mediterranean windpipe was loosened.

For the moment at least, he refused to be deflected. With more of the 15th Panzer in attendance, Battlegroup Knabe started off down the Trigh Capuzzo once more, and by noon had succeeded in pushing the British out of Sidi Azeiz. Bardia seemed within reach, but by this time all the other news reaching Rommel was bad. The attack on El Duda had been beaten off by artillery fire, some from the expected direction, some from a new enemy position on the other side of the Trigh Capuzzo. The impression was increasing among the German forces that their enemy was acquiring almost hydra-like properties – cut off one head and another simply appeared in its place. The 7th Armoured Support Group 'Jock columns' had been a persistent annoyance for some time, but it was more than that. British forces seemed to be cropping up all over the place. It was almost – perish the thought – as if each unit was a law unto itself, making up the battle as it went along.

And, as Rommel now discovered, two more had just cropped up, one lurking with intent on the road south of El Adem, the other launching a morning attack on the Italian-held positions around Bir el Gubi. With another serious threat to Tobruk apparently brewing south of Sidi Rezegh, he was left with no choice but to recall the 15th Panzer from Sidi Azeiz.

He needn't have bothered. With only Italians to beat, the 11th Indian Brigade had forsworn the need for reconnaissance, and paid the appropriate price. The Blackshirt *Coorto* battalion had shared in *Ariete*'s successful defence of Bir el Gubi fifteen days earlier, and it now displayed much the same determination and gallantry in a solo role; when night fell it was still clinging to one of two principal positions. The 4th Armoured Brigade could have been shifted a few miles south to settle things, but Knabe's advance on Bardia had shaken Ritchie, and by day's end he had finally decided to move his main armoured formation back towards the supposedly threatened frontier. 'To our great astonishment,' Bob Crisp wrote, 'we headed our tanks towards sunrise as soon as we woke, and rumbled straight back to our old stamping ground at Bir Berraneb.'[7]

Rommel was no nearer the frontier, Ritchie no nearer El Adem.

In Rome Ciano received a letter from General Gambara, hand-delivered by one of his intelligence officers. While Gambara had devoted most of his missive to criticizing Rommel and regretting Mussolini's decision to place the German in operational command, the intelligence officer had some real news to impart, 'that the exhaustion of our troops is noticeable, that enemy infiltrations reach every point of Cyrenaica, and that, finally, we are in no condition to resist another offensive by the British. "Our men go to their deaths gloriously," he concludes, "which does not change the fact that they die."'[8]

The war was about to expand, and following the Japanese appeal to their two governments, Ciano had been trying, without success, to tease a definite response out of Ribbentrop. The Germans, he thought, were less than thrilled by the prospect of American intervention.

He was mistaken. The lack of a favourable German response to Japan's request for unconditional backing had nothing to do with any reluctance on Ribbentrop's or Hitler's part. The latter, plane-hopping his way from Rastenburg to the Ukraine and back, had been out of communication with Berlin, and the former, despite ample prior authorization, had simply been too frightened to act on his own. After finally reaching Hitler on the scrambler phone that morning, and receiving yet another blank cheque in Tojo's name, Ribbentrop spent the rest of the day putting together a revised Tripartite Pact.

It arrived for Ciano's perusal at three the following morning. German Ambassador Mackensen, who had conveyed it across Rome in person, suggested they also wake Mussolini. 'I didn't do it,' Ciano wrote with pride, 'and the Duce was very pleased.'[9]

In London the War Cabinet resumed its discussion about what more assistance it should send to Russia. Churchill proposed an immediate dispatch of ten RAF squadrons from North Africa to the Rostov-Caucasus area, and comprehensively lost his temper when the consensus decided otherwise. The chiefs of staff had no ideas of their own, he raged, and all they could do was oppose his. Attlee and Eden tried to jolly him along, but it was no use. After indulging in a long and pointed sulk, the PM performed an harrumphing theatrical exit. It was, as Brooke wrote, 'pathetic and entirely unnecessary. It is the result of over-working himself and keeping too late hours . . . God knows where we would be without him, but God knows where we shall go with him!'[10]

That Thursday evening twenty-four prominent politicians and industrialists met for dinner at Washington's Carlton Hotel. The event was supposedly in honour of Vice-President William Wallace, but it had really been arranged to expedite the acceleration of the American war economy, and the first few after-dinner speeches were all about Democrats and Republicans pulling together and getting things done.

Then Navy Secretary Knox got up to speak. War was very close, he told his fellow diners; it might even have started that evening. But he wanted them to know that 'no matter what happens, the

United States navy is ready! . . . Whatever happens, the navy is not going to be caught napping.'

One little-known Washington bureaucrat found this all a little too much. Given the floor, Robert Wyman Horton described a visit to the Navy Department on the previous day, in which he'd almost been trampled in a mid-afternoon rush to the golf course. 'It seemed to me,' Horton said, 'that the high-ranking people in the department were knocking off work rather early, if we're so close to war.'

'Who is this son of a bitch?' Knox hissed at his neighbour.

Horton went on, describing a recent trip around Norfolk navy yard and Hampton Roads in a patrol boat. He and his companions had seen all the warships they wanted to see, even come ashore and wandered around the piers, but no one had seen fit to challenge their right to be there. 'We could have been spies, saboteurs, any-thing . . . we could have blown the whole place to pieces, for all the obstacles the navy put in our way.

'Mr Secretary,' Horton concluded by way of a punchline, 'I don't think your navy *is* ready.'[11]

In the northern Pacific, seas were rough and refuelling impossible. The fleet ploughed on, still unobserved, towards its target. And as Oahu drew ever nearer the chances of anything other than a diplo-matic breakthrough stopping Nagumo and his planes grew ever more remote. On the previous day he had told his fleet that war might 'explode' at any time, and that if it did break out before they reached their launch-point he fully intended, surprise or no sur-prise, to 'operate as scheduled' and attack Pearl Harbor.[12] At 10.40 he ordered that any ship encountered, whether enemy or neutral, should be prevented from sending a report of their presence. If the ship allowed a boarding party to destroy her communications equipment, well and good. If not, she should be sunk.

As the ships crashed their way through the heavy seas, the pilots continued their exercises, checking their planes, poring over the maps, playing 'spot the American battleship'. Assuming the fleet reached the launch-point undetected, the future of 20,000 men would rest with the 400 fliers who entered the lion's den, and they were not above enjoying their new celebrity status. Extra baths were drawn, extra rations of milk and eggs provided for the future heroes.

Flight Officer Genda had complete confidence in his pilots, rather less in his superiors Nagumo and Kusaka. He was particularly dismayed by their oft-repeated intention of beating a hasty retreat after only a single two-wave attack on Pearl Harbor. This was far too rigid an approach for Genda, who wanted to take any decision on what to do next after the results of that first attack had been assessed. The Americans might be waiting for them, and a swift withdrawal might be necessary, but there were also circumstances Genda could imagine in which a second attack might be necessary.

If they did achieve surprise, and the American ability to strike back at *Kido Butai* was severely compromised or altogether destroyed, then Genda saw every reason to ram home the Japanese advantage. The fleet could stay in the area for several days before returning by the northern route, or it could take its time sailing past Oahu on a more southerly course home – either would provide the opportunity for repeated attacks, and the comprehensive destruction of the American military presence on Oahu. An invasion might even be possible.

But could Genda persuade his superiors to take such options seriously? Since leaving Hitokappu Bay he had taken every opportunity to recommend flexibility, but Nagumo and Kusaka had, as yet, shown no inclination to listen.

FRIDAY 5 DECEMBER

In Tokyo Vice-Admiral Ito paid a visit to the Foreign Office. The note to the Americans should be delivered half an hour later than previously agreed, he told Togo. Why the change of mind?, the Foreign Minister wanted to know. A miscalculation, Ito told him blithely.

Togo asked again about the time interval between notification and attack, and though Ito again refused a direct answer he managed to convey the tightness of the timetable by stressing how important it was that the notification did not reach the Americans ahead of the scheduled time. As Ito knew and Togo did not, there was now only a half-hour gap between the scheduled delivery in Washington and Fuchida's intended arrival over Pearl Harbor.

If Admiral Ozawa had prayed to the weather gods, his prayers were now answered — as his Malaya invasion force headed south and south-west around the lowered head of Indo-China it found itself shrouded in dense curtains of tropical rain. Those scouring sky and sea for plane and submarine were able to relax, if only for a while, and add the dried eels bought in Formosa to the uninspiring ships' rations of bean soup and boiled rice.

If Force Z had sailed to the rescue of Malaya and Singapore, salvation would have to wait a while. With the relatively new *Prince of Wales* in dock for boiler repairs, *Repulse* departed for Darwin, where she could reassure the Australians and where the ship's vulnerability to air attack would not be an issue. Admiral Phillips took a Catalina to Manila for a long-arranged meeting with his American counterpart, Admiral Hart. If the Japanese attacked Malaya within the next few days, Force Z would be far from the front line.

Not, as Phillips' American hosts made clear, that such an eventuality was likely. General MacArthur and his chief of staff, General Sutherland, who joined the two admirals for their first session of discussions, told the dubious Phillips that his ships would be perfectly safe in Manila Bay. 'The inability of an enemy to launch his air attack on these islands is our greatest security,' MacArthur added, over-egging the proverbial pudding.[1]

Japanese test flights over the Philippines continued – a formation of Zeros sighted here, more unexplained radar blips there – but the only note of urgency in the American response was the final departure, soon after dark, of sixteen B-17s for Del Monte Field in the southern island of Mindanao. Brereton had proposed this move on 26 November, and the B-17s' new home was finally ready to receive them, albeit at a minimal level of comfort.

MacArthur and his staff had sanctioned this apparent retreat only with reluctance. Their skies might be full of Japanese planes, but their mental preparations still revolved around American air attacks on Japan, not Japanese air attacks on the Philippines.

The final word on Matador arrived in Singapore. Roosevelt had promised armed support in several contingencies, Churchill told Brooke-Popham, and proceeded to list them. He could send British forces into neutral Thailand if the Japanese did or tried to do the same, or if they attacked Malaya or the Dutch East Indies. Brooke-Popham could even implement Matador if he had 'good information that a Japanese expedition is advancing with the apparent intention of landing on the Kra Isthmus'.[2]

What seemed clear in Whitehall seemed less so in Singapore, at least as far as Brooke-Popham was concerned. If the Japanese invaded Thailand, he knew what to do. But what if they attacked Malaya and left Thailand alone? Should he, could he, still seize those positions in the Kra Isthmus which the army considered a necessary brick in Malaya's defensive wall? He felt in need of clarification.

Unknown to OKH, Stavka had succeeded over the last few weeks in amassing a formidable number of reserve formations. Many were units transferred from the Far East and Central Asia, freed by a combination of Sorge's intelligence and the knowledge that a successful Japanese attack this late in the Siberian year would be next to impossible. Some had already been fed into the front when dangerous breaches loomed, but most had been held back for this moment. At 03.00 on 5 December the Red Army launched the first moves of a powerful and wide-ranging counter-offensive against the unsuspecting Army Group Centre.

Stavka's plan was simple enough. It was Army Group Centre's converging pincers – the 3rd and 4th Panzer Groups to the north-west, the 2nd Panzer Army to the south-west – which had posed the greatest threat to Moscow, and the primary objective of the new Soviet counter-attacks was, at worst, to push them back, at best, to encircle and destroy them. Either side of Kalinin the Soviet 29th, 30th and 31st Armies were to strike south and south-westwards at the German 9th Army and the exposed flank of the overextended 3rd Panzer Group. Between Yakhroma and Krasnaya Polyana, the 1st Shock and 20th Armies would hit the eastern and southern sides of the salient held by the 3rd and 4th Panzer Groups, while south of Istra the 5th and 16th Armies would attack north-westwards into the 4th Panzer Group's rear. Further south, two other sets of Soviet pincers would attempt to pinch out the large Venev-centred pocket held by the 2nd Panzer Army east and north-east of Tula and the flatter bulge held by the German 2nd Army around Yelets.

It was a hugely ambitious programme, and it had more than

surprise going for it. The Soviets enjoyed only marginal superiority in numbers, but their men, tanks and aircraft were much better
equipped to withstand the conditions in which they had to operate. The men had camouflaged winterwear, goggles, skis and
automatic weapons that didn't freeze up; the tanks had wider tracks
and ran on cold-resistant fuel; the aircraft were kept in heated
hangars. Where German horses dropped dead from the cold, the
Russian steppe ponies kept going.

Stavka's idea was to stagger the opening of the counter-offensive
over several days, and hope to leave the Germans reeling from a
succession of widely spread blows. The first fell in the north, where
the 31st and 29th Armies launched their attacks at 03.00 and 11.00
respectively. The former gained more ground than the latter, but by
nightfall both armies had secured bridgeheads on the southern
bank of the frozen Volga, and the German 9th Army's hold on
Kalinin suddenly looked more precarious.

There were no further set-piece Soviet offensives on this day, but
other sectors were far from quiet, as each side sought to adjust
stretches of front line in its favour. In one regimental HQ a few
miles west of the Moscow–Volga Canal, the German commander
was optimistically examining a newly delivered city map of
Moscow with his company commanders when all hell broke loose:
'Furious machine-gun fire from three sides and the first hits right
in the village by anti-tank guns indicate that the enemy has
launched a counter-attack. In a second everyone is outside. The
roof of the headquarters hut is already in flames . . .'[3]

A few miles further south, the 2nd Panzer Division was forced
out of Katyushki. The 3rd Panzer Group was given somewhat
superfluous permission to go over to the defensive, while the 4th
Panzer Group's planned attack on the following day was unsurprisingly cancelled. Both panzer groups were told to make
preparations for a probable withdrawal to an Istra
Reservoir–Solnechnogorsk–Rogachevo line.

The 2nd Panzer Army was not under attack, and the 31st
Infantry made another forlorn attempt to link up with the 3rd
and 4th Panzer north of Tula – not so much a last throw as a

final fumble. With threats growing on his flanks, sixty-eight degrees of frost and no assistance from the neighbouring 4th Army, Guderian decided enough was enough. That evening he issued orders to suspend attacks and withdraw his foremost units to a generally defensible line. It was 'the first time during the war that I had had to take a decision of this sort, and none was more difficult . . . Our attack on Moscow had broken down. All the sacrifices and endurance of our brave troops had been in vain.'[4]

Army Group Centre, as von Bock's diary entry for the day made abundantly clear, remained unaware of what Zhukov had in store for it. Further west in the East Prussian forest, Halder noted the cancelled Panzer Group attacks and 'one enemy penetration east of Kalinin', but he was more concerned with the problems facing Army Groups North and South. Unconsciously hinting at what was to come, he remarked that 'a series of Führer orders' had 'caused some confusion' and mentioned, almost in passing, that von Brauchitsch had decided to resign as commander-in-chief of the army.[5] This resignation would be refused, but a second attempt a fortnight hence would prove successful. The failure in front of Moscow would be far from the army's last, but much of the blame thereafter would lie with the Führer, and his belief, confided to Halder, that 'this little matter of operational command is something anyone can do'.[6]

The Polish town of Novogrudok had fallen to the Germans in the second week of Barbarossa. Jews had lived there since the fifteenth century, and now formed a majority of the town's 12,000 population, with their own schools, hospital, orphanage, loan society and sports club. A hundred were killed almost immediately, and other small groups were taken away and murdered at regular intervals thereafter, but as far as the vast majority was concerned the Germans seemed content to harass and humiliate.

Early that morning all of the town's 7,000 Jews were ordered into the yard of the courthouse. They were left standing in sub-zero temperatures until dark, and then jammed into the courthouse itself, where space was so short that most were forced to stand. Tomorrow, they guessed, they would learn their fate.

In North Africa the day began with Rommel concentrating his armour and artillery just to the west of El Adem, prior to either beating off a British attack or launching one of its own in the direction of Bir el Gubi. Either way, he was anticipating a major and – hoping against hope – possibly decisive clash between the 4th Armoured Brigade and his woefully outnumbered but still potent *Afrikakorps*.

It was not to be. Ritchie had disobligingly moved the 4th Armoured Brigade out of the way – Crisp and Co. spent the day practising a new night leaguering system at Bir Berraneb – and Crüwell's panzers only ran over the 11th Indian Brigade on their way to relieve the Blackshirts at Bir el Gubi. Unaware that he was up against only a single infantry brigade, Crüwell failed to press his advantage, and the British, unaware that his meagre force was indeed the *Afrikakorps*, happily ordered the 22nd Guards Brigade to the 11th Indian's aid.

Had Crüwell known, and had the British adopted a hyper-cautious approach, the *Afrikakorps* might well have added the 11th Indian to its list of brigades recently shattered beyond immediate repair. But little else would have changed. The Axis forces would still have been outnumbered in men, tanks and guns. That evening Rommel had a visitor from Rome – one Colonel Montezemolo of the Italian Supreme Command. Montezemolo had given Rommel's nominal superior, General Bastico, the bad news on the previous evening, and now he laid it out for the *Panzergruppe* commander. Of the twenty-two Italian ships which had sailed for North Africa during November, fourteen had been sunk, along with sixty-two per cent of the total cargo. The loss of supplies was serious in itself, the loss of shipping even more so, and there was no chance of any major convoys setting out before early January, when *Luflotte 2* would be up and running in Sicily and able to offer meaningful protection. In the meantime Rommel would have to live and fight with what he had. There might be a modicum of fuel and ammunition, but no more men, no more tanks, no more air-craft.

Rommel told Montezemolo that he understood and accepted the situation, but questioned whether his superiors understood and accepted the likely consequences. With fewer than forty tanks still running, and insufficient fuel and ammunition for any more major battles, his forces would need to find a defensible line and sit behind it. And if they could not regain their original line on the frontier – which seemed most unlikely – then there was little chance of finding another one short of El Agheila. All of Cyrenaica would have to be abandoned.

A more amenable Churchill turned up at Friday's War Cabinet meeting and agreed that North African circumstances should determine when and if RAF squadrons were sent to help the Soviets. Brooke had meetings with all the foreign military attachés, including the Japanese. They seemed gloomy, causing him to wonder 'whether we shall have them with us for much longer'.[7]

Washington was still waiting for the Japanese government's formal reply to Hull's Ten Points. War was still expected, but there was little apparent urgency as to when, and no quick thinking as to where, it might erupt.

Anyone reading G-2's final pre-war estimate of Japanese intentions, issued that day, could have concluded that the threat had receded. The German difficulties in Russia had put such a damper on Japanese enthusiasm that '*she might disregard her obligations, and even withdraw from the Axis*'.* G-2 recognized the wide scope of Japanese ambition, but thought that nation's leaders were aware of the perils of military adventures; '*they want to avoid a general war in the Pacific*'.*

American preparations continued, with the military reinforcement of the Philippines having the highest priority. Over 130

---

* Italics in original.

bombers were due for dispatch over the next 10 weeks, and 52 dive-bombers were already en route, with an ETA around Christmas. Another batch of P-40 fighters were being shipped that day, and 21,000 troops were scheduled to leave in the coming week.

In the meantime another hint of the Imperial Navy's primary target went begging. This was the day that the Office of Naval Intelligence translated Tokyo's request for information on those ships that remained in Pearl Harbor, and decided that it merely reflected a Japanese passion for filling in details.

On Oahu Yoshikawa did another round of the military sights. From his usual vantage point above Pearl Harbor, he noticed that *Lexington*, the sole remaining aircraft carrier, and five heavy cruisers were no longer in port. They had, in fact, left that morning, the carrier loaded with marine planes for the reinforcement of Midway. They were not expected back until 9 December.

Kido Butai was less than a thousand miles from Pearl Harbor, and Honolulu radio stations were much easier to pick up than the ones back home. That morning, after a penultimate refuelling, the three tankers and one escort destroyer of Supply Group Two were left behind. As the crews waved the task force goodbye, one captain signalled his hope that the 'brave mission' would be 'honoured with success'. According to Chigusa, everyone was 'deeply moved'.[9]

The fear of discovery remained. On the previous evening Tokyo had picked up radio signals in the fleet's vicinity – a possible American submarine. Nagumo had fretted, convinced himself that his fleet was being tailed, and dragged Flight Leader Fuchida from his bed to get a second opinion. Fuchida was annoyed. 'If it was true,' he said later, 'he [Nagumo] should have taken appropriate measures. One could understand if he'd consulted the chief of staff [Kusaka], but for a commander-in-chief to summon his flight commander and ask him a thing like that was plain stupid . . .'[10]

No trace was found of the submarine, and none of the Soviet

merchantman that Tokyo also reported in the area. Nagumo had six fighters warmed up and ready to launch in case of a sighting, but he was not prepared to send them up and risk their being seen for anything less. Later in the day, a clear sign of the growing tension was a sudden scare over a mysterious light in the sky. This sent gunners rushing to their stations, but it turned out to be a lighted balloon sent aloft by *Kaga* to test the wind.

SATURDAY 6 DECEMBER

Two days earlier, the British military authorities in Singapore had ordered a step-up in reconnaissance flights from Khota Baru to Cape Cambodia, across the gaping throat of the Gulf of Siam. For forty-eight hours the weather had been prohibitive, but one of the Australian Lockheed Hudsons based at Khota Baru finally lifted off late that morning, and, despite the low cloud cover, managed to find what his superiors feared. The pilot's first sighting was of a cruiser and three transports, his second, half an hour later and 140 miles south-east of Cape Cambodia, was of Ozawa's main force of 18 transports and half as many warships. Careful to keep himself beyond the range of the Japanese anti-aircraft guns, the pilot reported what lay beneath him.

On his flagship *Chokai*, Ozawa could see the distant plane slipping in and out of the fast-moving clouds. Should he try to shoot it down, and start a war two days ahead of schedule? He could hardly let it shadow his fleet for hours, reporting every detail of the invasion force. Yes, he finally decided, he should shoot it down. But by then it was too late. Before an interceptor could be launched, the enemy plane had disappeared.

The news of his convoy's passage was out. The British might buy the deception, and believe it was headed only for Cambodia, but

Ozawa very much doubted it. They would recognize an invasion
fleet when they saw one and would work on the assumption that
it was headed their way.

News of the sighting reached Phillips in Manila that Saturday afternoon. He made arrangements to fly back to Singapore, and sent a
message recalling the Australia-bound *Repulse*. There was, by this
time, no chance of the battlecruiser returning in time to intercept
the convoy, if it was indeed a Japanese invasion force. Sending it
had been a mistake, the first of several.

Army Commander Percival received the news in Kuala Lumpur,
where he was meeting with General Heath, the commander of the
Matador-assigned III Indian Corps. After warning Heath that
orders for implementing Matador were likely to arrive at any
moment, Percival took the two-hour flight back to Singapore.
Reaching his own HQ soon after 18.30, the army commander
found to his astonishment that Brooke-Popham had not seen fit to
set the operation in motion.

Brooke-Popham had received news of the sighting soon after
14.00, and had been dithering ever since. The Japanese convoy
might be innocent, might be heading – or so his naval advisers
told him – for the shelter of Kao Rong Bay off Cambodia. One
group of ships had been seen heading in that general direction.
And even if they were heading west towards Thailand and Malaya,
the implications seemed far from clear. His requested clarification
had still not arrived from Whitehall, and, as the afternoon went by,
Brooke-Popham managed to convince himself that Matador was
inoperable in the event of a Japanese attack on Malaya which
avoided compromising Thai neutrality. No matter that, in the
event of a Japanese attack on Malaya, Thai anger towards the
British would be the least of the latter's worries. No matter that
the only British strategy for defending Malaya rested on denying
the Japanese an opportunity to put armies ashore in southern
Thailand and northern Malaya. Brooke-Popham would not
authorize Matador's incursion into Thai territory until he was
absolutely certain that the Japanese were also in the process of

invading Thailand. Or, to put it another way, until it was too late to prevent that invasion. He ordered further reconnaissance, but Catalinas sent north that evening and overnight failed to find the Japanese convoys.

After Phillips' hasty departure for Singapore, MacArthur held an off-the-record press conference. War was coming, he told the gathered journalists, but probably not until the new year. What the Japanese might gain from waiting was left unexplained.

He also sent off a confidential report to the War Department in Washington. MacArthur claimed his airbases were on alert, their planes appropriately dispersed, but his emphasis on guards around planes and installations, and on the ongoing organization of counter-subversive activities, should, like General Short's similar obsession, have raised a few doubts in Washington. The fact that these two generals still considered local saboteurs a greater threat than the Japanese air force was a sure sign that they were not paying attention.

If MacArthur was correct in claiming that his airbases were on alert, it was the alertness of chickens waiting for a fox in an open field. At the all-important Clark Field, trenches had been dug and oil drums filled with sand, but defensive shelters had been completed for only two of the remaining B-17s. Anti-aircraft guns ringed the field, but the continuing shortage of ammunition meant that few had been test-fired. And there was still insufficient room to disperse the B-17s, even with half the force gone to Del Monte. The fighters were either old and outmatched or new and essentially untried.

The situation at the other airbases was often worse. At Iba Field, for example, the fighters were unprotected by either anti-aircraft guns or shelter provision. The planes were new, and pilot training on them had been minimal. They had not yet been adapted for flight at altitudes over 15,000 feet, and their wing-guns had still not been test-fired. MacArthur's air force might be on alert, but it was far from ready.

And some were fully aware of that fact. Addressing a gathering of fighter pilots at the Fort Stotsenburg Officers' Club, Brereton's supply officer, Colonel George, advised them to make out and deposit their wills in the next few days. 'You are not necessarily a suicide squadron,' he told them, 'but you are goddamn near it.'[1]

In the early hours of Saturday, a few miles north of Soviet-held Dedovsk, a solitary KV tank forded the small river that marked the nominal front line between the armies. Its intended destination was the small village of Nefedyevo, where the 10th Panzer's remaining eighteen tanks were reportedly spending the night. Lieutenant Pavel Gudz and his crew of five had been given the job – a probable suicide mission – of destroying them in a dawn raid.

Gudz had already checked their route on foot, and as the KV moved closer to the German-held village a prearranged artillery bombardment of empty forest helped mask the sound of its approach. Lights were still burning inside some of the cottages, and when the tank swished to a halt on the village outskirts the sounds of German voices and an accordion rose out of the sudden silence. With dawn approaching, and the panzers visible in the half-light, Gudz and his crew opened fire. Eight were in flames before the Germans managed a response, and their shells bounced off the thick Russian armour, bruising and shaking the occupants without causing serious damage. As the German drivers moved the surviving panzers out of the firing line, their infantry headed for the KV, only to be knocked back by the tank's machine-gunner. When Soviet infantry appeared, the Germans decided to abandon the village. Gudz followed in their wake, firing at the retreating panzers until all his shells had gone.

This was an isolated attack, part of the preparation for the wider offensive planned for this sector on 8 December. Elsewhere whole Soviet armies were on the move, the 30th, 1st Shock and 20th Armies moving forward against the weak and over-extended flank of the 3rd Panzer Group. The much-reduced German 14th and 36th Motorized Divisions, strung out along the forty-mile stretch of front between Yakhroma and the area north of Klin, soon came under intense pressure from Lelyushenko's 30th Army. This was serious: Klin itself lay astride the 3rd Panzer Group's only escape route.

By evening, units of the 1st Shock Army had fought their way into Yakhroma. Further south, the rest of the 1st Shock and General Andrei Vlasov's 20th Army had secured more bridgeheads on the western bank of the Moscow–Volga Canal and were pushing forward against increasingly desperate resistance from the 3rd Panzer Group's infantry and artillery. Reinhardt, intent on securing Klin and covering his group's retreat, took the sensible course of pulling his armour back from the front line. In the process, he uncovered the left flank of the neighbouring 4th Panzer Group. It was finger in the dike time, and one hole plugged was another opened.

On the other side of Moscow, the Soviets made even better progress. The 10th Army, which enjoyed a 3:1 superiority over the forces guarding Guderian's right flank, claimed the biggest advances of the day, covering over fifteen miles, and the 13th Army, launching converging attacks on either side of Yelets, made threatening inroads into the German rear.

'At three o'clock we were suddenly woken from our restless half-sleep,' one German reported. The Soviets attacked, using what cover the undulating terrain offered to work their way forward into the German positions. 'Soon they were so close to us that we heard the rousing shouts of the officers and commissars and the heated battle cries of the Bolsheviks, with which they tried to raise their courage.' Running out of cover, the Soviets simply charged, and the German automatic weapons came into their own: 'We mowed down many of the attackers, either by shooting them or forcing them to the ground by the effect of our fire. It was a fantastic fire show. The straw stacks in front of our positions burst into flame. The light tracer ammunition whistled in the air from all sides with flashes of light bouncing off the stone-hard ground, catapulting into the air to buzz away aimlessly. Houses in the nearby villages, which the attackers used for cover, were covered in flames and lit up the battlefield.'[2]

This attack was beaten back, but many were not. Evicted from Yakhroma, von Luck and his men were now retreating down two hastily cleared routes. The snow had been piled high on either side of these 'roads', turning them into long canyons, and 'the effect of the enemy air attacks was devastating. Since no one on the retreat routes could escape, and since the Russians always came from the east, hence from behind, the infantry first caught the brunt of them. The next victims were the horse-drawn supply and artillery units. Before long, the narrow roads were choked with the cadavers of horses and broken-down vehicles. The men fought their way west on foot and were often attacked in the flank by Russian ski patrols.'[3]

The commander of the 39th Panzer Korps, which was still clinging to Tikhvin with its ice-encrusted fingernails, reported that his men had 'already gone beyond the bounds of physical endurance . . . the troops and now even individual company and battalion commanders are becoming listless and indifferent'.[4] As another long battle would put his four mobile divisions completely out of the action, the corps commander suggested an immediate withdrawal from the town.

That evening von Leeb's chief of staff, General Brennecke, telephoned OKH. Did Halder realize how serious the situation was at Tikhvin? Halder said that he did. The Führer, however, was insisting that the town be held.

That afternoon Hitler called a meeting to discuss the current situation and what should be done about it. He began by quoting statistics – 'he has the figures in his head,' Halder dryly noted – to prove the enemy's underlying weakness. The Red Army, he claimed, had lost between eight and ten million men, the Wehrmacht only half a million. The Russians, having lost 78,000 guns, had none left. 'If we have lost twenty-five per cent of our fighting power,' Hitler went on, 'the Russians have lost far more, despite their three hundred per cent increase in newly activated units.' And the proof: 'when our divisions can hold thirty kilometres [of front], it proves the deficient strength of the enemy. Numbers prove nothing,' he concluded without apparent irony.

Things were much better than they seemed. Tikhvin might appear endangered, but Hitler still hoped for a link-up with the Finns and the imposition of an unbreakable ring around Leningrad. Rostov might have fallen, but he had no intention of writing the city off for the winter – the enemy had suffered enormous losses and had worn itself out. As for the centre, 'the Russians have not abandoned any place voluntarily; we cannot do so either'.

'Decent weather' and 'continuous reinforcements' would do the trick. But where would the latter come from? Not from the west – the possibility of Anglo-American action already loomed large in his mind. Not from the Balkans, where the Italians and Hungarians were clearly unable to cope. There were spare German troops in Romania, but most of the reinforcements would have to come from Germany itself, from soldiers on leave and soldiers from motorized units which no longer had motors, from young workers in the mines and factories, whose work could be done by Soviet prisoners. The war was only twenty-seven months old, and Hitler was already scraping the barrel.

Finally, some six months too late, the Führer turned his attention to locomotives. The German Army in the East, the meeting was told, did not need perfect engines, merely 'the simplest ones which will last five years'.[5]

In Novogrudok German officers arrived to conduct a selection process. Questions were asked about professional skills and children, but the answers seemed irrelevant – one saddlemaker with two children was sent one way, another saddlemaker with two children sent the other. At the end of the process there was one group of 2,000 Jews, another of 5,000.

The first group was led off to the nearby village of Pereshike, squeezed into twenty-two stolen homes and put to work making gloves and boots for the glorious Wehrmacht. The second group was taken a mile further, to a ravine outside the village of Skridlewe, for immediate execution.

There were no survivors of this massacre, but some of Novogrudok's Jews had already saved themselves, escaping in ones and twos from the town over the previous months. These young men and women went on to become the nucleus of the Bielski partisan group, which would eventually provide underground homes for over 1,200 Jewish women and children in the nearby Nabilocka Forest.

Rommel remained reluctant to accept defeat. A combined attack by the Axis panzer and motorized divisions on the British forces around Bir el Gubi could still, he decided, produce a result. If it did not, 'then, in view of our own heavy losses in men and materiel, we shall have to consider breaking off the battle and withdrawing to the Gazala position, and later evacuating Cyrenaica altogether'.[6]

The 'combined' element of the proposed attack proved problematic. The Italians declared themselves exhausted, and asked in vain to be excused. Refused their sick day, they took it anyway, endlessly preparing for a journey that never got started. As Crüwell waited for them, the British formed a strong arc of forces – the 11th Indian, 22nd Guards, 1st South African and 4th Armoured Brigades – five miles or so to the south-east. For several hours the two sides contented themselves with probing patrols and exchanges of long-range artillery fire.

At 15.00 Crüwell gave up waiting for the Italians – his 'where is Gambara?' soon acquired the status of an *Afrikakorps* catchphrase – and launched an attack without them. The panzers succeeded in pushing the 22nd Guards Brigade back, but there was no breakthrough to justify the heavy losses from enemy shellfire – the 15th Panzer commander Neumann-Silkow was one victim – and soon after dark Crüwell was forced to call it a day. Aware that his hard-won wedge in the British line could turn into a trap, he asked permission to pull his forces back. This was refused – Rommel wanted one last try the following morning – but later that night the *Afrikakorps* commander was also instructed to reconnoitre possible withdrawal routes. Rommel was no longer expecting success, merely reluctant to rule out a miracle.

The British had finally realized that the eastern end of the Tobruk perimeter had been abandoned by its Axis occupants, and that evening a few 11th Hussar armoured cars re-established XIII Corps' connection with the garrison. They also knew, as Rommel did, that western Cyrenaica was bereft of defensible lines, and that any Axis retreat was doomed to be a long one.

Hermann Göring was back in Amsterdam for one last scouring of the erstwhile Jewish bazaars. 'Visits to arts dealers and shopping' was his own summary of a highly satisfactory day, and as his private train pulled out that evening the day's proceeds were neatly packed in one of the carriages (others contained a barber, hospital, theatre and outsized bath).[7] *Asia* was headed east towards Berlin, as if its owner had somehow sensed Nagumo's falling blade.

As dawn broke over Hawaii, *Kido Butai* began its last refuelling some 600 miles to the north. This was the time of maximum danger for Nagumo's task force, within range of Short's B-17s, yet still unable to reach Oahu with its own planes. But the seas were mercifully calm, and the job was finished inside three hours. The last four tankers and their escort destroyer dropped away as the war-ships plunged on.

At 11.30 they turned due south and picked up speed. As *Akagi* signalled Yamamoto's final message to the rest of the fleet – 'The fate of the empire rests upon this battle – every man will do his duty' – Admiral Togo's famous Z flag from Tsushima was hoisted aloft to rousing cheers. On each ship of the fleet every available man was mustered on deck to hear the message read aloud.

In wintry Washington a war between Japan and the United States still seemed hard to contemplate. At 10.40 that morning news arrived of the British sighting of Ozawa's convoy, causing Navy Secretary Knox to ask the assembled naval leaders whether the Japanese were going to hit them. 'No, Mr Secretary,' Rear Admiral Turner replied, 'they're going to hit the British. They're not ready for us yet.'[8]

Over at the Japanese embassy, Kurusu was also hoping for a stay of execution. Talking to Ferdinand Mayer, an old American friend, he explained that the occupation of Indo-China had been sanctioned by his government only because the military demanded action of some sort, and all the other options had seemed even more provocative. Kurusu wanted Mayer to make sure that Hull understood this, and not force Tokyo into a corner. Given time, he was sure that 'the better element in Japan was really on its way to control the situation'.[9]

It was now eight days since Roosevelt had suggested a personal message to the Japanese Emperor, and that afternoon he finally got around to writing it. No peoples, he wrote, could 'sit either indefinitely or permanently on a keg of dynamite', and since no other nation was interested in invading Indo-China he saw no point in the Japanese keeping troops there. 'I address myself to Your Majesty at this moment,' he continued, 'in the fervent hope that Your Majesty may, as I am doing, give thought in this definite emergency to dispelling the dark clouds.' Both of them, he concluded, had 'a sacred duty to restore traditional amity and prevent further death and destruction in the world'. He sent the message on to Hull, with instructions to 'shoot this to Grew'.[10]

While Roosevelt was writing this appeal, both Japanese and American decoders were hard at work on a new series of messages from Tokyo to the Japanese embassy. The first of these, the so-called 'Pilot message', arrived early in the day. This gave advanced warning of the second, a message in fourteen parts detailing the government's response to Hull's Ten Points, all but one of which arrived in stages through the morning. The embassy was instructed to 'put this in nicely drafted form', and to keep it secret, until a third message arrived with the proposed hour of delivery. An extra message forbidding the diplomatic staff from using a hired typist to create the 'nicely drafted form' caused some difficulty, in that only one of the officials could type, and not very well at that.[11]

The first thirteen parts of the fourteen-part message – which the Americans decoded faster than the Japanese embassy – contained a long and resentful retelling of recent events, with Japan and America in the respective roles of misunderstood peacemonger and arrogant imperialist. The peacemonger's preferred denouement would presumably be revealed in part fourteen.

This still hadn't arrived when Roosevelt and Harry Hopkins were given the rest to read that evening. 'This means war,' was the President's first reaction, warning Stark his second, but the Navy Chief of Operations was at the theatre, and dragging him out might cause 'undue alarm'.[12] When finally reached around 23.30, Stark saw no reason to take further action. They were already expecting a Japanese attack, so nothing had really changed.

Earlier that Saturday Stimson and Marshall had decided to proceed with the latest delivery of B-17s to the Philippines via Hawaii. In order to maximize fuel and mileage, the bombers were flying unarmed, but the possibility of their being attacked over the Pacific seemed sufficiently remote, and MacArthur's need sufficiently urgent, to sanction their departure that evening. Arriving over Pearl Harbor the following morning, they would offer up a definitive example of how to get caught in the wrong place at the wrong time.

More potential warnings were missed. In Washington Dorothy Edgers, a recent addition to the navy's cryptographic section, worked overtime on Saturday afternoon translating two recent messages from Tokyo and the consulate in Honolulu. Neither offered conclusive information of an imminent attack on Pearl Harbor, but both offered grounds for real suspicion, and her superiors' failure to follow them up was remiss. In Hawaii Yoshikawa sent off a final report, stressing the lack of barrage balloons and torpedo nets, and the opportunity this lack of protection offered for 'a surprise attack'.[13] The consulate was now reduced to using its simpler codes, but this particular message was still not translated until 8 December.

At Washington's Cosmos Club, Carnegie Institute President Vannevar Bush, scientist Arthur Compton and Harvard President

James Conant enjoyed a discursive lunch. Roosevelt had approved and arranged funding for their nuclear development programme, and before the check arrived the three men had settled on four ways forward. Three concerned different methods – gaseous diffusion, centrifuge and electric-magnetism – of extracting U-235 from uranium ore. The fourth involved a newly discovered element, which would eventually be named plutonium.

Driving home on Saturday evening from a charity dinner dance at the Schofield Barracks Officers' Club, General Short took in Pearl Harbour's panoramic spread of illuminated ships. 'What a target that would make!' he exclaimed to his companion, General Fielder.[14]

As *Kido Butai* sailed south through the hours of darkness, the last intelligence reports from Yoshikawa and the Japanese submarine cordon were received and absorbed. The news was mixed. On the one hand, there were no barrage balloons over Pearl Harbor to hinder low flying, no torpedo nets to protect the American warships, no air patrols to the north, no sign that the Americans were expecting or preparing for an attack. Eight battleships were at anchor. On the other hand, there were no warships at the Lahaina anchorage on Maui, where the water was deep enough to preclude the salvage of sunken ships. And, most important of all, there were no carriers in Pearl Harbor. This was a serious blow, one that caused some to openly question whether the attack was worth pursuing. Nagumo was not one of them. Having got this far, he had no intention of slinking back off to the west. Genda, who understood the importance of carriers better than any of them, managed to put the disappointment behind him. Up on deck in the hour before midnight, he suddenly 'felt very refreshed, as if all the uncertainties were cleared away'.[15]

The fleet was seven hours from the launch-point, and now travelling at around its top speed of twenty-four knots. The light cruiser *Abukuma* led the charge, some three miles ahead of the battleships and six ahead of the leading carriers. As navigation officers juggled direction, speed and distance to reach the designated spot of ocean at the designated time, pilots did their best to sleep, mechanics checked their planes and radio officers listened to soothing Hawaiian music on the KMGB station, alert for any sudden declaration of emergency.

SUNDAY 7–MONDAY 8
DECEMBER

Expecting further British reconnaissance flights that morning, Ozawa sent up a screen of planes to intercept them. When one Japanese pilot spotted a Catalina at 09.50, he engaged the better-armed British plane, drawing it away from sight of the convoy and keeping its occupants busy until Japanese fighters arrived to administer the coup de grace. No report was received in Singapore.

An hour or so later Ozawa's fleet reached the designated dispersal point and split into five; minor forces headed for Prachuab, Chumphorn/Badorn and Nakhorn in Thailand, major forces for Singora/Patani in Thailand and Khota Baru in Malaya. A Norwegian merchantman which ran into the Khota Baru force sent no message before she was boarded and scuttled, and three Lockheed Hudsons sent north failed to find any trace of the Japanese. It was early evening before a Blenheim finally caught sight of the Japanese flotillas homing in on Khota Baru and Patani and radioed the news back to Singapore.

There was no doubt now as to where the Japanese were headed, and one of their destroyers had actually opened fire on the Blenheim. The conditions for authorizing Matador had certainly been met, as even Brooke-Popham was willing to admit. It was, of course, too late. The Japanese would be ashore at Singora and

Patani by midnight, and, as Percival pointed out, there was no chance of the 11th Indian Division getting there before two in the morning. Matador was redundant, but Heath's men were left where they were until morning, just in case.

Army Group Centre seemed in danger of breaking into its constituent parts. Advanced units of the Soviet 30th Army reached within five miles of Klin, threatening not only the 3rd Panzer Group's lifeline but unravelling the seam that connected it to the 9th Army. The Panzer Group was in full retreat, spread out for tens of miles along roads and tracks running north-west towards Klin. Fifteen tanks, along with countless cars and lorries, had been left behind because they wouldn't start, either for want of fuel or due to the effects of cold. Three heavy howitzers and half a dozen anti-aircraft guns had been abandoned in situ, either frozen in place or lacking a tow. The Soviets followed cautiously behind, hardly believing their luck that finally, six months into hell, they had the Germans on the run.

Closer to Moscow, the right wing of Rokossovsky's 16th Army had joined Vlasov's 20th in assaulting those German units intent on a disciplined pull-back from the high-tide line that ran through Krasnaya Polyana, Lunevo and Klushino to Kryukovo. Here the seam between the 3rd and 4th Panzer Groups was in danger of ripping apart. Further south and west, the 16th Army's left wing began the reversal of its long retreat down the Volokolamsk highway, and the 5th Army set in motion a converging attack from the south-east. Five days later the two would join hands west of a retaken Istra.

Much further south, General Ivan Boldin's Tula-based 50th Army, so long under siege by the 2nd Panzer Army, mounted a breakout to the east, with the ambitious aim of meeting the westward-pushing 10th Army, and encircling its would-be encircler. Progress was slow, but Guderian's armoured spearheads, which only a fortnight earlier had been motoring north and north-west with such optimism, now seemed out on dangerous limbs, vulnerable to attack from all sides and in peril of amputation. On the situation maps, the extended fingers of these conquests took the shape of a splayed, despairing hand reaching in vain towards Moscow.

It had, Bock wrote, been a 'difficult day'. Setbacks were proliferating as the means to reverse them shrank. What were the 'causes for this serious crisis'? Bock listed three: the combination of weather and conditions which had prevented a swift exploitation of the Vyazma–Bryansk victories of early October, the virtual collapse of the railway supply system, and the underestimation of Soviet resources and resolve. Over the last three weeks twenty-four new Red Army divisions had appeared in the Army Group Centre sector; his divisions, by contrast, had seen their strength halved by the fighting and winter.

A fourth cause was eluded to. Continuing the offensive had been justified, Bock thought, 'as long as the Supreme Command believed that he was fighting for his life with the very last of his forces; the effort to defeat him in one short push was worth "the ultimate sacrifice" – as the Army High Command demanded'. But it was now evident that the Supreme Command had underestimated the enemy's strength, and Army Group Centre was 'now forced to go over to the defensive under the most difficult conditions'. The Führer clearly had no conception of the real situation, because 'only today' Bock had received orders to hold the railway line which ran through quasi-encircled Yelets.[1]

Guderian later criticized these 'repeatedly exorbitant demands being made on our fighting troops'. At this moment, the right course seemed obvious: 'a prompt and extensive withdrawal to a line where the terrain was suitable to the defence, and where there were already prepared positions.' As far as the 2nd Panzer Army was concerned, this meant retreating to the north–south course of the River Oka, where some defences had already been constructed. 'But this,' he later noted, 'was exactly what Hitler refused to allow.'[2]

The Führer was becoming part of the problem, as Halder was all too aware. It had been a 'heartbreaking and humiliating' day at the Wolfsschanze, with von Brauchitsch 'no more than a messenger boy, if that much'. Hitler was often bypassing his army commander completely and talking direct to the generals at the front. 'Worst of all,' Halder noted, the Führer 'does not realize the condition our troops are in and indulges in paltry patchwork when only big decisions could help.'[3]

Tikhvin was a case in point. As the German grip loosened, von Leeb bombarded Halder with telephone calls. He needed to give up the town, needed to pull his forces all the way back to the Volkhov River, the first defensible line to the west. Late in the day Hitler finally agreed to an evacuation of the city, but refused point-blank to countenance the forty-mile retreat. Tikhvin and the Leningrad railway must be kept within German artillery range.

At the front, Lieutenant Gruman recognized 'the impossibility of holding the defence line'. And he was all too aware of the condition of his fellow soldiers: 'Eighty men have been brought here, forty of whom have second- and third-degree frostbite. Swollen legs are covered with blisters, so that they are no longer legs, but rather some kind of formless mass. In some cases gangrene has already set in. Those who managed to make it through the deluge of shrapnel have become invalids here. What will become of us? What is it all for?'[4]

One sure indication of the resistance bubbling beneath the surface of the New Europe was the Nazi need to ratchet up the fear factor. The current punishments for those guilty of offences against the Reich – penal servitude or a hard-labour sentence – were no longer considered a sufficient deterrent by the political, SS and military leaderships. According to OKH chief Keitel, a 'more efficient and enduring intimidation' was necessary.[5]

The need was answered by the *Nacht und Nebel* (Night and Fog) decree, which Hitler issued that Sunday afternoon. Enemies of the Reich who were not immediately executed would vanish into the ether. Relations and friends would be told nothing of their whereabouts in custody, and nothing of their eventual fate or resting place.

★

In Riga a week had passed since the previous Sunday's 'Action'. At 16.00 the local police began banging on doors in the Jewish ghetto, advising the remaining inhabitants to gather their bags and line up in the street. Occasional bursts of gunfire encouraged obedience, and by 18.00 the whole population was lined up in ranks of five. They were left standing there for an hour, and then marched through the night streets to an already-crowded three-storey building. It was standing room only, and no one slept for fear of being trampled underfoot.

'If the enemy was not beaten today,' Rommel told Crüwell at the latter's HQ that morning, they 'would have to abandon the Tobruk front and go back to the Gazala position.' In reality, he had already abandoned any such hopes. The German and Italian infantry was already moving back, and Crüwell's real task was to 'keep the enemy off, and to counter-attack if the enemy pressed too hard'.[6] The panzer divisions were no longer seeking victory, merely covering the inevitable retreat.

This they did with their usual efficiency, the tanks sheltering behind the screen of their formidable artillery. An outflanking move by the 4th Armoured Brigade was fought off in late afternoon, and soon after dark the order was given to disengage. Crüwell's men had provided the day's grace which the *Pavia*, *Brescia* and *Trento* and 90th Light Infantry divisions needed to get one step ahead of a pursuing enemy. But there was no saving the Axis garrisons on the frontier, which would surrender one by one through January, and yield almost 14,000 prisoners.

Earlier in the day, Auchinleck had remarked to his chief of staff that 'the turning point may be near. I say "may", as the enemy has shown his wonderful powers of recovery more than once, and he may well do so again before we finish him off.'[7]

Ciano noted the 'dark news from Libya', and Mussolini's calm reaction. The Duce, it seemed, had more important matters on his mind. He was 'very much irritated' by the low Italian casualty rate in Abyssinia. Only sixty-seven men had fallen during the defence

of Gondar, but ten thousand prisoners had been taken. 'One does-
n't have to think very long,' Ciano mused, 'to see what these
numbers mean.'[8]

Night had fallen in eastern Asia. At the airbases in Formosa, and
aboard the carrier *Ryujo* in the Philippine Sea, the Japanese pilots
heard that tomorrow was the day. They would be taking off in the
middle of the night, with the objective of reaching their Philippine
targets in the half-hour after dawn.

In Manila that Sunday evening, the 27th Air Group was throwing a party in Brereton's honour, and the drink was flowing freely.
At 23.30 Brereton was called away – the radar at Iba had picked up
a flight of unidentified planes. Interceptors were sent up but failed
to make contact with the intruders. It was another false alarm.

In Washington the diplomatic endgame was under way. The last
part of Tokyo's fourteen-part reply arrived in the early hours, and
decoded versions reached the desks of G-2's Colonel Bratton and
ONI's Commander Kramer around 08.00. Kramer set off on his
delivery round, which took in Roosevelt, Hull and Knox. The
general reaction was anti-climactic. The fourteenth part contained
no declaration of war, merely an announcement that the negotiations had failed and would not be continued. There was not even
a severance of diplomatic relations. Had the Japanese got cold feet
at the last moment?

Back at his office Kramer found another decoded message waiting for him: 'Will the ambassador please submit to the United
States government (if possible to the Secretary of State) our reply to
the United States at 1.00 p.m. on the 7th, your time.'[9]

This changed everything. There was only one reason for putting
a precise time on the delivery of a diplomatic message, and that was
to coordinate it with some other action. Which, in the present circumstances, had to be military. One p.m. in Washington, Kramer
noticed, would be two or three hours before dawn in the South
China Sea, a good time for starting an amphibious landing. It
would also, he realized, be 07.30 in Hawaii.

He took the information to Admiral Stark, and then to the State Department and White House, but despite the suspicious timing neither Kramer nor any recipient of his news could bring themselves to believe in a Japanese attack on Hawaii. Malaya and possibly the Philippines seemed much more likely.

Over at G-2, Colonel Bratton had made the same connections, and felt the same alarm. He set off to find Marshall, but the general was out riding, and it was almost 11.30 when Bratton finally reached him with news of the 1.00 p.m. timing. Marshall agreed to send out further war warnings, and Stark, after first deciding that enough had already been sent, offered to let the army use naval channels. Marshall declined, whereby Stark asked him to include the naval opposite numbers in his army warnings. It was now almost 12.00, but the decision was taken to send the warnings by radio, despite the availability and better speed of the scrambler phones. Priority was given to the Philippines.

The warnings went out to Panama and Manila, but atmospheric conditions prevented transmission to Hawaii or San Francisco. The officer in charge of the army signal centre thought about taking the navy up on their offer, but decided instead to use Western Union, which had no direct line to Honolulu. It was 12.17 in Washington, 06.47 in Hawaii, and the message was not marked urgent.

At the Japanese embassy, in scenes that would not have gone amiss in *Duck Soup*, the staff were fighting and losing the battle to get the fourteen-part message typed and delivered on time.

After reaching Tokyo at noon on 7 December, Roosevelt's personal appeal to Emperor Hirohito had fallen victim to a recent regulation regarding the delivery of foreign cables, and spent the next ten hours in a Japanese in-tray. Ambassador Grew finally received it at 22.30 (08.30 in Washington), and reached Foreign Minister Togo's official residence with the decoded version at around 00.15 on 8 December.

Togo refused to arrange an immediate imperial audience for Grew, but promised to deliver Roosevelt's message in person. Once the ambassador had gone, he phoned Privy Seal Kido, who agreed to meet him at the palace. On the way he stopped off to see Tojo, who immediately asked if the message contained any American concessions. On discovering there were none, he simply shrugged his shoulders and expressed relief that it hadn't come several days earlier, when it might have had some effect on those of lesser resolve. As things stood, it was simply too little too late.

This, as Togo soon found, was also the view of the Privy Seal. There was no point in waking the Emperor.

As the first hints of light appeared in the eastern sky, the lifts on the six carriers were hard at work, bringing planes up from hangar decks to flight decks. It was a cloudy day, the sea rough for launching, but whatever the conditions, they had to be borne. The task of reaching this far unobserved – a task that Nagumo had once considered almost impossible – had been achieved. 'I have brought the task force successfully to the point of attack,' he told Genda. 'From now on the burden is on your shoulders and the rest of the flying group.'[10]

For breakfast the pilots ate *sekihan* – the rice and red bean concoction reserved for important occasions. Most were wearing freshly ironed uniforms and traditional *hashamaki* headbands; some stopped off for a moment's contemplation at the portable Shinto shrines and downed small glasses of sake. They studied the briefing room blackboards, updated since the previous evening with the results of Yoshikawa's final surveillance, and made their way up to the swaying flight decks, where the engines in their planes were already running.

Two seaplanes – one each from the cruisers *Chikuma* and *Tone* – had already disappeared into the southern clouds, one bound for Pearl Harbor, the other for Lahaina, where Nagumo still hoped to find a target. Dispatching them was a risk – if either was seen, the balloon would go up – but Fuchida's first strike would be only half an hour behind.

In the event it was more like fifty minutes. At around 05.50 the six carriers swung eastwards into the wind and increased speed, but it was 06.05 before the sea was calm enough to risk the first take-off.

The lead Zero dipped alarmingly close to the waves before soaring, but soar it did. Now take-off followed take-off on all six carriers, a hundred and eighty-three of them in fifteen minutes, with only one plane ditched. At 06.20, twenty minutes later than planned, Fuchida gave the signal for their departure to the south.

Fighters were launched to stand guard above the fleet, and the second wave of 167 planes was brought up from the hangar decks. This left at 07.15, as per schedule. Nagumo, Kusaka and Genda watched it fade into the southern sky and settled down to wait. In less than half an hour, if nothing went seriously wrong, Fuchida would be over a surprised Pearl Harbor.

The Japanese landings in Malaya and Thailand had been scheduled to coincide with the attack on Hawaii, but when, late in the planning stages, the latter was moved back ninety minutes to avert a launch in darkness, someone forgot to tell those in charge of the former, and the first 25th Army units hit the water around 23.10 on 7 December, almost two hours ahead of the attack on Pearl Harbor.

The outmatched Thai defenders of Singora would resist the Japanese for half a day, and offer in the process a hint of what Matador might have achieved, but all of Yamashita's other Thai targets would fall with hardly a fight. Takumi Force would have trouble in Khota Baru, as much from the choppy seas as the exertions of the British, but once the Japanese troops were ashore their greater number and efficiency would swiftly begin to tell.

Soon after midnight fog closed in on the Japanese naval airbases in southern Formosa, and it became obvious that the air offensive against the Philippines would suffer a delay. As the minutes and hours went by, concern steadily grew, particularly among those who knew what was happening five thousand miles to the east. The need for light had always condemned the Japanese to attacking the Philippines several hours later than Pearl Harbor, but they had expected that their planes would at least be in the air when the enemy discovered that war had broken out. If the fog persisted many hours longer, there was every chance the Americans would be taking off first and heading straight for them and the vulnerable troopships.

The five Japanese midget submarines were supposed to be lurking on the Pearl Harbor bottom by dawn, ready to sink whatever Fuchida's planes left on the surface, and by 03.30 four of the two-man crews had wished their larger submarine hosts goodbye, enjoyed a brief view of Honolulu's lights twinkling on the northern horizon and had begun their submerged journeys towards the Pearl Harbor entrance. None would return. The fifth submarine, beset by a broken gyrocompass, did not set out until 05.30 and would spend most of the day travelling in circles.

Two minesweepers were doing their job outside the harbour, and at 04.00 an officer aboard one of them spotted what looked like a periscope. He reported the sighting to the destroyer *Ward*, which spent a fruitless hour scouring what seemed the relevant patch of ocean. Two hours later, the conning tower of an unusual-looking craft was spotted by a supply ship captain, and *Ward* was once more called in. This time the submarine was easily spotted. Hit by gunfire, it faltered, slowed and ran right into a pattern of depth charges. As Fuchida had feared, the midgets had let the cat out of the bag.

Or not. The destroyer captain's report of the incident was logged at 06.53, almost an hour before the first Japanese planes arrived over Pearl Harbor. The buck was then passed, by telephone, up a lengthy chain of recipients. Each took several precious minutes to consider how serious or not the matter might be. In the end the decision was left to Kimmel, and by then it was too late. No one thought to inform the army.

The army was busy dropping its own ball. At 07.00 the two privates on duty at the Opana Radar Station in northern Oahu were finishing their night shift when one spotted an unusually large blip on the oscilloscope. It was a flight of at least fifty planes, they decided, and during the time it took Private Elliott to report the sighting to the information centre, those planes drew twenty miles closer.

The shift at the information centre also ended at 07.00, and only two inexperienced men were there to receive the call. While Lieutenant Kermit Tyler, the new pursuit officer, was listening to the report, he remembered that a flight of B-17s was due in from California that morning and would be arriving from roughly that direction. 'Don't worry about it,' he told the boys at the radar station.[11]

Chikuma and *Tone* sent in their reports: there were no ships at Lahaina, nine battleships at anchor in Pearl Harbor. The lowest clouds were at five thousand feet. It was turning into a beautiful morning.

News of the Japanese attack at Khota Baru reached Singapore at half-past midnight, over half an hour before Fuchida reached Oahu, but no one hurried to inform the Americans that another war had begun. Governor Shenton Thomas ordered the internment of all Japanese male residents and took coffee with Lady Thomas on the Government House balcony. He was, he said, confident that Percival's troops would 'shove the little men off'.[12]

Reaching the northernmost point of Oahu at 07.49, Fuchida sent the signal for charge or *tosugekiseyo* — *to, to, to* — and headed south-westwards above the coastline. Away to his left, the skies above the island were blissfully empty of warplanes — surprise had been achieved, and there was no need to send the fighters in ahead of the torpedo-bombers. A signals mix-up ensued, but had no adverse consequences. Within minutes the dive-bombers were over Wheeler Field, where the American planes, tightly grouped to frustrate saboteurs, were veritable sitting ducks. The different units took their prearranged paths, swooping south-eastwards across the island as they had so often mentally swooped across the model. About five minutes after Fuchida's first signal, Pearl Harbor was under attack from half a dozen directions, the torpedo-bombers lancing in across the bay at the lines of warships. Once they had had their say, wreaking havoc on the outer line of Battleship Row, the high-level bombers had theirs, wreaking havoc on the inner line.

In the meantime, Hickam Field, Ewa Field and the Kaneohe Naval Station had gone the way of Wheeler, their planes caught on the ground and mostly destroyed. Bellows Field was the last to suffer attack, and might have been ready to fight it off if the warning message from Kaneohe had not been taken as a practical joke. And amid all this carnage the B-17s from California finally arrived to a wholly unexpected welcome.

The Japanese first wave had barely departed when the second arrived, homing in on targets missed by its predecessor. The same ships and airfields were pounded, until all but Fuchida were on their way back to the carriers. He hovered high above the harbour for a few moments more, assessing the extent of the wreckage below.

News of the attack reached the White House at 13.47, and was passed on to Hull at the State Department about fifteen minutes later. Nomura and Kurusu were already waiting in the Diplomatic Reception room, breathing rather heavily after rushing over from the Japanese embassy. Hull was inclined not to see them, but settled for keeping them waiting until 14.20. When the two diplomats were ushered into his office, he declined to shake their hands or offer them a seat.

Nomura passed over the fourteen-point message. He had, he said, been instructed to deliver it at one p.m.

'Why at one p.m.?' Hull asked coldly.

Nomura admitted he didn't know.

Hull made a brief pretence of looking through the document, then launched into a self-righteous harangue. In all their mutual dealings he had never uttered 'one word of untruth', and here the Japanese were, presenting him with nothing with lies. Never in his 'fifty years of public service' had he seen such 'infamous falsehoods and distortions, on a scale so huge that I never imagined until today that any government on this planet was capable of uttering them'. Hull failed to mention that he had been intercepting and reading his guests' diplomatic mail for over a year, and happily accepting the advantage that this illicit knowledge gave him in their negotiations. He also neglected to tell his guests that Japanese forces had attacked Pearl Harbor, assuming, for no good reason, that they already knew.[13]

A somewhat shell-shocked Nomura and Kurusu made their way back to the embassy, where news of the attack had just arrived.

The United States had at least been favoured with some sort of Japanese declaration, late and vague as it was. The British, as befitted their newly subsidiary status, had received only bullets and bombs.

Around 02.30 on 8 December Brooke-Popham, two members of Percival's staff and Admiral Phillips met in conference at the naval base. Phillips announced that he was minded to send the *Prince of Wales* and *Repulse* against the Japanese beachheads and supply chains, provided that sufficient air cover could be provided. He also admitted that sailing his ships westwards and waiting for reinforcements would be the safer option.

In the discussion that followed, two contradictory things became clear − that Phillips' plan to engage the enemy was generally approved, and that sufficient air cover was unlikely to be forthcoming. A final decision was still to be taken when the meeting was cut short by the rising whine of air-raid sirens.

News of Pearl Harbor reached Manila from several sources in the hour between 03.00 and 04.00. MacArthur, woken by Sutherland, was still getting dressed when Washington called to confirm the attack. Brereton, also woken by Sutherland, alerted his fliers and went to ask MacArthur for permission to attack Formosa. By this time, shortly after 05.00, MacArthur was closeted in his office with Admiral Hart, and Sutherland refused to let Brereton see him. And only MacArthur, he insisted, could sanction such offensive action − Brereton would have to wait.

Brereton returned at 07.15, but Sutherland again refused access to MacArthur, who was now alone in his office. Leaving Brereton cooling his heels, Sutherland went in on his own and emerged a few minutes later with the commander-in-chief's second refusal to sanction an attack on Formosa. This was somewhat surprising, since by this time MacArthur had received a direct order to implement the Rainbow 5 contingency war plan, which called for exactly the sort of attack that Brereton wanted to launch. The commander-in-chief was still intent on not making the 'first overt act', Sutherland told Brereton, as if Pearl Harbor had not been overt enough. In these crucial hours MacArthur seemed intent on giving the best possible impression of a rabbit transfixed by oncoming headlights.

News of the Japanese attack reached Berlin around 22.30 on 7 December, and Hitler an hour or so later, when an excited press officer burst in on one of his late-night soirées. The Führer leaped to his feet, exultantly slapped his thighs and cried out that this was 'the turning point!' Eager to share the news, he rushed out into the frozen night in search of Keitel and Jodl. 'Now we cannot lose the war,' he told the hurrying-to-keep-up Walther Hewel; 'we now have an ally who has never been vanquished in three thousand years.'[14]

Perspicacious as ever, Ribbentrop refused to believe the news. It was 'a propaganda trick of the enemy', he told the bearer, and asked not to be woken again.[15] Second thoughts followed quite quickly, or perhaps just a chat with the Führer, because soon he was waking Ciano with the wonderful tidings.

Churchill, dining with the American ambassador at his official country residence, Chequers, was only half-listening to the radio when the news was announced, but soon received confirmation from his butler. His immediate impulse was to declare war on Japan, but he was dissuaded from doing so on the mere say-so of a radio newsreader. Seeking confirmation, the ambassador phoned the White House; receiving it, he put Churchill on to talk to

Roosevelt. 'It's quite true,' the President told the Prime Minister, 'they have attacked us at Pearl Harbor. We are all in the same boat now.'[16]

It was a shock, but one that could hardly have been more welcome. This, as Churchill knew, made victory inevitable. After all the terrible trials and tribulations of the last twenty-eight months – ejection from the Continent, a narrowly averted invasion, the bombing Blitz and the U-boat threat, the long Russian retreat – Britain had won the war. 'Once again in our long Island history we should emerge, however mauled or mutilated, safe and victorious. We should not be wiped out. Our history would not come to an end. We might not even have to die as individuals. Hitler's fate was sealed. Mussolini's fate was sealed. As for the Japanese, they would be ground to powder.' With America on board, all that was needed was 'the proper application of overwhelming force'.[17]

Around midnight, after an evening of *shogi* and a very brief sleep, Yamamoto took a seat in the Nagato operations room and settled down to what seemed an endless wait. It was finally rewarded at 03.19, when the ship's radio operator locked in on Fuchida's '*to, to, to*' message – surprise had been achieved. Over the next two hours report followed report, and by the time dawn had broken outside it was clear that the attack had been a triumphant success. Yamamoto's gamble had paid off, and the faces all around him were filled with jubilation.

His, however, was not. In fact, he looked strangely depressed. He knew what Churchill and Roosevelt knew: that as far as Japan was concerned, this was as good as it was likely to get.

Fuchida's plane touched down on the *Akagi* flight deck around noon. Summoned to the bridge, he gave his assessment: at least four battleships had been sunk, and another four badly damaged, but the dockyard installations and fuel tanks had hardly been touched. A third strike was both necessary and feasible – the damage already inflicted on the American defences would more than make up for the lack of surprise.

Fuchida was not alone – other flight leaders and carrier commanders had already urged such a strike. Genda was also in favour of further attacks, but not at that moment – the seas had grown rougher and the returning planes had been rearmed to face a possible attack by American carrier planes. He favoured staying in the area and seeing what transpired. If he could find the American carriers and sink them, that would be ideal. If they were not in the area, then further attacks on Oahu could be mounted without too much risk.

Nagumo and Kusaka believed and said that they had already risked enough. The attack had succeeded beyond their wildest expectations – why keep the First Air Fleet in harm's way for what seemed like marginal gains? They were heading home.

This was a major mistake. Operation Z had always been two gambles in one. The first – could they successfully attack Pearl Harbor? – had been answered in the affirmative. The second – could such a success create the conditions for a wider victory? – remained to be answered. Fuchida and Genda were right in believing that the destruction of the fuel and dockyard installations on Oahu, and/or the sinking of the two enemy carriers in the area, would have made life much more difficult for the Americans. The odds on the second gamble had always been incredibly long, and any means of shortening them had to be pursued.

But Nagumo and Kusaka were far from alone in their culpability. The prioritization of targets had been set in stone at the planning stage, and the foolishly low priority accorded the oil farms, repair facilities and power generators at Pearl Harbor reflected the same obsession with weaponry and neglect of logistics which were dooming the German wars in the Soviet Union and North Africa. If the installations which allowed Pearl Harbor to function as an air and naval base had been targeted and destroyed in the first attacks – if necessary, at the expense of leaving a few obsolete battleships afloat – the excessive caution of Nagumo and Kusaka would not have mattered.

From 06.00 on 8 December Japanese radio carried announcements of the outbreak of war, and at 11.45 the imperial authorization was read out over the air. The navy had their say at 13.00, claiming a 'crippling raid on USA naval and air forces in the Hawaii area', and Tojo made a short speech emphasizing Japan's unbeaten record over two thousand years.[18] This record alone was 'enough to produce a conviction in our ability to crush any enemy no matter how strong'. The stakes were high: according to Tojo 'the prosperity or ruin of East Asia literally depend upon the outcome of this war'.[19]

Some were convinced – years of 'patriotic education' had taken their toll. Many, like student Nogi Harumichi, 'felt a sense of relief more than anything else . . . the constraints of deadlock were broken and the way before Japan was clear'.[20] And there was also elation and pride, particularly as news of the Pearl Harbor triumph came through. According to Yoshida Toshio, who worked in the Navy Ministry, members of the operations section were 'swaggering up and down the halls, swinging their shoulders'.[21] Others were imagining what exotic opportunities the future might hold. Nodi Mitsuharu, serving aboard the *Nagato*, saw himself as head of accounts in the Japanese garrison in San Francisco.[22]

Some were more realistic. Machinist Kumagaya Tokuichi had a pretty good idea what was going to happen: 'Those who dealt with machinery realized what a gap there was between us and the Americans.'[23] Tanisuga Shizuo, who had fought in China, could hardly believe his ears when the news came through. 'How could such a country win with America and Britain as opponents? . . . War meant national suicide . . .'[24] On hearing of the Pearl Harbor sinkings, Onozuka Kiheiji, a former president of Tokyo's Imperial University, whispered to a colleague: 'This means that Japan is sunk too.'[25]

News of America's military involvement was greeted with relief in the Chinese Nationalist capital, Chungking. According to novelist Han Suyin, whose husband was about to take up the post of military attaché in London, Generalissimo Chiang Kai-shek sang operatic airs and played *Ave Maria* all day, while his generals congratulated each other and started making lists of what new toys they could expect from Washington. There was also more than a hint of glee – the 'fat boy' Americans, so used to criticizing the Chinese for their gross inefficiency, had really been caught with their pants down by the Japanese.

In Washington it was still 7 December. That evening the Cabinet gathered around the President's desk in the Oval Office. Roosevelt outlined the scope of the disaster at Pearl Harbor with suitable solemnity, but those who knew him well detected an underlying relief. The die had been cast, and he knew as well as Churchill how weighted it now was against the Axis.

Should America declare war on Germany and Italy? Would Pearl Harbor blow away public opposition to American involvement in the European war? Fortunately for Roosevelt and his colleagues, they knew from the intercepted messages between Oshima and Tokyo that Hitler had promised to join the Japanese and would almost certainly declare war on the United States in the next few days. In the meantime, and particularly in the Atlantic, they would act as if he already had.

On Formosa the fog slowly cleared. Between 08.30 and 09.45 192 planes – 108 Mitsubishi bombers and 84 Zeros – took off from the airfields at Takao and Tainan and headed south towards Clark and Iba Fields.

Back at his headquarters, Brereton was told around 08.00 that radar had picked up a large incoming formation. Both fighters and B-17s were scrambled, the former to intercept the intruders, the bombers because they would be safer circling Mount Arayat than stuck on the ground. They had not been up for long when news began reaching Manila of minor Japanese attacks in northern Luzon (committed by Formosa-based army planes whose strips had not been fogged in) and the far south (launched from the carrier *Ryujo*). Surely this was overt enough, Brereton argued, but Sutherland would still only sanction a photo reconnaissance mission over Formosa. The fact that one was needed – while the Japanese had a clear picture of American bases in the Philippines, the

Americans had only the blurriest notion of the Japanese bases on Formosa – spoke volumes about MacArthur's preparations for this long-anticipated moment.

And then, almost out of the blue at 10.15, MacArthur rang Brereton and gave him carte blanche to act as he saw fit. Over the next half-hour Brereton's staff completed the plan for a dusk strike by the B-17 force on the known Formosan airfields. The earlier alarm had proved false, and the bombers were ordered back down for refuelling and bomb-loading in preparation for a 14.00 departure. At around noon, Brereton also called the fighters down for refuelling. It was his first mistake of the day, and it would prove fatal.

At 08.00 Brooke-Popham received his answer from London – he had permission to authorize Matador even if the Japanese attacked only Malaya. Two hours later the plan was officially abandoned, but the 11th Indian Division was not apprised of this fact until 13.30, shortening still further the time it would have to improve the weak defensive positions around Jitra.

At the outbreaks of the first Sino-Japanese, Russo-Japanese and First World Wars, the Japanese Emperor had called on his subjects to respect internationally accepted conventions on the conduct of war and occupation. No such request was made on this occasion.

Ten weeks had passed since the dismantling and transportation of the Kharkov Tank Works east to the Urals, and the first new batch of T-34s was now rolling off the re-erected assembly line. Across Siberia and Central Asia many other relocated industries were getting back to work, dramatically expanding the Soviet war economy. Those ten weeks of non-production had represented a significant window of opportunity for the Germans. The last they would get.

The long-delayed German withdrawal from Tikhvin was a messy affair, coinciding as it did with the Soviet 4th Army's fighting entry. OKH and Hitler had almost left it too late, and an orderly retreat was the best von Leeb could hope for. There was certainly no possibility of holding a new defence line short of the Volkhov, and fulfilling Hitler's demand that the city be kept within artillery range. The wider ring around Leningrad, which the Führer had ordered to be tightened, had now been substantially loosened. The Soviet Union's second city would not be razed to the ground, and two-thirds of its three million residents would outlive the murderer of the other third.

Around the capital, the relief was more immediate. Only a week ago, news of fighting in Kryukovo and Krasnaya Polyana had been panic-inducing, terrifying proof of how close the Germans were. Over that week those towns had come to stand for defiance, and now, as the enemy was finally driven out, they were the names of victories. Solnechnogorsk would soon follow, and Istra, and Klin.

A few miles north-east of the last, General Ferdinand Schaal was reduced to lying behind a lorry and firing single rounds from a carbine when his 56th Panzer Korps HQ came under attack. These were desperate days, and discipline, as Schaal later remembered, 'began to crack. There were more and more soldiers making their own way back to the west, without any weapons, leading a calf on a rope, or drawing a sledge of potatoes behind them – just trudging westwards with no one in command. Men killed by aerial bombardment were no longer buried . . . Supply units were in the grip of psychosis, almost of panic, probably because in the past they had only been used to headlong advances. Without food, shivering in the cold, in utter confusion, the men moved west.'[26]

Von Luck's unit was also retreating. 'It was a grisly sight. Alongside dead horses lay dead and wounded infantrymen. "Take us with you or else shoot us," they begged. As far as space allowed, we took them on our supply vehicles to hastily organized dressing stations. The poor devils. Protected against the cold with makeshift foot-rags, they were now only a shadow of those who had stormed through Poland and France.'[27]

As they jolted their way eastwards on a rough road, Henry Metelmann and his comrades became aware of a distant rumbling – the guns at the front. Today they were only going to their billets, in a one-street village of mud-built cottages. Their orders were to take one cottage per crew and throw the family out. 'When we entered "ours",' Metelmann remembered, 'a woman and her three young children were sitting around the table by the window, obviously having just finished a meal. She was clearly frightened of us, and I could see that her hands were shaking, while the kids stayed in their seats and looked at us with large non-understanding eyes. Our sergeant came straight to the point: "*Raus!*", and pointed to the door.'

The woman objected, but to no avail. The sergeant gave her five minutes to gather their belongings, holding up that number of fingers in explanation. She did as she was told, dressed her children and led them out into the bitter cold. Watching them 'standing by their bundles in the snow, looking helplessly in all directions, not knowing what to do', Metelmann 'felt strange. In all my life I had never been in such a situation before. When I looked again a little later, they were gone; I did not want to think about it any more.'[28]

PQ6 left Hvalfjordur in Iceland. It would be the sixth of eighty-two convoys to reach either Murmansk or Archangel with supplies of mostly American weaponry, vehicles and food supplies for the Soviet Union.

Most of Rommel's army was now heading for the temporary safety of the Gazala line, but one division, *Pavia*, had suffered a severe and thoroughly unnecessary mauling in the process. Supreme Command in Rome had been shocked by Rommel's threat to abandon Cyrenaica, and Gambara, acting on his boss General Bastico's behalf, had shamefully sought to make a point at his own troops' expense. He had countermanded the German order to withdraw, and exposed *Pavia* to a heavy British attack.

This took place in the early hours, and it felt like a final straw to Rommel, who was still seething over *Ariete*'s no-show and Neumann-Silkow's subsequent death. When General Bastico arrived to see him that morning he kept his Italian superior waiting outside the Mammoth's door for fifteen minutes, and then treated him to a diatribe which the Führer would have appreciated.

The Crusader defeat was all the Italians' fault, Rommel told their startled commander. He intended to take his own divisions back to Tunisia and give himself up to the French.

An alarmed Bastico did his best to soothe the German and accepted, as Rommel probably intended he should, the humiliating notion of a total withdrawal from Italian Cyrenaica. This bout of bad feeling between allies would simmer for several days, the Italians complaining bitterly of Rommel's rudeness but lacking a coherent strategic alternative to the proposed retreat. They knew, as he did, that both Germans and Italians had fought well in the Crusader battles, and that fighting well had not been enough.

It was still dark in Riga when the Jews were ordered out of their temporary home. Latvian police at the door tried to steal a march on their German superiors by demanding jewellery and money, but were mostly ignored. An SS man swinging a wooden club told them to leave their carefully packed bag of belongings on the pavement, and was unanimously obeyed.

They were marched off through the city at a brisk pace, encouraged by occasional shots and the cracking of whips. When they reached the Moscow highway the pace seemed to increase – now they were almost running, and desperately trying not to slip on the icy ground and be shot where they fell.

As they neared the Rumbula Forest the sounds of shooting grew louder. The doubts were all gone, but what could they do, hemmed in by lines of police and SS? 'The situation was hopeless,' as Frida Michelson wrote later. 'We were all numb with terror and followed orders mechanically. We were incapable of thinking and were submitting to everything like a docile herd of cattle.'[29]

At the entrance to the forest there was a box for their money and valuables, and most obliged, despite the lack of any search. A little further on, they were ordered to add their overcoats to an already groaning pile.

Michelson went up to one of the policemen and tried to make a case for her own survival. 'Go show your diplomas to Stalin!' the man yelled at her, scattering her precious papers.

The shooting was louder now. 'We were nearing the end. An indescribable fear took hold of me, a fear that bordered on loss of mind. I started screaming hysterically, tearing my hair, to drown out the sounds of the shooting.'[30]

They were told to take off all but their underclothes, and Michelson tried to lose herself in the pile. Hauled back out, she was saved by a Latvian woman, who distracted the nearest guard with her own plea for special treatment. Michelson flung herself down on the ground, face gouged deep in the snow, and tried to play dead.

For several minutes she lay there, convinced it was only a matter of time before her imposture was discovered. But then something landed on her back, and something else again. It was shoes, she realized, shoes and boots and galoshes – she was disappearing under a mound of the ghetto's footwear.

Hours went by, hours of keening and moaning and shooting, until all that remained was one child crying for her mother, a last burst of shots and finally silence. Once darkness had fallen, Michelson worked her way out from under the pile and resumed her task of surviving the war.

In the small village of Chelmno, some thirty-miles north-west of Lodz in central Poland, eighty men were ordered out of the mansion where they'd spent the night and into the back of a large van. They and their 620 companions had been told that they were being sent 'East' to work, but this would be their last journey. As the van set off into the nearby forest, its redirected exhaust pipe began pumping carbon monoxide into the back. By the time it reached its destination in a remote clearing, the screaming and hammering had long since stopped, and the bodies could be tipped out for mass burial.

The van went back for more, on this and each of the next four days. By 11 December almost all of the 4,000 Jews who had lived in nearby Kolo were buried in the forest clearing. The Nazi genocide had entered its industrial phase, but the promised regularization of the process would have to wait a few weeks.

Afraid that recent events would require himself and others to attend a Reichstag session over the next few days, Heydrich reluctantly postponed the Wannsee meeting that was scheduled for Tuesday. It would be held in January.

Woken in the middle of the night by Ribbentrop – he was 'jumping with joy about the Japanese attack on the United States' – Ciano had resisted the temptation to dampen his caller's enthusiasm with expressions of doubt. But when, later that morning, King Victor Emmanuel also 'expressed his satisfaction' at the turn of events, the Foreign Minister allowed himself to suggest that a long war might allow America to mobilize all its potential strength. The King took this in and brilliantly observed that in the long run his Foreign Minister might be right.

As in Tokyo, the essential irrelevance of success in the short run was not quite grasped. Mussolini was also delighted with the news from Hawaii, and the 'clarifying' light it threw on the relationship between America and the Axis.[31]

The incoming flight of 192 Japanese fighters and bombers was picked up by radar. Warnings were sent to Clark Field by teletype, radio and phone. The first was missed because the operator was at lunch, the second because of static, the third because it was not passed on by its recipient.

At 12.35 the bombs started falling. Less than a hour later, as the last Japanese fighter turned for home, all but one of the vaunted B-17s and almost all of the American P-40 fighters were smoking wrecks. Buildings, installations and fuel tanks had been destroyed, and black smoke was pouring upwards into the Philippine sky, signalling disaster.

Hawaii, Malaya, the Philippines – in half a day three different command structures had been caught napping by the Japanese, a display of serial incompetence which almost beggars belief.

Phillips took the *Prince of Wales* and *Repulse* north that afternoon, intent on attacking the Japanese beachheads and supply lines. Seen from the air on the following day, he abandoned the idea, only to renew it when news of further landings reached him. No RAF support was provided, and when the Japanese bombers eventually found him on 10 December the result was entirely predictable. It was a British disaster, but, in retrospect, hardly a Japanese triumph. In sending Force Z to the bottom of the sea the pilots from Indo-China had done little more than demonstrate the new irrelevance of the battleship, and, by implication, the hollowness of their comrades' victory at Pearl Harbor.

According to the Wehrmacht's daily Eastern Front report, there were 'only local combat operations in progress'.[32] The German troops knew otherwise – the Red Army was steadily pushing them back, and in some areas seemed to be threatening a great deal more. But encirclements, and the wholesale destruction of large German formations, were still beyond the Red Army's capability. As Zhukov later admitted, had his Red Army commanders relied less on frontal assaults and more on bypassing enemy concentrations and striking at supply and communication lines, greater successes might have been achieved. But like the British in the desert, they were still learning how to fight a modern war. Only when the Allied armies had absorbed all the Germans could teach them would their economic superiority prove decisive.

Von Bock didn't know it, but he had made the cover of that week's *Time* magazine. It was clear to the article's author that the tide of the eastern campaign had turned, and the article's subject seems, finally, to have reached a similar epiphany. In the current situation, he told Guderian, 'either one held out, or let himself be killed. There were no other choices.'[33]

Hitler had reached the same conclusion. According to Führer Directive No. 39, issued before his departure for Berlin that day, 'the severe winter weather which has come surprisingly early in the East, and the consequent difficulties in bringing up supplies, compel us to abandon immediately all major offensive operations and go over to the defensive'.[34] Barbarossa had failed, and any slim chance of creating a European superpower capable of taking on the

United States and Britain had died with it. Nazi Germany, as Todt
and Rohland had all but told their Führer on 29 November, was a
dead man walking.

If Yamamoto doubted that his attack on Pearl Harbor had galva-
nized America resistance, he need only have listened to US Senator
Arthur Vandenberg's press conference that afternoon. A member of
the Senate Foreign Relations Committee for twelve years,
Vandenberg had advocated isolationism with a rare persistence. He
had done everything he possibly could to prevent the United States
being drawn into another war, to the extent of recommending
American recognition of Japanese rule over parts of China. But the
attack on Pearl Harbor had changed everything. From this moment
on, he told the assembled press corps, only one thing mattered:
'victorious war with every resource at our command.'[35]

EPILOGUE

There is far too much deference accorded by historians to political and military leaders, most of whom ally average
intelligence to above-average doses of the less desirable human
attributes. The history of these twenty-two days is replete with stu-
pidity, incompetence, short-sightedness and evil in high places,
and remarkably deficient in wisdom, simple competence, far-
sightedness or human empathy. Finest hours were thin on the
ground.

At one Stavka session in November 1941, Marshal Timoshenko
told his colleagues that oil was the crucial factor, and that all that
the Soviets needed to do was force the Germans to increase their
consumption while denying them access to fresh supplies. With the
enemy at the gates of the Soviet capital, he had the temerity to say
that 'the first phase of the war had actually been won by the Red
Army, however much a glance at the map may give a the public a
different impression'.[1] Timoshenko's ability to see beyond the map
was shared by Auchinleck, but not by many others. During
Barbarossa Timoshenko's colleagues in the Red Army were mostly
reliant on human sacrifice to slow the Germans, while Auchinleck's
subordinates were only saved by a relative surfeit of weapons and
fuel. The British military commands in the Far East made a com-

plete pig's ear of defending Singapore, the American military commands on Hawaii managed to misinterpret almost every signal they received, and MacArthur's culpability for the Philippines catastrophe was virtually complete.

Fortunately for the Allied commanders, their opponents were not much better. The German army group and army commanders in Russia did well enough with what they were given, but chose – or allowed the regime to impose – policies of war and occupation which inevitably strengthened their enemy. Their superiors had missed the basic point, that in the absence of a well-run war economy or anything to offer the peoples they conquered, any military successes were bound to be temporary.

The Japanese had the same problem. Yamamoto's attack on Pearl Harbor was daring, inspired and utterly irresponsible. Winning this particular battle meant next to nothing in the context of Japan's economic weakness and brutish occupation policies. And once the predictable reaction of the loser was taken into account, it meant even less. Yamamoto was fully aware of this. His opponent had all the high cards, yet still he opted for playing and losing.

The political leaders exercised no moderating influence on their military commanders. The Axis and Japanese leaders set their losing wars in motion, set its brutal tone, sacrificing millions of other nationals and eventually millions of their own. They made the essentially heartless mistake of believing that whole peoples could be subdued indefinitely by intimidation and violence, when all the evidence available to them actually suggested otherwise. Stalin was as reckless with lives in war as he had been in peace, Roosevelt made sure that nuclear science would be applied, first and foremost, to weapons of mass destruction, and Churchill gave his full backing to the strategic bombing policy which served as a precedent for so many later atrocities. Small wonder that the baleful legacy of the Second World War still lingers on.

Japan's only hope of victory – and a faint one at that – had lain in attacking the Soviet Union in July 1941. A reinforced Barbarossa might have knocked the latter out of the war without triggering an

American entry and set up a more equal global contest between the Anglo-American and Tripartite Pact powers. But the Japanese military had, not without reason, shrunk from such a step, and any chance of winning a war had long since passed when Nagumo set out from Hitokappu Bay. The Japanese success at Pearl Harbor had only a temporary impact, as Yamamoto had known it would. He had offered Prince Konoye a possible year of victories, but barely six months had passed when *Kido Butai*'s defeat at Midway ushered in the long and hopeless struggle to stave off defeat.

The initial Japanese onslaught had an impact elsewhere – Hitler was not entirely mistaken in thinking that a fresh enemy would make life more difficult for his opponents. The losses at Pearl Harbor and in the Philippines, and the strategic retreats that went with them, did shift American attention and productive capacity away from Europe for a while. The loss of Malaya and threats to Burma and India necessitated a weakening of British forces in the Middle East which a resupplied Rommel would make the most of. But the Germans would still end up fighting the first decisive battle at El Alamein with fewer than forty tanks, and the planes and U-boats brought in to protect Rommel's supply lines would be sorely missed in Russia and the Atlantic.

There was not enough to go around, and there never had been. It is often assumed that the German war in the east came to grief at Stalingrad, and while this is literally true, it shrouds the deeper truth, that Germany's failing war economy not only ruled out the repetition of a Barbarossa-scale offensive in 1942, but even precluded success on the limited scale envisaged for that summer. Stalingrad, like El Alamein, was a defeat waiting to happen. With the successful relocation of Soviet industry to the east, and the American entry into the war, each month that passed saw a widening of the relative disparity in military-economic strength. The only opponents whom the Nazis could still beat were those helplessly trapped behind German lines – the Jews and the Roma, the Communists and socialists, the mentally handicapped and the homosexuals.

By December 1941 there was no hope of reversing the tide; the war was already won and lost. Unfortunately, human beings still had to win and lose it. Two-thirds of the approximately fifty million people who died in the Second World War would do so after Japan's attack on Pearl Harbor. Many millions more would lose people who brought joy to their lives – husbands and wives, mothers and fathers, sons and daughters, brothers, sisters and friends. A generation maimed in body and soul, and all to demonstrate, for the umpteenth time, the futility of using violence in pursuit of national and racial aggrandizement.

REFERENCES

MONDAY 17 NOVEMBER
1. Ugaki, Matome, *Fading Victory* (University of Pittsburgh Press, 1991)
2. Quoted in Bartsch, William, *December 8, 1941* (Texas A&M University Press, 2003)
3. Quoted in Rzhevskaya, Elena, 'Roads and Days: The Memoirs of a Red Army Translator', *Journal of Slavonic Military Studies*, Vol. 14, March 2001
4. Quoted in Burdick, C., and Jacobsen, H.-A., *The Halder War Diary* (Greenhill, 1988)
5. Quoted in Haupt, Werner, *Assault on Moscow 1941* (Schiffer, 1996)
6. Quoted in Braithwaite, Rodric, *Moscow 1941* (Profile, 2006)
7. Ibid
8. Guderian, Heinz, *Panzer Leader* (Futura, 1974)
9. *Das Reich*, 16 November 1941
10. Quoted in Gilbert, Martin, *The Holocaust* (Fontana, 1987)
11. Ibid
12. Ibid
13. Quoted in Irving, David, *Hitler's War* (Hodder & Stoughton, 1977)
14. Crisp, Robert, *Brazen Chariots* (Corgi, 1960)
15. Quoted in Allen, Louis, *Singapore* (Davis-Poynter, 1977)
16. Quoted in Bryant, Arthur, *The Turn of the Tide* (Fontana, 1965)
17. *The Times*, 17 November 1941
18. *Daily Mirror*, 17 November 1941
19. *The Times*, 17 November 1941
20. *New York Times*, 17 November 1941
21. Hull, Cordell, *Memoirs* (Hodder & Stoughton, 1948)
22. Quoted in Prange, Gordon, *At Dawn We Slept* (Penguin, 2001)
23. Quoted in Heinrichs, Waldo, *Threshold of War* (Oxford University Press, 1988)

TUESDAY 18 NOVEMBER
1. Quoted in Deane, John Potter, *Admiral of the Pacific* (Heinemann, 1965)

2. Ugaki, Matome, *Fading Victory* (University of Pittsburgh Press, 1991)
3. Bek, Alexander, *The Volokolamsk Highway* (Moscow Foreign Languages, c. 1964)
4. Ibid
5. Ibid
6. Rokossovsky, Konstantin, *A Soldier's Duty* (Progress, 1970)
7. Ibid
8. Ibid
9. Quoted in Piekalkiewicz, Janusz, *Moscow 1941* (Arms & Armour, 1981)
10. Quoted in Haupt, Werner, *Army Group South* (Schiffer, 1998)
11. Quoted in Armstrong, John (ed.), *Soviet Partisans in World War II* (University of Wisconsin Press, 1964)
12. Quoted in Kershaw, Ian, *Hitler 1936–45: Nemesis* (Allen Lane, 2000)
13. Quoted in Heiber, Helmut, *Goebbels* (Robert Hale, 1973)
14. Crisp, Robert, *Brazen Chariots* (Corgi, 1960)
15. Ibid
16. *New York Times*, 18 November 1941

WEDNESDAY 19 NOVEMBER

1. Quoted in Muggenthaler, Karl, *German Raiders of World War II* (Pan, 1980)
2. Ibid
3. Quoted in Cook, H. T., and Cook, T. F., *Japan at War: An Oral History* (New Press, 1992)
4. Quoted in Wohlstetter, Roberta, *Pearl Harbor: Warning and Decision* (Stanford University Press, 1962)
5. Quoted in Prange, Gordon, *At Dawn We Slept* (Penguin, 2001)
6. Quoted in Burdick, C., and Jacobsen, H.-A., *The Halder War Diary* (Greenhill, 1988)
7. Ibid
8. Ibid
9. Guderian, Heinz, *Panzer Leader* (Futura, 1974)
10. Crisp, Robert, *Brazen Chariots* (Corgi, 1960)
11. Quoted in Agar-Hamilton, J., and Turner, L., *The Sidi Rezeg Battles 1941* (Oxford University Press, 1957)
12. Quoted in Walker, Ian W., *Iron Hulls, Iron Hearts* (Crowood, 2003)
13. Ibid
14. Moorehead, Alan, *The Desert War* (Hamish Hamilton, 1965)
15. Ibid
16. Mellenthin, F. W. von, *Panzer Battles* (University of Oklahoma, 1956)
17. Ibid
18. Crisp, Robert, *Brazen Chariots* (Corgi, 1960)
19. Ibid
20. Quoted in Burdick, C., and Jacobsen, H.-A., *The Halder War Diary* (Greenhill, 1988)

21. Quoted in Trevor-Roper, Hugh, *Hitler's Table Talk* (Weidenfeld & Nicolson, 1953)
22. Metelmann, Henry, *Through Hell for Hitler* (Stephens, 1990)
23. Quoted in Gilbert, Martin, *The Holocaust* (Fontana, 1987)
24. Ibid
25. Ciano, Count Galeazzo, *Diaries*, ed. Muggeridge, Malcolm (Heinemann, 1947)
26. Ibid

THURSDAY 20 NOVEMBER
 1. Quoted in Haupt, Werner, *Army Group South* (Schiffer, 1998)
 2. quoted in Salisbury, Harrison, *The 900 Days: The Siege of Leningrad* (Pan, 2000)
 3. Bock, Fedor von, *The War Diary* (Schiffer, 1996)
 4. Quoted in Tooze, Adam, *The Wages of Destruction* (Penguin, 2007)
 5. http://www.holocaust-education.de/resmedia/document/A028T04E.PDF
 6. Quoted in Kershaw, Ian, *Hitler 1936–45: Nemesis* (Allen Lane, 2000)
 7. Quoted in Trevor-Roper, Hugh, *Hitler's Table Talk* (Weidenfeld & Nicolson, 1953)
 8. Ciano, Count Galeazzo, *Diaries*, ed. Muggeridge, Malcolm (Heinemann, 1947)
 9. *Daily Mirror*, 20 November 1941
10. Quoted in Parkinson, R., *Blood, Toil, Tears and Sweat* (Hart-Davis MacGibbon, 1973)
11. Mellenthin, F. W. von, *Panzer Battles* (University of Oklahoma, 1956)
12. Crisp, Robert, *Brazen Chariots* (Corgi, 1960)
13. Ibid
14. Quoted in Macintyre, Donald, *Battle for the Mediterranean* (Batsford, 1964)
15. Ciano, Count Galeazzo, *Diaries*, ed. Muggeridge, Malcolm (Heinemann, 1947)
16. Quoted in Toland, John, *Rising Sun* (Penguin, 2001)
17. Ibid

FRIDAY 21 NOVEMBER
 1. Quoted in Prange, Gordon, *At Dawn We Slept* (Penguin, 2001)
 2. Quoted in Rzhevskaya, Elena, 'Roads and Days: The Memoirs of a Red Army Translator', *Journal of Slavonic Military Studies*, Vol. 14, March 2001
 3. Bock, Fedor von, *The War Diary* (Schiffer, 1996)
 4. Guderian, Heinz, *Panzer Leader* (Futura, 1974)
 5. Quoted in Erickson, John, *The Road to Stalingrad* (Weidenfeld & Nicolson, 1975)
 6. Quoted in Braithwaite, Rodric, *Moscow 1941* (Profile, 2006)
 7. http://en.wikipedia.org/wiki/Occupation_of_Denmark_by_Nazi_Germany

8. Quoted in Kershaw, Ian, *Hitler 1936–45: Nemesis* (Allen Lane, 2000)
9. Ibid
10. Quoted in Pitt, Barry, *The Crucible of War: Auchinleck's Command* (Cassell, 2001)
11. Quoted in Connell, John, *Auchinleck* (Cassell, 1959)
12. Crisp, Robert, *Brazen Chariots* (Corgi, 1960)
13. Quoted in Burdick, C., and Jacobsen, H.-A., *The Halder War Diary* (Greenhill, 1988)
14. Ibid
15. Quoted in Wohlstetter, Roberta, *Pearl Harbor: Warning and Decision* (Stanford University Press, 1962)

SATURDAY 22 NOVEMBER
1. Quoted in Wohlstetter, Roberta, *Pearl Harbor: Warning and Decision* (Stanford University Press, 1962)
2. Quoted in Prange, Gordon, *At Dawn We Slept* (Penguin, 2001)
3. Ibid
4. Quoted in Burdick, C., and Jacobsen, H.-A., *The Halder War Diary* (Greenhill, 1988)
5. Quoted in Rzhevskaya, Elena, 'Roads and Days: The Memoirs of a Red Army Translator', *Journal of Slavonic Military Studies*, Vol. 14, March 2001
6. Rokossovsky, Konstantin, *A Soldier's Duty* (Progress, 1970)
7. Quoted in Kirchubel, Robert, *Operation Barbarossa: Army Group North* (Osprey, 2005)
8. www.usswashington.com/worldwar2plus55/dl21no41.htm
9. Quoted in Gilbert, Martin, *The Holocaust* (Fontana, 1987)
10. Quoted in Crisp, Robert, *Brazen Chariots* (Corgi, 1960)
11. Ibid
12. Ibid
13. Quoted in Humble, Richard, *Crusader* (Leo Cooper, 1987)
14. Quoted in Macintyre, Donald, *Battle of the Atlantic* (Batsford, 1961)
15. Quoted in Muggenthaler, Karl *German Raiders of World War II* (Pan, 1980)
16. Quoted in Heinrichs, Waldo, *Threshold of War* (Oxford University Press, 1988)
17. Hull, Cordell, *Memoirs* (Hodder & Stoughton, 1948)

SUNDAY 23 NOVEMBER
1. Ugaki, Matome, *Fading Victory* (University of Pittsburgh Press, 1991)
2. Quoted in Prange, Gordon, *At Dawn We Slept* (Penguin, 2001)
3. Ibid
4. Quoted in Cook, H. T., and Cook, T. F., *Japan at War: An Oral History* (New Press, 1992)
5. Guderian, Heinz, *Panzer Leader* (Futura, 1974)
6. Rokossovsky, Konstantin, *A Soldier's Duty* (Progress, 1970)
7. Ibid

8. Ibid
9. Quoted in Erickson, John, *The Road to Stalingrad* (Weidenfeld & Nicolson, 1975)
10. Quoted in Burdick, C., and Jacobsen, H.-A., *The Halder War Diary* (Greenhill, 1988)
11. *Das Reich*, 23 November 1941
12. http://en.wikipedia.org/wiki/Occupation_of_Denmark_by_Nazi_Germany
13. Quoted in Irving, David, *The Trail of the Fox* (Weidenfeld & Nicolson, 1977)
14. Mellenthin, F. W. von, *Panzer Battles* (University of Oklahoma, 1956)
15. Ibid
16. Quoted in Connell, John, *Auchinleck* (Cassell, 1959)
17. Schmidt, Heinz W., *With Rommel in the Desert* (Harrap, 1953)
18. Crisp, Robert, *Brazen Chariots* (Corgi, 1960)
19. Quoted in Connell, John, *Auchinleck* (Cassell, 1959)
20. Quoted in Agar-Hamilton, J., and Turner, L., *The Sidi Rezeg Battles 1941* (Oxford University Press, 1957)
21. Mellenthin, F. W. von, *Panzer Battles* (University of Oklahoma, 1956)
22. Quoted in Lewin, Ronald, *Rommel as a Military Commander* (Batsford, 1968)
23. Mellenthin, F. W. von, *Panzer Battles* (University of Oklahoma, 1956)
24. Quoted in Guingand, Francis de, Operation Victory (Hodder & Stoughton, 1947)

MONDAY 24 NOVEMBER

1. Rokossovsky, Konstantin, *A Soldier's Duty* (Progress, 1970)
2. Ibid
3. Quoted in Rzhevskaya, Elena, 'Roads and Days: The Memoirs of a Red Army Translator', *Journal of Slavonic Military Studies*, Vol. 14, March 2001
4. Quoted in Burdick, C., and Jacobsen, H.-A., *The Halder War Diary* (Greenhill, 1988)
5. Ciano, Count Galeazzo, *Diaries*, ed. Muggeridge, Malcolm (Heinemann, 1947)
6. Quoted in Pitt, Barry, *The Crucible of War: Auchinleck's Command* (Cassell, 2001)
7. Quoted in Connell, John, *Auchinleck* (Cassell, 1959)
8. Moorehead, Alan, *The Desert War* (Hamish Hamilton, 1965)
9. Quoted in Young, Desmond, *Rommel* (Collins, 1950)
10. Crisp, Robert, *Brazen Chariots* (Corgi, 1960)
11. Quoted in Barnett, Corelli, *The Desert Generals* (William Kimber, 1960)
12. Curie, Eve, *Journey Among Warriors* (William Heinemann, 1943)
13. Crisp, Robert, *Brazen Chariots* (Corgi, 1960)
14. Quoted in Toland, John, *Rising Sun* (Penguin, 2001)
15. Ibid

16. Quoted in Feis, Herbert, *The Road to Pearl Harbor* (Princeton, 1950)
17. Quoted in Wohlstetter, Roberta, *Pearl Harbor: Warning and Decision* (Stanford University Press, 1962)

TUESDAY 25 NOVEMBER
 1. Quoted in Lord, Walter, *Day of Infamy* (Bantam, 1958)
 2. Quoted in Prange, Gordon, *At Dawn We Slept* (Penguin, 2001)
 3. Quoted in Allen, Louis, *Singapore* (Davis–Poynter, 1977)
 4. Quoted in Burdick, C., and Jacobsen, H.-A., *The Halder War Diary* (Greenhill, 1988)
 5. Zhukov, Georgi, *Reminiscences and Reflections* (Progress, 1985)
 6. Quoted in Irving, David, *Hitler's War* (Hodder & Stoughton, 1977)
 7. Ciano, Count Galeazzo, *Diaries*, ed. Muggeridge, Malcolm (Heinemann, 1947)
 8. Bock, Fedor von, *The War Diary* (Schiffer, 1996)
 9. Quoted in Connell, John, *Auchinleck* (Cassell, 1959)
10. Quoted in Humble, Richard, *Crusader* (Leo Cooper, 1987)
11. Crisp, Robert, *Brazen Chariots* (Corgi, 1960)
12. Hull, Cordell, *Memoirs* (Hodder & Stoughton, 1948)
13. Quoted in Toland, John, *Rising Sun* (Penguin, 2001)
14. Ibid
15. Ibid
16. Ibid
17. Quoted in Wohlstetter, Roberta, *Pearl Harbor: Warning and Decision* (Stanford University Press, 1962)

WEDNESDAY 26 NOVEMBER
 1. Quoted in Prange, Gordon, *At Dawn We Slept* (Penguin, 2001)
 2. Ibid
 3. Quoted in Agawa, Hiroyuki, *Yamamoto, Reluctant Admiral* (Harper & Row, 1979)
 4. Ibid
 5. Ibid
 6. Quoted in Prange, Gordon, *At Dawn We Slept* (Penguin, 2001)
 7. Ibid
 8. Quoted in Bartsch, William, *December 8, 1941* (Texas A&M University Press, 2003)
 9. Ibid
10. Zhukov, Georgi, *Reminiscences and Reflections* (Progress, 1985)
11. Rokossovsky, Konstantin, *A Soldier's Duty* (Progress, 1970)
12. Quoted in Bloch, Michael, *Ribbentrop* (Abacus, 2002)
13. Ciano, Count Galeazzo, *Diaries*, ed. Muggeridge, Malcolm (Heinemann, 1947)
14. Quoted in Murphy, W. E., *The Relief of Tobruk* (New Zealand government publication, 1961)

15. Ibid
16. Quoted in Kimball, Warren, *Churchill and Roosevelt: the Complete Correspondence* (Princeton University Press, *c.* 1984)
17. Hull, Cordell, *Memoirs* (Hodder & Stoughton, 1948)
18. Quoted in Heinrichs, Waldo, *Threshold of War* (Oxford University Press, 1988)
19. Hull, Cordell, *Memoirs* (Hodder & Stoughton, 1948)
20. Quoted in Wohlstetter, Roberta, *Pearl Harbor: Warning and Decision* (Stanford University Press, 1962)

THURSDAY 27 NOVEMBER
 1. Quoted in Toland, John, *Rising Sun* (Penguin, 2001)
 2. Guderian, Heinz, *Panzer Leader* (Futura, 1974)
 3. Ibid
 4. Luck, Hans von, *Panzer Commander* (Cassell, 2002)
 5. Rokossovsky, Konstantin, *A Soldier's Duty* (Progress, 1970)
 6. Quoted in Liddell Hart, B. H., The Other Side of the Hill (Cassell, 1951)
 7. Quoted in Friedlander, Saul, *The Years of Extermination* (Weidenfeld & Nicolson, 2007)
 8. Quoted in Hauner, M., *Hitler: A Chronology of His Life and Time* (Palgrave Macmillan, 2005)
 9. Quoted in Irving, David, *Hitler's War* (Hodder & Stoughton, 1977)
10. Quoted in Agar-Hamilton, J., and Turner, L., *The Sidi Rezeg Battles 1941* (Oxford University Press, 1957)
11. Quoted in Lewin, Ronald, *Rommel as a Military Commander* (Batsford, 1968)
12. Mellenthin, F. W. von, *Panzer Battles* (University of Oklahoma, 1956)
13. Quoted in Wohlstetter, Roberta, *Pearl Harbor: Warning and Decision* (Stanford University Press, 1962)
14. Ibid
15. Quoted in Rhodes, Richard, *The Making of the Atomic Bomb* (Touchstone, 1988)
16. Quoted in Wohlstetter, Roberta, *Pearl Harbor: Warning and Decision* (Stanford University Press, 1962)
17. Quoted in Prange, Gordon, *At Dawn We Slept* (Penguin, 2001)
18. Quoted in Wohlstetter, Roberta, *Pearl Harbor: Warning and Decision* (Stanford University Press, 1962)

FRIDAY 28 NOVEMBER
 1. Quoted in Feis, Herbert, *The Road to Pearl Harbor* (Princeton, 1950)
 2. Quoted in Bartsch, William, *December 8, 1941* (Texas A&M University Press, 2003)
 3. Ibid
 4. Quoted in Allen, Louis, *Singapore* (Davis-Poynter, 1977)
 5. Bock, Fedor von, *The War Diary* (Schiffer, 1996)

6. Ibid
7. Ibid
8. Quoted in Porter, Cathy, and Jones, Mark, *Moscow in World War II* (Chatto & Windus, 1987)
9. Ibid
10. Michelson, Frida, *I Survived Rumbuli* (Holocaust Library, *c.* 1979)
11. http://emperors-clothes.com/archive/mufhitler.htm
12. Ciano, Count Galeazzo, *Diaries*, ed. Muggeridge, Malcolm (Heinemann, 1947)
13. Quoted in Friedlander, Saul, *The Years of Extermination* (Weidenfeld & Nicolson, 2007)
14. Ibid
15. Quoted in *The Times*, 28 November 1941
16. Ibid
17. Ibid
18. Ibid
19. Ibid
20. Ibid
21. Quoted in Shirer, William, *The Rise and Fall of the Third Reich* (Pan, 1964)
22. Quoted in Hastings, Max, *Bomber Command* (Pan, 1999)
23. Quoted in Wohlstetter, Roberta, *Pearl Harbor: Warning and Decision* (Stanford University Press, 1962)
24. Ibid
25. Ibid
26. Ibid
27. Quoted in Prange, Gordon, *At Dawn We Slept* (Penguin, 2001)

SATURDAY 29 NOVEMBER
1. Quoted in Toland, John, *Rising Sun* (Penguin, 2001)
2. Ibid
3. Ibid
4. Ibid
5. Ibid
6. Quoted in Newton, Steven H., *Hitler's Commander* (Da Capo, *c.* 2004)
7. Bock, Fedor von, *The War Diary* (Schiffer, 1996)
8. Quoted in Erickson, John, *The Road to Stalingrad* (Weidenfeld & Nicolson, 1975)
9. Quoted in Bek, Alexander, 'The Map', in Sevryuk, Vladimir (ed.), *Moscow–Stalingrad: Recollections* (Progress, 1970)
10. Rokossovsky, Konstantin, *A Soldier's Duty* (Progress, 1970)
11. Quoted in Anders, W., *Hitler's Defeat in Russia* (Henry Regnery, 1953)
12. Bock, Fedor von, *The War Diary* (Schiffer, 1996)
13. Quoted in Rzhevskaya, Elena, 'Roads and Days: The Memoirs of a Red Army Translator', *Journal of Slavonic Military Studies*, Vol. 14, March 2001
14. Quoted in Braithwaite, Rodric, *Moscow 1941* (Profile, 2006)

15. Michelson, Frida, *I Survived Rumbuli* (Holocaust Library, *c.* 1979)
16. Ibid
17. Quoted in Kershaw, Ian, *Hitler 1936–45: Nemesis* (Allen Lane, 2000)
18. Quoted in Breitman, Richard, *The Architect of Genocide* (Bodley Head, 1991)
19. Metelmann, Henry, *Through Hell for Hitler* (Stephens, 1990)
20. Quoted in Hauner, M., *Hitler: A Chronology of His Life and Time* (Palgrave Macmillan, 2005)
21. Quoted in Kershaw, Ian, *Hitler 1936–45: Nemesis* (Allen Lane, 2000)
22. Quoted in Tooze, Adam, *The Wages of Destruction* (Penguin, 2007)
23. http://www.revolutionarydemocracy.org/Rdv7nl/Bose.htm
24. Quoted in Irving, David, *Hitler's War* (Hodder & Stoughton, 1977)
25. Quoted in Pitt, Barry, *The Crucible of War: Auchinleck's Command* (Cassell, 2001)
26. www.usna.edu/LibExhibits/Archives/Armynavy/An1941.htm
27. Quoted in Wohlstetter, Roberta, *Pearl Harbor: Warning and Decision* (Stanford University Press, 1962)
28. Quoted in Prange, Gordon, *At Dawn We Slept* (Penguin, 2001)
29. Ibid

SUNDAY 30 NOVEMBER

1. Quoted in Prange, Gordon, *At Dawn We Slept* (Penguin, 2001)
 2. Ibid
 3. Quoted in Burdick, C., and Jacobsen, H.-A., *The Halder War Diary* (Greenhill, 1988)
 4. Quoted in Blumentritt, Gunther von, *Von Rundstedt* (Odhams, 1952)
 5. Quoted in Burdick, C., and Jacobsen, H.-A., *The Halder War Diary* (Greenhill, 1988)
 6. Zhukov, Georgi, *Reminiscences and Reflections* (Progress, 1985)
 7. Bock, Fedor von, *The War Diary* (Schiffer, 1996)
 8. Quoted in Haupt, Werner, *Army Group South* (Schiffer, 1998)
 9. Ibid
10. Quoted in Carell, Paul, *Hitler's War on Russia* (Harrap, 1964)
11. Quoted in Nagorski, Andrew, *The Greatest Battle* (Aurum, 2007)
12. Quoted in Haupt, Werner, *Army Group South* (Schiffer, 1998)
13. Zhukov, Georgi, *Reminiscences and Reflections* (Progress, 1985)
14. Bock, Fedor von, *The War Diary* (Schiffer, 1996)
15. Quoted in Burdick, C., and Jacobsen, H.-A., *The Halder War Diary* (Greenhill, 1988)
16. Quoted in Trevor-Roper, Hugh, *Hitler's Table Talk* (Weidenfeld & Nicolson, 1953)
17. Michelson, Frida, *I Survived Rumbuli* (Holocaust Library, *c.* 1979)
18. Quoted in Macksey, Kenneth, *Rommel* (Arms & Armour, 1979)
19. Quoted in Agar-Hamilton, J. and Turner, L., *The Sidi Rezeg Battles 1941* (Oxford University Press, 1957)

20. Ibid
21. Ibid
22. Ciano, Count Galeazzo, *Diaries*, ed. Muggeridge, Malcolm (Heinemann, 1947)
23. Quoted in Parkinson, R., *Blood, Toil, Tears and Sweat* (Hart-Davis MacGibbon, 1973)
24. Ibid

MONDAY 1 DECEMBER
1. Quoted in Ike, Nobutaka (ed.), *Japan's Decision for War* (Stanford University Press, 1967)
2. Ibid
3. Ibid
4. Ibid
5. Ibid
6. Ibid
7. Ibid
8. Quoted in Manchester, William, *American Caesar* (Arrow, 1979)
9. Brereton, Lewis H., *The Brereton Diaries* (William Morrow, 1946)
10. Quoted in Burdick, C., and Jacobsen, H.-A., *The Halder War Diary* (Greenhill, 1988)
11. Ibid
12. Ibid
13. Ibid
14. Bock, Fedor von, *The War Diary* (Schiffer, 1996)
15. Quoted in Burdick, C., and Jacobsen, H.-A., *The Halder War Diary* (Greenhill, 1988)
16. Simonov, Konstantin, *The Living and the Dead* (Greenwood, 1968)
17. Quoted in Reinhardt, Klaus, *Moscow: The Turning Point* (Berg, 1992)
18. Crisp, Robert, *Brazen Chariots* (Corgi, 1960)
19. Ibid
20. Quoted in Humble, Richard, *Crusader* (Leo Cooper, 1987)
21. Mellenthin, F. W. von, *Panzer Battles* (University of Oklahoma, 1956)
22. Ciano, Count Galeazzo, *Diaries*, ed. Muggeridge, Malcolm (Heinemann, 1947)
23. Quoted in Trevor-Roper, Hugh, *Hitler's Table Talk* (Weidenfeld & Nicolson, 1953)
24. Quoted in Gilbert, Martin, *Finest Hour: Winston Churchill 1939–41* (Heinemann, 1983)
25. Ibid
26. Ibid
27. Ibid
28. Ibid
29. Quoted in Parkinson, R., *Blood, Toil, Tears and Sweat* (Hart-Davis MacGibbon, 1973)

30. Ibid
31. Quoted in Bryant, Arthur, *The Turn of the Tide* (Fontana, 1965)
32. Quoted in Parkinson, R., *Blood, Toil, Tears and Sweat* (Hart-Davis MacGibbon, 1973)
33. Quoted in Parkinson, R., *Blood, Toil, Tears and Sweat* (Hart-Davis MacGibbon, 1973)
34. Quoted in Gilbert, Martin, *Finest Hour: Winston Churchill 1939–41* (Heinemann, 1983)
35. Quoted in Wohlstetter, Roberta, *Pearl Harbor: Warning and Decision* (Stanford University Press, 1962)

TUESDAY 2 DECEMBER
 1. Tsuji, Masanobu, *Singapore: The Japanese Version* (Mayflower-Dell, 1966)
 2. Quoted in Agawa, Hiroyuki, *Yamamoto, Reluctant Admiral* (Harper & Row, 1979)
 3. Quoted in Wohlstetter, Roberta, *Pearl Harbor: Warning and Decision* (Stanford University Press, 1962
 4. *Malaya Tribune*, 2 December 1941
 5. Quoted in Thompson, Peter, *The Battle for Singapore* (Portrait, 2006)
 6. Quoted in Blumentritt, Gunther von, *Von Rundstedt* (Odhams, 1952)
 7. Quoted in Reinhardt, Klaus, *Moscow: The Turning Point* (Berg, 1992)
 8. Bock, Fedor von, *The War Diary* (Schiffer, 1996)
 9. Reese, Willy Peter, *A Stranger to Myself* (Farrar Straus Giroux, 2006)
10. Quoted in Lewin, Ronald, *Rommel as a Military Commander* (Batsford, 1968)
11. *Daily Mirror*, 2 December 1941
12. Quoted in Parkinson, R., *Blood, Toil, Tears and Sweat* (Hart-Davis MacGibbon, 1973)
13. *New York Times*, 2 December 1941
14. Quoted in Ketchum, Richard, *The Borrowed Years* (Anchor, 1991)
15. Quoted in Prange, Gordon, *At Dawn We Slept* (Penguin, 2001)
16. Ibid
17. Quoted in Agawa, Hiroyuki, *Yamamoto, Reluctant Admiral* (Harper & Row, 1979)

WEDNESDAY 3 DECEMBER
 1. Quoted in Prange, Gordon, *At Dawn We Slept* (Penguin, 2001)
 2. Ibid
 3. Quoted in Tsuji, Masanobu, *Singapore: The Japanese Version* (Mayflower-Dell, 1966)
 4. Quoted in Bartsch, William, *December 8, 1941* (Texas A&M University Press, 2003)
 5. Quoted in Hauner, M., *Hitler: A Chronology of His Life and Time* (Palgrave Macmillan, 2005)
 6. Quoted in Haupt, Werner, *Assault on Moscow 1941* (Schiffer, 1996)

7. Ibid
8. Ibid
9. Ibid
10. Quoted in Burdick, C., and Jacobsen, H.-A., *The Halder War Diary* (Greenhill, 1988)
11. Quoted in Reinhardt, Klaus, *Moscow: The Turning Point* (Berg, 1992)
12. Quoted in Burdick, C., and Jacobsen, H.-A., *The Halder War Diary* (Greenhill, 1988)
13. Metelmann, Henry, *Through Hell for Hitler* (Stephens, 1990)
14. Ciano, Count Galeazzo, *Diaries*, ed. Muggeridge, Malcolm (Heinemann, 1947)
15. *Daily Mirror*, 3 December 1941
16. Quoted in Agar-Hamilton, J. and Turner, L., *The Sidi Rezeg Battles 1941* (Oxford University Press, 1957)
17. Quoted in Bryant, Arthur, *The Turn of the Tide* (Fontana, 1965)
18. Quoted in Toland, John, *Rising Sun* (Penguin, 2001)
19. *Honolulu Advertiser*, 3 December 1941

THURSDAY 4 DECEMBER
1. Quoted in Tsuji, Masanobu, *Singapore: The Japanese Version* (Mayflower-Dell, 1966)
2. Brereton, Lewis H., *The Brereton Diaries* (William Morrow, 1946)
3. Bock, Fedor von, *The War Diary* (Schiffer, 1996)
4. Ibid
5. Quoted in Reinhardt, Klaus, *Moscow: The Turning Point* (Berg, 1992)
6. Ibid
7. Crisp, Robert, *Brazen Chariots* (Corgi, 1960)
8. Ciano, Count Galeazzo, *Diaries*, ed. Muggeridge, Malcolm (Heinemann, 1947)
9. Ibid
10. Quoted in Bryant, Arthur, *The Turn of the Tide* (Fontana, 1965)
11. Quoted in Ketchum, Richard, *The Borrowed Years* (Anchor, 1991)
12. Quoted in Prange, Gordon, *At Dawn We Slept* (Penguin, 2001)

FRIDAY 5 DECEMBER
1. Quoted in Bartsch, William, *December 8, 1941* (Texas A&M University Press, 2003)
2. Quoted in Allen, Louis, *Singapore* (Davis-Poynter, 1977)
3. Quoted in Piekalkiewicz, Janusz, *Moscow 1941* (Arms & Armour, 1981)
4. Guderian, Heinz, *Panzer Leader* (Futura, 1974)
5. Quoted in Burdick, C., and Jacobsen, H.-A., *The Halder War Diary* (Greenhill, 1988)
6. Quoted in Strawson, John, *Hitler as Military Commander* (Sphere, 1973)
7. Quoted in Bryant, Arthur, *The Turn of the Tide* (Fontana, 1965)
8. Quoted in Wohlstetter, Roberta, *Pearl Harbor: Warning and Decision*

(Stanford University Press, 1962)
9. Quoted in Prange, Gordon, *At Dawn We Slept* (Penguin, 2001)
10. Quoted in Agawa, Hiroyuki, *Yamamoto, Reluctant Admiral* (Harper & Row, 1979)

SATURDAY 6 DECEMBER
1. Quoted in Bartsch,William, *December 8, 1941* (Texas A&M University Press, 2003)
2. Quoted in Haupt, Werner, *Assault on Moscow 1941* (Schiffer, 1996)
3. Luck, Hans von, *Panzer Commander* (Cassell, 2002)
4. Quoted in Reinhardt, Klaus, *Moscow: The Turning Point* (Berg, 1992)
5. Quoted in Burdick, C., and Jacobsen, H.-A., *The Halder War Diary* (Greenhill, 1988)
6. Quoted in Agar-Hamilton, J., and Turner, L., *The Sidi Rezeg Battles 1941* (Oxford University Press, 1957)
7. Quoted in Irving, David, *Göring* (Macmillan, 1989)
8. Quoted in Toland, John, *Rising Sun* (Penguin, 2001)
9. Quoted in Prange, Gordon, *At Dawn We Slept* (Penguin, 2001)
10. Ibid
11. Ibid
12. Quoted in Toland, John, *Rising Sun* (Penguin, 2001)
13. Quoted in Prange, Gordon, *At Dawn We Slept* (Penguin, 2001)
14. Ibid
15. Ibid

SUNDAY 7–MONDAY 8 DECEMBER
1. Bock, Fedor von, *The War Diary* (Schiffer, 1996)
2. Guderian, Heinz, *Panzer Leader* (Futura, 1974)
3. Quoted in Burdick, C., and Jacobsen, H.-A., *The Halder War Diary* (Greenhill, 1988)
4. Quoted in Rzhevskaya, Elena, 'Roads and Days: The Memoirs of a Red Army Translator', *Journal of Slavonic Military Studies*, Vol. 14, March 2001
5. http://en.wikipedia.org/wiki/Nacht_und_Nebel
6. Quoted in Lewin, Ronald, *Rommel as a Military Commander* (Batsford, 1968)
7. Quoted in Connell, John, *Auchinleck* (Cassell, 1959)
8. Ciano, Count Galeazzo, *Diaries*, ed. Muggeridge, Malcolm (Heinemann, 1947)
9. Quoted in Wohlstetter, Roberta, *Pearl Harbor: Warning and Decision* (Stanford University Press, 1962)
10. Quoted in Prange, Gordon, *At Dawn We Slept* (Penguin, 2001)
11. Quoted in Toland, John, *Rising Sun* (Penguin, 2001)
12. Quoted in Thompson, Peter, *The Battle for Singapore* (Portrait, 2006)
13. Quoted in Toland, John, *Rising Sun* (Penguin, 2001)
14. Quoted in Irving, David, *Hitler's War* (Hodder & Stoughton, 1977)

15. Quoted in Weintraub, Stanley, *Long Day's Journey into War* (Lyons, 2001)
16. Churchill, Winston, *The Second World War, Vol. 3, The Grand Alliance* (Penguin, 1985)
17. Ibid
18. Agawa, Hiroyuki, *Yamamoto, Reluctant Admiral* (Harper & Row, 1979)
19. www.bookmice.net/darkchilde/japan/tojo3.html
20. Quoted in Cook, H. T., and Cook, T. F., *Japan at War: An Oral History* (New Press, 1992)
21. Ibid
22. Ibid
23. Ibid
24. Ibid
25. Quoted in Ienaga, Saburo, *The Pacific War* (Pantheon, *c.* 1978)
26. Quoted in Newton, Steven H., *Hitler's Commander* (Da Capo, *c.* 2004)
27. Luck, Hans von, *Panzer Commander* (Cassell, 2002)
28. Metelmann, Henry, *Through Hell for Hitler* (Stephens, 1990)
29. Michelson, Frida, *I Survived Rumbuli* (Holocaust Library, *c.* 1979)
30. Ibid
31. Ciano, Count Galeazzo, *Diaries*, ed. Muggeridge, Malcolm (Heinemann, 1947)
32. Quoted in Haupt, Werner, *Assault on Moscow 1941* (Schiffer, 1996)
33. Bock, Fedor von, *The War Diary* (Schiffer, 1996)
34. http://www.geocities.com/Pentagon/1084/hitler_directives/dir39.htm
35. Quoted in Ketchum, Richard, *The Borrowed Years* (Anchor, 1991)

EPILOGUE

1. Quoted in Irving, David, *Hitler's War* (Hodder & Stoughton, 1977)

SELECT BIBLIOGRAPHY

EAST ASIA AND THE PACIFIC

Agawa, Hiroyuki, *Yamamoto, Reluctant Admiral* (Harper & Row, 1979)

Allen, Louis, *Singapore* (Davis-Poynter, 1977)

Bartsch, William, *December 8, 1941* (Texas A&M University Press, 2003)

Brereton, Lewis H., *The Brereton Diaries* (William Morrow, 1946)

Chapman, John, 'The Imperial Japanese Navy and the North–South Dilemma', in Erickson, J., and Dilks, D., *Barbarossa, the Axis and the Allies* (Edinburgh University Press, 1994)

Cook, H. T., and Cook, T. F., *Japan at War: An Oral History* (New Press, 1992)

Costello, John, *Days of Infamy* (Pocket, 1994)

Deane, John Potter, *Admiral of the Pacific* (Heinemann, 1965)

Farrell, Brian P., *The Defence and Fall of Singapore* (Tempus, 2006)

Feis, Herbert, *The Road to Pearl Harbor* (Princeton, 1950)

Hoyt, Edwin, *Yamamoto* (McGraw-Hill, 1990)

Ike, Nobutaka (ed.), *Japan's Decision for War* (Stanford University Press, 1967)

Layton, Edwin, *'And I was there'* (Greenhill, 2006)

Lord, Walter, *Day of Infamy* (Bantam, 1958)

Manchester, William, *American Caesar* (Arrow, 1979)

Prange, Gordon, *At Dawn We Slept* (Penguin, 2001)

Smith, Carl, *Pearl Harbor* (Osprey, 2001)

Thompson, Peter, *The Battle for Singapore* (Portrait, 2006)

Toland, John, *Rising Sun* (Penguin, 2001)

Tsuji, Masanobu, *Singapore: The Japanese Version* (Mayflower-Dell, 1966)

Ugaki, Matome, *Fading Victory* (University of Pittsburgh Press, 1991)

Willmott, H. P., *Pearl Harbor* (Bison, 1981)

Wilson, Dick, *When Tigers Fight* (Hutchinson, 1982)

Wohlstetter, Roberta, *Pearl Harbor: Warning and Decision* (Stanford University Press, 1962)

RUSSIA

Anders, W., *Hitler's Defeat in Russia* (Henry Regnery, 1953)

Armstrong, John (ed.), *Soviet Partisans in World War II* (University of Wisconsin Press, 1964)

Bek, Alexander, *The Volokolamsk Highway* (Moscow Foreign Languages, c. 1964)

Blumentritt, Gunther von, *Von Rundstedt* (Odhams, 1952)

Bock, Fedor von, *The War Diary* (Schiffer, 1996)

Braithwaite, Rodric, *Moscow 1941* (Profile, 2006)

Burdick, C., and Jacobsen, H.-A., *The Halder War Diary* (Greenhill, 1988)

Carell, Paul, *Hitler's War on Russia* (Harrap, 1964)

Clark, Alan, *Barbarossa* (Hutchinson, 1965)

Colvin, John, *Zhukov* (Weidenfeld & Nicolson, 2004)

Creveld, Martin van, *Supplying War* (Cambridge University Press, 1977)

Dallin, Alexander, *German Rule in Russia* (Macmillan, 1957)

Erickson, John, *The Road to Stalingrad* (Weidenfeld & Nicolson, 1975)

Forczyk, Robert, *Moscow 1941* (Osprey, 2006)

Freidin, S., and Richardson, W. (eds.), *The Fatal Decisions* (Michael Joseph, 1956)

Glantz, David, *Barbarossa 1941* (Tempus, 2001)

Grenkevich, L., *The Soviet Partisan Movement 1941–44* (Frank Cass, 1999)

Guderian, Heinz, *Panzer Leader* (Futura, 1974)

Haape, Heinrich, *Moscow Tram Stop* (Collins, 1957)

Haupt, Werner, *Army Group South* (Schiffer, 1998)

Haupt, Werner, *Assault on Moscow 1941* (Schiffer, 1996)

Keitel, William, *Memoirs* (William Kimber, 1965)

Kirchubel, Robert, *Operation Barbarossa: Army Group South* (Osprey, 2003)

Kirchubel, Robert, *Operation Barbarossa: Army Group North* (Osprey, 2005)

Luck, Hans von, *Panzer Commander* (Cassell, 2002)

Merridale, Catherine, *Ivan's War: The Red Army 1939–45* (Faber and Faber, 2005)

Metelmann, Henry, *Through Hell for Hitler* (Stephens, 1990)

Nagorski, Andrew, *The Greatest Battle* (Aurum, 2007)

Newton, Steven H., *Hitler's Commander* (Da Capo, c. 2004)

Overy, Richard, *Russia's War* (Penguin, 1998)

Piekalkiewicz, Janusz, *Moscow 1941* (Arms & Armour, 1981)

Porter, Cathy, and Jones, Mark, *Moscow in World War II* (Chatto & Windus, 1987)

Reese, Willy Peter, *A Stranger to Myself* (Farrar Straus Giroux, 2006)

Reinhardt, Klaus, *Moscow: The Turning Point* (Berg, 1992)

Reinhardt, Klaus, 'Moscow 1941', in Erickson, J., and Dilks, D., *Barbarossa, the Axis and the Allies* (Edinburgh University Press, 1994))

Rokossovsky, Konstantin, *A Soldier's Duty* (Progress, 1970)

Rzhevskaya, Elena, 'Roads and Days: The Memoirs of a Red Army Translator', *Journal of Slavonic Military Studies*, Vol. 14, March 2001

Sajer, Guy, *The Forgotten Soldier* (Weidenfeld & Nicolson, 1971)

Salisbury, Harrison, *The 900 Days: The Siege of Leningrad* (Pan, 2000)

Seaton, Albert, *The Battle for Moscow* (Stein and Day, 1971)

Seaton, Albert, *The Russo-German War* (Barker, 1971)
Sevryuk, Vladimir, (ed.) *Moscow–Stalingrad: Recollections* (Progress, 1970)
Simonov, Konstantin, *The Living and the Dead* (Greenwood, 1968)
Werth, Alexander, *Russia at war* (Barrie & Rockcliff, 1964)
Zhukov, Georgi, *Reminiscences and Reflections* (Progress, 1985)

NORTH AFRICA
Agar-Hamilton, J., and Turner, L., *The Sidi Rezeg Battles 1941* (Oxford University Press, 1957)
Barnett, Corelli, *The Desert Generals* (William Kimber, 1960)
Carell, Paul, *The Foxes of the Desert* (Bantam, 1962)
Connell, John, *Auchinleck* (Cassell, 1959)
Crisp, Robert, *Brazen Chariots* (Corgi, 1960)
Curie, Eve, *Journey Among Warriors* (William Heinemann, 1943)
Humble, Richard, *Crusader* (Leo Cooper, 1987)
Kriebel, Rainer, *Inside the Afrika Korps* (Greenhill, 1999)
Lewin, Ronald, *Rommel as a Military Commander* (Batsford, 1968)
Mellenthin, F. W. von, *Panzer Battles* (University of Oklahoma, 1956)
Moorehead, Alan, *The Desert War* (Hamish Hamilton, 1965)
Murphy, W. E., *The Relief of Tobruk* (New Zealand government publication, 1961)
Pitt, Barry, *The Crucible of War: Auchinleck's Command* (Cassell, 2001)
Rommel, Erwin, *The Rommel Papers* (Collins, 1953)
Schmidt, Heinz W., *With Rommel in the Desert* (Harrap, 1953)
Strawson, John, *Battle for North Africa* (Batsford, 1969)
Walker, Ian W., *Iron Hulls, Iron Hearts* (Crowood, 2003)
Young, Desmond, *Rommel* (Collins, 1950)

GENERAL
Bryant, Arthur, *The Turn of the Tide* (Fontana, 1965)
Burns, J. M., *The Lion and the Fox* (Secker & Warburg, 1956)
Ciano, Count Galeazzo, *Diaries*, ed. Muggeridge, Malcolm (Heinemann, 1947)
Deighton, Len, *Blood, Tears and Folly* (Pimlico, 1995)
Gilbert, Martin, *Finest Hour: Winston Churchill 1939–41* (Heinemann, 1983)
Gilbert, Martin, *The Holocaust* (Fontana, 1987)
Gilbert, Martin, *Never Again* (HarperCollins, 2000)
Hastings, Max, *Bomber Command* (Pan, 1999)
Hauner, Milan, *Hitler: A Chronology of His Life and Time* (Palgrave Macmillan, 2005)
Heinrichs, Waldo, *Threshold of War* (Oxford University Press, 1988)
Hull, Cordell, *Memoirs* (Hodder & Stoughton, 1948)
Irving, David, *Hitler's War* (Hodder & Stoughton, 1977)
Jungk, Robert, *Brighter Than a 1000 Suns* (Penguin, 1960)
Kershaw, Ian, *Hitler 1936–45: Nemesis* (Allen Lane, 2000)

Ketchum, Richard, *The Borrowed Years* (Anchor, 1991)

Liddell Hart, B. H., *History of the Second World War* (Pan, 1973)

Macintyre, Donald, *Battle of the Atlantic* (Batsford, 1961)

Macintyre, Donald, *Battle for the Mediterranean* (Batsford, 1964)

Michelson, Frida, *I Survived Rumbuli* (Holocaust Library, *c.* 1979)

Muggenthaler, Karl, *German Raiders of World War II* (Pan, 1980)

Parkinson, R., *Blood, Toil, Tears and Sweat* (Hart-Davis MacGibbon, 1973)

Rhodes, Richard, *The Making of the Atomic Bomb* (Touchstone, 1988)

Roskill, Stephen, *The War at Sea* (HMSO, 1957)

Shirer, William, *The Rise and Fall of the Third Reich* (Pan, 1964)

Tooze, Adam, *The Wages of Destruction* (Penguin, 2007)

Trevor-Roper, Hugh, *Hitler's Table Talk* (Weidenfeld & Nicolson, 1953)

Weintraub, Stanley, *Long Day's Journey into War* (Lyons, 2001)

Woodman, Dorothy, *Europe Rises* (Victor Gollancz, 1943)

INDEX